S0-ADW-175

**COMPUTER BOOK SERIES FROM IDG**

# *Microsoft Works For Windows® 95 For Dummies®*

*Cheat Sheet*

## Navigating in Almost Any Document

| To Do This ... | Do This ... |
|---|---|
| Scroll up/down | Use vertical scroll bar |
| Scroll sideways | Use horizontal scroll bar |
| Right, left, up, down | Press arrow key |
| End of column/next paragraph | Press Ctrl+down arrow |
| Start of column, paragraph | Press Ctrl+up arrow |
| One screen up/down | Press PgUp / PgDn keys |
| Beginning/end of line or row | Press Home / End keys |
| Beginning/end of document | Press Ctrl+Home / Ctrl+End keys |

## General Stuff

| To Do This ... | Do This ... |
|---|---|
| Start Works | Double-click on Works Shortcut icon |
| Exit Works | Press Alt+F, X |
| Start a new document | Press Ctrl+N |
| Save a document | Press Ctrl+S |
| Open a document | Press Ctrl+O |
| Close a document | Press Ctrl+W |
| Choose document window | Press Alt+W, then 1 or 2 or 3 ... |
| Print Preview | Press Alt+F, V |
| Print | Press Ctrl+P |

## Editing Almost Everywhere

| To Do This ... | Do This ... |
|---|---|
| Select text | Click and drag |
| Select text with keys | Press Shift+navigation key |
| Select graphic | Click |
| Delete | Press Delete key or Backspace key |
| Cut selection to Clipboard | Press Ctrl+X |
| Copy selection to Clipboard | Press Ctrl+C |
| Paste from Clipboard | Press Ctrl+V |
| Move selection | Drag frame |
| Create & move a copy | Press Ctrl+drag frame |

## *. . .For Dummies: #1 Computer Book Series for Beginners*

COMPUTER
BOOK SERIES
FROM IDG

# Microsoft Works For Windows® 95 For Dummies®

Cheat Sheet

## Miscellaneous Spreadsheet Stuff

| To Do This ... | Do This ... |
| --- | --- |
| Sum column or row | Press Ctrl+M, Enter - or - Sigma icon in toolbar, Enter |
| Change column width | Click and drag right edge |
| Insert row | Press Alt+I, R |
| Insert column | Press Alt+I, C |

## Number Formats in Spreadsheets and Databases

| To Do This ... | Press This ... |
| --- | --- |
| Dollars | Ctrl+4 ($ key) |
| Percent | Ctrl+5 (% key) |
| Comma at thousands | Ctrl+, (comma) |

## Formatting in the Word Processor

| To Do This ... | Press This ... |
| --- | --- |
| Add or Remove space before paragraph | Ctrl+0 (zero) |
| Indent | Ctrl+M |
| Un-indent | Ctrl+Shift+M |
| Hanging indent | Ctrl+Shift+H |
| Un-hang indent | Ctrl+Shift+T |

## Formatting Almost Everywhere

| To Do This ... | Press This ... |
| --- | --- |
| Choose font | Ctrl+Shift+F |
| Choose font size | Ctrl+Shift+P |
| Bold | Ctrl+B |
| Italic | Ctrl+I |
| Underline | Ctrl+U |
| Center | Ctrl+E |
| Left-align | Ctrl+L |
| Right-align | Ctrl+Shift+R |
| Remove font styles | Ctrl+spacebar |
| Insert page break | Ctrl+Enter |
| Change margins, page | Alt+F, G |

## Date and Time Almost Everywhere

| To Do This ... | Do This ... |
| --- | --- |
| Insert today's date | Press Ctrl+; |
| Insert time now | Press Ctrl+Shift+; |

## . . .For Dummies: #1 Computer Book Series for Beginners

 ®

# References for the Rest of Us! ®

## COMPUTER BOOK SERIES FROM IDG

Are you intimidated and confused by computers? Do you find that traditional manuals are overloaded with technical details you'll never use? Do your friends and family always call you to fix simple problems on their PCs? Then the *...For Dummies*® computer book series from IDG Books Worldwide is for you.

*...For Dummies* books are written for those frustrated computer users who know they aren't really dumb but find that PC hardware, software, and indeed the unique vocabulary of computing make them feel helpless. *...For Dummies* books use a lighthearted approach, a down-to-earth style, and even cartoons and humorous icons to diffuse computer novices' fears and build their confidence. Lighthearted but not lightweight, these books are a perfect survival guide for anyone forced to use a computer.

Already, hundreds of thousands of satisfied readers agree. They have made *...For Dummies* books the #1 introductory level computer book series and have written asking for more. So, if you're looking for the most fun and easy way to learn about computers, look to *...For Dummies* books to give you a helping hand.

™

**IDG BOOKS WORLDWIDE**

# MICROSOFT® WORKS
## FOR
# WINDOWS® 95
## FOR
# DUMMIES®

# MICROSOFT® WORKS FOR WINDOWS® 95 FOR DUMMIES®

### by David C. Kay

IDG Books Worldwide, Inc.
An International Data Group Company

Foster City, CA ♦ Chicago, IL ♦ Indianapolis, IN ♦ Braintree, MA ♦ Southlake, TX

**Microsoft® Works For Windows® 95 For Dummies®**

Published by
**IDG Books Worldwide, Inc.**
An International Data Group Company
919 E. Hillsdale Blvd.
Suite 400
Foster City, CA 94404

Library of Congress Catalog Card No.: 95-81428

ISBN: 1-56884-944-3

Printed in the United States of America

10 9 8 7 6 5 4 3 2

1A/SX/QS/ZW/IN

Distributed in the United States by IDG Books Worldwide, Inc.

Distributed by Macmillan Canada for Canada; by Computer and Technical Books for the Caribbean Basin; by Contemporanea de Ediciones for Venezuela; by Distribuidora Cuspide for Argentina; by CITEC for Brazil; by Ediciones ZETA S.C.R. Ltda. for Peru; by Editorial Limusa SA for Mexico; by Transworld Publishers Limited in the United Kingdom and Europe; by Al-Maiman Publishers & Distributors for Saudi Arabia; by Simron Pty. Ltd. for South Africa; by IDG Communications (HK) Ltd. for Hong Kong; by Toppan Company Ltd. for Japan; by Addison Wesley Publishing Company for Korea; by Longman Singapore Publishers Ltd. for Singapore, Malaysia, Thailand, and Indonesia; by Unalis Corporation for Taiwan; by WS Computer Publishing Company, Inc. for the Philippines; by WoodsLane Pty. Ltd. for Australia; by WoodsLane Enterprises Ltd. for New Zealand.

For general information on IDG Books Worldwide's books in the U.S., please call our Consumer Customer Service department at 800-762-2974. For reseller information, including discounts and premium sales, please call our Reseller Customer Service department at 800-434-3422.

For information on where to purchase IDG Books Worldwide's books outside the U.S., contact IDG Books Worldwide at 415-655-3021 or fax 415-655-3295.

For information on translations, contact Marc Jeffrey Mikulich, Director, Foreign & Subsidiary Rights, at IDG Books Worldwide, 415-655-3018 or fax 415-655-3295.

For sales inquiries and special prices for bulk quantities, write to the address above or call IDG Books Worldwide at 415-655-3200.

For information on using IDG Books Worldwide's books in the classroom, or ordering examination copies, contact the Education Office at 800-434-2086 or fax 817-251-8174.

For authorization to photocopy items for corporate, personal, or educational use, please contact Copyright Clearance Center, 222 Rosewood Drive, Danvers, MA 01923, or fax 508-750-4470.

is a trademark under exclusive license to IDG Books Worldwide, Inc., from International Data Group, Inc.

# About the Author

## David C. Kay

Dave Kay is a reformed engineer who spent his teenage years fascinated by electronics, watching his ham radio equipment glow in the dark of his basement. Hoping to make a career out of that fascination, he became an electrical engineer, only to end up doing more teaching, talking, and writing than engineering. A decade or so later, he now runs BrightLeaf Communications, doing promotional writing and creating websites for the software and electronics industries. Kay enjoys "being able to tell the unadorned truth about software" through ...*For Dummies* books.

This is Kay's eighth computer book, including *Works 3 For Windows For Dummies,* and multiple editions of *WordPerfect For Windows For Dummies*, *More WordPerfect For Windows For Dummies*, and *Graphics File Formats*.

In his spare time, Kay likes to do "art stuff" — playing with paint and charcoal, melting blobs of glass, and building virtual reality worlds on the computer — and "nature stuff." Some day he'd like to write and teach about animal and human tracking, which he calls "finding data in the dirt." Says Kay, "I'm almost good enough to track farm equipment now. Another couple of decades and I expect to move on to animals — probably starting with the heavier mammals, though, like whales." Kay lives with his wife, Katy Weeks, and their golden retriever, Rusty, in the apple-growing country of Massachusetts. You can send mail to him at *works@dummies.com*.

Welcome to the world of IDG Books Worldwide.

IDG Books Worldwide, Inc., is a subsidiary of International Data Group, the world's largest publisher of computer-related information and the leading global provider of information services on information technology. IDG was founded more than 25 years ago and now employs more than 7,700 people worldwide. IDG publishes more than 250 computer publications in 67 countries (see listing below). More than 70 million people read one or more IDG publications each month.

Launched in 1990, IDG Books Worldwide is today the #1 publisher of best-selling computer books in the United States. We are proud to have received 8 awards from the Computer Press Association in recognition of editorial excellence and three from Computer Currents' First Annual Readers' Choice Awards, and our best-selling ...*For Dummies*® series has more than 19 million copies in print with translations in 28 languages. IDG Books Worldwide, through a joint venture with IDG's Hi-Tech Beijing, became the first U.S. publisher to publish a computer book in the People's Republic of China. In record time, IDG Books Worldwide has become the first choice for millions of readers around the world who want to learn how to better manage their businesses.

Our mission is simple: Every one of our books is designed to bring extra value and skill-building instructions to the reader. Our books are written by experts who understand and care about our readers. The knowledge base of our editorial staff comes from years of experience in publishing, education, and journalism — experience which we use to produce books for the '90s. In short, we care about books, so we attract the best people. We devote special attention to details such as audience, interior design, use of icons, and illustrations. And because we use an efficient process of authoring, editing, and desktop publishing our books electronically, we can spend more time ensuring superior content and spend less time on the technicalities of making books.

You can count on our commitment to deliver high-quality books at competitive prices on topics you want to read about. At IDG Books Worldwide, we continue in the IDG tradition of delivering quality for more than 25 years. You'll find no better book on a subject than one from IDG Books Worldwide.

*John J. Kilcullen*

John Kilcullen
President and CEO
IDG Books Worldwide, Inc.

IDG Books Worldwide, Inc., is a subsidiary of International Data Group, the world's largest publisher of computer-related information and the leading global provider of information services on information technology. International Data Group publishes over 250 computer publications in 67 countries. Seventy million people read one or more International Data Group publications each month. International Data Group's publications include: **ARGENTINA:** Computerworld Argentina, GamePro, Infoworld, PC World Argentina; **AUSTRALIA:** Australian Macworld, Client/Server Journal, Computer Living, Computerworld, Digital News, Network World, PC World, Publishing Essentials, Reseller; **AUSTRIA:** Computerwelt, PC TEST; **BELARUS:** PC World Belarus; **BELGIUM:** Data News; **BRAZIL:** Annuário de Informática, Computerworld Brazil, Connections, Super Game Power, Macworld, PC World Brazil, Publish Brazil, SUPERGAME; **BULGARIA:** Computerworld Bulgaria, Networkworld/Bulgaria, PC & MacWorld Bulgaria; **CANADA:** CIO Canada, ComputerWorld Canada, InfoCanada, Network World Canada, Reseller World; **CHILE:** Computerworld Chile, GamePro, PC World Chile; **COLUMBIA:** Computerworld Colombia, GamePro, PC World Colombia; **COSTA RICA:** PC World Costa Rica/Nicaragua; **THE CZECH AND SLOVAK REPUBLICS:** Computerworld Czechoslovakia, Elektronika Czechoslovakia, PC World Czechoslovakia; **DENMARK:** Communications World, Computerworld Danmark, Macworld Danmark, PC World Danmark, PC World Danmark Supplements, TECH World; **DOMINICAN REPUBLIC:** PC World Republica Dominicana; **ECUADOR:** PC World Ecuador, GamePro; **EGYPT:** Computerworld Middle East, PC World Middle East; **EL SALVADOR:** PC World Centro America; **FINLAND:** MikroPC, Tietoverkko, Tietoviikko; **FRANCE:** Distributique, Golden, Info PC, Le Guide du Monde Informatique, Le Monde Informatique, Reseaux & Telecoms; **GERMANY:** Computer Business, Computerwoche, Computerwoche Extra, Computerwoche Focus, Electronic Entertainment, GamePro, I/M Information Management, Macwelt, PC Welt; **GREECE:** GamePro, Macworld & Publish; **GUATEMALA:** PC World Centro America; **HONDURAS:** PC World Centro America; **HONG KONG:** Computerworld Hong Kong, PCWorld Hong Kong, Publish in Asia; **HUNGARY:** ABCD CD-ROM, Computerworld Szamitastechnika, PC & Mac World Hungary, PC-X Magazine; **INDIA:** Computerworld India, PC World India, Publish in Asia; **INDONESIA:** InfoKomputer PC World, Komputek Computerworld, Publish in Asia; **IRELAND:** ComputerScope, PC Live!; **ISRAEL:** PC World 32 BIT, People & Computers; **ITALY:** Computerworld Italia, Computerworld Italia Special Editions, Lotus Italia, Macworld Italia, Networking Italia, PC Shopping, PC World Italia, PC World/Walt Disney; **JAPAN:** Macworld Japan, Nikkei Personal Computing, SunWorld Japan, Windows World Japan; **KENYA:** East African Computer News; **KOREA:** Hi-Tech Information/Computerworld, Macworld Korea, PC World Korea; **MACEDONIA:** PC World Macedonia; **MALAYSIA:** Computerworld Malaysia, PC World Malaysia, Publish in Asia; **MEXICO:** Computerworld Mexico, GamePro, Macworld, PC World Mexico; **MYANMAR:** PC World Myanmar; **NETHERLANDS:** Computable, Computer! Totaal, LAN Magazine, Macworld, Net Magazine; **NEW ZEALAND:** Computer Buyer, Computerworld New Zealand, MTB, Network World, PC World New Zealand; **NICARAGUA:** PC World Costa Rica/Nicaragua; **NIGERIA:** PC World Africa; **NORWAY:** Computerworld Norge, Computerworld Privat, CW Rapport Klient/Tjener, CW Rapport Nettverk & Telecom, CW Rapport Offentlig Sektor, IDG's KURSGUIDE, Macworld Norge, Multimedia World, PC World Ekspress, PC World Nettverk, PC World Norge, PC World's Produktguide, Windows Spesial; **PAKISTAN:** Computerworld Pakistan, PC World Pakistan; **PANAMA:** GamePro, PC World Panama; **PARAGUAY:** PC World Paraguay; **P. R. OF CHINA:** China Computerworld, China Infoworld, Computer & Communication, Electronic Product World, Electronics Today, Game Camp, PC World China, Popular Computer Week, Software World, Telecom Product World; **PERU:** Computerworld Peru, GamePro, PC World Profesional Peru, PC World Peru; **POLAND:** Computerworld Poland, Computerworld Special Report, Macworld, Networld, PC World Komputer; **PHILIPPINES:** Computerworld Philippines, PC Digest, Publish in Asia; **PORTUGAL:** Cerebro/PC World, Correio Informático/Computerworld, Mac•In/PC•In Portugal; **PUERTO RICO:** PC World Puerto Rico; **ROMANIA:** Computerworld Romania, PC World Romania, Telecom Romania; **RUSSIA:** Computerworld Rossiya, Network World Russia, PC World Russia; **SINGAPORE:** Computerworld Singapore, PC World Singapore, Publish in Asia; **SLOVENIA:** MONITOR; **SOUTH AFRICA:** Computing S.A., Network World S.A., Software World; **SPAIN:** Computerworld España, COMUNICACIONES WORLD, Dealer World, Macworld España, PC World España; **SWEDEN:** CAP&Design, Computer Sweden, Corporate Computing, MacWorld, Maxi Data, MikroDatorn, Nätverk & Kommunikation, PC/Aktiv, PC World, Windows World; **SWITZERLAND:** Computerworld Schweiz, Macworld Schweiz, PCtip; **TAIWAN:** Computerworld Taiwan, Macworld Taiwan, PC World Taiwan, Publish Taiwan, Windows World; **THAILAND:** Thai Computerworld, Publish in Asia; **TURKEY:** Computerworld Monitör, MACWORLD Turkiye, PC WORLD Turkiye; **UKRAINE:** Computerworld Kiev, Computers & Software Magazine, PC World Ukraine; **UNITED KINGDOM:** Acorn User, Amiga Action, Amiga Computing, Amiga, Appletalk, CD Powerplay, CD-ROM Now, Computing, Connexion, GamePro, Lotus Magazine, Macaction, Macworld, Open Computing, Parents and Computers, PC Home, PC Works, The WEB; **UNITED STATES:** Cable in the Classroom, CD Review, CIO Magazine, Computerworld, Computerworld Client/Server Journal, Digital Video Magazine, DOS World, Electronic, InfoWorld, I-Way, Macworld, Maximize, MULTIMEDIA WORLD, Network World, PC World, PUBLISH, SWATPro Magazine, Video Event, WebMaster; **URUGUAY:** PC World Uruguay; **VENEZUELA:** Computerworld Venezuela, GamePro, PC World Venezuela; and **VIETNAM:** PC World Vietnam

10/17/95

# Dedication

This book is dedicated to my wife, Katy Weeks: spouse *extraordinaire,* environmental-engineer-to-be, and best friend.

# Credits

**Senior Vice President
and Publisher**
Milissa L. Koloski

**Associate Publisher**
Diane Graves Steele

**Brand Manager**
Judith A. Taylor

**Editorial Managers**
Kristin A. Cocks
Mary Corder

**Product Development Manager**
Mary Bednarek

**Editorial Executive Assistant**
Richard Graves

**Editorial Assistants**
Constance Carlisle
Chris Collins
Kevin Spencer

**Production Director**
Beth Jenkins

**Production Assistant**
Jacalyn L. Pennywell

**Supervisor of
Project Coordination**
Cindy L. Phipps

**Supervisor of Page Layout**
Kathie S. Schnorr

**Supervisor of Graphics and
Design**
Shelley Lea

**Production Systems Specialist**
Steve Peake

**Reprint/Blueline Coordination**
Tony Augsburger
Patricia R. Reynolds
Todd Klemme
Theresa Sánchez-Baker

**Media/Archive Coordination**
Leslie Popplewell
Melissa Stauffer
Jason Marcuson

**Project Editor**
Bill Helling

**Editor**
Diana R. Conover

**Technical Reviewer**
Jim McCarter

**Project Coordinator**
Valery Bourke

**Graphics Coordination**
Gina Scott
Angela F. Hunckler
Carla Radzikinas

**Production Page Layout**
Brett Black
Kerri Cornell
Maridee V. Ennis
Jill Lyttle
Jane Martin
Drew R. Moore
Kate Snell
Michael Sullivan

**Proofreaders**
Joel Draper
Christine Meloy Beck
Gwenette Gaddis
Dwight Ramsey
Carl Saff
Robert Springer

**Indexer**
Liz Cunningham

**Cover Design**
Kavish + Kavish

# Acknowledgments

I would like to thank my ever-supportive friends and family, especially Doug Muder, who saved my brain from certain meltdown by co-editing this book on short notice. I would also like to thank Matt Wagner of Waterside Productions and the insightful and hardworking editorial team at IDG Books: project editor Bill Helling, copy editor Diana R. Conover, and technical editor Jim McCarter.

(The Publisher would like to give special thanks to Patrick J. McGovern, without whom this book would not have been possible.)

# Contents at a Glance

# Cartoons at a Glance

## By Rich Tennant

*page 102*

"I JUST BOUGHT THIS NEW COMPUTER THAT COMES WITH ADDITIONAL MEMORY, AND FOR AN EXTRA $100 DOLLARS, IT'LL CARRY A GRUDGE. BUT SERIOUSLY FOLKS, ..."

*page 236*

"WE OFFER A CREATIVE MIS ENVIRONMENT WORKING WITH STATE-OF-THE-ART PROCESSING AND COMMUNICATIONS EQUIPMENT, A COMPREHENSIVE BENEFITS PACKAGE, GENEROUS PROFIT SHARING, STOCK OPTIONS AND, IF YOU'RE FEELING FUNKY AND NEED TO CHILL OUT AND RAP, WE CAN DO THAT TOO."

*page 290*

"I WISH SOMEONE WOULD EXPLAIN TO PROFESSOR JONES THAT YOU DON'T NEED A WHIP AND A LEATHER JACKET TO FIND A LOST FILE."

*page 71*

"... AND HERE IS OUR FOCUS GROUP THAT DECIDES WHAT FEATURES GO INTO THE NEXT VERSION OF WORKS."

*page 9*

After spending hours trying to get the system up and running, Carl discovers that everything had been plugged into a "Clapper" light socket when he tries to kill a mosquito.

*page 267*

*page 205*

I DON'T KNOW - MY SPREADSHEET TELLS ME WE SHOULD BASE OUR OVERHEAD BUDGET ON SALES FIGURES RATHER THAN FIXED, MY PLOT CHART INDICATES WE SHOULD ESCALATE OUR MARKETING THRUST, AND MY PSYCHOANALYSIS PROGRAM TELLS ME I DEPEND TOO MUCH ON OUTSIDE INPUT AND SHOULD TRUST MY INSTINCTS MORE.

*page 145*

*page 309*

"It was at this point in time that there appeared to be some sort of mass insanity."

*page 347*

# Table of Contents

# Introduction

● ● ● ● ● ● ● ● ● ● ● ● ● ● ● ● ● ● ● ● ● ● ● ● ● ● ● ● ● ● ● ● ● ● ● ● ● ● ● ● ● ● ● ● ● ● ● ● ●

Congratulations! You have already proven your superior intelligence. Rather than blowing several hundred bucks on the biggest and most muscle-bound word processor, database program, spreadsheet program, graphics, and communications software you can find, you're using Microsoft Works — a program that can do probably everything you need for a lot less trouble and money. Heck, you're so smart that you may have bought a PC with Works already installed.

So then why, exactly, should you be reading a book *For Dummies?* Because Dummies are an underground group of people smart enough to say, "OK, so I'm not a computer wizard. So sue me. Call me a dummy if you will. I still want to use this stuff." The ... *For Dummies* books are for people who:

✔ Want to learn about their software without being bored silly.

✔ Feel like there should be a manual to explain the software manual.

✔ Actually want to get some work done. Soon. Like today.

✔ Don't want to wade through a lot of technical gibberish.

✔ Don't think like computer software engineers seem to think.

## What's in This Book

This book describes how to use all the tools of Microsoft Works, separately and together, plus some introductory things on Windows, disks, and other basics. It includes:

✔ Window basics (opening, closing, and painting them shut).

✔ Word processing (like food processing, only messier).

✔ Spreadsheets (for soft, comfortable naps on your spreadbed).

✔ Databases (for storing all your baseless data).

✔ Communications (for teaching your computer to talk).

✔ Graphics (for charting uncharted waters and general doodling).

# What's Different about This Book

Unlike software manuals, this book doesn't have to deliver a positive message about the software, so it doesn't breathlessly try to show you everything you could possibly do. Instead, it focuses on the everyday things you have to do, points you towards shortcuts, and steers you around some of the stuff you probably don't need.

*Microsoft Works For Windows 95 For Dummies* doesn't assume that you already know about software. Heck, it doesn't even assume that you know much about Windows. If you are already comfortable with your PC and Windows 95, that's great, and this book won't bore you to tears. But if — like a lot of new PC users — your soundest PC skill so far is finding the ON switch, there's a whole introductory section and a Works installation appendix to get you going. Plus, this book doesn't rely on special terms to describe how to do something. It uses the terms so you get to know them, but it doesn't force you to go look them up.

# Who Do I Think You Are, Anyway?

Apart from thinking that you are a brilliant and highly literate person (evidenced by the fact that you have bought or are considering buying this book), here's what I assume about you, the esteemed reader:

- Your PC has Windows 95, a mouse or trackball, and enough memory and disk space to install Works. (If your PC is new, it probably has all this.)

- You don't really give a gnat's eyebrow about Windows except what you absolutely need for your daily work.

- You don't necessarily have great skill with Windows and mice, except perhaps to put screens on the windows in the summertime to keep the mice out.

- Heck, you may even have thought that Works was part of Windows, if it came with your PC. (It's not.)

- If you're on a computer network, you have a computer and network guru available — an expert whom you can pay off in cookies or pizza.

- You're *not* one of those people who are secretly hoping Works will let you do desktop publishing, relational databases, multilevel spreadsheets, and 3-D graphics and rendering for under a hundred bucks. (You people know who you are.)

Apart from that, you could be darn near anybody. I know of mathematicians, computer scientists, business people, and daycare center managers who use Works quite happily.

# How to Use This Book

Nobody, but nobody, wants to sit down and read a book before they use their software. So don't. Instead, just look something up in the index or table of contents and "go to it." Don't just read, though. Follow along on your PC, using this book as a tour guide or road map. I use pictures where necessary, but I didn't throw in a picture of everything because you have the pictures right there on your PC screen, and they're even in color.

If you're already fully fenestrated (Windows-cognizant), just march right along to the Part on your favorite tool. Since Works is an *integrated* package of several tools, you'll find that they have a lot in common. If you're still figuring out what the heck all this stuff is on your computer screen, check out Part I, Survival Skills.

This is mainly a reference book, so you don't have to read it in any particular order. Within each part, though, the earlier chapters cover the more fundamental stuff. So if you want, you can just read the chapters in order (in each part) to get from the simple to the more complex.

# How This Book Is Organized

Unlike some computer books, which seem to be organized alphabetically by gadget, this book is organized by what you are trying to learn. It doesn't, for example, explain each command as it appears on the menu. Unless you are one of those compulsive people who, say, actually learns all the buttons on their VCR remote control before using it, that sort of organization is pretty useless.

No, what this book does is break things down into the following useful parts, including one part for each tool. In each tool's part, there's something for everyone, whether you've never used a similar tool before or you're an old hand who just needs to learn how Works does it.

## Part 1: Survival Skills

If you're currently beating your head against Windows, files, directories, mice, or disks, or you're just trying to get under way with Works, Part I is the place to turn. Here's how to start Works, make your various windows behave, and get basic keyboard and mouse skills.

Part I is also the place to go for things that work pretty much the same everywhere in Works: opening and closing files, getting help, cutting and pasting, and changing the appearance of things.

## Part II: The Wily Word Processor

The one tool that nearly everyone uses — the word processor — can also be rather elusive. In this part, you discover its wiles and ways. This part covers everything from basics, such as how to use the keyboard, to subtle and elusive facts, such as where paragraph formatting hides. Learn how to get the document you want and save work by avoiding old-fashioned typewriter habits. Later chapters introduce editing techniques and essential bells and whistles like page numbers, tables, borders, lines, headers, footers, and footnotes.

## Part III: Setting Sail with Spreadsheets

Yo, ho, ho! Stay the mizzen! Batten down the poop deck! Here's how to put the wind in your spreadsheets and computerize your calculations. Even if your feelings for calculation are more "oh, no" than "yo, ho!", Part III shows you how to have a nice cruise. From the basics of entering stuff in cells and navigating around, to the secrets of creating and copying formulas, to the subtleties of date and time arithmetic, Part III is your port of call.

## Part IV: Doing Active Duty at the Database

As some old soldier once said, "There's the right way, there's the wrong way, and there's the Army way." Well, in Works there's the Works database way. If you've never used a database before, Part IV will give you your basic training. If you've already done a hitch with other database software, Part IV will help you understand the slightly quirky Works way of doing and talking about databases. This part explores fields, records, data entry, different *views,* making changes, filtering, and creating basic reports.

## Part V: Exploring the Communications Wilderness

There's an information highway out there all right, but it's a bumpy road through a vast communications wilderness. This part shows you where to catch the bus for the information highway, how to survive if the bus breaks down, and how to make yourself at home in the wilderness if you want an extended stay. From Works' Easy Connect feature, to communications procedures, setups, and *protocols,* Part V shows you how Works can connect your computer to another one for fun and profit.

## Part VI: Creating Great Works of Art: Graphics

A mercenary artist friend of mine says, "a picture is worth a thousand bucks." Well, your pictures might be worth that, but with Works they'll cost a lot less. Works provides easy charting and other forms of graphics, from "blob art" with the Draw tool, to WordArt and ClipArt. Part VI first shows how to quickly transform a spreadsheet into a bar, pie, line, area, or other kind of chart, complete with labels and legends and charty stuff like that. Then it shows you how to use Works' drawing tool for creating your own diagrams and other works of art. Finally, it takes you on a brief tour of Works' ClipArt Gallery and the swoopy, loopy world of the WordArt tool.

## Part VII: The Part of Tens

The part of tens? Why not the part of eights? Who knows, but thanks to the perfectly ridiculous act of fate that gave humans ten fingers, every ...*For Dummies* book has a part of tens. Here are Ten Golden Rules, Ten Nifty Tricks, Ten Things NOT to Do, and other suggestions and recommendations that will make your life easier.

# Icons Used in This Book

You'd think we were in Czarist Russia from the popularity of icons in the computer world. Everything from toasters to VCRs has got icons instead of words now, which is no doubt responsible for all those sleepy folks sticking bread into the tape slot at breakfast time. (That's not a problem at your house?) Anyway, not to be left behind, this book uses icons, too — only ours are much cuter than the ones on your toaster. Here's what they mean:

If there's an easier or faster way to do something, or if there's something really cool, you'll find one of these target-thingies in the margin.

If there's something that you really shouldn't miss, this icon appears to let you know about it.

This icon reminds you that you shouldn't forget to remember something — something that was said earlier but is easily forgotten.

This icon cheerfully tells you of something that might go wrong, with consequences ranging from mild indigestion to weeping, wailing, and gnashing of teeth.

You won't see too much of Mr. Science here (alias the *Dummies* guy) in this book. When he does appear, he indicates that here's a little inside information on how things work that you just might want to know. But, if you give him a miss, you won't be much worse off.

If there's something important somewhere else in the book, this icon lets you know about it. Because a lot of Works tools work alike, there are a bunch of these guys.

# The One Shortcut Used in This Book

This book always uses genuine English words to descibe how things work! Well, almost always (sorry). There's one important exception. When you see an instruction that looks something like this,

"Choose Blah⇨Fooey from the menu bar . . ."

it means, "Click on Blah in the menu bar, and then click on Fooey in the menu that drops down." (If you don't know what *click on*, *menu bar*, or *menu* mean, that's okay — see Chapters 1 and 2.)

This sort of instruction crops up so often that, if we didn't use that shortcut, you'd be bored silly by Chapter 3 — and IDG Books would have to slaughter another forest worth of trees to get the extra paper to print the book!

# Where to Go from Here

If Works is already installed on your PC, you probably have tried to do something with it. You are probably already perplexed, annoyed, or intrigued by something you've already seen. Look it up in the table of contents or the index and see what this book has to say about it. If you're just trying to start a document in Works, see Chapter 1. If you're trying to master some of the basics, such as controlling windows and moving around, see Chapter 2.

If Works isn't already installed on your PC, fear not. Go to the installation appendix, Appendix B, at the end of this book. If *Windows 95* isn't already installed, and you have to do it yourself, pick up a copy (well, buy a copy) of *Windows 95 For Dummies* by Andy Rathbone.

Otherwise, drag a comfy chair up to your PC, bring along a plate of cheese for your mouse, and thumb through the book until you find something fun. Feeling whimsical? Check out Part VI, "Creating Great Works of Art: Graphics." Got some junk mail to send? Turn to Appendix A, "Wisdom and Wizardry for Common Tasks." You may end up with something useful, and — in any event — it beats the heck out of working!

# Part I
## Survival Skills

**The 5th Wave**     By Rich Tennant

"...AND HERE IS OUR FOCUS GROUP THAT DECIDES WHAT FEATURES GO INTO THE NEXT VERSION OF WORKS."

# In this part . . .

*T*he old recipe for bear stew read: "First, catch a bear."
This was great as long as the reader was pretty well up
to speed on bears. Otherwise the prospective stew-er
became the stew-ee more often than not.

If you think most computer books, like that recipe, leave out
some pretty important fundamentals, Part I of this book is
where you want to start. Here's where you can find out how
to use and control the windows on your PC; how to start
programs like Works; what all those weird keys are on your
keyboard; what your mouse or trackball is all about; how to
create folders on your computer; and all those other
fundamentals that other books assume you know all about.

"Though this be madness, yet there is method in't."

*Hamlet*, Wm. Shakespeare

# Chapter 1

# Starting

· · · · · · · · · · · · · · · · · · · · · · · · · · · · · · · · · · · · · · · · · · ·

## In This Chapter

▶ Using your keyboard

▶ Using your mouse or trackball

▶ Starting Works

▶ Using and losing the Task Launcher

▶ Starting new documents

▶ Files, disks, folders, and directories

▶ Starting with an existing document

▶ Finding documents

· · · · · · · · · · · · · · · · · · · · · · · · · · · · · · · · · · · · · · · · · · ·

*L*ots of software books jabber away about keyboards, mice, files, disks, folders, and directories as if you had spent your childhood with a mouse in your hand and had used a keyboard for a pillow. (If you were born before about 1980, the only way that this circumstance could have happened is if you had lived in a rodent-infested typewriter shop. If you were born after 1980, you are probably genetically hardwired to use a computer and need only a quick refresher.)

This book does things a little differently. Here you can start at the beginning, if starting at the beginning is what you need to do. This chapter talks about some things that few software books ever tell you, such as what's what on your keyboard, how to use your mouse, and what icons, files, disks, folders, and directories are.

If you're already keyboard-qualified, rodent-ready, and file-familiar, thumb ahead in this chapter to the section on starting Works. (If you haven't already installed Works, however, check out Appendix B, "Installation.") If you've already managed to get Works started, read on about Works' Task Launcher, which helps you create new documents and find where your existing ones are hiding in that vast expanse of your disk drive.

# *Using Your Keyboard*

Take a look at your keyboard. I bet it looks something like Figure 1-1. If you're using a laptop computer, all bets are off. The laptop manufacturers put stuff where they feel like putting it, so you have to check your manual.

- ✔ **Function keys:** These keys are usually located along the top of the keyboard and are labeled F1 through F10 or F12. The function keys carry out one set of commands when you use them by themselves; these same keys carry out other commands when you use them with the *shift keys:* Alt, Ctrl, and Shift.

- ✔ **Typewriter keys:** Your old Royal typewriter had most of the same characters, numbers, and punctuation keys. The computer people added a few new ones to jazz things up. You use these keys mostly to type stuff in, but you can use them with the Alt, Ctrl, and Shift keys to issue commands.

- ✔ **Navigation keys:** These keys are to the right of the typewriter keys. Four of the keys have arrows on them and move the cursor when you're typing or move the highlight that appears when you're using Windows menus or scroll bars. The others, marked Home, End, PgUp (or Page Up), and PgDn (or Page Down), are keys that move you around in a document in large gulps. Nearby are a Delete key (which deletes stuff) and an Insert key (which doesn't actually insert anything). Try not to hit the Insert key. If you do, it makes you type over existing text; hit the Insert key again to type normally.

- ✔ **Numeric keypad:** The keys on this keypad basically duplicate the number keys and useful math symbols that are across the top of your keyboard. On many computers, the numeric keypad also duplicates the Enter key. The keypad can alternatively perform the function of the navigation keys if you press the Num Lock button, located somewhere nearby.

- ✔ **Enter key:** Generally labeled Enter or marked or with a funny L-shaped arrow, this key is used mostly to signal that you've finished typing a paragraph or some data. You generally *do not* use the Enter key the way that you do on a typewriter, to end every line.

- ✔ **Esc key:** Called the Escape key, this little guy lets you back out of commands you didn't mean to get into.

- ✔ **Shift keys:** The keys in this shifty bunch don't do anything by themselves — they work only in combination with other keys, sort of like the pedals on a piano. When the Shift, Alt, and Ctrl (pronounced Control) keys are held down, they impart new meanings to other keys.

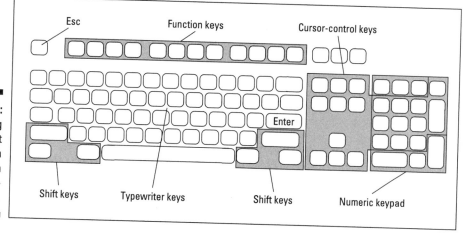

Esc — Function keys — Cursor-control keys

Enter

**Figure 1-1:**
Interesting
keys, most
of which
weren't on
your Smith-
Corona.

Shift keys — Typewriter keys — Shift keys — Numeric keypad

When you use shift keys, use them in the right sequence, as shown in these steps:

1. **Press a shift key (Shift, Alt, or Ctrl, as directed) first and hold it down.**
2. **Press the other key (the F6 key, for example).**
3. **Finally, release both keys.**

    If your fingers don't work well together, release the shift key last.

These types of combinations are written as Shift+F6, for example, or Ctrl+F6 or Alt+F6 (if F6 is the other key being pressed).

Sometimes, you must press more than two keys. Such an instruction is written as Ctrl+Shift+F6, for example; but the instruction may as well be written Shift+Ctrl+F6 because the order in which you press the Ctrl and Shift keys doesn't matter. Just get both of 'em down before you press the last key and release 'em all at once.

# Using Your Mouse or Trackball

That strange rodent-shaped object with push buttons on the top, plugged into your computer by its tail, is probably a *mouse*. If you have something with a ball on the topside, you probably have a *trackball*. If you don't seem to have a mouse or trackball, check the manuals that came with your computer and find out how to install one or the other. Using Windows or Works without a mouse or a trackball is practically impossible.

TIP

## *Really* basic basics

If you have a mouse, it goes on a pad on your desk, not on the floor. You operate the mouse with your hand, not your foot. The curved, button side goes up.

If you have a trackball, it also goes on your desk and needs to be kept from sliding around. The ball side goes up. Operate the ball and buttons with your fingers, not any other extremity. (If a ball is protruding from the surface of your laptop, it's probably the trackball, and its buttons are next to it.)

Any other modes of operation require a level of dexterity not known to exist in Earth fauna and are probably illegal between consenting adults in several states. This is not to say that otherwise intelligent people have not tried them.

## *Mouse anatomy and behavior*

The mouse or trackball is the modern, polite, and mature way to do what you did as a toddler: point at what you want. Now, however, you point by moving a *mouse pointer* or *mouse cursor* (typically an arrow, although its shape changes) that appears on your screen. You move the mouse pointer by moving the mouse around on your desk (preferably on a *mouse pad*) with your hand. With a trackball, you move the cursor by spinning the ball of the trackball with your fingers. After the pointer is over the thing you want, you *click* — that is, you press a button on the mouse/trackball.

The mouse (or trackball) generally wears two buttons. Really snazzy dressers may sometimes sport three. If you have a third, middle button, consider it a vestigial remnant of the days when giant, Jurassic-era mice roamed the country-side and intimidated each other with their vast arrays of buttons.

In Works and all other Windows programs, the left button is the most important one. (If you're left-handed, you can ask your computer guru to make the right button the most important one.)

The right mouse button, in Works, brings up a menu of commonly-used editing commands such as Copy and Paste. You can find the same editing commands elsewhere in Works, but this feature puts these commands conveniently at your fingertips.

## *Mouse skills*

The first mouse skill you need in order to control a Windows program is the ability to *point and click,* so here's exactly what this term and related terms mean:

✔ **To point:** Move the mouse pointer or cursor by pushing your mouse around or spinning the trackball. Move the pointer so that its tip is anywhere on top of, or very near, the thing that you're pointing at.

✔ **To click something (also called clicking "on" something):** Point to it and then press and release the button (traditionally the left one) on the mouse.

✔ **To double-click:** Press and release the button twice in rapid succession. Discovering just how fast you need to click may take a bit of time.

✔ **To click and drag:** Press the mouse button down and hold it down. Then move the mouse while holding down the button; this action *drags* something, such as the edge of a highlighted area, around on the screen. When you're done dragging, release the button.

# Understanding Files, Disks, Folders, and Directories

Besides keyboards and mice, another subject that lots of beginners are in the dark about is — what are the basic lumps of stuff that software is made of? Well, here's an overview of the fundamental atoms and molecules that make up that mysterious substance called *software.*

✔ *Files* are how your computer stores programs, your documents, and other forms of information. Each file has a *filename*, given either by you or by the program that created the file, so that you and the PC can both identify it.

✔ Your PC usually keeps its files on a *hard disk* that lives permanently in your PC. You can also keep copies of files on *diskettes* (those little flat plastic things that are often simply called *disks*) if you like, either for backup (in case your hard disk breaks) or to give to other people. The diskette drives (the places you put diskettes) are called *A:* and *B:* (you may have only *A:*). The hard disk is called *C:*. If you have a second hard disk or a CD ROM drive, it's drive is usually called *D:*. (Why the colons? It's ancient PC tradition.) If your computer is on a network, you can store things on disk drives on someone else's computer; talk to the person who manages your network in order to find out how you can do this task.

✔ You organize your files by using *folders*, analogous to file folders in a file cabinet. These computer file folders (sometimes called *directories* or *subdirectories*) have names, too. Some folders are created and named automatically by Windows 95 — other folders you have to create and name yourself. Works lets you create a new folder at the same time that you save a file, so that you can easily organize your documents. Folders are usually within folders within folders on your PC — a hierarchy of folders. To go *up* the hierarchy is to open the folder that contains the currently-open folder.

✔ Whenever you save your work in a file, you give your file a filename. In Works 4 and other programs that are designed for Windows 95, you can give files nice, readable filenames with spaces and punctuation in them, such as *Letter To Mom About Cookies*. (You can't, however, use any of these characters: * ? " < > | : / \.) If you have friends or colleagues who are still using earlier versions of Windows and you want to share your files with them, using filenames that are less than eight characters long is best (and use just letters and numbers — no spaces or punctuation).

✔ Files also have an *extension* to their name; an extension can be up to three characters long. The extension is added by the program that you use, such as Works, to help Windows identify what program made the file and what's in the file. You may, if you like, specify the extension yourself; but generally letting Works or whatever program you are using take care of specifying the extension is best. When Works asks you for a file or document name, don't bother adding the extension to the end.

✔ When you want to tell your computer in detail about a specific file in a specific location, you can put all the preceding information together into one line called a *path*. You start with the disk drive; then you add the directory (folder) name, any subdirectories' names (folders within that folder), filename, and finally the file extension. It goes something like this:

```
c:\letters\mom\cookies.wpd
```

# *Finding and Starting Works*

First things first — you need to wake Works up and get it running. What's that? Works is not installed? If you just bought Works and it's still sitting in a box on your desk, turn to Appendix B for all that you need to know in order to install Works on your own.

If you installed Works by using the recommendations in Appendix B, finding and starting Works is very easy. Look on your screen for the *icon* (tiny picture) labeled Shortcut to Microsoft Works 4.0 and double-click that icon. Figure 1-2 shows that icon and some of the other things that are probably on your screen.

If you can't find that Shortcut to Microsoft Works 4.0 icon, here's how to find and start Works:

1. **Click the Start button (shown in Figure 1-2).**

2. **In the menu that springs up, point with your mouse pointer to Programs and pause there.**

   Another menu appears next to the first one.

**Figure 1-2:**
The Start
button, the
Works
shortcut
icon, and
some of the
other icons
that may be
on your
screen.

3. **Move your pointer horizontally until it's on the new menu. Then move the pointer vertically to point to a folder icon labeled Microsoft Works 4.0.**

   Yet another menu appears. At this point, your screen has begun to resemble Figure 1-3.

4. **Again, move your pointer horizontally until it's on the latest menu. Then move your pointer down to point to another icon labeled Microsoft Works 4.0. Click that icon.**

Hey, you did it! You got Works running, and the Works window appears on your screen. You know that the window is the Works window if the title Microsoft Works appears on the top line. (All windows have a top line like this one, called the *title bar* of the window, that gives the name of the program or file that appears in that window.)

**Figure 1-3:**
Where
Works lurks:
menus
within
menus
within
menus.

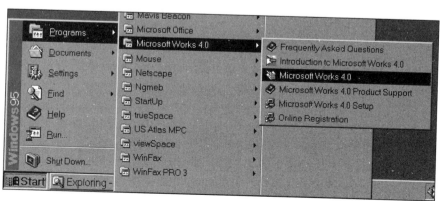

# Using and Losing the Task Launcher

As shown in Figure 1-4, when you first start Works, it displays a rectangular area entitled Works Task Launcher. Works Task Launcher helps you find files, choose the tool you need, or create a new document with a TaskWizard (an automated program).

You can call up the Task Launcher at any time while you're using Works. Simply choose File⇨New from the menu bar at the top of the screen or press Ctrl+N.

This book uses a shortcut way to describe choosing something from the *menu bar*, that list of words marching across your Works window just under the title bar. When this book says, "Choose *blah⇨fooey* from the menu bar," it means, "Click on the word *blah* in the menu bar; then click on the word *fooey* in the menu that drops down."

The Works Task Launcher gives you three ways to get going, represented as three *index cards,* whose tabs you see in Figure 1-4, with the TaskWizards card on top. Click one of the other tabs to see the contents of that card. The three ways to get going are to:

Click categories (in bold) for more TaskWizards.

Click tabs for other ways to start working.

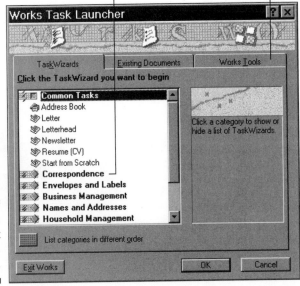

**Figure 1-4:**
The Works
Task
Launcher,
displaying
TaskWizards
— one of
three ways
to get
started on a
document.

✔ Have a TaskWizard create a new document for you.

✔ Choose a document from a list of recently-worked-on documents or find an existing document.

✔ Go directly to one of the four main Works tools.

The Task Launcher is a helpful feature when you are starting out, but later you may prefer to simply open the file that you need. To get rid of the Task Launcher, you can press the Esc key, click the Cancel button, or click the button marked X on the top-right corner of the dialog box.

If you don't use TaskWizards much, you would probably rather have Works display something other than the TaskWizards card when you start Works. To change the card that is initially displayed when you start Works, you use the Options tool. The following magic commands take you through the changing process:

1. **Press Esc to clear the Task Launcher.**

2. **Then choose Tools ⇨ Options from the menu bar and click on the Views tab in the Options dialog box.**

3. **Then press either Alt+X to choose the Existing Documents card for startup, Alt+K to choose the Works Tools card, or Alt+B to make Works remember the last card that you used.**

4. **Press the Enter key when you're done.**

# Starting New Documents with TaskWizards

*TaskWizards* are automated programs that ask you a few questions; they then automatically build (or at least begin to build) the document that you need. TaskWizards are great for keeping things simple, if you don't mind Works making some of your decisions for you.

There are lots of TaskWizards, in several categories, waiting to do your bidding. To use a TaskWizard, start from the Works Task Launcher. (If the Task Launcher is not on your screen, choose File⇨New from the Works menu bar or press Ctrl+N.) Choose the TaskWizards card and then:

✔ To see what TaskWizards are in a category (in bold type), click the category. (Click the category again to close it.)

✔ To see a description of the task, click its TaskWizard.

✔ To start a TaskWizard, double-click it.

TaskWizards generally just get you started — you still have to make changes to the document afterward. Some of these changes can be tricky, so for more information on using TaskWizards to do some of the more common tasks, such as creating mailing lists and newsletters, see Appendix A.

# Opening Existing Documents

If you have recently created or worked on a document in Works, Works remembers.

If you're using the Task Launcher when you get the urge to return to one of these recently-created-or-worked-on documents, click the Existing Documents tab in the Works Task Launcher, and you see a list as shown in Figure 1-5. (To get the Task Launcher on your screen, choose File⇨New from the Works menu bar or press Ctrl+N.)

To choose a document from this list, click on the document name and then click the OK button of the Task Launcher. Or you can just double-click the document name.

If you are already working on a document, you can find a short list of recently-opened documents by clicking File in the Works menu bar. Click one of the documents listed to open it.

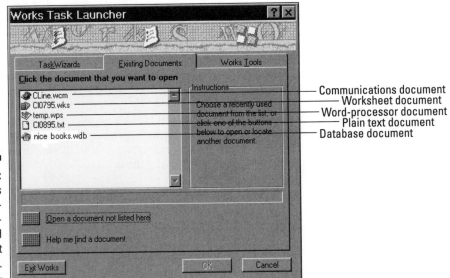

**Figure 1-5:**
Works lists your most-recently-used document first.

# Opening Existing Documents Not Listed on the Task Launcher

It is possible to have a document on your PC, but not have it show up on the Existing Documents card of the Task Launcher. This happens when you haven't used the document in awhile, or your copy of Works has never seen the document before, so Works doesn't know about it. For example, the document may have been created on another computer and brought over to your PC, the document may have been created by another program, or the document may have been created before you installed Works for Windows 95.

If you think that you know which folder your document is in, you can use the Existing Documents card of the Task Launcher to browse around and find the document.

If the Task Launcher is on your screen, click the Existing Documents tab; then click the Open a document not listed here button.

Clicking this button takes you to a dialog box called Open (short for *open a document*).

If the Task Launcher is not currently on your screen, choose File⇨Open from the Works menu bar or press Ctrl+O (that's the letter O, not the number 0). This procedure also takes you to the Open dialog box (as shown in Figure 1-6).

Look in any higher-level folder or disk drive.

The "Up One Level" button.

This is the folder you are looking in.

Show filenames only.

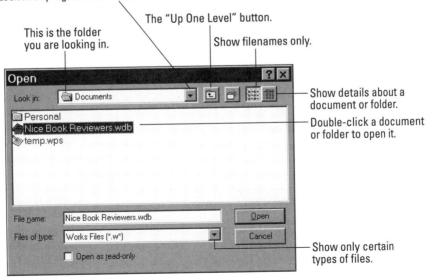

**Figure 1-6:**
The Open dialog box displays the contents of one folder at a time and starts you out in Works' Documents folder.

Show details about a document or folder.

Double-click a document or folder to open it.

Show only certain types of files.

## Browsing through the folders

The Open dialog box shows you the contents of whatever folder you looked in last. This dialog box displays the name of the folder at the top of the dialog box, in the area marked Look in.

- ✔ If you see the document that you want, double-click it (or click it and click the Open button).

- ✔ To open any of the folders displayed, double-click it.

- ✔ To open the folder that contains the folder Works is currently showing you, click the "Up One Level" button, at the top of the dialog box. (See Figure 1-6.)

- ✔ To go more than one level up the folder hierarchy, click the down-arrow button to the right of the Look in box. Click any folder in the list that appears.

- ✔ To look on a diskette (or to look at the very top of the folder hierarchy on your hard disk), click the down-arrow button to the right of the Look in box. In the list that appears, click disk drive *C:* for your hard disk, *A:* or *B:* for your diskette. (*D:* is typically your CD-ROM drive, if you have one, but you probably won't find any Works documents there.)

When you first start Works, it opens a folder called Documents and shows you what's inside the Documents folder. This Documents folder is within a folder called MSWorks, which is in another folder called Program Files.

## Looking for different types of documents

Works creates four main types of *documents* (or *files*), one type of document for each of the four main tools. Different types of documents have different icons, and their names end in unique three-letter combinations called *extensions*. The Works document types and their extensions are:

- ✔ database: wdb
- ✔ word processor: wps
- ✔ worksheet: wks
- ✔ communications: wcm

The Open dialog box initially displays all of these file types. (In fact, the Open dialog box displays any file with an extension beginning with the letter *w;* some of these files may come from another program, and Works may or may not be able to read them.)

If you want to see any other type of file (or if you are interested only in, say, Works spreadsheets), click the down-arrow to the right of the Files of type box and select one of the other types from the list that appears. If you are trying to open a file created by another program, your best choice is All files (*.*).

# Finding Documents with the Task Launcher

It won't take too long before you're knee-deep in documents and folders and need a little help finding the document that you want. Your buddy, the Task Launcher, can come to your rescue. (If the Task Launcher is not displayed, choose File⇨New from the Works menu bar or press Ctrl+N.)

With the Task Launcher on your screen, click the Existing Documents tab and then click the button labeled Help me find a document.

The Find dialog box springs into view. The Find dialog box may look familiar to you if you have used the Find tool in Windows 95. This familiarity exists because the tools are the same! (You get the Find dialog box directly from Windows 95 by using Start⇨Find⇨Files or Folders from the Windows 95 Taskbar.) For the full, gory details of using the Find dialog box, see *Windows 95 For Dummies* (IDG Books Worldwide, Inc.).

The Find dialog box has multiple *cards* like the Task Launcher has; click a named tab to select a card. Here are the most useful things to know, organized by card:

✔ **If you know part of the name:** Choose the Name & Location card.

First, press the Del key to delete what's there and type the part of the name that you remember in the Named box. Substitute the * (asterisk) character for any other part that you don't remember. So, for example, if you're looking for an invoice, and you know that the file begins with *inv,* type **inv\***. To look only for Works documents, add a Works three-letter extension to the end: .wps for a word processing file, .wks for a worksheet file, .wdb for a database file, or .wcm for a communications file.

✔ **If you know when the file or folder was created or last modified:** Choose the Date Modified card.

First, click Find all files created or modified. Then specify the date, either by editing the between fields or by specifying a number of preceding months or days.

✔ **If you know any text that the file or folder contains:** Choose the Advanced card.

This selection is *really* useful because you don't have to remember anything about the document's name or location! If you wrote a letter to

Mr. Smith about condominiums, just enter either Smith or condominium into the Containing text box. Try to choose a unique word or phrase.

✔ **After you have specified something on any or all of these cards: Press the Enter key or click Find Now.**

A list of documents appears at the bottom of the Find dialog box — just double-click the document you want in order to open it!

# Starting by Choosing a Tool

Some of us simpler-minded types prefer to skip all this helpful Task-Launcher stuff — such as TaskWizards and lists of recently-used files — and just start by choosing the tool that we want. If that's the way you work, too, just click the Works Tools tab on the Task Launcher and pick your tool. (To get the Task Launcher if it's not on your screen already, choose File⇨New from the Works menu bar or press Ctrl+N.)

Works has four main tools, and the Tools card gives you brief descriptions of what these four tools do. Click one of the four buttons to use a tool. For more details on each tool, see that tool's section in this book. For an overview of these tools, see Chapter 2.

# Chapter 2

# Getting Around

· · · · · · · · · · · · · · · · · · · · · · · · · · · · · · · · · · · · · · ·

*In This Chapter*

▶ Understanding the tools of Works

▶ Controlling Windows

▶ Understanding menus and toolbars

▶ Using the keyboard command shortcuts

▶ Getting around in your document

▶ Using dialog boxes

▶ Using and controlling Help

▶ Saving files and creating folders

▶ Exiting Works and shutting down your PC

· · · · · · · · · · · · · · · · · · · · · · · · · · · · · · · · · · · · · · ·

*I*f cars had as many gadgets and doodads as Windows software does, we'd all be taking the bus. Works for Windows 95 tries to be helpful about it, but sometimes even the help can be a little bewildering. So this chapter tries to point out the stuff you need for day-to-day survival, including some Windows basics that nobody may have pointed out to you before.

## The Tools of Works

Works is a program made up of smaller programs called *tools*. When Microsoft built Works, it put in a bunch of tools that they think most folks are likely to need sometime. No matter how you start a document — even if you start it by using a TaskWizard — you are using one of these tools. These tools include:

✔ a word processor for writing letters and other documents

✔ a spreadsheet for creating tables and doing calculations

✔ a database tool for storing large amounts of information and helping you find it easily

- ✔ a communications tool that lets your computer talk to other computers
- ✔ a charting tool for making charts out of the information in spreadsheets and tables
- ✔ a drawing tool called Microsoft Draw
- ✔ a tool called WordArt for doing artistic things to words and letters
- ✔ a bunch of other little tools, such as a spell checker and a thesaurus

The first four are what I call the Big Four; the others are sort of helper tools, like elves. I talk about each of the Big Four and various elves in detail in Parts II through V. Right now, I show you what the tools have in common.

As with a Swiss Army knife, you usually have only one tool open at a time, although there's nothing to stop you from having several tools open at once. Sometimes having more than one tool open at a time is helpful. You may, for example, want to create a drawing (using the drawing tool) to be inserted into a document that you're working on (using the word processor). You still *use* only one tool at a time, but you want to switch back and forth between them quickly and easily.

Each tool is a specialist: it works only on its own kind of thing. The drawing tool is for working on drawings; the spreadsheet tool is for tables and spreadsheets. But these tools do work together. For example, when you need to create a drawing in a document, the word processor calls in Microsoft Draw as a specialist. When you need to put a spreadsheet in a document, the word processor calls in the spreadsheet tool.

The things that these tools work on are all called *documents* by Microsoft, which therefore forces us to talk about word-processor documents, spreadsheet documents, database documents, and so on. What a bore. Most of the time in this book, I rebel and call the spreadsheet documents *spreadsheets* and the database documents *databases* and the graphics documents *graphics*. Radical, huh?

As with the Swiss Army knife (and I promise to drop this analogy soon), the individual tools in Works are not the *best* — in the sense of being the most fully featured — of their kind. Just as a professional carpenter would probably prefer a solid screwdriver to the folding one in the knife, a professional financial analyst would probably prefer a more fully featured spreadsheet program, such as Excel, Quattro Pro, or Lotus 1–2–3, to the one in Works. Nonetheless, the Works tools are perfectly fine for most of what the vast majority of people want to do, and they cost less and need less memory and disk space on your computer. In a way, Works' tools *are* the best because they don't have a lot of extraneous features that you don't need and that would only trip you up.

Because all these tools are part of the same Works package, they look and work very much alike. When you go to print a spreadsheet, for example, you do it almost exactly the same way that you would print a word-processor document. Certain things may be different, but the similarities are very helpful. You don't have to relearn the basic commands for each tool.

# Controlling Works' Windows

After you start working on a document, you're often confronted with a window full of confusing stuff. What's more, the window is probably an inconvenient size and is covering up something important on your screen.

Works' windows behave like every other program's windows that runs under Windows 95. You can refer to _Windows 95 For Dummies_ (IDG Books Worldwide, Inc.) for the full gory details on handling windows, but the basics are here.

Here's how to manage Works' windows:

## Controlling Works' program window

To get your Works window under control, belly up to the _title bar_. Every window in Windows has a bar (called the title bar) at the top that describes what that window is all about. Whenever you are working in a particular window, its title bar gets colored in. Otherwise, it remains a sleepy, dull gray. To select a window, just click in the blank area of the title bar.

The title bar also contains (in the right-hand corner) buttons useful for controlling the size of your program window, as shown in Figure 2-1.

Figure 2-1 shows you how to minimize, maximize, and close Works, and defines what those terms mean. Here are a few other things you can do:

**Figure 2-1:**
The Works title bar heads your Works window and provides buttons to control window size.

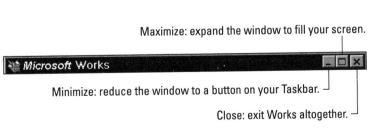

Maximize: expand the window to fill your screen.

Minimize: reduce the window to a button on your Taskbar.

Close: exit Works altogether.

**To shrink a "maximized" Works window:** When you have expanded the window to its maximum, Windows replaces the "maximize" button by one that looks like this:

Click this guy to restore your Works window to an intermediate size.

**To enlarge/reduce the window's width or height:** Click an edge or corner of the window (where your cursor turns into a two-headed arrow) and drag the edge or corner in any direction.

**To restore the window after it's been shrunk to a Microsoft Works button on the Taskbar:** Click that button. (The Works button has the Works icon on it; the Taskbar is that gray bar in Windows 95 with the Start button on it.)

**To move the Works window:** Click the title bar, but not on any of the buttons or the Works icon at the far left. Hold down the mouse button, drag the window where you want it, and release the mouse button.

You can also control the Works window by clicking the Works icon at the far left of the title bar and then clicking a selection in the menu that drops down.

## Controlling Works' document windows

Like one of those Russian dolls that's full of more dolls (a *Matroishka*, I think), the Works window contains even more windows. Whenever you create or open a document or create a drawing or graph, that document, drawing, or graph gets its own window. (Most of the time, you have only one document open.)

If you open more than one document at a time, things may get a little more confusing. Look at the Works program window in Figure 2-2, which shows the Works window with four different document windows (plus the Help window) open at once.

Here are the important facts to know about managing document windows:

- ✔ **Only one document can be active at a time:** The *active document* is the one whose title bar is in some exotic designer color, such as blue.

- ✔ **To make a document active:** Click the document anywhere — but preferably on the blank area of the title bar so that you don't accidentally change something.

- ✔ **To bring any document window to the top:** Click any part of that document that you can see. If you can't see the document at all, click <u>W</u>indow and then click the name of the document, which is listed in the bottom part of the menu that drops down.

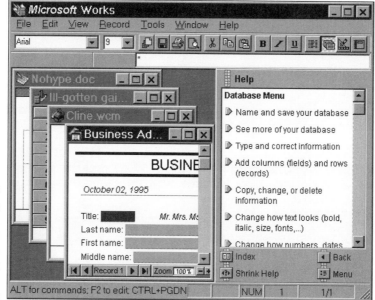

**Figure 2-2:**
Works with
several
documents
open at
once.

✔ **Works automatically switches to the right kind of tool for a document when you choose that document:** The menu bar and the tool bar change subtly when you choose a different type of document.

✔ **To shrink or enlarge a document window:** You can control a document window the same way that you control the Works program window: use the buttons in the upper right-hand corner of the window. The buttons look the same as for the Works window.

✔ **When you minimize a document window:** The document window becomes a little rectangle in the bottom-left corner of the Works window. Click the little rectangle to reinflate the document window.

If your document window is maximized (and that's how documents usually start out), the tiny buttons that shrink and enlarge that window don't appear in the title bar (for reasons known only to Microsoft). Nope, they appear instead just under the minimize/maximize/close buttons for Works, on the Works *menu bar,* for cryin' out loud! They look like this:

See how nice and neat the document windows are in Figure 2-2? You don't think that *I* did that, do you? Not a chance. You should see my office. I can't even see my desktop. No, such neatness is a product of the Window menu in the Works menu bar.

**To arrange documents neatly overlapping as in Figure 2-2:** Click Window⇨Cascade (in the menu that drops down).

**To arrange documents side by side, like tiles:** Click Window⇨Tile (in the menu that drops down).

**For any other arrangement:** You have to do the arranging yourself by shrinking, enlarging, and moving windows. Whichever window is active is always displayed on top.

# Zooming

"If you can't raise the bridge, lower the water." This saying has served many people well over the years, despite the fact that it is complete gibberish. Continuing in this vein, an alternative to making a window bigger so that you can see more is to make the document text smaller, known as zooming out. (Or is it zooming in?) Never could remember, but never mind; it's zooming, anyway.

The important thing to realize is that zooming has absolutely no effect on your document. Zooming just makes the text look bigger or smaller. Your document prints out the same.

Here's one way to zoom:

**Click View⇨Zoom:** The Zoom dialog box zooms into view and lets you choose a magnification expressed as a percentage. You can either click one of the standard percentages listed there, such as 75%, or type a percentage in the Custom rom. Click the OK button in this dialog box when you're done.

**To shrink a document in a window:** Use a percentage less than 100%.

**To magnify a document in a window:** Use a percentage greater than 100%.

Here's another way to zoom:

**Click the minuscule + or – buttons next to the Zoom button at the bottom-left corner of your document window.** The + button enlarges your document; the – button shrinks it.

# Getting Around in Your Document

The smoothest way to get around in your document is to slide! At the side and bottom of each document window are scroll bars (which I think should be called "sliders") that let you move the document around within the document window.

To see farther up or down in your document, use the vertical scroll bar, which looks like Figure 2-3:

✔ **To slide the document up or down in little increments:** Click the arrows at top and bottom.

✔ **To slide the document with a lot more speed:** Click and drag the box in the middle up or down. (Or click above or below the box.) The position of this box on the scroll bar gives you a rough idea of how far down in the document you are. If the box is large, nearly filling the scroll bar, that means most of your document is visible in the window.

✔ **To slide the document horizontally (in case your window isn't wide enough to display the entire width of the document):** A horizontal scroll bar at the bottom of the window works the same way as the vertical one.

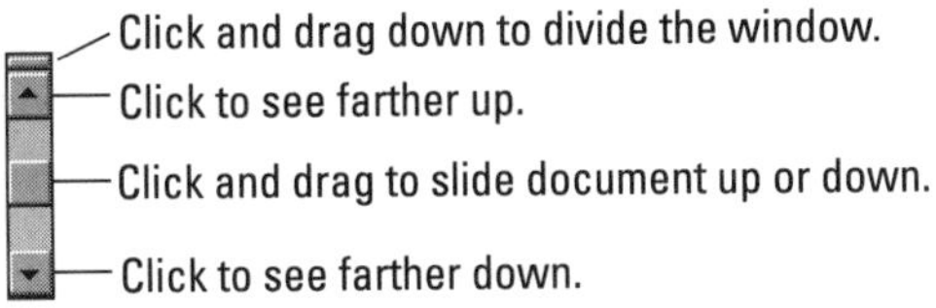

**Figure 2-3:**
The vertical scroll bar.

Click and drag down to divide the window.
Click to see farther up.
Click and drag to slide document up or down.
Click to see farther down.

A little-known feature of the vertical scroll bar is the capability to divide the document window into two parts. This feature is great if, for example, you want to see two distant parts of your document at once. To perform this trick, click and drag the tiny bar at the top of the scroll bar downward; stop about halfway down the document window. When you release the mouse button, your document window divides into two parts. Each of these subwindows has its own scroll bars so that you can view two different parts of your document! To return to a single window, click and drag the bar back up to the top.

Another easy way to get around in your documents is to "navigate"! For this technique, use the *navigation keys* on your keyboard: the arrow keys plus the PgUp and PgDn keys. The navigation keys move the blinking cursor that defines where editing takes place, and your document slides around to keep that cursor visible in the window. The arrow keys move one step at a time, but the PgUp and PgDn keys move one window's worth at a time.

If you use the scroll bars to move around in your document, make sure that you click in the new location before you begin typing or editing. The scroll bars move your viewpoint around, but the scroll bars do not move the blinking cursor that defines where the editing action takes place. Put that cursor where you want it by clicking before you type. Otherwise, your cursor jumps back to its preceding location as soon as you press a key.

# Ordering from the Menu Bar

The main way to place your orders in Works is to use the menu bar, shown in Figure 2-4. Click any of the words in the menu bar, and a menu of commands drops down. Click one of these commands to execute it. You may not even be done before another menu or a dialog box springs up!

The sequential process of choosing things from menus is pretty boring to write about (and even more boring to read about) without using some kind of shortcut notation. I could say, "Click File on the menu bar; then click Save on the menu that drops down," but this kind of talk would drive you batty after a while. So in this book (and in ...*For Dummies* books in general), I say the same thing using this kind of notation:

Choose File⇨Save

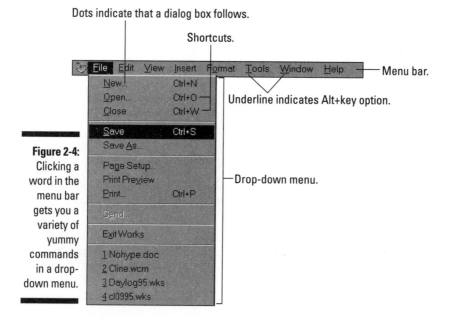

**Figure 2-4:** Clicking a word in the menu bar gets you a variety of yummy commands in a drop-down menu.

Just like the menu in your local sandwich shop, a large portion of the Works menu bar always appears the same. This regularity is true no matter what tool you are using — the menu bar appears very much the same. However, each of the words on this menu bar leads to a set of commands, some of which change with different tools. So if ever the commands on a menu look unfamiliar to you, it is probably because you have different types of documents open in Works, and you have switched from one type to another. This book goes into detail on the more important differences in the tool-specific Parts II through V.

Here's generally what you can do in each of these menu bar selections:

**File:** Open, close, and save documents; set up the page layout; and print.

**Edit:** Copy text and numbers, move them, find them, replace them; also (and very important) undo whatever change you just made to the document.

**View:** See things differently or otherwise change the way the screen looks (but without changing the document itself), such as by turning the toolbar on or off.

**Insert:** Plug stuff into your document, such as illustrations from another document or file.

**Format:** Change the appearance of text and numbers and how they line up.

**Tools:** Use the spell checker or other little helpers to the Big Four tools.

**Window:** Arrange the document windows or make a different window active.

**Help:** Read help information about Works or turn the Help feature on or off.

# Keep your eye on the bottom line!

If, before you choose any of the commands in a drop-down menu, you would like a reminder of what the command does, keep your eye on the Works status bar. No, the status bar is not some high-status watering hole in, say, trendy Foster City, California (home of IDG Books) — the status bar is the bottom line of the Works window.

After you click File or any of the other words in the menu bar, a drop-down menu appears. Without clicking any buttons on your mouse, move your mouse slowly in the "down" direction. As you do this, you move the colored highlight down the drop-down menu. The status bar tells you what the highlighted command does. Click to choose that command.

Part I of this book deals with the commands that remain the same in each of these menus. For anything in these menus unique to a particular tool, see that tool's part later in this book.

# Command Shortcuts Using the Keyboard

If you don't want to take the time to order from a menu, here's a shortcut. Some commands in the drop-down menus have a key combination (such as Ctrl+S) shown on the same line. That means you don't even have to make that menu drop down in order to use that command — just press the key combination. Ctrl+S, for example, saves your document as a file. You can find these shortcuts easily because they are listed in the drop-down menu whenever you click a menu selection. See Figure 2-4 for examples.

If you're more comfortable using a keyboard than a mouse, Windows gives you another way to use menus. See all those underlined letters in the menu bar? Press the Alt key *and* the underlined letter key on the menu bar, and the drop-down menu springs cheerfully up (so to speak) under that word. To choose a command from the drop-down menu, just press the letter *without* the Alt key.

The Ctrl+key combinations work immediately, without going through the menu. The Alt+key combinations let you pick items off whatever menu is currently displayed so that you use the key combinations sequentially; for example, use *Alt+F* to open the File menu followed by *S* to save a file.

## When commands go gray

One aspect of Windows that occasionally gives new users gray hairs is the "graying out" of certain commands on a drop-down menu or in a dialog box. An example of graying out is the Send command in Figure 2-4.

When commands are grayed out, they are temporarily inactive, not applicable, or otherwise unavailable for comment. Generally, you won't care; but sometimes you really, really *want* Works to execute that command. Well, to do so, you have to figure out *why* that command is currently deactivated. Why doesn't it apply in this case? For example, the Send command in Figure 2-4 is inactive because I don't have networking on my PC, and I can't send the document anywhere. Generally, something is grayed out because the action that command is responsible for can't be done at the time or the item the command relates to just isn't present in your document (or in the area of your document that you have selected).

# Toiling with Toolbars

The Works menu bar is lovely, full of genuine English words and lots of drop-down menus. Although the Works menu bar is quite nice, it's just a tad tedious to use sometimes. You click the menu bar, you click the drop-down menu, you click the dialog box . . . pretty soon your eyes glaze over and you just sit there and click . . . click . . . click — until you are found and revived, days later, by the *Mouse-Induced-Stupor (MIS) Patrol.*

After having had to resuscitate a few afflicted colleagues, the engineers at Microsoft did something about this grave problem. They employed the classic engineering technique of going to a bar. In this case, they went to a tool bar (known in Works parlance as the toolbar).

The *toolbar,* shown in Figure 2-5, is the line of stuff just under the menu bar — the toolbar is the one that's as full of icons as a Russian museum. If you find the toolbar aesthetically displeasing or just plain don't want it around, you can click View⇨Toolbar to remove it from the screen. If you later decide that you want it back, do the same thing.

Each *icon* is a shortcut alternative to some command in the menu bar — a command that the folks at Microsoft thought that you may use a lot. Just click the icon once, and stuff happens: your file gets saved, for example, or you print something out. No more click, click, click. Just click.

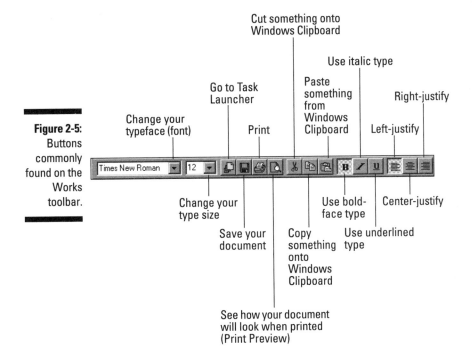

**Figure 2-5:** Buttons commonly found on the Works toolbar.

Cut something onto Windows Clipboard

Use italic type

Go to Task Launcher

Paste something from Windows Clipboard

Right-justify

Change your typeface (font)

Print

Left-justify

Change your type size

Use bold-face type

Center-justify

Save your document

Copy something onto Windows Clipboard

Use underlined type

See how your document will look when printed (Print Preview)

The selection of icons in the toolbar changes a bit. Some icons appear in all of the Big Four tools of Works; others appear only for a particular tool. For example, the Save icon appears in each toolbar because you always need to be able to save your work. On the other hand, the Insert Record icon appears only with the database tool. That icon makes no sense anywhere else. The toolbar changes along with your tool, so if you switch your active window from a database document to a spreadsheet document, the toolbar changes.

The icons that appear most frequently are shown in Figure 2-5.

If you forget what an icon is supposed to do, just move your mouse cursor over it (don't click). A tiny yellow square appears with a one-word description of the icon's function. The status bar at the bottom of the Works window gives you a few more words about the icon.

For more about the editing, formatting, and file operations that these buttons actually do, see Chapters 3 and 4.

For each tool in Works, as it turns out, you can customize which icons appear on your toolbar. I'm not going to fool with telling you how to customize your icons in this book. If you want to take matters into your own hands, the command for changing icons is Tools⇨Customize Toolbar.

# Dealing with Dialog Boxes

*Dialog boxes* tend to crop up all over the place. A command that ends in three dots (...) warns you that you're about to have to deal with a dialog box. The dialog box's purpose in life is to let you specify important details about the command, such as what to name something you want to store and where to put it.

On the surface, dialog boxes look like windows, but you can't shrink or expand dialog boxes. (You can drag them around by their title bars, though, if they are in the way.) Internally, dialog boxes can look like darn near anything. Here, in Figure 2-6, is an example from Works. Fortunately, certain internal gadgets (I prefer the technical name, "thingy") reappear regularly.

Following is how this dialog box stuff works. Don't try to memorize all the names and distinctions of the thingies. I certainly don't use the names any more than I have to. Just refer back here if you get confused about a dialog box.

**Explanation button (question mark):** Click this button in the title bar, and a question mark attaches itself to your mouse cursor. "Gee, how useful!" you say. But wait — the excitement is yet to come: if you *then* click a button or setting in the dialog box, you'll see an explanation of that item. Click in a plain area of the dialog box to clear the explanation off the screen.

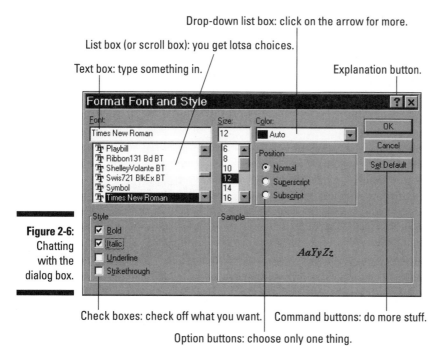

Drop-down list box: click on the arrow for more.

List box (or scroll box): you get lotsa choices.

Text box: type something in.

Explanation button.

**Figure 2-6:**
Chatting
with the
dialog box.

Check boxes: check off what you want.  Command buttons: do more stuff.

Option buttons: choose only one thing.

**Text box:** You can type something in a text box, but often a quicker way (such as clicking something in a *list box* immediately underneath the text box) is available to accomplish the same task. When you open a text box, it usually has something in it as a suggestion. You can delete that suggestion by pressing the Delete key, or you can change the suggestion by clicking anywhere in the box to get a typing cursor. Type or press the Backspace or Delete keys to erase stuff. Do *not* press the Enter key when you're done typing unless you don't need to do anything else in this dialog box!

**List or scroll box:** List boxes or scroll boxes show you a list of choices. Click one of the choices, and your choice generally appears in a text box above the list. Double-click on one, and the computer not only chooses that item, but it also tells the dialog box, "I'm done; go and do your thing!" If more text is in the list than fits in the box, a scroll bar appears alongside the list box. (Such scroll bars work like the scroll bars in your document window.)

**Drop-down list box:** A drop-down list box is like a list box, but you have to act to make it appear. To make a drop-down list box reveal itself, click the down-pointing arrow alongside the box.

**Check boxes:** Check boxes are like tax forms, but even more fun. Check off one or more things by clicking them or the box next to them. A check mark appears when an item is selected. Click the item (or the box next to it) again to deselect it.

**Option buttons:** These buttons allow you to click only one thing in the list. The center of the button appears black when the button has been selected (is "on").

**Command buttons:** The most important command button is OK. Click the OK button when you're done with a task. If you want to back out of a command, click Cancel. Other command buttons may take you to yet more dialog boxes.

# Hollering for Help

We all need a little assistance now and then. A *little* assistance, I say, not necessarily the squadron of very eager helpers that have been built into Works. The helpers are all very nice, but they can be a bit overwhelming if you don't know how to keep them under control. In this section, I try to sort them all out and make the Help features of Works a little more, um . . . helpful.

The Help feature is a little bit like having a manual in your computer. The nice thing is that Works can sometimes put you on the right page of Help automatically, based on what you're doing at the time. (This feature, called *context-sensitive help,* is found in most Windows programs.) Even when Works doesn't put you on the right page automatically, you can look through the equivalent of a table of contents or an index and zap yourself to the right page.

## Kinds of help

Two basic kinds of help are available in Works:

- ✔ **Brief explanations of dialog box thingies:** When confronted with a dialog box that looks only slightly less complex than the cockpit of a jet fighter, here's how you can find out what the various buttons and settings do: click the ? button in the upper right-hand corner of the dialog box and then click the button or setting. A brief explanation appears; to make the explanation go away, click a blank area of the dialog box.

- ✔ **Detailed documentation on how to do things:** This form of help appears in the panel that pops up automatically in Works whenever you start a new document, and it sets up shop in the right-hand side of the Works window. I describe this type of help in the rest of this section.

## Getting . . . and getting rid of . . . Help

One of the first things you may want to do with Help is put it away! If you don't need Help, the pop-up panel is, after all, taking up valuable real estate on the right side of your Works window. To put Help away, click the ? button labeled Shrink Help at the bottom of the Help panel. That button then retreats to the lower-right edge of your Works window; click this button again to restore the Help panel. Alternately shrinking and restoring the Help panel is a good way to follow the Help instructions without the Help panel itself getting in your way.

You can call the Help squadron into action by doing any of the following:

- Press the F1 key to get help related to whatever you're currently doing.
- Choose Help⇨Contents from the menu bar to choose help for a particular tool.
- Choose Help⇨Index from the menu bar to get help on darned near anything.
- Click the button with the tiny book-like icon in the lower-right edge of the Works window (this icon, too, takes you to the Help Index).

 These commands not only bring up the panel that displays the actual Help information as shown in Figure 2-7, they also bring up the Help Topics dialog box. This dialog box is helpfully designed to help you find the help you need. (Oh, Help!) See "Help on what? Using Help's Index and Contents," coming up soon.

Click buttons for help.

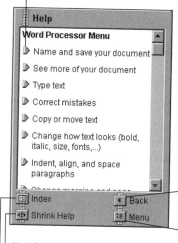

**Figure 2-7:** The Help panel being its helpful self.

Use Back to back up to previous Help page.

Use Menu to see top-level Help on this tool.

Use Shrink Help to get Help off your screen.

Use Index to type in a request.

# Pinky finger alert!

Touch typists, keep your pinky fingers under control. Pinky fingers tend to want to press the Enter key or the Esc key, either of which can make a dialog box go away. When you press Enter, the dialog box goes off and does stuff, even if you're not ready for that stuff to be done. When you press Esc, the dialog box just goes away quietly, as if you never started the command (pressing Esc is the same as clicking the Cancel button).

## Navigating Help

Works' Help feature has a series of levels that you navigate by clicking the arrow-like bullets next to each topic. Each bullet is a link to another page of Help. Your goal is to get a set of numbered instructions. The levels go as follows:

Menu of Help topics for a tool (word processor, spreadsheet, database, or communications)— (To return here, click the Menu button at the bottom of the Help panel.)

   Subtopics, such as "To type text in the header or footer"

      Maybe more subtopics

         Your goal: step-by-step instructions and
         links to related topics or subtopics

## Help on what? Using Help's Index and Contents

Works tries to use what you are currently doing to figure out what topic you are interested in. For example, when you start a new word-processor document, Works puts up the word processor Help information.

If you want help on something other than what's displayed in the Help panel, choose either the Help Contents or the Index.

   ✔ **To type in a subject you want help on or to select a subject from an amazingly long list:** Choose Help⇨Index from the menu bar or click the Index button at the bottom of the Help panel.

   ✔ **To choose Help for a different tool than the one you're currently using:** Choose Help⇨Contents from the menu bar.

Either command brings up the Help Topics dialog box, which has two tabbed *cards* like the Task Launcher has. One of these cards is the Index, and the other card is the Contents.

The Index is the most helpful Help helper (so to speak). When the Index appears, simply type in a word or phrase describing what you want help on. As you type, Works looks at what you've typed so far and scrolls the list of topics to match the letters you have typed to a topic, if it can. When you see the subject that you want, just click it. (If the subject has a folder icon, the icon can open up and reveal subtopics.) The subject appears either in the Works Help window or in a separate dialog box.

# Saving Files and Creating Folders

Existence is fleeting and fragile, especially for Works documents. They flicker into life when you create them, but they cannot survive when Works is not running or your PC is off. To preserve Works documents, you have to save them as files on a disk. See "Understanding Files, Disks, Folders, and Directories" in Chapter 1 for more on files and their residences.

Works won't let you exit the program without asking you whether you want to save your work as a file, so you don't have to worry about that; but you never know when someone's going to trip over the power cord to your PC, so save your work to a file often.

There are three ways to save your document as a file — choose your favorite:

- ✔ Choose File➪Save from the menu bar.
- ✔ Press Ctrl+S.
- ✔ Click the button with the diskette icon (on the toolbar).

When you use these commands to save a document for the first time, Works gives you the Save As dialog box, as shown in Figure 2-8, so that you can give the file a name and a location. After you have saved the document for the first time, Works subsequently saves it with the same name and to the same location.

To make a copy of the file and give it a different name, different location, or even a different *file type*, use the File➪Save As command to get to the Save As dialog box. This procedure is helpful if you need slightly different versions of the same file (for example, if you are sending the same letter to three different people).

The Save As dialog box is a close relative of the Open dialog box described in Chapter 1. A twin, in fact. These two dialog boxes work in almost exactly the same way: you need to tell Works where the file is to go and what its name should be.

## Telling Works where the file should go

Unless you tell Works otherwise, it puts all your documents in one single folder. Like the extended-wear diaper, having all your documents in the same folder is not a particularly good idea. Both examples result in a rather full and untidy storage situation. You wouldn't put all your documents in a single folder in your file cabinet, would you? If you continually use this Works default, Works puts all your documents in its Document folder. (The Document folder is located within the MS Works folder, within the Program Files folder on your hard disk, in case you need to find it from another program.)

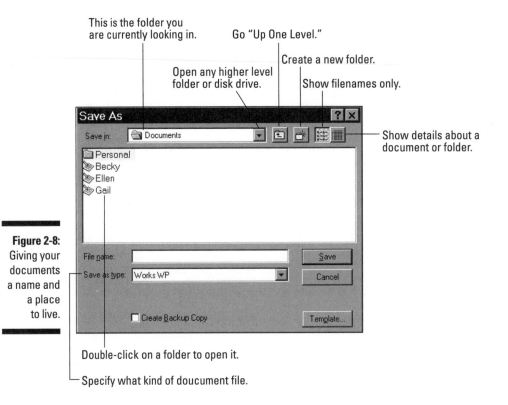

This is the folder you are currently looking in.

Go "Up One Level."

Open any higher level folder or disk drive.

Create a new folder.

Show filenames only.

Show details about a document or folder.

**Figure 2-8:**
Giving your documents a name and a place to live.

Double-click on a folder to open it.

Specify what kind of doucment file.

You have the choice of putting your document in any existing folder or creating a new folder for your document. You can create folders with the Documents folder, if you like. Here's how to specify what folder the document should go into:

- ✔ **To put your document in any of the named folders displayed in the big white box:** Double-click that folder.

- ✔ **To open the folder that contains the current folder:** Click the *up-one-level* button, at the top of the dialog box (see Figure 2-8).

- ✔ **To go more than one level up the folder hierarchy:** Click the down-arrow button to the right of the Save in box. Click any folder shown.

- ✔ **To use a disk or to open the very top of the folder hierarchy on your hard disk:** Click the down-arrow button to the right of the Look in box. Click a disk drive: *C:* for your hard disk; *A:* or *B:* for your diskette.

- ✔ **To create a new folder in the folder that's currently open (shown in the Save in box):** Click the New Folder button (see Figure 2-8). A new folder, cleverly named New Folder, appears; just type a name to replace that name.

## Naming your file

To name your file, put a name in the File name box. Just click there and type in a new name. (Leave off the three-letter extension; Works supplies it automatically according to the file type.)

You can choose to use the name of an existing file; just click the existing file's name in the big white area of the Save As dialog box. If you use a file that already exists, you overwrite the file, and its original contents are lost. Works warns you about this situation, however, and gives you a chance to change your mind.

For veterans of earlier Windows and DOS software, Windows 95 is cause to rejoice! You are no longer stuck with filenames of eight characters or less, with no spaces or funny characters! Now you can use filenames up to 255 characters long, with whatever you please for characters. Before you go wild, however, consider whether you're going to be giving files to some poor colleague still stuck in Windows 3.1 or DOS. If you are going to do that, stick to the old naming rules. Also, choose Works for Windows 3.0 — or whatever the name of the software is that your colleague is running — in the Save as type box.

# Works Stoppage

Why stop Works from running at all? Why not just minimize Works to a button on the Taskbar? Well, maybe you need to use some other program that takes a lot of memory. (You'd know that was the case because Windows would complain that it had insufficient memory when you tried to run the other program, or else all your programs would run very slowly.) Or, hey! Maybe you even want to shut off your PC and go to bed! (What a concept!)

Any one of the following can cause you to exit Works:

- ✔ Shut down your computer (using the Windows 95 Start⇨Shut Down command on the Taskbar).
- ✔ Click File⇨Exit Works.
- ✔ Click the button with the *X* in the upper right-hand corner of your Works window.
- ✔ From the Task Launcher, click the Exit Works button.

Works stops running, and the Works window disappears from your screen.

Except . . . if you've been working on something and haven't saved your work as a file, a dialog box pops up at this point. The dialog box asks whether Works should save changes to the file you're working on and gives you three choices: Yes, No, or Cancel.

✔ If you click Yes, whatever you've been doing in Works is saved with the filename you gave in the Save As dialog box. (Works makes up a name such as "Unsaved Document 1" if you never created a name for this document.) If you've been changing an existing file, the changes overwrite the old contents of that file; the process is just like recording over a videotape.

✔ If you click No, whatever you've been doing in Works goes to that big bit-bucket in the sky and is lost forever. If you've been working on an existing file, that file goes back to the way it was before you started working on it. If you had created a new file, you end up with nothing.

✔ If you click Cancel, nothing happens to your document. You don't exit Works, and nothing is saved.

This dialog box may appear several times, once for each different document you are working on. Each time this dialog box appears, it asks only about a single file. When all the open documents are saved, Works disappears from your screen.

# Chapter 3
# Basic Editing and Formatting

· · · · · · · · · · · · · · · · · · · · · · · · · · · · · · · · · · · · · · · · · · · · · · · · · · · ·

· · · · · · · · · · · · · · · · · · · · · · · · · · · · · · · · · · · · · · · · · · · · · · · · · · · ·

*Y*ou there, with the eyeshade and the ink stains. Yeah, you — you're an editor, believe it or not. In computerese (geek-speak), whenever you change a document, you have *edited* it. And, as it turns out, many of the basic editing operations are the same in the different tools of Works.

But before you whip out your blue pencil and go a-editing, you have to be able to do one really basic thing: tell Works exactly *what* text you want to edit — what to delete or move or underline, or whatever your editorial instincts induce you to do. This procedure is called *selecting*, or sometimes *highlighting*, text. Read on.

# Selecting (Highlighting)

*Selecting* is pointing out to Works exactly what in your document you want it to operate on: what text you want in bold or what illustration you want to delete or what cells in the spreadsheet you want to copy.

Selecting is really pretty simple. To select a bunch of stuff (text, spreadsheet cells, whatever) with your mouse, do the following mouse-based highlighting process:

1. **Click at one end of the text you want to select but keep your mouse button pressed; don't let it up.**

2. **Move your mouse pointer to the other end of the text you want to select.**

As you do this action, a black, rectangular area extends out in the direction you're moving, enveloping your text like an ominous fog. Incongruously, this fog is sometimes called the highlight. (In the word processor, the fog envelopes one character at a time until you extend it beyond one word; then it hungrily envelopes one word at a time!) If any illustrations are in the middle of your text, they're selected, too.

When you select multiple lines of text, don't go to the end of the line and then back to the beginning of the next, and so on; you can drive yourself buggy doing that. Like driving in Boston, just go directly toward your final destination, ignoring all intervening pedestrians and other distractions.

3. **Release the mouse button.**

The text is now selected, and your mouse cursor is free to do other stuff, like click editing commands or buttons. (If you're in the word processor, the word *drag* attaches itself parasitically to your cursor whenever the cursor passes over your selected text. Ignore that for now.)

If you didn't quite get the end point where you wanted it when you released the button, you can cleverly adjust the end point by using the arrow keys on your keyboard. (See the sidebar, "Text selection without rodents.")

# Text selection without rodents

If you're working while skydiving, bungee-jumping, or doing other tasks where mice are impractical, inaccurate, or downright hazardous, a mouse-free way to select text or adjust your selection is available:

1. **Use the navigation keys (arrow keys, plus Home, End, PgUp and PgDn) to position the insertion point at one end of the text you want to select.**

2. **Then hold down the Shift key and again use any navigation key to move the end point of the selection. Keep the Shift key down and press navigation keys repeatedly until you've selected the text that you want.**

In the word processor, this keyboard selection technique is useful in that — unlike selecting with the mouse — the highlight extends itself by only one character at a time. (If you want to extend it one word at a time, hold down both the Ctrl and Shift keys while you press navigation keys.)

This distinction lets keyboard selection serve as a clever trick for adjusting the end point of a selection you made with the mouse. Hold down the Shift key and press a navigation key, and you can adjust the end point of a selection you just made. Sorry, you can adjust only the end point, not the starting point.

Here are a few special cases. For more information on tool-specific special cases, see the chapter on that tool.

 ✔ **To select a word:** Double-click it. In the word processor are more such click-tricks that let you select lines and paragraphs. Check out Chapter 9 about the word processor.

 ✔ **To select the entire document:** Click <u>E</u>dit in the menu bar and then click Select <u>A</u>ll in the menu that drops down.

 ✔ **To select an illustration or chart or some other solitary chunk of stuff in your document:** Just click it once.

 ✔ **In a spreadsheet, just click a cell to select it.** Use the highlighting process to select multiple cells, though; a border makes a little corral around the selected area.

 ✔ **Likewise, to select a single field in a database, just click the field.** Selecting stuff in List view works just like in a spreadsheet.

# *Being Bold (or Italic): Quick Text Styles*

**B**/<u>u</u>? Or be I not you? That is the question. And if I *were* you, I'd want to know what these **B**, *I*, and <u>u</u> buttons in the Works toolbar are all about. Here's the answer:

(Warning! The following text contains material that may be offensive to anyone with poetic sensitivities or other forms of good taste.)

 **B** is for bold, as all writers should be,

 *I* is for italic, from Italy across the sea,

 <u>u</u> is for underline, when emphasis is key, and

 ***<u>this</u>*** is what you get when you use all three!

(See what writing computer books does to your brain? You have been warned!)

Bold, italic, and underlining are three really basic ways you can change the appearance (*format*) of your text. This particular form of text formatting is called *character formatting*, or more specifically, *changing the font style.*

## Changing the style for text that you've already typed

Here are the incredibly complex and sophisticated instructions for making text bold, italic, underlined, or all three:

1. **Select some text. (See preceding section.)**

2. **Click the B, *I*, and/or u button on the toolbar.**

You can turn this formatting on or off. Notice that the button that you clicked now appears to be depressed. In a fit of perverse psychology, these buttons look depressed while they are *on*. This is the case whenever your current insertion point is amidst or upon bold, italic, or underlined text. Why the buttons should be so unhappy, I don't know. But if you later select that same text and click the depressed button, the formatting is undone, and the button no longer appears depressed (it goes *off*).

## Changing the style for text that you're currently typing

If, instead of typing first and then formatting as I just described, you prefer to type directly in bold, italic, or underlined text, follow these even more incredibly complex and sophisticated instructions:

1. **Click the B, *I*, and/or u button on the toolbar to turn on formatting.**

2. **Type.**

3. **Click the same button again to turn off formatting.**

## Changing the style without buttons

The preceding two highly complex procedures work in any tool where the **B**, *I*, and u buttons appear in the toolbar. (Where they don't appear, you don't need them. Trust the folks at Microsoft. They know what you need.) If, perchance, the toolbar is not visible (perhaps you turned it off), or you just don't like using the mouse, you can use the following key combinations rather than clicking on the buttons:

- Press Ctrl+B for bold.
- Press Ctrl+I for italic.
- Press Ctrl+U for underline.

Another way of specifying the font style (besides using these buttons and key combinations) is available. This other procedure is rather more complicated, involving the <u>F</u>ont and Style command in the <u>F</u>ormat drop-down menu. I get into this procedure in the upcoming section, "Using the Format Font and Style dialog box."

## Reading the buttons

Even if you don't use the buttons, they still continue to reflect the style of your text by looking depressed. Don't take it personally; it's their job. Their depressed look occurs whenever your current insertion point is amidst or upon bold, italic, or underlined text, in whatever tool that you're using.

In the word processor, the buttons have yet another trick. If you have selected a bunch of text, and some of it has a style applied, but some does not, the appropriate button takes on a peculiar, hollow look, as if it were engraved, not depressed. (Wouldn't you be depressed, too, if you were engraved?) If you click the button, Works applies that style to all of the selected text. Click it again, and Works removes the style.

## Removing styles

If you want to get rid of any and all styles, you can use Ctrl+spacebar. To unformat a block of text, select the text first and then press Ctrl+spacebar. To begin typing with unformatted text, press Ctrl+spacebar; then start typing.

Ctrl+spacebar also changes the font and size back to the original, except in the word processor. In the word processor, no quick way to go back to the original font and size is available. You have to re-specify the original font and size by using either the font and size boxes on the toolbar or on the Format Font and Style dialog box.

# Fooling with Fonts

You may have noticed a rather tedious consistency in Works. A lot of the type looks the same. The way type looks is called its *font*. (The way type looks used to be called the typeface, but the computer industry has transmogrified the terminology.) Works has a rather boring preference for using two fonts called Times New Roman — a truly dumbfounding name — and Arial (incorrectly calling to mind Disney's *The Little Mermaid*, if you're a parent). How can you bring a ray of sunshine into this dreary world of fonts?

# Changing font and size with the toolbar

If you're using any of the Big Four tools except the communications tool, take a gander at your toolbar. If you're not using any tools at the moment, redirect your gander and any other waterfowl you may have lying around at Figure 3-1, where you can see a piece of the toolbar with a drop-down menu.

**Figure 3-1:**
Grab a more interesting font from the toolbar's font area.

The font box on the toolbar, together with its sidekick, the font size box (the one with the 12 in it in Figure 3-1), lets you brighten up your document with any font that's installed on your computer.

Here are two quick steps to change the font you're currently typing in:

1. **Click the down-arrow next to the font box.**

   Works shows you each font by name. The name is written in that font to give you an example of what it looks like.

   To see more fonts, use the scroll bar on the right of the menu. See Chapter 2 for more on scroll bars.

2. **Click any font in the drop-down menu.**

To change the font of text that you've already typed, select the text first and then do the preceding two-step.

Changing font size works the same way. To change the size you're currently typing in, click the down-arrow to the right of the font size box for a drop-down list of sizes. Click any size in the menu that drops down from the box. To change the size of text that you've already typed, select that text first.

## Wisdom of the font

Where the heck do fonts come from, anyway? Although it seems that fonts ought to be just lying around, like air, ready to be used, they actually have to come from somewhere. Most of your fonts probably came with Windows. Sometimes, when you install other programs on your computer, those programs add some fonts to the ones you already have. You can also buy additional fonts, often called *font libraries*, and install them yourself. Your printer may also have come with fonts, either built in or on a diskette for you to install. To install them, use Start⇨Settings⇨Control Panel, then double-click Fonts in the Control Panel and use File⇨Install New Font.

Except for printer fonts, most of the fonts live in a place where all the Windows programs know to look for them. That's why, if you have another program besides Works, that program shows you the same fonts.

When you see a double-T icon in front of a font, this icon indicates that the type is a *TrueType* font, a kind of font that Windows knows a lot about and can depict accurately both on your computer screen and on your printer. If no icon appears in front of the font, that means that Works is going to do the best it can to make the screen match the printed text, but Works makes no promises. If an icon of a printer is in front of the font, the font lives in the printer and is usually available only in certain sizes.

## *Using the Format Font and Style dialog box*

The main command for changing font, style, and all other type-related stuff is Format⇨Font and Style, which brings up the Format Font and Style dialog box of Figure 3-2. The Format Font and Style dialog box does the same things as the font, size, and style features on the toolbar, plus a little bit more. You can choose an additional style here, ~~strikethrough~~; choose a color for your type (at least on the screen and on the printer, too, if you have a color printer); and if you're using the word processor, you can choose a *position,* either subscript or superscript.

This dialog box also lets you save your font and style selections as the initial (or *default*) selections for certain types of new documents. See the next section, "Changing the font and style that Works starts with."

In the spreadsheet tool and in the database tool, it's technically not the Format Font and Style *dialog box,* but the Font *card* of the Format Cells dialog box — but it looks and works basically the same as what I describe here.

Position options (word processor only).

Make settings standard.

Click on a font here.

Click on a size here.

Sample window shows the effect of your choices.

Click on a style here.

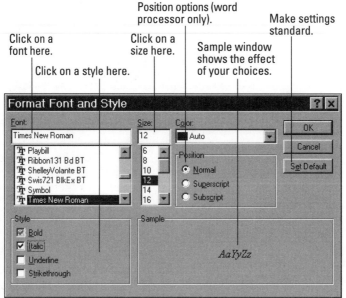

**Figure 3-2:**
The Format Font and Style dialog box does it all: font, size, style, and more.

Here's how to format characters using the Format Font and Style dialog box:

1. **If you're formatting text that you've already typed, select that text.**

   If you just want to start typing in a new font or style, skip this step.

2. **Click Format⇨Font and Style in the menu that drops down.**

   The Format Font and Style dialog box arrives on your screen.

3. **Click the font and/or size that you want.**

   To see more fonts or sizes, click the arrows in the adjoining scroll bars.

4. **If you want a special style such as Bold, click it.**

   The Style selections of bold, italic, and underline (the ones you get using the buttons B, *I*, and u in the toolbar) appear in the dialog box as check boxes in the lower left of the dialog box. (Another style, strikethrough, is also listed; strikethrough is used for editing and has a line through the middle. Weird, huh?)

   If a given style is currently *on* (being applied to text that you're typing or to text that has been selected), you see a check mark in its check box. If the box is gray, as is the Bold selection in Figure 3-2, that means that some of the currently selected text has that style and some does not. To turn a style *off*, click on that style again.

5. **For colored type, click the** Color **box.**

Zowie! Color! Click the color you want in the drop-down menu that appears. (Click the down-arrow in the scroll bar to the right of the menu for more colors.) But don't get too excited unless you have a color printer. Colored type comes out as black on a black-and-white printer. Still, color can be useful for distinguishing certain parts of your document, such as editorial comments, on your screen.

6. **If you need superscript or subscript, click it.**

You can do superscript or subscript only while you're using the word processor. The area marked Position in Figure 3-2, where these selections hang out, doesn't appear with any other tool. Clicking Superscript raises text above the normal line, as is used for footnote numbers and exponents. Subscript lowers text below the normal line.

To remove sub- or superscripting, click Normal.

7. **After you've set up everything the way that you want it, click the** OK **button.**

In the word processor tool, you can choose superscript or subscript right from the keyboard without using a dialog box. Press Ctrl and the = (equal) key for subscript, and press Ctrl+Shift and the = (equal) key for superscript.

## *Changing the font and style that Works starts with*

Okay, you can now change the font that you're working with in your current document. But what about the next time you create a document? Works is stuck on this Times New Roman/Arial shtick, so Times New Roman/Arial is what you get every time you create a new document. If you don't care for these fonts, you can change the font every time, but what a bore! Instead of changing the font every time you create a new document, however, you can change Works' *default* font and style (the font and style it starts a new document with).

To specify the default, do the following. Before you begin, make sure that you're working in a document of the same type for which you want to specify future default fonts. For example, if you want to specify the default font for, say, spreadsheet documents, you should be currently working with a spreadsheet document. (That is, a spreadsheet document should be the *active* one in the Works window.)

1. **Summon up a Format Font and Style dialog box by choosing Format⇨Font and Style.**

2. **Specify your font, size, style, and other stuff in the dialog box. (See the preceding section.)**

3. **Click the S̲et Default button in the dialog box.**

   An impertinent little dialog box crops up, asking in bold type whether you really, truly want to change the default font to whatever font, size, style, and color you specified in Step 2 (cryptically stated as something like Arial 10, Bold, Auto). Click the Y̲es button.

Now, the next time you create a new document of the same type you're currently working in, you'll start out using that font and style.

# Cutting, Copying, and Pasting

Finally, this sentence was written. Subsequently, this sentence. First, this sentence was written. Paragraph sense make does this? No? Then you (or somebody) needs to edit it.

The particular editing features in Works that can make short work of such scrambled writing are the cut, copy, paste, and drag features. The first three features are practically universal among Windows programs. Employing, as they do, a Windows feature called the Clipboard, these features even let you transfer things *between* Windows programs using that Clipboard as a vehicle.

The Windows *Clipboard* is a temporary storage area that holds only one thing at a time; text and illustrations and all kinds of things can be copied to the Clipboard. The contents of the Clipboard can then be pasted into any document in any Windows program.

Besides carrying things between Windows programs, this Clipboard also serves as a vehicle to move things around *within* a Works document or *between* Works documents. Works' drag feature does not use this Windows Clipboard, so the drag feature works only within Works — either to move something or to copy something.

## Copy and paste

You can copy any text or illustration onto the Windows Clipboard and then insert it (*paste* it) somewhere else. In fact, after you have copied the text or illustration onto the Windows Clipboard, you can paste the text or illustration as many times as you like. This feature can be very useful if you are repeatedly typing something lengthy, such as Dinglehausen-Schneitzenbaum Furniture Prefabrication Company.

Here's the procedure for copying:

1. **Select the text or illustration that you want to copy.**

2. **Press Ctrl+C, or**

   **Choose Edit⇨Copy from the menu bar, or**

   **Click the Copy button in the toolbar.** (The Copy button is normally next to the button with the scissors, and the icon on the Copy button shows two overlapping documents.)

   This procedure copies the selected stuff onto the Windows Clipboard. These commands do the same thing in most other Windows programs, by the way.

3. **Click where you want a copy to appear.**

   This spot can be in the document that you're working on, some other Works document, or even something that you're working on outside of Works, in another Windows program that's currently running. You can take your time opening documents or whatever you need to do.

   Whatever you copy stays on the Clipboard only until you copy or cut something else or turn off your computer.

4. **Press Ctrl+V, or**

   **Choose Edit⇨Paste from the menu bar, or**

   **Click the Paste button in the toolbar.** (The Paste button shows a clipboard with a document.)

   This procedure copies stuff off the Windows Clipboard and pastes it into the new location. The Ctrl+V (paste) command is the same in most Windows programs.

You can repeat Steps 3 and 4 as many times as you like, until you put something new on the Clipboard. Dinglehausen-Schneitzenbaum Furniture Prefabrication Company. Dinglehausen-Schneitzenbaum Furniture Prefabrication Company. See, it works!

If you want to make only a single copy of some text or an illustration, you may find it easier to use the drag feature, coming up soon.

## *Cut and paste*

If you want to move something, one way to move it is to cut and paste it. This procedure is exactly like the copying and pasting just described, except that the original text is removed from your document. This method is particularly useful for moving something a long distance: over several pages or between documents. Within Works, you can also just drag something to move it, as I show you in a minute.

Here's the procedure for cutting and pasting:

**1. Select the text or illustration you want to move.**

**2. Press Ctrl+X, or**

   **Choose Edit⇨Cut from the menu bar, or**

   **Click the Cut (scissors) button in the toolbar.**

   This procedure copies the selected stuff onto the Windows Clipboard and deletes it from your document. These commands do the same thing in most other Windows programs, by the way.

   The next two steps are the *paste* procedure, identical to the procedure you use in copying and pasting.

**3. Click where you want a copy to appear.**

**4. Press Ctrl+V, or**

   **Choose Edit⇨Paste from the menu bar, or**

   **Click on the Paste button on the toolbar.**

As with the copy procedure described previously, you can repeat Steps 3 and 4 as many times as you like until you put something new on the Clipboard.

## Drag

As even Og the Caveman knew, dragging is often an easy way to move something a short distance. A short distance, in this case, means within Works only, over a distance of a couple of pages or so within a document, or between documents that are already open in a document window.

The cut (or copy) and paste method is better if you have to move or copy something for a distance of many pages, to a document that's currently closed, or to some program other than Works.

Here's how to move or copy something by dragging it:

**1. Select the text or illustration you want to move.**

**2. Place your mouse cursor over the highlighted area.**

Note that the word *drag* attaches itself, lamprey-like, to your cursor. This word is merely a suggestion, but follow it.

3. **Press down the mouse button (don't let go) and drag the selected text to where you want to move it.**

   If you want to copy, not move, the selected text, press and hold the Ctrl key down at this point. The word *drag* changes to the word *copy*.

   If your destination is not visible in the document window, drag to the window's edge in the direction that you'd like to go. When your cursor hits the edge, the window scrolls.

   If your destination is in another Works document, that document has to be open in a window.

4. **Release the mouse button at your final destination.**

# Yikes! Undoing What's Been Done

Yikes! You just accidentally pasted a double-cheesecake recipe into your non-dairy diet book! What now?

One way in which Works improves on real life is that Works lets you undo your mistakes. Works doesn't allow you to undo all mistakes, mind you, but most editing mistakes, such as changes that you make to the contents of an open document. Works doesn't undo mistakes that you make with files, mistakes such as deleting, replacing, renaming, and file-ish stuff like that.

Works also doesn't undo any more than the last thing that you did. If you made two mistakes, Works only undoes the last one. If you undo again, your undo gets undid (which sounds as if it would be your undoing, but it's not; you can just undo again). Typing or deleting a succession of characters counts as one single mistake, not a bunch of them. If you type a sentence, then undo it, the entire sentence goes away.

To undo, click Edit⇨Undo (*something*) in the menu that drops down. The *something* is whatever you last did: typed, entered a number, deleted, formatted. A faster way to undo is to press Ctrl+Z.

If Works can't undo your mistake, it tells you so by graying out the Undo command line and displaying **Can't undo** in the command's place.

# Checking Your Spelling

One of the helpful little gnomes that scurry around in Works is the Spelling Checker (or *spell checker*, although that sounds more wizardish than gnome-like). Unlike the rest of the help squad described in this chapter, the spell checker actually does something instead of just informing you about things. Specifically, the spell checker helps you eliminate typographical errors (typos) and misspellings. Actually, what the spell checker does is make sure that your document contains 100 percent genuine words (or words that it thinks are genuine).

The spell checker does not, however, make sure that you use words write. Like just then — the word *write* is absolutely and indisputably a word; it just happens to be in the wrong place at the wrong time. The spell checker doesn't turn up anything wrong with that that sentence.

The spell checker, however, does catch the repeated word *that* in the last sentence of the preceding paragraph, which can be nice for people like me who pause in the the middle of a sentence and often repeat articles such as *the* — repetitions that are hard to see. The spell checker also catches capitalization and hyphenation errors.

The Spelling Checker runs like this: The spell checker looks for words that it doesn't have in its dictionary (a list of words). If the spell checker finds any such unrecognized words, it points out the word and lets you change it. If you know that the word is okay, you can just tell the spell checker to ignore the word and continue checking. You can also tell the spell checker to add this word to its dictionary so that it always ignores the word thereafter.

Here's the inside scoop on snaring misspellings:

1. **If you are just going to check a single word or block of text, select the word or text block by highlighting it.**

   Otherwise, to check your whole document starting where your insertion point or spreadsheet cursor is, go on to Step 2.

2. **Click on Tools⇨Spelling.**

   In the word processor, you can alternatively click the Spelling Checker button on the toolbar (the check mark with ABC on it).

   If the spell checker doesn't find any words that it can't recognize, a little box tells you that the spell-checking process is done; click the OK button in that box.

   Otherwise, you get the Spelling dialog box shown in Figure 3-3.

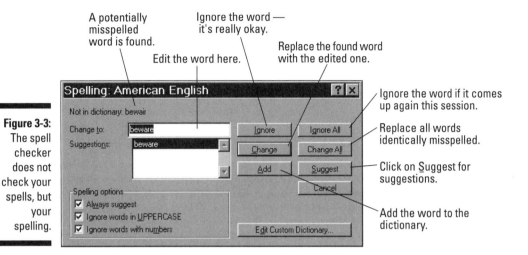

A potentially misspelled word is found.

Ignore the word — it's really okay.

Edit the word here.

Replace the found word with the edited one.

Ignore the word if it comes up again this session.

Replace all words identically misspelled.

Click on Suggest for suggestions.

Add the word to the dictionary.

**Figure 3-3:**
The spell checker does not check your spells, but your spelling.

### 3. See if the word the Spelling Checker found is really incorrect.

The word is shown at the top of the Spelling dialog box, where it says, `Not in dictionary`. Works suggests a replacement in the `Change to` text box.

### 4. If the word is okay, ignore it or add it to the dictionary.

If the word is okay this particular time but may be a typo or misspelling if it appears again in this document or any other document, click Ignore. If the word comes up again during this spell-checking session, it gets flagged again.

If the word is okay in this document (as *Snark* may be in a document about sailboats) but may be a typo or misspelling in some other document, click `Ignore All`. The word is ignored until the next time that you use the Spelling Checker.

If the word is a real word (such as *uvula*) that you might use in any document, click on `Add`. The word is then added to the spell checker's Custom Dictionary and is thereafter and forever ignored in any document that you check. Be certain that the word is really spelled correctly before you do this!

If you have acronyms such as *NAVCOM*, the Spelling Checker ignores them. If you want the spell checker to point out such uppercase-only words to you as errors, click the check box marked `Ignore words in UPPERCASE` so that the check mark disappears from the check box.

If you have terms that have numbers in them, the Spelling Checker ignores them. If you want the spell checker to point out terms with numbers to you as errors, click on the check box marked `Ignore words with numbers` so that the check mark disappears from the check box.

After you act on one of the preceding tasks, the Spelling Checker moves on to check the remainder of the document.

5. **If the word suggested by Works in the Change to box is not correct, edit it.**

If you know the correct word, click the Change to text box and edit the word. Or other suggestions may be in the Suggestions box; click one of these suggestions, and it fills the Change to box.

If you don't like this suggestion stuff, clear the check mark in Always suggest by clicking that check box. Otherwise, Works lists suggestions for every misspelling that it finds.

6. **Click the Change button to replace the original word in your document with the one in the Change to box.**

You don't get to watch this replacement happen because the action happens so fast. The spell checker moves right along to your next apparent blunder, and you're back at Step 3.

Eventually, the spell checker reaches the end of your document and puts up a little box letting you know that the spell-checking process is done. Click OK in this box.

If you didn't start spell checking at the beginning of your document, Works asks whether it should do so. Click OK in this box if you would like to check the first part of your document. Click on Cancel if you're done.

## Where is this dictionary?

Most dictionaries are hard to miss. The one in your PC is hard to see. (Oops, make that *the several* dictionaries in your PC.) In the U.S. of A., your copy of Works comes with a dictionary in good ol' A-Merican, plus another in that fancy British stuff, where they talk like they invented the language or something. (To change the language orientation of your dictionary, press Alt+T and O, click the tab labeled Proofing Tools, and click the dictionary of your choice in the Choose dictionary text box. Then press Enter.)

Works maintains yet another dictionary where it stuffs the words you Add during spell checking.

This second dictionary is called the Custom Dictionary. If you would like to add or remove works to that dictionary, click on the Edit Custom Dictionary button in the Spelling dialog box. To add a word to the Custom Dictionary, type the word into the Word text box and click the Add button. To delete a word from the Custom Dictionary, find it in the big white list box, click it, and then click on the Delete button. Whichever task you do, click on the Done button when you've finished.

# Chapter 4

# Basic Printing

• • • • • • • • • • • • • • • • • • • • • • • • • • • • • • • • • • • • • • • • • • • • • • • • • •

## In This Chapter

▶ Setting margins, paper size, and orientation

▶ Using measurements other than inches

▶ Reusing the same setup all the time

▶ Previewing your document before printing

▶ Printing on paper

▶ Stopping printing

▶ Selecting or installing a printer

• • • • • • • • • • • • • • • • • • • • • • • • • • • • • • • • • • • • • • • • • • • • • • • • • •

*A*ccording to some accounts, computers were supposed to lead to the paperless office. No more of this cutting down forests, flattening them into paper, smearing ink all over them, and then dumping them into landfills where typos are preserved like mummies for the critical eye of posterity. Hah! As my fellow technology skeptic (and coauthor on other books) Margaret Levine Young is fond of saying, "The paperless office of the future is just down the hall from the paperless bathroom of the future."

No, computers actually have increased paper consumption. And you, too, can join the parade with your own printer. Fortunately, features such as Works' Print Preview can at least minimize the amount of paper that you waste.

Printing is something that you can do in the word-processor, database, and spreadsheet tools, and printing works about the same way in each one. In each tool, the commands that have anything to do with printing (including page setup such as margins and orientation) have been forced by Microsoft to live with evil relatives in the File menu. Perhaps, someday, some handsome royalty from the kingdom of Microsoft will rescue them and give them their very own Print condominium on the menu bar.

## The special world of envelopes

Unless you really like figuring out the nuts and bolts of how things work, you probably shouldn't attempt to print envelopes without help from Works. Works has a special envelope tool (which also serves as the envelope TaskWizard) that works with the word-processor tool and takes care of all your page setup and printing needs.

Because this special envelope tool uses the word processor to create the envelope, I've put the discussion of how to print a single, simple envelope in Chapter 7. For a discussion of using the envelope tool/TaskWizard to create multiple envelopes for mass mailing, see Appendix A.

# *Setting up the Page*

Ever since humankind moved from scrolls to pages, things have been going downhill. Now we have to worry about top and bottom margins as well as side margins. Even worse, now we can print the darn pages sideways! Back to scrolls, I say!

But, in the meantime, I suppose that we have to deal with all this stuff. Fortunately, the controls for page margins, page size, and orientation work the same for all the different Works tools.

You don't have to set up the page every time you print — just set up the page once for each document. Your page setup is saved as part of the document file. In fact, you may be quite happy with the margins and other page setup stuff that Works uses automatically. In that case, you don't have to bother with setting up your pages at all! Skip ahead to "Previewing Coming Attractiveness," later in this chapter, which describes how to see what your document looks like before you print it. If you like the way your document looks, don't bother fooling with Page Setup.

## *Marginal settings*

Margins in Works are defined as the spaces between the edge of the page and the regular body text and footnotes of the document. Headers and footers (including page numbers) go within these margins, and you specify their positions separately using the Header margins.

Choose File⇨Page Setup to get a Page Setup dialog box; then click the Margins tab. The Margins card then graces you with its presence, as shown in Figure 4-1:

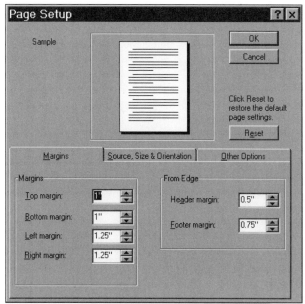

✔ **To increase or decrease a margin:** Click on the up-arrow or down-arrow next to the value. The sample changes as you do.

✔ **To type in a specific margin value:** Double-click that margin's white box and type in a new number. If you want inches (or whatever your default units are), you can just type in the value and leave off the units (for example, type **2.5** for 2.5 inches). You can type in other units, too, such as **cm** for centimeters, **mm** for millimeters, **pi** for picas, and **pt** for points.

When you type a margin value into a box, the Sample doesn't show the result until you click within some other margin box. Works then knows that you have finished typing the value.

✔ **To set header or footer margins:** Headers and footers are text that appears in the margins on the top or bottom of every page. The header distance is measured from the top edge of the page to the bottom of the header text; so the header distance must be set to a value no larger than the top margin. The footer distance is measured from the bottom edge of the page to the top of the footer, so the footer distance must be set to a value no larger than the bottom margin.

## Hooked on metrics

Let's face it: inches are silly, but that's what we all grew up with here in the good old U.S. of A. If you live in a country where people have discovered that they have ten fingers and toes, you probably prefer the metric system. Or perhaps you've worked in the typing, publishing, or printing businesses, where they have really silly measurements, such as the pica (which I always thought was a rodent).

If you want Works to use your favorite *metrics* (units of measure), do this:

**1. Click the** Cancel **button in any dialog box that's open, such as in the Page Setup dialog box.**

**2. Click on** **Tools**⇨**Options. A somewhat intimidating Options dialog box springs up; click on the General tab and then focus your attention on the upper-left corner marked** Units.

**3. Click whatever unit you want Works to use by default.** (That is, the unit you want Works to use when you don't specify a unit, just a number.)

**4. Click on the** OK **button in this Options dialog box.**

## *Source, size, and orientation settings*

You may print 99% of your work on standard-sized paper in the *normal,* or *portrait,* orientation. Still, for spreadsheets, signs, certain kinds of flyers, and other work, you may want your printer to print sideways, in the *landscape* orientation. (Note that landscape orientation does *not* mean that you put the paper sideways into your printer!) Also, many printers require you to manually insert the paper for special-sized paper. For this special printing to work, you should tell Works about it on the Source, Size & Orientation card of the Page Setup dialog box, shown in Figure 4-2.

Choose File⇨Page Setup to get a Page Setup dialog box; then click the Source, Size & Orientation tab.

✔ **To set page orientation:** Click the Source, Size & Orientation card. Then click on either Landscape or Portrait in the lower-left corner. The page icon (with the letter A) illustrates how type will be printed on the page.

✔ **To tell Works that you are using a special paper source on your printer:** On the Source, Size & Orientation card, click the box marked Paper Source. If you need to use a special paper-feeding place on your printer, such as a single-sheet feed slot, you can click that source in the list that drops down. After you indicate the source, Works prompts you at the right time to put the paper in for manual feeding; for automatic feeding, Works tells the printer to use that special source.

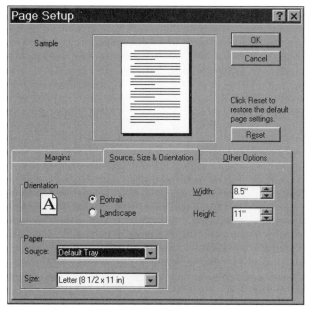

**Figure 4-2:**
Getting
sourced,
sized, and
oriented all
at once.

🖚 **To tell Works that you're using a special paper size or an envelope:** On the Source, Size & Orientation card, click on the box marked Paper Size. Click the paper size in the box that drops down. If you're using a paper size that's not shown in the drop-down box, double-click the box marked Width and type in a new value; then do the same for Height. (Width always refers to the direction a line of text will run.) When you're done, check the Sample to see if things look roughly correct. Click on the Reset button to return to the default paper size.

## Starting page number and other options

Each type of Works document has certain special options for page setup, so see the individual tool sections in this book for more information on those options. One "other option" that they all have in common is the capability to specify what page number should appear on the first page of your document. The main use for this process is when you are writing a document with lots of sections and chapters, and each Works document is a section. In that case, you want to set the first page number to something other than 1.

Here's how:

1. **Choose File⇨Page Setup to get a Page Setup dialog box; then click the Other Options tab.**

2. **Either click the** `Starting page number` **box and type in a value, or click the adjoining up-arrow to increase the page number setting.**

## Reusing the same setup all the time

Because your page setup only affects the current document, the situation can be a little frustrating if you want to use the same settings all the time. (You have to set the settings up each time that you want to use them.) One solution to the problem is to create a custom template. A *template* is a sort of proto-document that is all set up to do a particular type of document. After you have created a template, you can start a new document based on this template by choosing from User Defined Templates, a category that now appears on the list of TaskWizards in the Task Launcher. For more on templates, see "Creating and Using Templates" in Appendix A.

# Previewing Coming Attractiveness

You've formatted your document, and you think that it will look quite attractive on paper. But how do you know? The time for a preview of coming attractiveness has arrived. Specifically, it's time for Print Preview, which shows you how Works thinks your document will look in print, without wasting paper. (See Figure 4-3 for a preview of Print Preview.)

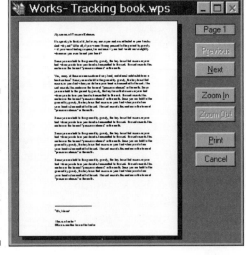

**Figure 4-3:**
Works shows you teeny-tiny print on a minuscule page. Click the page to zoom in.

You can get into Print Preview in one of three ways:

- ✔ **Click File⇨Print Preview in the menu bar.**
- ✔ **Click the button in the menu bar that looks like a document with a monocle.** (To see if you're on the right button, place your mouse cursor over the button without clicking, and Works puts up a tiny label saying Print Preview.)
- ✔ **In the word processor, press Ctrl+P and then click the Preview button in the Print dialog box that appears.**

Whichever way you use, you get a Print Preview dialog box that initially shows you a tiny, illegible picture of your document. (The picture may be illegible, but this initial, bird's-eye view is actually helpful for checking margins and overall layout.)

Here are some of the things you can do in this dialog box:

- ✔ **To see other pages:** Click Next to see the next page or click Previous to see the preceding page. If no next or preceding page exists, the buttons are grayed out.
- ✔ **To enlarge the view of the document:** Position your mouse cursor over a location in the document you want to see; then click. Click a second time for greater magnification. Clicking the Zoom In button also enlarges the view of the document. Use the vertical and horizontal scroll bars to view parts of the document that extend beyond the window.
- ✔ **To shrink the document:** Keep clicking on it. The document returns to its original size after a total of three clicks. Or hold down the Ctrl button and click. Clicking the Zoom Out button also shrinks the view.
- ✔ **To actually print the document on paper (what a stunning concept!):** Click the Print button. (When you print, how big the document looks in Print Preview doesn't matter. The document prints at normal size.)
- ✔ **To return to the document window:** Click the Cancel button or press the Esc key.

# Printing on Actual Paper!

What will they think of next? Imagine being able to actually see words and graphics on paper rather than on a computer screen!

Printing is a little different *for* each tool in Works; and sometimes printing is even different *within* that tool, depending on exactly what you're doing (for example, printing a document with an envelope page). For some of the most important printing variations within each tool, see the chapters on that tool.

Printing is pretty simple when things go right:

1. **Turn on your printer.**

2. **Wait until it comes online**.

   Most printers have an indicator light somewhere that is marked On Line. If this indicator light lights up, the printer is telling you that it has had its morning coffee and is ready to roll.

3. **To print the whole document without further ado, click the Print button on the Works toolbar.**

   (The Print button has a picture of a printer on it.)

   At this point, you're essentially done. Read "Stop Printing!" later in this chapter if you've changed your mind about printing the document.

4. **If you want to print a part of the document or print multiple copies, click File⇨Print or press Ctrl+P. (Pressing Ctrl+P does the same thing.)**

   The Print dialog box comes to your aid.

5. **For multiple copies, click the** Number of copies **box and type the number of copies that you want (but don't press the Enter key).**

   Or, you can click on the up- or down-arrows next to that box to change the page count.

6. **To print a specific group of pages, click** Pages **in the Print dialog box and enter the starting and ending page numbers.**

7. **To print faster but with less quality, click on** Draft quality printing **in the Print dialog box.**

8. **Click the** OK **button (or press the Enter key).**

   If all goes well, you can now just close your eyes and wait for your document to be printed. If you change your mind about printing — quick, read "Stop Printing!"

# Stop Printing!

Stopping a printer is like trying to catch a bus that's just left the bus stop. If you're really fast, you can flag the bus down. Otherwise, you have to run to the next bus stop.

Don't just turn off the printer. Your paper may get stuck halfway and need to be carefully extracted, your PC will get confused and start tossing complaints on your screen, and when you start the printer up again, your first page may be a mess.

Three bus stops are on the printing route. First, the document goes to the printing part of the program, which displays the Print dialog box. Then as that part of the program prepares each page for printing, the document goes to the Windows' Print Manager. Finally, the print manager delivers each page, one at a time, to the printer. To stop printing, you can interrupt the process at any point.

**Stop 1.** If you move fast enough, you can click on the Cancel button in the Printing dialog box. This box disappears fairly quickly, though, and you may not be able to move fast enough to stop the first page or two.

**Stop 2.** If you miss the opportunity to cancel printing in Works, you can still catch the bus in the Windows print manager. At the other end of the Taskbar from the Start button (down by the current time display), a printer icon appears. Double-click it to open it. Click on the name of your document in the list shown there and then click the Delete button. After a pause, the document name no longer appears. Click the X button on the top right of the dialog box to exit.

**Stop 3.** If you know where the online/offline button is on your printer, you can press that button. The Print Manager eventually discovers your action and displays a box complaining that The printer on LPT1 is offline or not selected or some such stuff. Click the Cancel button in this box. Next, follow the directions for Stop 2. Finally, press the online/offline button on your printer again.

# Selecting or Installing a Printer

There's a good chance that Works already knows what printer you have and how you want that printer to work. No, Works hasn't been snooping in your credit card records. When you (or your friendly local software guru) installed Windows, you installed the printer there, too: you told Windows what printer or printers you would be using, and you loaded some software. If you said that you may use more than one printer, you may also have specified one printer as the standard (or *default*) printer. Unless you tell Works otherwise, it uses this default printer.

Here are the main circumstances under which you may need to tell Works or Windows something about a printer:

✔ If you just installed a new printer (or a fax modem), you need to tell Windows about it.

✔ If you are switching to another printer or if you want to send a fax with your fax modem and fax software (which makes Works think that the fax modem is a printer), you need to tell Works about these actions.

## Selecting a printer in Works

After a printer has been installed (both physically and in software), Works can use it. If you have more than one printer installed and you want to switch to another printer, you have to choose the other printer from Works. Although you probably don't have more than one real printer, you may have a fax modem that transmits faxes; the fax modem installs and works like a printer. To use the fax modem, you have to choose it.

Here's how to select an installed printer:

1. **Choose File➪Print in the menu bar or press Ctrl+P.**

   The Print dialog box winks into existence on your screen.

2. **In the Print dialog box, click the down-arrow on the Name box.**

   This action displays the list of installed printers.

3. **Click the printer of your choice in the list.**

   After a brief delay, you're done.

Before you print, you may want to check the document's appearance with Print Preview. Different printers can affect the document's appearance somewhat.

## Installing a new printer

Here's how to go about installing a new printer and telling Windows about it. You may need to have your Windows 95 installation disks or CD handy; or if your printer came with a disk containing *printer drivers,* you may need that disk.

1. **Physically unpack and set up the printer.**

   Remove all the tabs, Styrofoam chunks, and rubber bands that the manufacturer tells you about. Read the instruction manual and do your best to follow the instructions. In the process, you'll either plug the printer into a *parallel port* or a *serial port* on your PC.

2. **Choose Start➪Settings➪Printers from the Windows 95 Taskbar.**

3. **In the Printers dialog box that appears, double-click the Add Printer icon.**

4. **An Add Printer Wizard appears; click the Next button and follow the directions.**

Now you are all set with your shiny new printer — probably color, too, you lucky person.

# Part II
# The Wily Word Processor

"I WISH SOMEONE WOULD EXPLAIN TO PROFESSOR JONES THAT YOU DON'T NEED A WHIP AND A LEATHER JACKET TO FIND A LOST FILE."

## *In this part . . .*

So, you're ready to dash off that important report or write that long-awaited letter in Works word processor? Well, Works makes it pretty easy — but as with all word-processing software, it's still a bit wild. Don't expect to just walk right up and pounce on it. It's a good idea to sidle up to it, nice and easy, and know what sort of interesting behavior to expect when you finally lasso it and put it to use.

This part covers everything from basics, like how to use the keyboard, to subtle and elusive facts, like where paragraph formatting hides. Learn about the word-processing habitat: why it's important to replace your old typing habits with new word-processing habits. Finally, learn how to teach your newly-tamed word processor advanced tricks, like page numbers, tables, borders, lines, headers, footers, and footnotes.

# Chapter 5

# In Search of the Wily Word Processor

So, you're ready to hunt down the wily word processor? Well, pack up your safari gear and you can get to know the wiles and ways of this wacky wordivorous wonder. Soon, you, too, will be able to write such annoying alliterative allegories as this one — and then avoid embarrassment by quickly deleting them again, as I should have — without the trials of typewriter ribbons and whiteout.

# What's the Big Deal?

Three being a magical number, there are, of course, three big deals about word processing:

**Big Deal 1.** You can make documents that you would never even attempt to create with a typewriter, such as two-column newsletters or presentation transparency foils (those see-through thingies that you put on an overhead projector) using big type.

**Big Deal 2.** Your documents look better and fancier, without pain and strain, when you use nice typefaces of different size and style, centered or indented text, borders, and graphics.

**Third and Final Big Deal.** Playing around with things until you like the results — changing words or sentences, moving paragraphs, or changing margins and page breaks — is really easy in word processing.

In addition, some tiny little deals, such as copying text from one place to another, automatic spell-checking, sending documents over the phone lines, and being able to add word processing to your résumé, are available. So word processing is a good deal all around.

## What's different from a typewriter?

You can do lots of things with a word processor that you can't do with a typewriter. (Word processors don't make that cool clickety-clack sound, but what the heck?) But even for doing things that you're accustomed to doing, there are a few differences to be careful of:

- ✔ Do not, *absolutely* do NOT, use the Enter key like the carriage return key, pressing it at the end of every line of text. This habit all but guarantees a bitter, contentious relationship with your word processor. Pressing Enter after every line is like buying a car, hooking up your horse to it, and cursing this newfangled means of transportation because your miles-per-bushel-of-hay goes down.

- ✔ Think twice before using the Tab key and the spacebar to position text. There are a lot of cool automatic formatting features, such as automatic centering or justifying of a line of text, for example. Strange things can appear on the page when your tab-and-space formatting starts to interact with the automatic formatting. Works provides better ways to do the indentations and positioning that you want.

- ✔ Some keys, such as the Backspace key and Caps Lock key, work a bit differently. See the section, "Keyboard tips and peculiarities," later in this chapter.

✔ Text flows around on your screen like spilled coffee on a desktop. (At least the text doesn't soak through to other documents.) When you add something or remove it, the remaining text moves away or flows in to fill the gap. For example, if you remove the special marks that keep paragraphs separate, the paragraphs merge together. Paragraphs are supposed to behave this way. You just have to go with the flow.

✔ Your screen doesn't always show you *exactly* what your document would look like if you printed it. You can work in two *views,* Normal and Page Layout; Normal view lets Works respond a bit more quickly as you type, and Page Layout view is closer to the final appearance. Print Preview, described in Chapter 4, is even more accurate.

✔ Do not use dashes and other symbols to make lines. Heavens, no — this way of making lines is far too tacky. There are lots of other, cleaner ways to do lines and borders.

## *What can you do with a word processor?*

The Works word-processor tool lets you make documents, including simple letters and memos, newsletters, scholarly reports, or even things that need big letters, such as signs or transparency foils for presentations. Here are some of the things that this tool lets you do with documents:

✔ Automatically move text around as you type new text in or delete old text

✔ Move text and graphics, or copy them, from one place or one document to another

✔ Use any of a wide variety of typefaces, in sizes from barely legible to utterly humongous — even in color, if you have a color printer

✔ Automatically indent, center, left-justify, or right-justify your paragraphs

✔ Quickly set or change line spacing or spacing between paragraphs

✔ Automatically add bullets to lists (such as this one)

✔ Automatically put page breaks in the right places

✔ Automatically floss your teeth

✔ Put your socks in the correct drawer

✔ Use charts, tables, and illustrations

✔ Automatically number footnotes and keep them on the correct page as you move text around

✔ Automatically search for certain words or phrases — and even replace them with other text, if you want. (For example, you may want to find all occurrences of "you pompous old windbag" and replace them with "Mr. Wiggins.")

✔ Automatically check your spelling

✔ Find synonyms for words using a built-in thesaurus

✔ Walk your dog

✔ Print envelopes

✔ Automatically put headers or footers on each page (as in this book, where each page has a header identifying the chapter number or part)

Just kidding about the teeth, the socks, and the dog, but the rest is true. And more.

## When shouldn't you use a word processor?

What shouldn't you do with the word processor? You shouldn't do anything nasty or impolite or ungrammatical. Doing so would reflect badly on us, your fellow Dummies. But apart from that, you shouldn't do anything using the word processor that you can do better with another tool. For example:

✔ Lists are better done with the spreadsheet or database tool.

✔ Records, such as inventories or sales prospects, are better kept by using the database.

✔ Business forms, such as invoice forms or bill-of-sale forms, are sometimes better done by using the spreadsheet tool. This tool lays things out on a nice grid, and it lets you fill in the blanks by using Works, if you want, rather than manually on paper.

## Getting Started

Enough preamble. Time to gird your loins and stroll onto the word-processing wrestling mat.

To find out about starting Works and the different ways of starting a word-processor document, see Chapter 1. Likewise, turn there if you're a little shaky on using the mouse or keyboard. For background on windows, menus, and dialog boxes, check out Chapter 2.

Otherwise, fire up Works and get the Task Launcher in your Works window. (If you've already been using Works and aren't currently looking at that screen, press Alt+F and then N.) From the Task Launcher, you can start a new word-processor document with a TaskWizard, if you like; but if you'd prefer to start with a nice, shiny, untrammeled new document:

> **Click the** Works Tools **tab of the Task Launcher; then click the** Word Processor **button on the Tools card.**

You are now gazing at the word-processing window, its toolbar, and other assorted paraphernalia.

# *The Word-Processing Window and Toolbar*

Figure 5-1 shows you what's what in your *word-processing window.* ("Word-processing window" is my name for how the Microsoft Works window looks when you use the word processor.) A document with one of the dweeby sort of startup names Works gives new documents, "Unsaved Document 3," is on the screen. (You'd think they'd baptize these documents or something, so that they would be saved.) Then there's the usual Works menu bar (with all the commands) near the top of the Works window, and the word-processing toolbar is underneath that.

You may also find a Help panel occupying the right-hand side of your Works window. If you find this panel helpful, leave it there. Otherwise, click the Shrink Help button in its bottom-left corner. For more on Help, see Chapter 2.

Don't try to memorize all the names in Figure 5-1. Stick a pencil here (or turn back the corner of the page) and come back here whenever you need to refresh your memory.

Make a mental note that you're looking at one of two possible views of your document here — this view is called *Normal view,* and the other view is called *Page Layout view.* The Normal view doesn't waste space showing you your margins. The Page Layout view does, but it gives a somewhat more accurate picture of what your document really looks like. I get into these views more in the section "Seeing What Your Document Really Looks Like," later in this chapter.

Menu bar.
Word-processing toolbar.
Document window title bar.
Ruler bar.

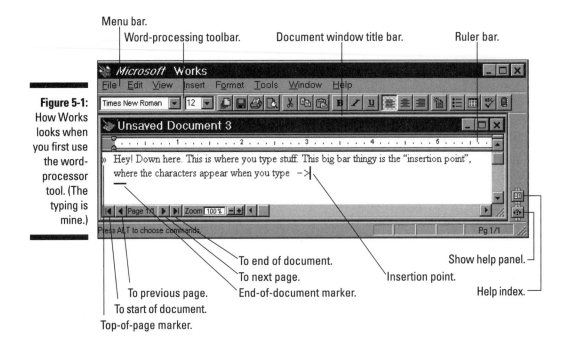

**Figure 5-1:**
How Works
looks when
you first use
the word-
processor
tool. (The
typing is
mine.)

To end of document.
To next page.
End-of-document marker.
Insertion point.
Show help panel.
Help index.

To previous page.
To start of document.
Top-of-page marker.

The ruler bar and toolbar are optional. You can turn them off or on. To turn
them off, click View in the menu bar and then click Toolbar or Ruler in the menu
that drops down — whichever one of these bars you want to turn off. To turn
that bar back on, do the same thing again. Everything else is pretty permanent.

The word-processing toolbar (as shown in Figure 5-2) is similar to the toolbars
in other Works tools. For more on Works' toolbars, see Chapter 3.

Most of the toolbar buttons are the usual suspects mentioned in Part I for
starting, saving, printing, doing basic cut-and-paste edits, changing fonts, and
getting help. The remaining toolbar buttons are more specific to word processing and are discussed in the following places:

✔ **Align Left/Align Right, Center, Justify:** see "Pretty Paragraphs" in
Chapter 7.

✔ **Bullets for lists:** see "Bulleted Lists" in Chapter 8.

✔ **Make a table:** see "Doing it by the Numbers: Tables, Spreadsheets, and
Charts" in Chapter 8.

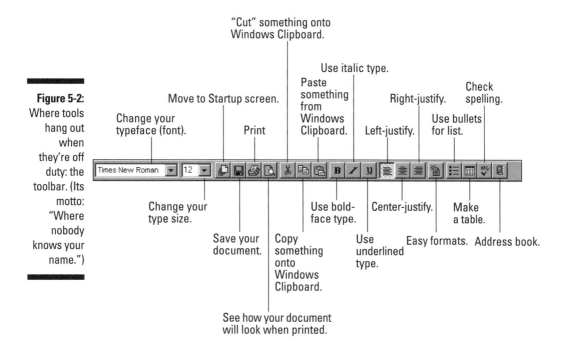

**Figure 5-2:** Where tools hang out when they're off duty: the toolbar. (Its motto: "Where nobody knows your name.")

"Cut" something onto Windows Clipboard.

Use italic type.

Paste something from Windows Clipboard.

Check spelling.

Right-justify.

Move to Startup screen.

Use bullets for list.

Change your typeface (font).

Print

Left-justify.

Change your type size.

Use bold-face type.

Center-justify.

Make a table.

Save your document.

Copy something onto Windows Clipboard.

Use underlined type.

Easy formats.   Address book.

See how your document will look when printed.

> ✔ **Check spelling:** see "Finding Helpp With Typos and Speling" in Chapter 7.
>
> ✔ **Easy formats:** see "Having it their way with Easy Formats" in Chapter 7.
>
> ✔ **Address book:** see "Creating an Address Book" in Appendix A.

# Typing and Deleting

Typing and deleting are the big existential deals of word processing: existence and nonexistence; calling into creation and returning to the void. All else is illusion (or maybe illustration).

## Typing

If you're now looking at a word-processing window, away you go. Just start typing. All the regular keys on the keyboard — the letters, numbers, and punctuation — put characters on the screen when you press them.

Keep on typing and do NOT press the Enter (or Return) key when you get to the end of the line. The text you type automatically starts on the next line, a phenomenon called *line wrap*. When you get to the bottom of the document window, the document *scrolls up*, like paper in your typewriter. Press the Enter key when you get to the end of a paragraph — NOT BEFORE!!!

If you want space between your paragraphs, you can press the Enter key twice at the end of the paragraph, but there's a better way, called *paragraph format-ting,* that I get into in "Spaced-out paragraphs" in Chapter 7. For now, try this technique: If you want a line's worth of space above the paragraph that you're currently typing (and a line's worth of space above subsequent paragraphs), press Ctrl+0 (that's zero, not the letter *O*). If you want that line to go away, press Ctrl+0 again.

## *The insertion point*

As you type, you start pushing around that big vertical bar, the *insertion point.* Its main function in life is to mark where the next character appears when you type or where a character disappears when you delete.

You can nudge the insertion point up, down, or sideways by pressing the arrow and other navigation keys on your keyboard. Or you can teleport the insertion point: just click the mouse pointer at the place in your document where you would like to start typing. See "Getting Around in Your Document," later in this chapter.

Notice what happens to your mouse pointer when you move it into the white area where you type. The mouse pointer changes into a mouse cursor, an *I-beam* shape that's a little easier to fit in between characters than the pointer is.

---

## Beware the insidious Insert key

There are two ways to type in Works: *insert mode* and *overtype mode*. (Actually there's a third, *a la mode,* when your ice cream drips onto the keyboard.) Normally you're in insert mode, which means that if you move the insertion point into the middle of text and type, the existing text scoots to the right to make room. If, however, you should accidentally press the Insert key (which lives over by your navigation keys, just waiting to be pressed accidentally), you find yourself trans-ported to the parallel dimension of overtype mode. (A little OVR shows up in the bottom-right corner of your window.) Now if you move the insertion point into the middle of text and type, the existing text vanishes as you type over it. If you find you are typing over existing text, you have probably pressed Insert. Press Insert again to return to your home dimension.

Don't confuse your mouse cursor (where you're pointing) with the insertion point (where you're typing). The mouse cursor is the one that you move with your mouse. Clicking the mouse moves the insertion point to where the mouse cursor is.

## Deleting

You can delete stuff either with the Backspace key or with the Delete key. To delete a character you just typed, press the Backspace key (usually on the upper-right corner of the typewriter keys). Technically speaking (geek-speak), the Backspace key deletes the character *before* the insertion point, and the Delete key deletes the character *after* the insertion point.

To delete a character in the middle of a line of text, you can use either the Backspace key or the Delete key — your preference. Click just after the character, and you can use the Backspace key. Click just before the character, and you can use the Delete key (which hangs out near your navigation keys).

To delete a block of text, select the text by clicking and dragging your mouse cursor across it; pressing either the Backspace key or the Delete key deletes the selected text. The selected area can span as many words, lines, paragraphs, or even pages as you want. For more on selecting text, see "Selecting Your Target" in Chapter 6.

To undelete (that's un-delete, not *undulate*, sorry) something that you deleted by accident, press Ctrl+Z. You have to do this immediately, like cardiopulmonary resuscitation, or you lose the patient. To untype something you just typed, you can also use Ctrl+Z.

## Rapping about wrapping

If you've never used a word processor before, here's something about line-wrapping that may catch you by surprise: Lines *unwrap* when you delete, just like they wrapped when you were typing. Try it. Type a couple of lines; then move the insertion point to somewhere in the second line and start deleting by pressing the Backspace key. When the insertion point gets back to the beginning of the line, don't let up. The insertion point jumps back up to the end of the first line and starts gobbling characters there. (The backspace key on your typewriter definitely did not work this way.)

The same thing happens when you move the insertion point with the arrow keys. If you're at the end of a line and go right, you wrap down to the beginning of the next line. If you're at the beginning of a line and go left, you wrap up to the end of the preceding line.

## Typing invisible characters

You probably have already suspected that your document is haunted by powerful, invisible beings. What you probably didn't know is that you're the one who put them there. Yes, indeedy. You pressed the keys that brought them into existence.

Some of these characters, such as the space character, are familiar and fairly innocuous. (You know, like Commander Data of *Star Trek: The Next Generation*. What a space character!) Other characters, such as the tab mark that you get when you press the Tab key, are somewhat more mysterious.

The spacebar puts a space mark (character) in your text. Unlike the space on a typewriter, the word processor's spacebar gives you a very skinny space (much thinner than most other characters you type). The space mark's width depends on the *font* (typeface and size) that you're currently using.

When you press the Tab key, you insert a tab mark. The tab mark creates space in your text starting from where the insertion point is and ending where the next *tab stop* is. See "The Tab Stops Here" in Chapter 7.

The elite of these invisible beings, the paragraph mark that you get when you press the Enter key, is so powerful that it gets its own section. I come back to the paragraph mark in a couple of pages.

"What tab mark? What paragraph mark?" you say. Well, these marks are *invisible*, of course, which is why they don't stand out in a crowd. They're easy to overlook when you format or delete. But they do affect the way your document looks and can cause weird, spooky, inexplicable things to appear, such as big gaps in your text (due to a tab mark or a line of spaces you didn't know was there) or a paragraph merging with another (when a paragraph mark gets deleted) or a font for your text that you didn't expect (when the insertion point gets plunked down next to an invisible character that has a different font attached to it).

For all these reasons, you need to be able to see these invisible characters, at least occasionally. Read on.

## Seeing invisible characters

I discuss the why and how-not-to of these mysteries later, but for now just follow this simple step to see these creepy invisible guys:

Click View➪All Characters.

AAAaaggghh! Your document is filled with nasty dots and funny marks! In fact, it looks almost as bad as the document shown in Figure 5-3! What a mess! Aren't you glad that these characters are normally invisible? Those dots between your words are spaces. The little backwards-P-looking thing is a paragraph mark, and it hangs out with the text that precedes it. If you have any tab marks, they look like arrows with a deodorant-failure problem (lots of space around them). Manually inserted page breaks are dotted lines.

Now, if any of these invisible dudes are giving you trouble, just revoke their existence (delete them). Put the insertion point in front of them and press the Delete key. The visible text moves around to fill the gap.

To make these characters invisible again, click <u>V</u>iew➪A<u>l</u>l Characters again. Frankly, however, until you get used to having these characters lurking around, your life may be easier if you leave the characters visible.

**Figure 5-3:**
Invisible
characters
are lurking
in your
document.

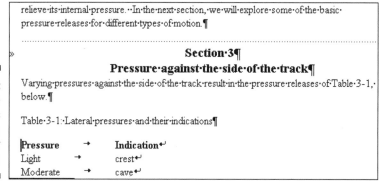

## *Paragraphs and paragraph marks*

Your English teacher told you what a paragraph is, right? Topic sentence? Two or more related sentences? Well, Works has its own idea about paragraphs. A Works paragraph is created when you press the Enter key and create one of those secret, invisible paragraph marks that I talked about in "Typing invisible characters" earlier in this chapter.

That paragraph mark is very powerful, as invisible beings tend to be. There are three extremely, very, very important, and utterly critical things to know about the paragraph mark.

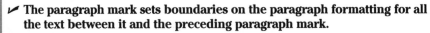

✔ **A paragraph mark tells Works, "Do not line wrap beyond this point; start a new line."**

A paragraph mark is the thing that keeps paragraphs apart.

✔ **The paragraph mark sets boundaries on the paragraph formatting for all the text between it and the preceding paragraph mark.**

Paragraph formatting is indentation, spacing between paragraphs, tab stops, alignment, justification, and other stuff that I talk about in "Pretty Paragraphs" in Chapter 7. When you format a paragraph, all this formatting information is *owned* by the paragraph mark and applies to the text preceding it. (The paragraph mark does *not,* however, specify type: typeface [font] or any aspect of type, such as style or size.) So if you copy a paragraph mark and paste it somewhere else, *it brings its paragraph formatting with it!*

✔ **Every time that you press the Enter key (creating a new paragraph mark), the new paragraph mark inherits all the paragraph formatting of the paragraph you were just in.**

The indentation, the spacing, the tab stops, and all the other paragraph stuff will be the same.

What these points mean for you is the following:

✔ Don't press the Enter key at the end of every line; only press it at the end of your paragraph. Otherwise your paragraph is actually a bunch of Works paragraphs. If you go to do something paragraphy, such as indenting everything but the first line, the format won't work properly because (as far as Works is concerned) every line *is* the first line!

✔ Do press the Enter key at the end of short lines in a list, such as this one.

✔ You can split one paragraph into two by putting the insertion point where you want the split and pressing the Enter key. The two new paragraphs will have identical paragraph formatting.

✔ To create a new paragraph to precede the one that you're currently in, move your insertion point to the beginning of the current paragraph and press Enter.

✔ To create a new paragraph to follow the one that you're currently in, move your insertion point to the end of the current paragraph (click the last line and press the End key to be sure) and press Enter.

✔ If you delete text that includes a paragraph mark (for example, if you select and delete text crossing two paragraphs), two paragraphs merge. The remaining single paragraph takes on the paragraph formatting of the bottom of the original pair. Try pressing Ctrl+Z to undo whatever you did; also see the sidebar, "Spooky formatting changes," in Chapter 7.

## Unfriendly mergers and takeovers of paragraphs

The Backspace and Delete keys delete invisible characters in the same way that they delete visible characters. If your insertion point is at the beginning of a paragraph and you press the Backspace key, you delete the preceding character: the invisible paragraph mark at the end of the preceding paragraph! Likewise, if you press the Delete key at the end of a paragraph, you delete the paragraph mark. Without a paragraph mark to hold it back, the first paragraph spills into the following one and forms one humongous paragraph. What's worse, if the two paragraphs were formatted differently — say that one paragraph was centered and the other paragraph wasn't — both of them are now formatted like the second paragraph.

You can get out of this mess by pressing Ctrl+Z (or clicking Edit⇨Undo) immediately. Another option is to reinsert the paragraph mark by clicking where you want the paragraph break and pressing the Enter key, but you still may need to reformat the first paragraph.

## *Keyboard tips and peculiarities*

For the big picture on the keyboard, see Chapter 1. Here are a few tips and peculiarities of the keyboard that are important to word processing:

- The two Shift keys work just like they do on a typewriter. To type a capital letter, hold down one of the two Shift keys while you type. Shift also gives you the upper set of characters on the top row of keys.

- CapsLock works *almost* like it does on a typewriter. To type a whole bunch of capital letters, press the CapsLock key and release it and then type. CapsLock does NOT, however, give you the upper set of characters on other keys. Your keyboard has a little light somewhere that tells you that CapsLock is on, and the word CAPS appears in the bottom-right corner of the Works window.

- If you hold down a key long enough, it *autorepeats*; that is, it repeatedly and rapidly types the character.

- The Backspace key doesn't just backspace; it deletes at the same time.

# *Getting Around in Your Document*

Sometimes you just want to take a spin around your document and check things out. Other times you want to move the insertion point and get down to work.

## Looking around

You can scroll around to look at one part of the document, maybe to review something you wrote earlier (which I never do, personally), while leaving your insertion point (that vertical bar) where you're typing. Leaving your insertion point in place is convenient because, while you look around, you don't lose your place. To perform this trick, scroll the document with the scroll bar on the right side or bottom of the document window. (See Chapter 2 for information on the scroll bar.)

If you type a word or if you press Delete, however, your view suddenly returns to the insertion point, because that's where you just typed. Works figures that, if you're working somewhere, you ought to be looking at what you're doing.

## Moving around

To work someplace different, you move your insertion point. To move your insertion point by using the mouse, just click somewhere in your document. To move to another page, click the arrow buttons (shown back in Figure 5-1) to the left of the scroll bar at the bottom of the document window. (Your view changes, too.)

To move your insertion point by using the keyboard, press the arrow or other navigation keys, like PgUp and PgDn. Table 5-1 shows you how to move the insertion point by using the keyboard. See "Rapping about wrapping," earlier in this chapter, to read how the insertion point moves from one line to another.

| Table 5-1 | Navigating with Keys |
|---|---|
| *Navigation Key* | *Where It Moves the Insertion Point* |
| Left-arrow/right-arrow | One character's worth left or right |
| Up-arrow/down-arrow | One line's worth up or down |
| PgUp/PgDn | One window's worth up or down |
| Home | Beginning of the line |
| End | End of the line |
| Ctrl+Home | Beginning of the document |
| Ctrl+End | End of the document |

## "Drink me" — making things bigger and smaller

If your Works window is so small that working in it is like looking down a rabbit hole, remember the antidote from Chapter 2.

You can make the document window bigger by clicking the maximize button in the uppermost right corner, and then you can do the same for the Works window. Refer to Figure 5-1 at the beginning of this chapter to distinguish between the two windows. See Chapter 2 for more information on program windows and document windows in general.

Another way to see your document better is to zoom. Click View➪Zoom and choose a magnification. See Chapter 3 for details.

# Seeing What Your Document Really Looks Like

One of the weird things about word processors is that they're all a little reluctant to show you *exactly* what your document looks like. In Works' word processor, there are three main ways of looking at your document (apart from printing it).

When you first start up the word processor, it shows a view of your work that is pretty close to, but not exactly, what you see when you print. For example, this first view doesn't show any page margins. It considers this view to be *Normal.* Humph.

A second view, called *Page Layout,* is a bit more exact. You can see your page breaks and margins realistically; also, if you use page numbers, headers, or footers, Page Layout view shows them. The Normal view doesn't. The Page Layout view is a bit slow to use, however: Works takes longer to show your changes as you make them.

Finally, the *Print Preview* feature lets you see something that's as close to the paper printout as Works can manage. You can't work on the document while looking at it in Print Preview, however. For more on this feature, see Chapter 6.

✔ To switch to the more realistic view, Page Layout, choose View➪Page Layout in the menu bar.

✔ To return to the Normal view, choose View➪Normal in the menu bar.

As you add and delete text in your document, the page breaks move fairly often. In the Normal view, the top of each page is marked by an unobtrusive little >> symbol. In the Page Layout view, your pages actually break. A gap and dividing line appear between one page and the next. This gap makes working in the vicinity of the page break, doing things like selecting text across the break, rather awkward. You probably want to use Normal view for most of your composing and then switch to Page Layout for final editing.

# Printing

Ahh, printing. Where the ink meets the paper. So visceral, so satisfying, so . . . confusing! At least it is sometimes. When everything works well, printing is fun. But getting everything to work the way that you want it to work can be a bit exasperating.

Fortunately, printing is pretty much the same for all the tools of Works. That's why the place to read all about printing is in Chapter 4, not here. Here, I just give a quick executive summary and point out what's different about printing a word-processor document.

The executive summary goes like this:

- ✔ You can print your whole document or any set of pages in it.
- ✔ The easiest way to print a single copy of the whole document is to click the Print button in the toolbar.
- ✔ To print a portion of your document, click File➪Print, or press Ctrl+P, and specify (in the Print dialog box) the pages that you want to print.

The main peculiarity of printing using the word processor is the *envelope* tool (or TaskWizard). For information on the envelope tool, see "The Envelope, Please" in Chapter 8.

# Saving Your Document

Saving your word-processing document is just like saving any other Works document, so see Chapter 2 for information about saving documents.

The executive summary on saving is:

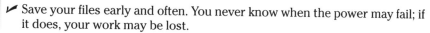

- ✔ Save your document either by clicking the Save button on the toolbar (the one with the diskette icon), choosing File⇨Save from the menu bar, or pressing Ctrl+S.

- ✔ Unless you save your document as a file on a disk, the document vaporizes when you stop Works from running or turn off your PC.

- ✔ Save your files early and often. You never know when the power may fail; if it does, your work may be lost.

# Exiting the Word Processor

To exit the word processor, all you have to do is close your word-processing document. Click on the X at the top-right corner of the document window. (Do not click the X in the top-right corner of the Works window, unless you want to exit Works completely.)

If you just want to switch to another open document, you do not need to close the active document. Just click the other open document's window. Or click Window in the menu bar and then click the other document's name on the menu that drops down.

To work on another new document of any kind, just create it in any of the usual ways (see Chapter 1). You don't need to close your word-processor document.

If your current document is still unsaved, or if it has changed since the last time you saved it as a file on a disk, Works puts up a dialog box to ask you if you want to save changes to your document. Click the Yes button, unless you really want to throw away what you've done since the last time you saved your work. If that's the case, click No.

# Chapter 6

# Hacking through the Jungle of Your Text

. . . . . . . . . . . . . . . . . . . . . . . . . . . . . . . . . . . . . . . . . . . . . .

### In This Chapter

▶ Selecting text

▶ Deleting, moving, and copying text

▶ Finding words and phrases

▶ Replacing words and phrases

▶ Looking up alternative phurds and wrases

▶ Checking your spelling

. . . . . . . . . . . . . . . . . . . . . . . . . . . . . . . . . . . . . . . . . . . . . .

*H*as your document become a tangle of misplaced paragraphs, wrong-headed words, and excessively long, lengthy, redundant, and duplicate descriptions? Time to sharpen up the old machete and cut an editorial swath through the underbrush.

Here's how to find and target such text, move it, copy it, delete it, replace it, or at the very least, spell it correctly. Gird your loins, buckle your swash, and have at it.

## Selecting Your Target

In order to do anything to the text you've typed, such as move it or copy it, you have to be able to tell Works exactly which text you're talking about. This process is called *selecting* or *highlighting* text; and because selecting works pretty much the same in all the Works tools, it is covered in detail in Chapter 3. Recall that the following two methods of selection work anywhere in Works:

✔ **Mouse method:** Click and drag the mouse cursor across the text you want to select. Release the mouse button when done.

> ✔ **Keyboard method:** Position the insertion point at one end of the text and then press the Shift key concurrently with an arrow key or another navigation key to expand the highlight. Release the keys when done.

The word processor has a few little peculiarities about selecting text with these two methods:

> ✔ When you use the mouse, you can select one individual character at a time within the first word, but after you have selected more than one word, you get one word at a time. Why? Go figure. If you like working this way, fine. But if not, you can fix it. Listen carefully: Click Tools➪Options. That leaves you looking at one of six index cards. The card that you want is called Editing. If the Editing card is not already the top card, click on the Editing tab to bring it to the top. On this card is an entry called Automatic word selection. Click the check mark in the box next to this entry, and the check mark goes away. Fixed. (Or you can just select big swaths of text with the mouse and then switch to the keyboard method for single-character control.)
>
> ✔ To select big gobs of text, press Shift+PgUp or Shift+PgDn; then switch to Shift+arrow keys for precision.
>
> ✔ To select from where the insertion point is to the beginning of the line, press Shift+Home; to select to the end of the line, press Shift+End.
>
> ✔ To select from where the insertion point is to the beginning of the document, press Ctrl+Shift+Home; to select to the end of the document, press Ctrl+Shift+End.

And here are some methods that are specially designed for word processing:

> ✔ To select a line, click in the white area to the left of that line; to select several lines, hold down the mouse button and drag.
>
> ✔ To select a paragraph, double-click anywhere in the white area to the left of the paragraph. (It doesn't matter which line you're next to.) To select several paragraphs, hold down the mouse button upon the second click and drag across the paragraphs.
>
> ✔ Finally, to select the whole document click on Edit➪Select All.

# Chopping Up Your Text: Moving, Copying, and Deleting

Remember the machete that you strapped on at the start of this chapter? Time to unbuckle it. And put on your pith helmet, because now's the time to cut that editorial swath through your pithy prose.

To aid you in this worthwhile endeavor, the Works word processor provides a variety of features that let you move text around, delete blocks of text, and copy text that is too tedious to retype every time it needs to appear.

These features are pretty much the same in every tool in Works. So rather than repeat them here, I suggest that you look at "Cutting, Copying, and Pasting" in Chapter 3. Here's the executive summary of how to edit text:

✔ To delete a block of text, select it; then press the Delete or Backspace key.

✔ To move text, select it; then click it again and drag it with the mouse.

✔ To copy text, do the same thing as for moving text, but hold the Ctrl key down while you drag.

✔ To make multiple copies, select something and then press Ctrl+C; click wherever you want a copy of that something and press Ctrl+V.

✔ To remove something and put a copy of it elsewhere, select it and then press Ctrl+X; then click wherever you want a copy to appear and press Ctrl+V.

You can use the buttons on the toolbar in place of the key combinations:

Ctrl+C is Copy, the button that shows two documents overlapping.

Ctrl+V is Paste, the button that shows a clipboard.

Ctrl+X is Cut, the button with the scissors.

Or you can find Copy, Paste, and Cut on the drop-down menu that appears when you click Edit.

# Finding Elusive Fauna (or Where's that Word?)

In the jungle of words that is the typical document, it's easy to lose track of important words and phrases. Perhaps way back somewhere in a 70-page tome, you had a discussion of the fauna of temperate transition zones (such as the Chicago suburbs). You'd like to cross-reference that discussion at this point, but you can't remember quite where it was.

Finding a word or phrase is no problem for your efficient and jungle-wise guide, the Find dialog box.

Here's how to give this trusty companion its marching orders:

1. **If you're sure that what you seek is somewhere before your insertion point, press Ctrl+Home.**

   This action puts your insertion point at the start of the document. Because Find starts searching from your insertion point and goes forward, starting from the beginning in this way can save you some time.

   If you have no idea where to look, skip to Step 2.

   If you know that what you seek is in a certain area, highlight (select) that area. Find restricts its search to the selected area.

2. **Click Edit⇨Find or press Ctrl+F.**

   The Find dialog box springs into action and presents itself for duty, as shown in Figure 6-1.

**Figure 6-1:**
Tell Find to
go forward
and seek a
word or
phrase.

3. **Type the word or phrase that you want to look for in the Find what box.**

   If you know that the word or phrase you want has some capital letters, capitalize them here and turn on the Match case feature. (You turn Match case off and on by clicking the Match case check box. The Match case feature is *on* if the check box has a check mark in it.) If, for example, you know that you are looking for the section entitled *Wildebeest,* (or *wildeBeest,* or even *wILDebeeST*), use the capitals. This step keeps Find from reporting on all the uncapitalized or miscapitalized *wildebeest*s (who should talk to their bankers).

   On the other hand, maybe you don't remember how the word was capitalized. (Maybe it was at the beginning of a sentence, or maybe not.) Then make sure that Match case is off and don't worry about the capitals. This action tells Find to look for *Wildebeests*, *wildebeests*, and *wILDebeeSTs* alike.

If the word or phrase you want to find includes a question mark, put the symbol ^ (Shift+6 on your keyboard) in front of the question mark. As it turns out, the ? symbol, when used here, means "any character." By putting a ^ (pronounced "^") in front of the question mark, you tell Works, "No, I really mean a question mark. Sheesh."

**4. Click F̲ind Next or press Enter.**

Find scurries forward into the underbrush, looking for *wildebeests* or whatever. When Find finds one, it highlights (selects) the *wildebeest* so that you can do stuff to it if you want to: delete it, format it, copy it, or just observe it in its habitat.

If Find can't find your word or phrase, it runs smack into either the end of your document or the end of the text you selected for the search. Rubbing its forehead, Find puts up a little box to ask if it should continue searching from the beginning of your document. Click Y̲es if you think that the *wildebeest* may be somewhere behind you. Otherwise, click N̲o to return to the Find dialog box so that you can revise your marching orders.

If Find has searched the entire document (or all of the text that you had selected) without success, it puts up a box saying Works did not find a match. which is Workspeak for "Back to the drawing board." Click OK in this box to return to the Find dialog box.

**5. To find another instance of the word or phrase, click F̲ind Next or press the Enter key again.**

Remember that your document may be swarming with *wildebeest*s. Keep searching until you find the right one.

**6. To find something different, edit your search word or phrase in the Fi̲nd what box.**

**7. Click the Cancel button in the Find box when you're done with your searching.**

## Whole wildebeests or pieces?

Is it wildebeest or wildebeast? If you're not sure how to spell what you're searching for (or not sure that you spelled it right when you used it before), try typing in just the portion of the word or phrase that you are sure of. You can just type *wilde,* and you can be pretty certain of finding wilde-whatevers. This trick also works if you're simply lazy and don't want to type the beest/beast part. Sloth is not a sin in finding words. (Though when you're finding sloths — well, never mind.) This method also works if you want both singular and plural *wildebeest(s)*: just leave off the *s.*

## Sticky boxes and words

The check boxes in the Find dialog box, such as Match case, are *sticky.* No matter which way you leave them when you quit Find (checked or not checked), that's how they appear when you use Find again, later. Always look to be sure that the check box is marked correctly before you begin searching. The word that you type is also sticky (as are the words that you type when using the Replace dialog box).

For any of these tricks to work, however, you have to make sure that the check box marked Find whole words only (in the Find dialog box) does *not* have a check mark in it. Click that check box if it does have a check mark.

## Searching for wildebeests and finding Oscar Wilde

Sometimes it's not such a good idea to search for pieces of a word. The Find feature may return from the hunt with Oscar Wilde instead of a wildebeest. Very embarrassing. Alas, no option to tell Find, "Do not find dead poets," is available.

So if there's a chance that your document includes both the fragment (*Wilde*) and the whole word (*wildebeest*), tell Find to search for whole words only. (A *whole word* is a bunch of characters set off by spaces or punctuation.) This whole-word option is very useful for short words, such as *an,* that crop up now *an*d again as fragments of other words.

To tell Find to search for whole words only, make sure that the check box marked Find whole words only has a check mark in it. Click that check box if it does not.

## Searching for invisible beasts

Your document is teeming with invisible, microscopic life — you know, like pond scum. (See "Typing Invisible Characters" in Chapter 5.) You can search for these invisible characters by using special *codes* — two-character combinations that begin with the carat symbol, ^ — or Shift+6 on your keyboard. For regular spaces, you can just type a space. But for tab marks, you can't just type a tab into the Find what text box. You have to use the special codes given in Table 6-1.

**Table 6-1    Codes to Use to Find Invisible Beasts in Your Document**

| Invisible Character | Codes to Use |
| --- | --- |
| Tab | ^T |
| Paragraph | ^P |
| End-of-line | ^n |
| Manual page break | ^d |
| Tabs or spaces | ^w |

Two invisible beasties — the paragraph mark and the tab mark — are so frequently searched for that Word thoughtfully provides special buttons for them in the Find dialog box. The arrow (for tab) and backwards-P (for paragraph) in Figure 6-1 are for that. If you click one of them, it inserts the appropriate code (^T or ^P) into the Find what box.

# Replacing Wildebeests with Whelks

If you've been typing along about wildebeests and suddenly realize that you meant *whelks,* not wildebeests, you have some problems that go beyond word processing, and I will not attempt to deal with them here. I can, however, tell you how to replace *wildebeest* with *whelk.*

Your companion on this environmentally dubious quest of replacing mammals with shellfish is not Find, but Find's twin, Replace. To use the Replace dialog box, you do exactly as you do with Find, giving a word or phrase to look for, except that you also give Replace something new to replace that word or phrase with. As Replace finds instances of the original word, you have the option of replacing each instance. You can also replace all instances. "Instancely."

Here's how to replace some text with other text:

1. **Narrow the area for your search and replace, if you can.**

   Like Find, the Replace command starts searching from your insertion point and goes forward. Click just before the area in which you want to replace text. If you know what you seek is in a certain area, highlight (select) that area. Replace restricts its search to the selected area.

2. **Click Edit⇨Replace or press Ctrl+H.**

   The Replace dialog box springs into action and presents itself for duty, as shown in Figure 6-2.

**Figure 6-2:**
Wantonly
replacing
wildebeests
with whelks.

**3. Type the word or phrase that you want in the Find what box.**

See "Finding Elusive Fauna (or Where's That Word?)" earlier in this chapter; the comments about capitalization, whole words, question marks, and invisible characters apply here as well.

**4. Type the replacement word or phrase in the Replace with text box.**

Unless you specifically want the replacement word to always be capitalized, using all lowercase letters is best. If the original text is capitalized, Replace cleverly capitalizes the new text.

See "Finding Elusive Fauna (or Where's That Word?)" earlier in this chapter; the comments about invisible characters apply here as well.

**5. Click the Find Next button or press Enter.**

Replace scurries forward into the underbrush, looking for *wildebeest*s to replace. When Replace finds one, it highlights (selects) the *wildebeest* so that you can see if this particular *wildebeest* is one that you want to replace.

If Replace can't find your word or phrase, it runs into the end of your document and, like its sibling, Find, asks if you want it to search from the start of the document. If this seems like a good idea, click Yes. If Replace has searched the entire document without success, it puts up a No Match Found box. Click OK in this box.

**6. To replace the highlighted text, click the Replace button.**

Poof! Your wildebeest is a whelk and happy as a clam.

Or to replace all instances of the search text, click the Replace All button. Replace doesn't pause for each instance to ask; it just does the replacement. If you selected a region of text back in Step 1, only that region is affected.

If you don't want to replace the particular instance that's currently highlighted, move on to Step 7.

7. **To find another instance of the word or phrase, click the** Find Next **button or press Enter again.**

   Remember that your document may be swarming with *wildebeest*s. Keep searching until you find all the ones that you want to replace.

   Replace lets you know when it has finished searching the whole document (or whatever text you selected).

8. **When you're done with your replacing, click the** Cancel **button or the** X **in the upper-right corner of the Replace dialog box.**

Here are a few tips and tricks for replacing:

✔ To replace a noun throughout your document, use the singular form (say, *wildebeest* or *whelk*) and make sure that the check box marked Find whole words only does NOT have a check mark in it. (Click the check box, if it does.) Where you once had *wildebeests*, you now have *whelks*. (This trick doesn't work if you're changing *wildebeests* to *octopi*, however.)

✔ As with the Find command, if you are searching for text that includes a question mark, precede that question mark with a ^ symbol, like this: ^?

✔ If you have a document that awkwardly uses lots of tabs and spaces for its formatting (instead of the nice paragraph formatting described in Chapter 7), you can get rid of those tabs and spaces by Replacing. Switch to *viewing all characters* by pressing Alt+V and then pressing A. See what invisible characters are being used, such as a row of spaces for indenting. Using ^t for tabs, and spaces for spaces, search for these and replace them with nothing in the Replace with text box.

✔ If your document uses blank lines (extra invisible paragraph marks) to create space between paragraphs, and you'd rather use Works' paragraph spacing features (see Chapter 7), get rid of the blank lines by Replacing two paragraph marks (**^p^p**) with one (**^p**).

The Replace All button can be dangerous. Use it carefully and make sure that you are only replacing what you want to replace. If you want to change *days* to *weeks*, make sure that you're not changing *Sundays* to *Sunweeks*.

# *Meeting the Mighty Thesaurus*

Among the various critters roaming around in the word processor is a thesaurus. Although not quite as mighty as the brontosaurus, the thesaurus is, perhaps, superior in intelligence. Its basic job is to help you find alternative words. (Note, Star Trek fans, that is alternative *words*, not alternative *worlds*. Stay with me, here.)

This thesaurus is nice and convenient, but it can't really hold a candle to a printed thesaurus (which is good, because they are generally flammable). Still, when you're stuck for a word, the Works thesaurus is good to have around.

The basic idea is to select (highlight) a word and then let the thesaurus look up alternatives. You can even select compound words, such as *blow up*. If the word can have several very different meanings (as the word *balloon* can have, for example), the thesaurus lists those and also lists alternative words within each meaning. You can explore alternatives for any of these words if you like. At any point, you can choose a word to replace the selected one.

Here's the click-by-click description of how to use the thesaurus:

1. **Select (highlight) the word you want to look up.**

2. **Click Tools⇨Thesaurus.**

   The Thesaurus dialog box of Figure 6-3 lumbers out of the wilderness and wants to be your friend.

**Figure 6-3:**
The baby thesaurus in Works is not purple, but it still wants to be your friend.

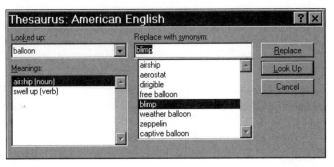

3. **Click any likely looking word or phrase in either the Meanings box or in the list of synonyms just below the Replace with synonym box.**

   Your substitute word can come from either list. If you click a *meaning,* you get a new list of synonyms to play with.

4. **To look for synonyms to your synonyms, click anything in either list and then click the Look Up button.**

   You can keep up like this all day. From *balloon* you can eventually float to almost anywhere. What fun! (If at any point you think "How the heck did I get here?" click the down-arrow next to the Looked up window, and the whole list of what you've looked up so far drops down.)

5. **When, in either list, you see a good substitute word or phrase, click it and then click the** Replace **button.**

   Your original word or phrase in the document is replaced.

Your new word or phrase may not be any better than your old one, but what a good time you've had. Beats working!

# Snaring Your Misspellings

Typos and misspellings sneak unnoticed into the undergrowth of any word-processing document. You may be amazed at how many errors you make that Works' spelling checker can discover and help you correct.

Because the Works spelling checker is one of those helpful features that is available for several tools, you can find it written up in detail in Chapter 3. The executive summary is as follows:

- ✔ Press Ctrl+Home to start at the beginning of your document; or select some text to be checked.

- ✔ Click the Spelling Checker button (the check mark with ABC) on the toolbar, press the F7 function key, or choose Tools⇨Spelling from the menu bar.

- ✔ The Spelling dialog box shows up if a word that it doesn't recognize (or capitalization or hyphenation that it doesn't approve of) appears.

- ✔ Make sure that the correctly spelled word is in the Change to box and then click Change or Change All. If you like what you had originally, click Ignore, Ignore All, or Add. (If you don't know which one you want to click, see Chapter 3.)

- ✔ When the checker puts up a little box telling you that it's done, click OK in that box.

# The 5th Wave

## By Rich Tennant

# Chapter 7

# Keeping Up Appearances

. . . . . . . . . . . . . . . . . . . . . . . . . . . . . . . . . . . . . .

## In This Chapter

▶ Formatting text

▶ Indenting and aligning paragraphs

▶ Setting spacing between lines and paragraphs

▶ Setting tab stops

▶ Using the ruler

▶ Setting page margins

▶ Printing sideways

▶ Using different sizes of paper

▶ Inserting page breaks

. . . . . . . . . . . . . . . . . . . . . . . . . . . . . . . . . . . . . .

*E*ven when on safari in the world of word processing, one must keep up appearances. There's no excuse for frumpy fonts, untidy indentation, improper alignment, unkempt tab stops, and mismanaged margins. Indeed, those who format fastidiously can even print sideways and control page breaks.

In this chapter, I show you how to attain all those niceties of civilization — first-line indentation, line spacing, paragraph spacing, and more — automatically, without typing a bunch of tabs and blank lines. I work from the small to the large — from characters to paragraphs to documents — and explore how Works can help give your document a civilized and smart look.

## Charming Characters

When your characters are losing their charm, it's time to look for a prettier face — typeface, that is (or *font*, as it is misnamed in the geeky world of computers). Works can put your type in any face (just what the world needs, more in-your-face typing) that you happen to have lying around on your PC, from the stodgy Times New Roman to swirly Script. Not only that, but Works can make the type large enough to see from across the room or small enough to be mistaken for flyspecks on your contracts. But wait! There's more! You can also easily change your font's *style,* making it **boldface**, *italic*, underlined, super-script, subscript, or ~~strikethrough~~!

All told, you have three different kinds of formatting to play with: font, size, and style. These different aspects of type are sometimes called *character formatting.* (No, character formatting is not a new kind of therapy.)

Changing the font, size, and style of your characters is one of those things that works the same way for all the tools of Works. So for full details, turn to Chapter 3. The executive summary goes like this:

Works offers three alternative techniques to change the way your type looks. First select some text you want to look different and then:

> **Alternative 1.** Use the toolbar. The Font Name box is at the far left end of the toolbar, and the Font Size box is right next to it. The Bold, Italic, and Underline buttons are just right of the center of the toolbar. For the other styles, you have to use Alternative 2.

> **Alternative 2.** Choose font, size, and style from something called the Font and Style dialog box. To get this dialog box, click Format⇨Font and Style.

> **Alternative 3.** (To change style only) Press Ctrl+B for bold, Ctrl+I for italic, and Ctrl+U for underline.

You can also use these alternatives with no text selected. In that case, you are changing the formatting of the insertion point. Any new characters that you type have the same formatting that the insertion point has. (To find out what the current formatting of the insertion point is, just look up at the toolbar.)

One tricky thing about character formatting is this: whenever you plunk the insertion point down somewhere by clicking the mouse cursor, the insertion point takes on the format of the first character to its right — even if that character is invisible! See the sidebar "Spooky formatting changes" (in this chapter) for more on this topic.

## *The Tab Stops Here*

You know all about tab stops, right? Those things that you used to set on your Smith-Corona where, when you pressed the Tab key, you moved to the next stop. Nice and simple. Well, tabs are simple no more. But although they're a tad (or a tab) more complex, they also do nice things. Right now, you're probably asking yourself, "Wait a second. I thought that tabs went out with buggy whips when Microsoft came up with this indentation thing." True, but (a) some people may never abandon their tabs, and (b) tabs are nice for doing, um . . . tabular stuff, such as certain simple types of tables.

## Spooky formatting changes

Sometimes you plunk your insertion point down, thinking to do a little work in the middle of, say, Times New Roman text, and suddenly find yourself typing in, say, Oz Handicraft font. You recall having done a little Oz work the other day, but you had changed your mind and reformatted back to Times New Roman.

Your problem probably is that something invisible is lurking in your text (something invisible that you didn't reformat because you couldn't see it). And your text is still in Oz. (And you're beginning to feel as if you are, too!) Your insertion point is in front of this invisible thing, so your typeface is Oz. The invisible thing is probably either a *space mark* or *paragraph mark,* and you need to exorcise it with the Delete or Backspace key. See "Typing invisible characters" in Chapter 5.

## *Newfangled tab stops*

Works (like most word processors) has four kinds of tab stops:

- ✔ **Left tab stop:** The conventional tabs that you're accustomed to are called left tabs in a word processor because what you type after the tab begins after the stop; therefore the text has its left edge at that point.

- ✔ **Decimal tab stop:** For columns of numbers, you may want to use the decimal tab stop, which aligns every number at the decimal point. You set the tab in the position where you want the decimal point to be (or at the end of a number without a decimal point). When you type a number (having first set up the tab stop and then tabbed over to this stop), Works types, oddly enough, to the left of this stop. Works does so until you type a decimal point; then it types to the right of the stop.

- ✔ **Right tab stop:** Unsurprisingly, the right tab stop is the opposite of the traditional or left tab stop. Instead of the left edge of text aligning with this stop, the right edge does. When you type (having first set up the tab and then tabbed over to this stop), Works shifts text over to the left, keeping the right edge of the text aligned with the tab stop.

- ✔ **Center tab stop:** When you set up one of these guys and then tab over to it and type, Works shuffles your characters left and right as you go, in order to keep your text centered on the tab position. Whatever you type ends up centered under the tab stop.

To see these beasties in action, skip way ahead in this chapter and check the examples in Figure 7-5.

## Dialoging about tab

If you find the ruler bar all too squinty for setting tab stops, or if you want something other than a left tab, the time has come to have a little dialog. Box, that is. Check out Figure 7-1.

The general idea is to work on one tab stop at a time (identified by its position), change its alignment or *leader* (the character that fills the space the tab creates — usually none), and then click the Set button. As you create new stops, they are listed in the larger box under Tab stop position. Later, you can delete a tab stop or change its alignment by clicking it in that box.

To add a new tab stop or change an existing one:

1. **Select the paragraphs whose stops you want to set or change.**

   If you don't select anything, Works assumes that you want to format the paragraph where the insertion point is. Select multiple paragraphs to give them all the same tab stops.

2. **Get a Tabs dialog box, if you haven't already.**

   You have two ways to get a Tabs dialog box (sounds like a diet breakfast cereal, doesn't it?):

   • Click Format⇨Tabs. (Or press Alt+O and then press T.)

   • Double-click the top of the ruler bar (where the numbers are).

3. **To add a new tab stop, type in its position in the Tab stop position box.**

   Click the box immediately under the Tab stop position label and type the tab's position from the left margin. The other controls in the dialog box — Alignment and so on — now refer only to this tab stop.

4. **Or to modify an existing tab stop, click it in the list box under Tab stop position.**

5. **Click an alignment for this tab stop in the Alignment area.**

6. **Click Set to put this tab stop in your paragraph.**

7. **If you decide you don't want this tab stop, click Clear.**

8. **To clear out all the tab stops in this paragraph, click Clear All.**

9. **Repeat with additional tab stops until you have just the tab stops you want in the Tab stop position list box.**

   To review the tabs' alignments, just click them in the list box.

10. **Click the OK button.**

Click the type of tab stop that you want.

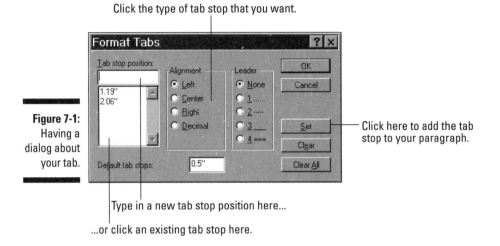

**Figure 7-1:**
Having a
dialog about
your tab.

Click here to add the tab
stop to your paragraph.

Type in a new tab stop position here...

...or click an existing tab stop here.

The Format Tabs dialog box also says something about a *leader*. No, the tabs have not formed a political system. Normally, when you're typing on a typewriter and press the Tab key, you get a blank area up to the position of the tab stop. That's not necessarily true in Works. A leader is what Works puts in this area. For example, in a table of contents, you may want a line of dots or something between the topic and the page number. To have a leader associated with a tab stop, click 1, 2, 3, or 4 in the Leader area; otherwise, click None.

Finally, if you really don't want to set a bunch of individual tab stops but would like to change the spacing of the tab stops that Works provides (the default tab stops), just type a new spacing in the Default tab stops text box. These tab stops are important because Works uses them for indenting paragraphs when you choose an indented format. "What's an indented format?" I hear you ask. (I have great ears, haven't I?) An indented format is a kind of paragraph formatting. What's paragraph formatting? Well, funny you should ask (or convenient at the very least). You're about to find out.

# Pretty Paragraphs

There's no accounting for taste. (In fact, there's no Personnel, Purchasing, or any other department for taste.) Some folks like the first line of their paragraphs indented. Others, perhaps plumbing professionals, like them *flush right*. Some folks like their lines double-spaced, and maybe they like bigger spaces between paragraphs, too. All this stuff is called *paragraph formatting,* which all boils down to a few things you can fool with:

✓ **Indentations:** How far the paragraph's margins should be from the page's margins. Also how far from the left page margin the first line of the paragraph should be.

✓ **Alignments:** How the paragraph's text lines up with the margins.

✓ **Breaks:** Whether to split up a paragraph when it crosses over onto the next page or to keep the paragraph as one solid lump; also, sometimes you may want two paragraphs, like marriage partners, to stay with each other on the same page.

In Works (a program which is trying, after all, to be all things to all people) there are generally two or three ways to do anything. Well, lots of ways are available to do paragraph formatting. Buttons, keystrokes, dialog boxes, the ruler bar, direct mind-to-chip control — you name it, it works. (Okay, I made one of them up.) Which ones you may like may depend on whether you prefer pictures or lists, how picky you are about getting things to look just the way you want, your astrological sign, and so forth. So if in the course of this chapter you find yourself saying, "There's got to be an easier/more precise/better way than that," keep reading. There probably is.

## Alignments: making your lines line up

Alignments are the simplest kind of paragraph formatting, so I get them out of the way first. Works has four kinds of alignment.

Left, left, left, left, left, left, left, left, left, left, left, left, left, left, left, left, left, left, left, left, left, left, left, left, left, left, left, left.

Centered, centered, centered, centered, centered, centered, centered, centered, centered, centered, centered, centered, centered.

Right, right, right, right, right, right, right, right, right, right, right, right, right, right, right, right, right, right, right, right, right.

Justified, justified, justified, justified, justified, justified, justified, justified, justified, justified, justified, justified, justified, justified, justified, justified, justified, justified, justified, justified, justified.

There are two really easy ways to change alignment. First select the paragraphs you want to realign and then *either:*

✓ **Click one of the three alignment toolbar buttons.**

These toolbar buttons are right up there above the ruler, between the 4-inch and 5-inch marks. The buttons are, in order, Align Left, Align Right, and Align Center. For reasons best known to Microsoft, no Justify button is on the toolbar.

> ✔ **Or press the appropriate key on the keyboard.**
>
> > Ctrl+L for align left
> >
> > Ctrl+Shift+R for align right
> >
> > Ctrl+E for align centered
> >
> > Ctrl+J for justified

If you happen to find yourself using the Format Paragraph dialog box for some other reason, you can click one of the four alignment buttons there. The Format Paragraph dialog box is explained later in this chapter and is shown in Figure 7-3.

## Indenting left and right edges

If you're used to typing on a typewriter, you're used to using the Tab key to indent stuff. Using the Tab key is okay for the first line of a paragraph, but if you have to indent a whole paragraph, tabbing gets pretty tedious. The clever folks who make word processors said, "Hey," (they always start like that) "how about we just let folks tell the word processor how they want the paragraph indented, instead of using all this tab stuff?" While the word processor folks were at it, they came up with a way for you to indent the right side, too. So lay off the Tab key; the modern, turn-of-the-millennium way to indent is with paragraph formatting.

> If your paragraph is just an average Joe, kind of laid back with no particular need for fancy indentation, its left and right edges are at the left and right page margins. But if your paragraph wants to stand out and strut its stuff, it needs indented left and right edges, such as this paragraph has.

The fastest way to do indentations is with the keyboard. Click the paragraph that you want to indent; to do several paragraphs at once, select the whole group.

> ✔ **To indent the left side:** Press Ctrl+M; the paragraph indents to the first built-in *default* tab stop (at $1/2$ inch). Press Ctrl+M again, and your paragraph indents another $1/2$ inch, and so on.
>
> ✔ **To do *hanging* indents (indent everything but the first line):** Press Ctrl+Shift+H.
>
> ✔ **To undo hanging (or any other left-side) indentations:** Press Ctrl+Shift+M; this action undoes indentation by one tab (moves the left edge of the paragraph left $1/2$ inch).

Having a keyboard combination to indent the first line would be nice, but one isn't available.

The next-fastest way to do indentations is with the ruler bar. Check out "Son of Having it your way — the ruler," later in this chapter.

## Spaced-out paragraphs

Space is the final frontier of paragraph formatting. If you need a little air in your text, you can always ventilate your paragraph by double-spacing or adding space between paragraphs. But *don't* add spaces the way you did on your old Dumbrowski-Stanowitz steam-powered typing machine:

- Don't press the Enter key twice at the end of every line to double-space. (Don't even press it once.)
- Don't press the Enter key twice at the end of every paragraph to get spaces between your paragraphs.

The quick way to get space between paragraphs is by pressing Ctrl+0. (That's zero, not the letter *O*.) This puts one line's worth of space before the current paragraph if there isn't one there already. If one line's worth of space is already there, this action takes it away. You can also use keyboard commands to set the line spacing within a paragraph:

- **Ctrl+1** single spaces the current paragraph (where your insertion point is).
- **Ctrl+2** double spaces the current paragraph.
- **Ctrl+5** imposes one-and-a-half-line spacing on the paragraph. Why 5? Well, in the strange math of Works, 5 = 1.5. Or at least it does here.

You can also do this stuff (and lots more) with the Format Paragraph dialog box. See "Having it your way — the Format Paragraph dialog box," later in this chapter.

## Having it their way with Easy Formats

If your taste in paragraph formatting is at all like the taste of most other humans on the planet, you're in luck. (Actually you're in luck even if your taste is pretty weird, as long as it matches the taste of somebody at Microsoft.) Works has a couple dozen real pretty, off-the-shelf formats, called Easy Formats, that you can choose from. To use an Easy Format:

1. **Select the paragraphs you want to format.**

   If you don't select anything, Works assumes that you want to format the paragraph where the insertion point is.

**2. Click the Easy Formats button.**

It's the one near the right end of the toolbar. (The icon looks like a document with a gleam.) What you get is a menu with Create From Selection at the top, More Easy Formats at the bottom, and five strange-looking names in between.

Those five names refer to the five most-recently-used paragraph formatting styles. Bet you never thought of paragraph formatting styles as having names; but unlike all those poor Unsaved Documents, they do. ("Prestige body" is my favorite. Want one? Just a click is all it takes.)

**3. If you like one of the five listed formats, click it.**

Done. Your paragraph is reformatted. Don't like it? Undo it by pressing Ctrl+Z and go back to Step 1.

**4. If none of the listed formats appeal to you, click** More Easy Formats.

Now you see the Easy Formats dialog box, pictured in Figure 7-2. On the left is the complete list of format names. The Sample box in the center gives a hazy rendition of how the selected format looks on a page. The Description box gives you the technical details of the selected format.

**5. Select a format from the Easy Formats dialog box.**

You do this step by clicking the format's name in the list on the left side of the box. Check out the Sample box to see if your selection makes the text look like what you want. If your selection does not suit you, click another format name. After you've gotten one that looks promising, move to Step 6. Or you can decide that reformatting was all a bad idea and click Cancel, which returns you to your pristine, unreformatted paragraphs.

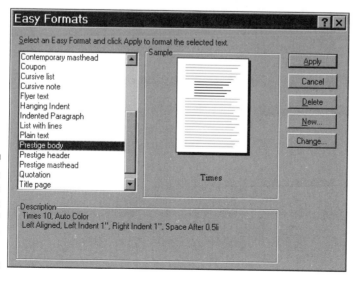

**Figure 7-2:**
Easy
Formats, the
fast food of
paragraph
formatting.

6. **Click the** Apply **button.**

The Easy Formats dialog box goes away, and your reformatted paragraphs await you.

If you're hunting for something amusing to do instead of working, cruise through some of the Easy Formats. The Coupon format is a hoot, and so is Cursive note.

An Easy Format consists of a paragraph format *plus* character formatting for all the characters in the paragraph. If you're fond of the font that you've been using, make sure (by looking at the Font Name and Font Size boxes on the toolbar) that you didn't change it unintentionally with an Easy Format. If you did change your font, you can just change it back. See "Charming Characters" earlier in this chapter.

Until you have confidence that you know what you're doing, stay away from the Change or New buttons in the Easy Formats dialog box. These buttons transport you to the cleverly named Change Easy Formats or New Easy Formats dialog boxes, which have more power than most of us really ought to wield. (Do you think that a Prestige body paragraph would look nicer with a magenta box around it? No problem.) The Change Easy Formats box changes the formats permanently, which may not be such a great idea. The New Easy Formats box allows you to create your own Easy Formats. But I show you a simpler way to do this task after I discuss the Format Paragraph dialog box. (See "Having it your way all the time: creating your own Easy Formats" later in this chapter.)

## *Having it your way — the Format Paragraph dialog box*

If those standard formats just don't get your blood racing, you can have custom-tailored paragraphs by using the Format Paragraph dialog box, shown in Figure 7-3 and 7-4. This dialog box provides one-stop shopping for all your paragraph formatting needs. Indentations, alignments, breaks, mufflers — you can do it all here.

You can get a Format Paragraph dialog box in two ways:

✔ Click Format⇨Paragraph. (Or press Alt+O and then press P on the key-board.)

✔ Double-click the left or right indent marks on the ruler bar.

The box looks like two index cards, one named Indents and Alignment, and the other named Spacing (which does breaks). You can switch between them by clicking the tab of the hidden card. Both cards have a Sample box, which shows you what the reformatted paragraph may look like on a page.

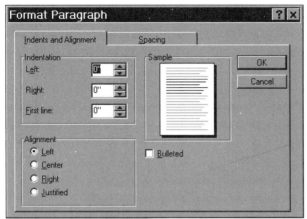

**Figure 7-3:**
The Indents
and
Alignment
card from
the Format
Paragraph
dialog box.

You use the Format Paragraph box by making whatever changes you want on the two cards and then clicking the OK button. Nothing is changed in your document until you click OK. If at any time you click the Cancel button, you return to your paragraph unchanged.

The Indents and Alignment card has an Indentation box, an Alignment box, a Sample box, and a Bulleted check box. The Indentation box is really three boxes, which control the distance between the left paragraph margin and the left page margin, between the right paragraph margin and the right page margin, and between the left page margin and the beginning of the first line. (By using these commands, paragraphs can be indented automatically, without using tabs. You can also do this automatic indentation with the ruler bar, as you soon see.) You can type a number into any of the three boxes and get that many inches of indentation. Or you can click the up-/down-arrows beside the boxes to raise or lower the number inside.

You can get any of the four basic alignments (Left, Center, Right, Justified) by clicking the white dot next to the alignment's name. (If you've forgotten what these terms mean, see "Alignments: making your lines line up" earlier in this chapter.)

•   If the check box next to Bulleted has a check mark in it, your paragraph has a black dot next to it and is indented a little, like this paragraph is. Clicking an empty check box puts a check mark in it if it is empty, or clicking the check box makes it empty if it had a check mark in it.

The Spacing card (as shown in Figure 7-4) tells Works how this paragraph gets along with its neighbors. Type numbers into (or click the up-/down-arrows next to) the Before and After boxes to tell Works how many lines to skip before or after the paragraph. Similarly, the Line spacing box tells Works how many lines to skip between lines of the paragraph. Setting Line spacing to 2, for example, double-spaces the paragraph.

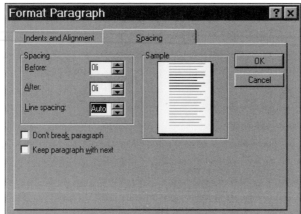

**Figure 7-4:**
The Spacing
card from
the Format
Paragraph
dialog box.

Putting a check mark in the `Don't break paragraph` check box prevents Works from putting part of the paragraph on one page and part on the next. Putting a check mark in the `Keep paragraph with next` check box makes sure that this paragraph and the next stay on the same page if at all possible. (Of course, if the paragraphs are more than a page long, there is no way to keep them on the same page.)

## *Having it your way all the time: creating your own Easy Formats*

If you find yourself using the same combination of character and paragraph formatting again and again (and the combination is not already an Easy Format), you can put it on the Easy Format list. All you have to do is:

1. **Select a paragraph that is already formatted the way that you want.**

2. **Click Easy Formats⇨Create From Selection.**

   This step invokes the New Easy Format dialog box, with most of its buttons grayed out.

3. **Name your format by typing in the box with the blinking cursor.**

4. **Click the** `Done` **button.**

Now your newly named format can appear on the Easy Formats menu. (See "Having it their way with Easy Formats" earlier in this chapter.)

# *Son of Having it your way — the ruler*

Nothing keeps order like a good ruler, so the Works word processor comes equipped with a royal one. Sometimes Works' ruler is a royal something else, but mostly it's a benevolent monarch.

If your ruler is missing, click View⇨Ruler. Don't be shy; if a cat can look at a king, you can View your Ruler.

The ruler reigns over indentations, alignments, and tab stops. A modest kingdom, perhaps, but an important one. See how it rules the indentations, alignments, and tab stops in Figure 7-5.

Notice how the left side of the paragraph aligns with the paragraph indent mark. Also, the first line aligns with the first line indent mark. (Pretty reasonable, huh?) The author of the document in Figure 7-5 entered tabs to position things. Dates in the table are aligned along their left edges because this clever author used a particular kind of tab stop, called the *left tab stop*. For the numbers, he used a *decimal tab stop,* which caused the numbers to align along their decimal points. And the locations align along their right sides because of (everyone together now — yes, that's right) the *right tab stop.* Finally, the whole line comes to a stop at the right paragraph indent mark. And now this paragraph comes to a stop. Not a minute too soon.

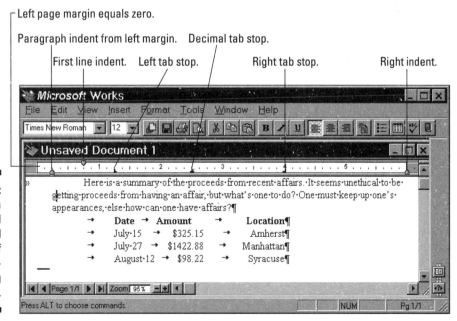

**Figure 7-5:**
The ruler: a kindly and powerful monarch of the word-processing realm.

The ruler shows you what's going on in the paragraph where your insertion point currently resides. Or, if you select a paragraph, the ruler tells about the paragraph you selected. The ruler can apply itself to only one paragraph at a time. If you select a bunch of paragraphs, it shows you the first one.

The totally, utterly cool thing about the ruler is that it not only *shows* you the paragraph stuff, it lets you *control* the paragraph stuff. I know; this news is pretty exciting, right? (Not quite as cool as slide rules, but what can you expect? It's the '90s.) Calm down; I can take this description a bit more slowly. Read on.

### Reading the ruler

As any good subject knows, it is important to understand your ruler. In particular, with this ruler, understanding what the tick marks and numbers correspond to is vital. Looking at the zero-inch mark, for example, you may well say, "Zero inches to what?"

Well, zero is where the left margin of your page is. All points on the ruler are measured from this left margin.

The tick marks are at $^1/_8$-inch intervals if you're using inches. (You can set your indentations and tab stops at even more precisely measured intervals than $^1/_8$ inch.) To use units other than inches, choose Tools⇨Options. See "Hooked on metrics" in Chapter 4 for details.

The tiny, little T leaves — I mean, T-shaped marks — at $^1/_2$-inch intervals, are the built-in tab settings. You can put in your own tab marks, too, where you want them; but the tab marks you insert look like Ls, not upside-down Ts. More on tabs in a minute.

If you decide to look at your document in the Page Layout view, your ruler changes a bit. Suddenly, there are negative numbers off to the left of zero. The only purpose of the negative numbers is to show how big your page margin is; you can't put anything in the margin. (That would violate its marginosity.) For more on Page Layout, check out "Seeing what your document really looks like," in Chapter 5.

### Indenting with the ruler

The cool thing about using the ruler for indents is that the ruler lets you do them graphically. Just click the left or right indentation mark and drag it. You change the edges of the paragraph that your insertion point is currently on. To set the edges of a bunch of paragraphs, select the paragraphs before you drag the marks. These edges are technically called the *left and right paragraph indentations*, not paragraph margins. Not thinking of them as margins is hard, but that would be marginal thinking.

The tricky thing about the two indentation marks on the left side is that they are related, like twins. These marks are like a split version of the right indent mark. The top half of this split triangle controls only the first line of the paragraph. The bottom half of the triangle controls the entire paragraph. The weird result of this split triangle is that when you move the bottom half, the top half always moves along with it! The idea is, apparently, that you probably want to keep the first line indent the same when you change the paragraph indent.

So having said all that, here's the blow-by-blow on changing paragraph indentations with the ruler:

1. **Select the paragraphs you want to indent.**

   If you don't select anything, Works assumes that you want to format the paragraph where the insertion point is.

2. **To indent the first line, drag the top triangle of the pair of triangles on the left of the ruler bar.**

3. **To indent the whole paragraph, drag the bottom triangle of the pair.**

4. **To indent the right side of the paragraph, drag the triangle on the right side of the ruler bar.**

You can also change indentations by using a dialog-box approach. The dialog box is not as cool and graphical as the ruler; but the dialog box is easier to use for those of us who are riding in a car across Connecticut at the moment, with a mouse that keeps falling off our knees as we try to move those tiny triangles around. See "Having it your way — the Format Paragraph dialog box" earlier in this chapter.

### Tab stops on the ruler

For setting nice, normal tab stops of the conventional sort that you would approve marrying into your family (left tab stops, I mean), the ruler is ideal. For anything newfangled and outlandish, such as decimal or right tab stops, see "The Tab Stops Here," earlier in this chapter. The ruler bar shows you these crazy newfangled tabs, but it quite stodgily refuses to have anything else to do with them (other than remove them, that is).

Works already provides a nice set of built-in tab stops, spaced about every $1/2$ inch (if you're using inches). (The built-in tab stops are the little upside-down T marks under the tick marks.) If you want more tab stops, just follow this complicated instruction:

**Click where you want your tab, in the bottom half of the ruler.**

That's all.

Your (left) tab marks look like tiny arrows that go left and then up. (An arrow that goes straight up is a center tab stop; if the arrow has a decimal point next to it, the tab is a decimal tab; and if the arrow goes right and then up, the tab is a right tab. (Refer to Figure 7-1.) Here's what to do with the tabs when you've got them.

✔ To move your tab marks around, drag 'em. The built-in marks that fall before or between your marks conveniently vanish.

✔ To remove one of your tab marks, drag it off the ruler and into the document, where it evaporates in the rarefied atmosphere of your prose.

✔ To go for an exotic *right, center,* or *decimal* tab mark, double-click the lower half of the ruler bar and see the section "The Tab Stops Here" in this chapter.

# Formatting Your Overall Document

All this stuff about letters and paragraphs and stuff is just dandy, but what about the *document?* How big is a page, what's on what page, and what are the margins? Good questions.

Works begins (as usual) by assuming a bunch of stuff about the page, the *page defaults:*

✔ You're using 8 ½ x 11-inch paper, oriented the normal way for a letter.

✔ Top and bottom margins are 1". Left and right margins are 1.25". If you're using headers and footers, they are .5" from the top and .75" from the bottom, respectively.

The places where Works puts page breaks follow from these settings and from how big and airy you want to format your characters and paragraphs. You can change these page breaks if you like.

Most of this formatting-of-the-overall-document stuff is tucked away inside the Page Setup dialog box.

## Page Setup

To set up your document's overall appearance (which is not to imply that it looks like a pair of old overalls), do the following:

Click File⇨Page Setup. (Or press Alt+F and then press G.)

This action wins you a Page Setup dialog box. When you first use this Page Setup command, the top card is the Margins card shown in Figure 7-6. These cards all deal with different aspects of page setup and printing. Click a card's tab, sticking out at the top, to choose it. (If you change to another card before quitting the Page Setup dialog box, that card is on top the next time that you use this dialog box.)

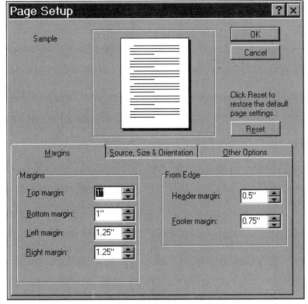

**Figure 7-6:**
Page Setup stuff looks like Mom's recipe card file, but without the blueberry-pie stains. This is the card for Margins.

 Each card in the dialog box also shows you a Sample, to give you a rough idea of what your document can look like using the changes you make. One quirk to be aware of is that if you type something into a box, the Sample doesn't show your changes until you click in a *different* box.

## Margins

Using the Page Setup dialog box in Figure 7-6 (press Alt+F and then G, if the Page Setup dialog box is not already up), click the tab marked Margins.

 To change one of the margins listed on this card, click the box for a margin and edit the margin setting or type in a new number. If you're not sure how to do that, see "Dialog Boxes" in Chapter 1.

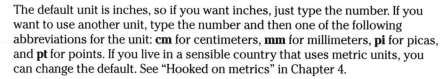

The default unit is inches, so if you want inches, just type the number. If you want to use another unit, type the number and then one of the following abbreviations for the unit: **cm** for centimeters, **mm** for millimeters, **pi** for picas, and **pt** for points. If you live in a sensible country that uses metric units, you can change the default. See "Hooked on metrics" in Chapter 4.

The Sample doesn't show your changes until you click in a *different* box from the one you just edited. The Sample box is just weird that way.

To go back to using the default margin values, click the Reset button.

Click OK if you're all done setting up the page.

## Sideways documents

If you want to print sideways, most PC printers these days let you do that. Because you can't normally put paper sideways into your printer, your printer has to be able to type sideways — which your printer can probably do, unless it uses type-wheels like some typewriters use. You just have to let Works know that sideways printing is what you have in mind. Use the Page Setup dialog box (press Alt+F and then press G, if the box is not already up).

In the Page Setup dialog box, click the tab marked Source, Size & Orientation. Then click Landscape in the lower-left corner to print sideways. (Portrait is the usual orientation, like the *Mona Lisa*.) The page icon, with the letter *A*, illustrates how type is to be printed on the page. The Sample also changes to show you how the lines of text run.

Click OK unless you need to set up something else, such as the paper size.

## Different-sized documents

If you're using anything other than 8 ½ x 11-inch paper (or if you're using an envelope), you need to tell Works about it. (Works has special features for envelopes. See "The Envelope, Please" in Chapter 8.) Use the Page Setup dialog box (to pull it up, press Alt+F and then press G).

1. **In the Page Setup dialog box, click the tab marked** Source, Size & Orientation.

2. **On the** Source, Size & Orientation **card, click the box marked** Size.

   Use the scroll bar to find more.

3. **Click one of the standard paper or envelope sizes in the box that drops down.**

   If you're using a paper size that's not shown here, click the box marked Width and type in a new value; then do the same for Height. (Width always refers to the direction that a line of text runs.) After your last change, click in a different box from the one that you're in and check the Sample to see if things look roughly correct.

4. **Click the Reset button if you want to return to the default paper size.**

5. **Click OK if you're all done setting up the page.**

## *Page breaks*

When you fill one page, Works begins another page automatically as you're typing. If you want the page to break at an earlier location, you can put in a page break yourself. If you want the page to break later, forget it. Works can't squeeze any more on a page unless you change some formatting.

If you use a smaller font size, smaller spaces between lines or paragraphs, or smaller margins, you can get more text on a page. (Of course, if you get carried away, you may produce a document that can be read only under an electron microscope. The wonders of technology!)

Most of the time Works' automatic page breaks are just fine because Works counts lines and measures spaces much better than you can. (It being a computer program and all.) But occasionally you know something that Works doesn't, such as the fact that this particular line is the start of a new chapter and really needs to come at the top of a page. Then you want to be able to put in a page break by hand. (Well, by typing on the keyboard or something.) This is what has happened in Figure 7-7.

You can avoid an inconvenient page break when it breaks up a paragraph or breaks between two consecutive paragraphs that you really want to keep together. Look at "Having it your way — the Format Paragraph dialog box" and Figure 7-4, both in this chapter.

You can also use page breaks to make a blank page (by putting in a pair of them) or to force a page to appear on the left or right side in a bound document (such as this book). Don't try this last trick until you have finished making all the edits. (Otherwise, you may have to repaginate the entire book.)

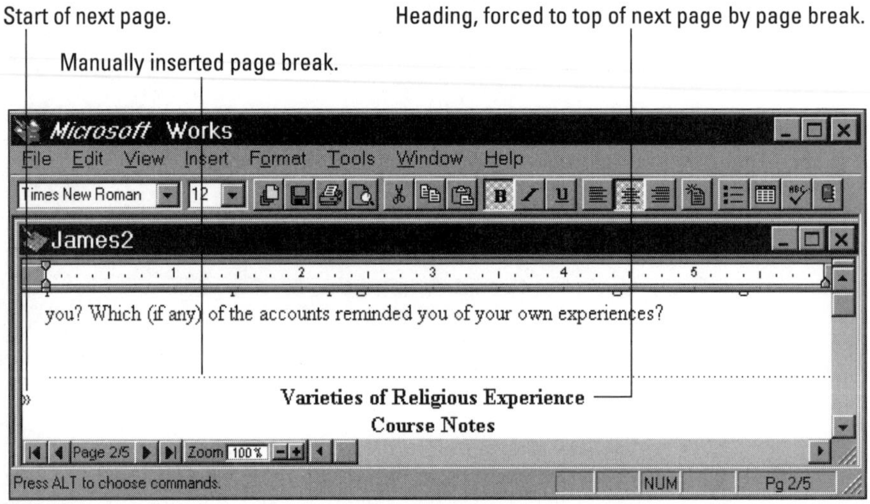

Start of next page.

Heading, forced to top of next page by page break.

Manually inserted page break.

**Figure 7-7:**
Give
yourself a
break — a
manual
page break.

> **Microsoft** Works
>
> File Edit View Insert Format Tools Window Help
>
> Times New Roman | 12 | | | | | | | | X | | | | B | I | U | | | | | | | | | |
>
> **James2**
>
> . . . . . . 1 . . . . . . 2 . . . . . . 3 . . . . . . 4 . . . . . . 5 . . . .
>
> you? Which (if any) of the accounts reminded you of your own experiences?
>
> Varieties of Religious Experience
> Course Notes
>
> | Page 2/5 | | Zoom 100% | |
>
> Press ALT to choose commands. | NUM | Pg 2/5

Here's how to put in your own page break:

### 1. Click exactly where you want the page break to occur.

If the page break is to occur between paragraphs, clicking at the beginning of the first line of the paragraph that's going on the next page is best — clicking *after* the last text on the current page is not good. Clicking at the beginning of the first line avoids problems with invisible paragraph marks.

### 2. Press Ctrl+Enter. Or click Insert⇨Page Break.

A dotted line appears; this is your page break symbol, as shown in Figure 7-7. You can delete, cut, paste, or drag the page break symbol just like any other symbol on the page. To select the page break by itself, click the left margin, next to the symbol.

Your manual page break appears on the screen as a faint dotted line. After your page break, Works continues to do its own normal, automatic page-breaking thing. In the Normal view, Works' automatic page breaks can be a little hard to find. The only indication is the little >> mark in the left margin at the top of a page. In Page Layout view, page breaks are really obvious. See "Seeing what your document really looks like" in Chapter 5.

Don't do any more page-breaking than you absolutely must. If you try to do your own break for every page, you can have a mess on your hands if you add or delete text later. If you add or delete text later, you must then reposition every page break!

# Chapter 8

# Fancier Word-Processing Documents

*I*t's payoff time! You've paid your dues. You've editorially slashed your way through the jungles of text and stood your ground in the face of pouncing paragraphs, rampaging thesauruses, and terrible tab stops. Now's the time to have a little fun. (Fun in the highly abstract, metaphoric sense of the word, that is. If you really find yourself looking forward to changing tab stops on the ruler, you may want to consider enlisting the aid of some competent professional.)

## Bulleted Lists: Shooting from the Toolbar

It's a jungle out there, and a few bullets may come in handy — bulleted lists, that is. Bulleted lists are made up of indented paragraphs, each with a little dot next to its first line. The paragraphs may be single- or multi-line (regular) paragraphs; Works doesn't care.

If you want simple big-black-dot style bullets, you can get them easily from the Bullets button on the toolbar. (The Bullets button looks like a bulleted list.) All you have to do is type your paragraphs in the usual way, select the ones you want to bulletize, and then click the Bullets button.

The Bullets button indents your paragraph to the first default tab stop — the stops marked with little upside-down Ts; not tab stops that you have created. To change these tab stops, see Chapter 7. If that indentation is not the indentation that you had in mind, you can adjust it from the keyboard. Each time you press Ctrl+M, the indentation will increase by one tab stop. Pressing Ctrl+Shift+M does the opposite — it shrinks the indentation by one tab stop.

You can also remove those bullets without an anesthetic — just select the proper paragraphs and hit the Bullets button again. This step gets rid of the black dot, but does not restore whatever fancy paragraph formatting (such as an indented first line, for example) that you had attached to the paragraph before you put the black dot there to begin with. If you need to reformat the paragraph, see "Pretty Paragraphs" in Chapter 7.

Bullets are a paragraph-format kind of thing. So you can get a new, prebulleted paragraph by pressing Enter within any bullet-formatted paragraph. This feature lets you type with bulleting *on* and spawn new, bulleted paragraphs as you go.

# *Heavy Ammo: The Format Bullets Dialog Box*

Bullets of any make and caliber are available from the Format Bullets dialog box, seen in Figure 8-1. The left side of the dialog box contains the Bullet style box, which lets you choose the little markers that you want to appear to the left of your paragraphs. The usual black dot is in the upper-left corner of the Bullet style box. If you want some other marker, just click its icon. Below the Bullet style box is the Bullet size box. You can choose the bullet size by either typing a number into the box or by clicking the up-/down-arrows next to the box. You can choose any size from 4 points (defined to be the exact size of a dust speck at sea level) to 127 points (which takes up about a third of the width of an ordinary page). Please use this awesome power responsibly.

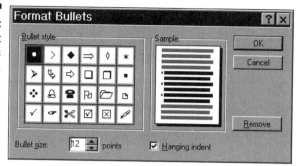

**Figure 8-1:**
The Format
Bullets
dialog box,
where
Works
stores its
heavy
ammunition.

Your paragraph has a hanging indentation if a check mark is in the Hanging indent check box. (See "Indenting Left and Right Edges" in Chapter 7.) If the Hanging indent check box is checked, then all the lines of text begin where the text of the first line begins. If this check box is not checked, all the lines after the first one line up under the bullet.

You can disarm your paragraph by clicking the Remove button in the Format Bullets dialog box. The box closes and the bullet disappears.

When you decide that you have the bullet that you want, click the OK button. The box disappears, allowing you to see your newly bulleted paragraph. Otherwise, you can click the Cancel button, which closes the box and returns you to where you were before you opened the box.

# Headers, Footers, and Page Numbers

You probably don't need to be told what page numbers are. *Headers and footers* are chunks of text that appear on every page of a document in a special location at the top (for headers) or at the bottom (for footers). Headers and footers are typically used for chapter or section titles or to remind everyone who the author is. You probably don't think of page numbers this way, but they are just a special kind of footer (or sometimes header).

## Inserting headers and footers

Usually the text of a header or footer is the same on every page. But there are a couple of exceptions. One is for page numbers. (For every page to have the same number would be kind of useless.) Another exception is for the first page of a document. You can, if you like, have a header or footer on every page *except* the first one.

To put a header or footer into your document, just follow these instructions:

1. **Click View⇨ Header (or Footer). (Or if you are in Page Layout view, you can just move the insertion point to the header or footer box by clicking it.)**

   This step does a couple of things. First, it puts your document into Page Layout view. Second, it moves the insertion point to the header (or footer) box on the current page.

2. **Type the text that you want to appear on each page.**

   Anything that you can put in ordinary text, you can put in a header or footer. Bold, italic, giant fonts, alignments, Easy Formats — anything goes. You can have multiple paragraphs, even. Heck, you could fill the whole page with headers and footers and leave only a line or two for text. (What an easy way to write a ten-page term paper!)

3. **If you want page numbers, the date or time, or the document name to appear in your header or footer, move the insertion point to the place you want your choice to appear, click Insert on the menu bar, and make a selection from the drop-down menu.**

   If you then click `Page Number` or `Document Name`, a special code appears in the header or footer box. (These special codes look like *page* and *filename*. But oddly enough, just typing *page* or *filename* from the keyboard won't do the trick.)

   If you want your first page to be some number other than one, you need to use the Page Setup dialog box. Move to Step 4.

   Clicking `Date and Time` takes you to a list of many, many possible date and/or time formats. Click the format you like, and it gets inserted into the header or footer. The outcome may look like something you could easily have typed yourself, such as "4:15 Wednesday." But every time you print or print preview your document, the date and time are updated.

4. **If you want to prevent header or footer text from appearing on the first page, click File⇨ Page Setup.**

   The Page Setup dialog box appears. (You can see it in Figure 7-6 in Chapter 7.) The Page Setup dialog box has three cards on it. Click the tab that says `Other Options`. This action exposes the `Other Options` card. On this card's left side are three check boxes: `No header on first page`, `No footer on first page`, and `Print footnotes at end`. Click the one(s) that you want.

   The `Other Options` card of the Page Setup dialog box also allows you to select whatever number you want to appear on your first page. (All right, all right, the number has to be an integer. You can't choose a number like $\pi$. Geez.) Type a number into the `Starting page number` box at the top of the card, or click the up-/down-arrows.

   When you are done with the Page Setup dialog box, click `OK`.

## Single-line headers and footers (with page numbers)

The header and footer boxes come equipped with their own special tab stops: a center tab in the center and a right tab on the right margin. These tabs make life easy if you just want a one-line header (or footer) that has something on the left, something in the center, and something on the right. So the following is what you can do if you want a header that has, say, the document name on the left, a page number in the center, and the date on the right:

1. **Click View ⇨ Header.**

   Or click Footer if you want to do a footer. Everything else is exactly the same.

2. **Click Insert⇨Document Name.**

   This step inserts the code *filename* into the left side of the header box.

3. **Press the Tab key.**

   The insertion point should now be in the center of the line.

4. **Click Insert ⇨ Page Number.**

   This action puts the code *page* into the center of the line. If you want, you can get fancy and type the word "Page" right before the code. This means that the fourth page says "Page 4", rather than just "4". (If you do this optional step, remember to leave a space before the code. Otherwise you get "Page4".)

5. **Press the Tab key.**

   Now the insertion point should be on the right edge of the line.

6. **Click Insert⇨Date and Time.**

   This action opens up a list of date and time formats. Click one.

High-quality books (like this one) have different headers on the left and right pages. Don't even try to do that in Works; you're likely to sprain your head (or foot). If Microsoft had put every possible feature into Works, how would they sell their higher-priced word processor?

## Header and footer margins

Anybody who has ever slept in a short bed is sensitive to having suitable margins for their headers and footers. To change your header or footer margin, choose File⇨Page Setup to get the Page Setup dialog box. Click the tab marked Margins and type in a new margin value for your header or footer.

Headers are supposed to appear within the top and bottom page margins. So in the Page Setup dialog box, you must make sure that the header margin is less than the top page margin and that the footer margin is less than the bottom page margin. Otherwise, you're back to the short-bed situation, and nobody's happy — least of all, Works. (What actually happens is that Works simply ignores you and resets the margins while you're not looking.)

# Footnote Fundamentals

When I get old (which should be by next Friday, at the very latest), I won't bore younger people with tales of how I trudged miles to school in the deep snow. Oh, no, I plan to bore younger people by telling them how we used to do footnotes before there were word processors. But if you want to be bored, you don't need me; you can just read the manual. (Besides, how can I tell whether you're younger than I am?)

Here's how to do automatically numbered footnotes:

1. **Put the insertion point just after the text you want to footnote.**

2. **Click Insert ⇨ Footnote.**

   The footnote footman (in the form of an Insert Footnote dialog box) comes to your aid.

3. **Click the Insert button in the Insert Footnote dialog box.**

   The Works footman switches you to Page Layout view (if you weren't there already) and transports you to a mysterious region: the footnote area at the bottom of your current page. The insertion point is waiting, right after an automatic reference number that Works provides.

4. **Type in your footnote text, beginning with a space (for appearances).**

5. **Press the PgUp key or scroll up to get back to where you were typing.**

If you don't like numbers and would rather use asterisks or something else, all you need to do is to change Step 3. Click the Special Mark check box in the Insert Footnote dialog box. Then type the mark that you want (usually * or **) in the Mark box and click the Insert button.

To delete any footnote, just delete its reference mark in the text. The mark *and* the footnote go away, and the remaining footnotes are renumbered.

If you find yourself doing really heavy-duty footnotes, as you would if you were writing a scholarly thesis of some sort, there are a few TaskWizards you should check out. (You find TaskWizards by clicking the Task Launcher button on the toolbar.) Works provides you with a School reports/thesis wizard and a Bibliography wizard.

# Doing It by the Numbers: Tables, Spreadsheets, and Charts

When you want your word processor document to display a bunch of numbers in an attractive, comprehensible way (or at least in as attractive and comprehensible a way as numbers allow), Works calls in its numbers specialist, the spreadsheet tool. It does this fairly unobtrusively; but if you aren't expecting to see the spreadsheet tool in a word-processor document, the table and chart capability can appear a little intimidating.

To take full advantage of all the cool features Works provides for tables and charts, you need to know how to use the spreadsheet and charting tools. Check out Part III and Part VI, respectively, for more on these tools. On the other hand, you may be saying, "Just let me get this table into my report, and I promise I'll never, ever go near a number again." In that case, pretend that you're a quick executive and read this quick executive summary, which skips a lot of useful but inessential details.

You've got some choice about how deeply you want to wade into this stuff. If you don't want to deal with the spreadsheet tool at all, just try doing your table typewriter style. Works has some cool tab stops that make this process easier than creating a table or chart on a typewriter.

If you just want some help lining up some numbers and formatting them so that they look pretty, then you should use the Insert Table dialog box.

But what if you need to do something more complicated? What if, say, your numbers have some mathematical relationship to each other, and you may want to update the whole lot of them when the new sales figures come in. Or what if you want to use them to create graphs and charts? Then you need the Insert Spreadsheet dialog box.

Finally, you may already have a spreadsheet, either because you made it yourself or because the folks in Accounting handed you one on a disk. You can insert this ready-made spreadsheet the way it is, or you can create cool charts from it and insert them.

## Typing a table without a license

If you want only a very simple table, with no gridlines and no easy way to chart its numbers, then Works doesn't need to know what you're up to. You can make an "unofficial" table as you would on a typewriter. Each line of the table is just a funny-looking paragraph, as far as Works is concerned. You can see an example of such a table in Figure 7-5 in Chapter 7.

To create an "unofficial" table, start with a new paragraph; you can use it for the first row, including your column headings. Format your paragraph with tab stops for columns. Use left or center tab stops for this header text. (See "New-fangled Tab Stops" in Chapter 7.) Type the column headers in this paragraph, separating them by pressing the Tab key; you may want to use bold text for the column headers throughout. Make sure to keep your lines short enough so that Works doesn't wrap them onto the next line. (Remember that Works doesn't know what you're doing, so it can't help you.)

Press the End key to go to the end of this first line; then press the Enter key to make a new paragraph that has exactly the same tab stops as your first paragraph. Use this new paragraph for your first line of *data* in the table. If some columns have numbers, you may consider changing the tabs for those columns to decimal tabs.

Press the End key to go to the end of this second line; then press the Enter key to make a new paragraph that has exactly the same tab stops as paragraph that preceded it. (A pattern emerges, no?) This third paragraph is for your second line of data. Continue on like this until your table is done.

To dress up your table with horizontal lines, you can apply a bottom border to each of the row paragraphs (and maybe even a heavier border across the column-headings row). See "Lines, Borders, and Shade" later in this chapter.

## Creating a table the official way

A table in Works is a spreadsheet's younger brother — affable and good-looking, but not nearly so hard-working. When you make a table, you're actually using the spreadsheet tool, but Works does its best to hide the ugly details from you. Sounds lovely, but Work's habit of hiding details can lead to problems if you need to do a lot of updating or if you want to make a chart of the data later on.

Here's the shortcut rundown on making tables:

**1. Move the insertion point to the place in your document where you want a table.**

**2. Click the Insert Table button in the toolbar.**

The Insert Table button is the one over on the right that looks like a tiny, illegible calendar. (Or you can click Insert ⇨ Table.) The Insert Table dialog box appears on the scene. See Figure 8-2.

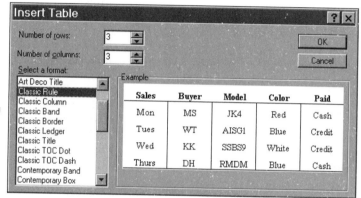

**Figure 8-2:**
The Insert
Table dialog
box.

**3. Size and format your table.**

Type the number of rows and columns into the two boxes at the upper left of the Insert Table dialog box. (Don't forget to add a row for your column heads and a column for your row heads.) The Example remains five-by-five — its function is to show off the formats, not the sizes.

On the left side of the dialog box is a list of possible formats. Each time you click a name, the Example box on the right changes to show you how that format looks. There are a gob of them, so you're bound to find one you like.

**4. Click OK.**

You now see a window that's cut up into rows and columns like a spread-sheet. This window is your table-to-be (see Figure 8-3). This table-to-be looks a little too big for the space, and it has some junk around the outside that you really don't want. But don't worry; the junk all goes away by the time that you're done.

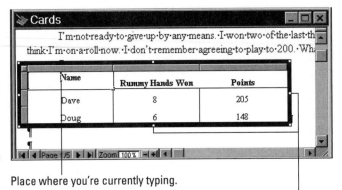

**Figure 8-3:**
High-tech
tables in
the word
processor.

Place where you're currently typing.

Handles to grab for expanding window.

**5. Type in the contents of your table.**

The square (*cell*) that you're currently typing in is the outlined one (the *active cell*). To move to another cell, either press any of the arrow keys on the keyboard or click another cell with your mouse.

The format that you chose in Step 3 takes care of all those nasty details like what gets centered and what font and style to use in any given cell. You can change these details with all the usual text editing commands, but if you've chosen a good format, you probably won't want to do much.

**6. Size the window that contains the table.**

You can grab the little handles on the sides of the window (see Figure 8-3) and push or pull on them to make the window larger or smaller. You keep the same number of rows and columns, but they get bigger or smaller to fit the space you decide upon.

**7. Click anywhere on your document outside of the table window.**

Wow! After a brief wait, all the spreadsheet-like stuff goes away, and you're left with a table!

To cut, paste, or copy the table, select it by clicking it; and then use the usual editing tools, such as Ctrl+X to cut or Ctrl+V to paste.

You can't edit the table just by selecting it and typing, though. To edit the table, you have to put it back into its spreadsheet form. Double-click anywhere on the table to do that.

When you're working on a table in the word processor, you are actually using the spreadsheet tool, so don't be surprised if the menus that drop down from the menu bar are a little different from the word-processor menus.

# Creating a spreadsheet

In the previous version of Works, spreadsheets and tables were the same things. They're still not all that different. Tables are designed to make getting the right display a little easier, and spreadsheets are designed to make manipulating the numbers a little easier. For more details, read about spreadsheets in Part III. Meanwhile, here's how you insert a spreadsheet into a word-processing document.

1. **Make a blank line for your spreadsheet.**

   Click the last line of the paragraph that you want the table or chart to appear *after*, press the End key to move the insertion point to the very end of that paragraph, and then press the Enter key.

2. **Click Insert⇨Spreadsheet.**

   The Insert Spreadsheet dialog box appears. The bottom part of the box allows you to specify a region from an already existing spreadsheet, which I describe later on. For now we're interested in the first option: Create a new spreadsheet. If this option isn't already the selected option, click it.

3. **Click OK.**

   Whoa! What's all this?! And why does it have its fat little edges splotted all over my text, you ask. "This-all" is a tiny window on a spreadsheet. This tiny window looks sort of like a table if you ignore all the letters and numbers around the outside edges. Naturally, the letters and numbers mean something, but if you're getting that deeply into creating a spreadsheet, you ought to read about spreadsheets in Part III.

4. **Expand the spreadsheet window to the size you need.**

   The spreadsheet window has little handles just like the table window shown in Figure 8-3. But with spreadsheets, the handles do something different. If you remember, the handles on the table window controlled just appearances: the table kept the same number of rows and columns. Reshaping the window just gave the table's rows and columns more or less space. The handles on the spreadsheet window, on the other hand, control content: the spreadsheet's cells stay the same size, but you get more or fewer of them. For more columns, click the tiny black handle in the center of the right edge and drag it to the right. For more rows, click the handle in the center of the bottom edge and drag it down.

5. **Type in the contents of your table.**

   The square that you're currently typing in (the *cell*) is the outlined one (just like the table in Figure 8-3). To move to another cell, either press any of the arrow keys on the keyboard or click another cell with your mouse. In this window, your mouse cursor is a big fat + symbol.

Numbers may change appearance when you change cells. Controlling the appearance of numbers is a bit tricky. The easiest way to pretty-up your table is to use the AutoFormat command in the Format menu; read about formatting spreadsheets in Chapter 11.

To make type boldface or change fonts or even right-justify text, just click a cell and then use any of the usual formatting methods, such as pressing Ctrl+B for bold or using the buttons on the toolbar.

If you already have a table and you want to turn it into a spreadsheet, you don't have to retype all the information. Just double-click the table, press Ctrl+A, and then click the Copy button on the toolbar. Now double-click your empty spreadsheet, select the upper-left cell, and click the Paste button on the toolbar. Works pastes all the table info into the spreadsheet.

6. **Click anywhere on your document outside of the table window.**

Check it out. All those letters and numbers around the outside go away, and you're left with something that looks an awful lot like a table, although maybe not quite so pretty. Your creation still has some funny edges with handles, but it looks better. The funny edges are visible because your spreadsheet has been *selected*. To make the edges go away, click once again anywhere on your document outside the spreadsheet.

To cut, paste, or copy the spreadsheet, select it by clicking it; and then use the usual editing tools, such as Ctrl+X to cut or Ctrl+V to paste. While the spreadsheet is selected, you can also use the handles to show more or fewer columns (as you did in Step 3). To edit the spreadsheet, first double-click it to put it into an editable mode.

## Inserting a spreadsheet from a file

If the spreadsheet already exists as a Works file, getting all or part of it into a word-processor document is easier than if you have to create the spreadsheet on the fly. (Creating anything on a fly is tough — they're just too small.) Basically, you just copy the cells from the spreadsheet document and paste them into the word-processor document. Here's the step-by-step on that:

1. **Open the spreadsheet file.**

   I'm assuming that your word-processor document was already open. To open the spreadsheet file, press Ctrl+O and look through your filing system for the file and then double-click its name or icon.

2. **Select the block of cells that you want to display in the word-processor document.**

   If you want to display all of the cells, press Ctrl+A. Otherwise select the cells you want to display with the mouse or navigation keys.

3. **Click the Copy button on the toolbar.**

4. **Switch back to the word-processor document.**

   Click Window from the menu bar and then click the name of the document where it appears in the drop-down menu.

5. **Move the insertion point to the place where you want to display the block from the spreadsheet.**

6. **Click the Paste button on the toolbar.**

## Creating charts

To do charts in Works, you have to start with a spreadsheet. (If you don't have one, go back to "Creating a spreadsheet" earlier in this chapter. Creating a basic bar or pie chart from data in a spreadsheet is pretty easy. For anything more than that, though, you really need to read about charting in Chapter 19.

1. **Double-click your spreadsheet.**

2. **Highlight one row of numbers (or several adjoining rows of numbers) in your table.**

   Click the leftmost cell of the first row that you want to chart; hold down the mouse button and drag to the rightmost cell of the last row that you want to chart. Release the mouse button.

   If you include a first row or column of words, they are used as labels for the chart. If you want them to be used differently, though, or you don't like the way they look, go to Chapter 19 for further information.

3. **Click the tiny, squinty bar chart icon in the lower-left corner of the spreadsheet.**

   Wow! Up pops the rather large New Chart dialog box. A lot of stuff is in this New Chart dialog box, and you can read about it in Chapter 19 on charting. For a simple bar chart, though, you don't really need to be concerned with most of those options.

   Well, concern yourself with just the following option:

4. **If you want a pie chart, click the square that looks like a pie chart.**

5. **If the chart in the New Chart dialog box meets with your approval, click the OK button there.**

   If it doesn't look good, click the Cancel button in this dialog box. In your spreadsheet/table, check to see that you've highlighted at least one entire row of data, beginning with the first column (typically containing row headings), but no more columns to the right than are actually filled with data. Try again with Step 3.

You should end up with nice bars and a legend. (If not, I know of some nice bars with legends in Key West; drop me a line.)

Click in your document anywhere outside of the chart window to make your chart look closer to its final appearance. To change the size of the chart, click one of the handles (little black squares) around the periphery and drag it. (Drag the ones along the sides sideways and the ones along the top and bottom vertically.)

Click somewhere in the text of your document to deselect the chart and see the final effect.

To change the chart data, double-click the chart; then click the tiny icon that looks like an illegible calendar in the lower-left corner of the chart window. This move turns the chart back to a spreadsheet, which you can edit.

# Lines, Borders, and Shade

Nothing like a few good lines to liven up the party! Works has got 'em, in the form of *borders* around paragraphs. You want a horizontal line? A horizontal line is a *bottom* or *top* border on a paragraph. A vertical line? A vertical line is a *left* or *right* border alongside your paragraph. If you want to box in your paragraph or box in a set of paragraphs, you use an *outline* border. You can even draw a border around your whole page. Want to give your paragraph some shade? (It can get awfully hot down there by the border.) No problemo.

How far do these border lines go? Horizontal borders run from the left to the right indent of the paragraph (which, for normal paragraphs, is from the left to the right page margin). Vertical borders run the height of the paragraph for as many lines as are in the paragraph.

What about a line by itself? To get a stand-alone horizontal line, like the *rule* across a letterhead, use a blank line (single-line paragraph) with a top or bottom border. This step lets you set the line width independently of the width of your surrounding paragraphs. Unfortunately, there's really no such thing as a stand-alone vertical line, like you may want to have for a typing-style table (see "Typing a table without a license" earlier in this chapter). You can do tricks with columns, but those tricks must wait for another book.

Because these borders are actually a part of paragraph formatting, if you create a new paragraph by pressing the Enter key while working in a bordered paragraph, the new paragraph is bordered, too. (By *working*, I mean where you have your insertion point, but it sounds so nerdy to say so.)

# *Marking your borders*

Here's how you, too, can create borderline documents, just like the pros:

1. **For a horizontal line by itself, create a new paragraph.**

   Click the last line of your current paragraph, press the End key, and then press the Enter key. If the line is to be shorter than the space between the page margins, drag the left and right indent marks (the inward-pointing triangles) on the ruler to mark the length of the line you want to insert.

   or

   **For a border around a group of paragraphs, select them.**

   For this technique to work, the selected paragraphs should all have the same left and right indents. Drag the left and right indent marks (the inward-pointing triangles) on the ruler to change indents.

   or

   **For a border on a single paragraph, click anywhere within it.**

2. **Click Format⇨Borders and Shading.**

   The Border patrol arrives on the scene in its three-card, four-wheel-drive dialog box. Have your passport ready.

3. **Click the tab of the** Bor\_ders **card if it isn't already displayed.**

4. **Click as many borders as you want in the Border dialog box.**

   Click the check boxes of the Border area of the dialog box: \_Left, \_Right, \_Top, Bottom, or all the way around (\_Outline) — whatever. A check mark indicates which border is selected. The only choice that needs an explanation here is Outline \_with shadow, which not only outlines your paragraph but gives it the illusion of three dimensions by giving it a shadow on the page. (This effect is either "way cool" or "to gag on," depending on your taste.)

   If you select a bunch of paragraphs and want an outline around the bunch, click Outline. If you want each paragraph to have its own border, as in the rows of a table, select the sides individually; ignore the gray in some check boxes.

5. **Click the line style you want in the** L\_ine Sty\_le **area of the dialog box.**

   If you have a color printer, click the box labeled \_Color and choose a color from the list that drops down.

6. **Click the** OK **button in the dialog box.**

To remove a border, do Steps 1 – 3 to get the Borders card back. The check boxes on the lower right should describe the current borders of the paragraph. (Any border that is on should have a check mark in its check box.) Click the check mark in the check box of any border that you want to get rid of. Click OK in that dialog box when you're done.

## Shady paragraphs

If you have a really red-hot paragraph, you can draw the reader's attention to it by putting it in the shade. Here's how:

**Do the same thing that you did in the preceding section for borders.**

You should now be looking at the Borders and Shading dialog box.

1. **Click the tab of the** Shading **card if it isn't already displayed.**

2. **Click a shading pattern in the box on the left side of the card.**

3. **If you have a color printer (or just want to make the document look cool on the screen), click foreground and background colors.**

   Watch the sample box to make sure that you aren't creating something hideous. Hideosity happens — there's a little Dr. Frankenstein in all of us.

4. **Click the** OK **button in the dialog box.**

## Framing your pages

You can put a border around your entire page, just to spiff things up a little. Allowing you to border each page differently would be a little too anarchic even for Works, so it gives you two choices: You can put the same border on all the pages, or you can put a border on just the first page and leave the others unbordered. Here's how to do both:

**Do the same first two steps as you did to get paragraph borders.**

(See "Marking your borders" a page or two ago.) You should now see the Borders and Shading dialog box.

1. **Click the tab of the** Page **card if it isn't already displayed.**

2. **Click the line style you want in the** Line Style **area of the dialog box.**

   If you have a color printer, click the box labeled Color and choose a color from the list that drops down.

3. **Select a distance from the page edge.**

   You can type into the boxes on the lower-right part of the card or click the up-/down-arrows there. Horizontal and vertical distances are chosen separately.

   When you make these choices, remember where your margins are. (See "Margins" in Chapter 7.) Works does not stop you from doing something stupid here, like drawing a border line right through your text. (Is it stupid, or is it Art?)

**4. Look at the check boxes on the** Page **card.**

Two check boxes are on the Page card. One puts the border only on the first page and leaves the other pages alone. The other puts a shadow around the right and lower edges of the border, giving it that three-dimensional look. A check in the box means that the corresponding feature is on. Click the box again to turn it off if you want.

The Sample on the Page card grossly exaggerates the size of the shadow. It's actually a sedate little shadow, and it does not go anywhere near the edge of the page.

**5. Click the** OK **button in the dialog box.**

Page borders don't show up at all in Normal view, and they don't look all that realistic even in Page Layout view. You have to click the File menu and select Print Preview to get a good idea of what your page borders really look like.

# *Pictures and Other Graphics*

Pictures! You say that you want pictures in your document? That's like going to the Louvre and asking your tour guide to show you some art. Boy, have they got art.

Likewise, Works has got lots of ways to put pictures in documents. And you can either study the 80-bazillion types of graphics and ways to use them or stick to a couple of simple methods at first. I suggest the latter.

I suggest that you stick to two basic categories of graphics at first: the functional and the decorative. Functional art is what I call business blob art: mostly boxes and lines and labels that you create yourself. Decorative art is my term for clip art, which comes in various forms. Works comes with a bunch of *clip art*: sketches and drawings of people, furniture, whale uvulae, atl-atls, and other things of normal everyday life.

For information on using clip art, see Part VI.

To insert a piece of business blob art into your document, do the following:

**1. Click where you want the art to go.**

As in the Louvre, putting your works of art in their own spaces is usually best: in this case, a blank line (paragraph). Click the last line of your current paragraph, press the End key, and then press the Enter key to get a blank line. Now you're ready.

(You can put artwork elsewhere; but then you have to work on making the text come out right, which is tricky and must wait until I can put it into another book.)

2. **Click Insert ⇨ Drawing.**

   You are pthwapped into Microsoft Draw. Don't worry: your document is still around; it's just on the back burner while you doodle a picture.

3. **See Chapter 22 for information on creating your own artwork with Microsoft Draw and exiting from Microsoft Draw.**

   Stick a Post-it or the generic sticky-pad paper of your choice here so that you know where to come back to.

4. **When you are done, a drawing is in your document. Click anywhere on the document outside the drawing to see how the drawing looks in its final form.**

   You can change the size of the drawing: Click once on the drawing to select it. (A faint frame with tiny squares called handles appears around the edge.) Drag any of the handles along the sides horizontally to make the drawing wider or narrower; drag the handles along the top or bottom vertically to make the chart taller or shorter. Deselect the drawing by clicking somewhere else in your document.

To delete a picture in your document, click immediately to the left of it; your insertion point indicator becomes as tall as the picture. Press the Delete key.

To move a picture or chart to the right side of the page, right-align the paragraph that the picture or chart is in. Just click the picture or chart and then click the right-align button in the toolbar. For a center-aligned picture or chart, use the center-align button instead.

# The Envelope, Please!

May we have the envelope please? Lets see . . . the winner is . . . you! You win because printing envelopes is one of the dirty little jobs that Works makes easier than it used to be. In the dark ages of word processing (five or six years ago), printing an envelope was a job that took a squadron of software engineers, five phone calls to the printer and software vendors, four Tylenol, and, ultimately, a ball-point pen. (That's something else I can bore younger people with when I get old.)

## The Works envelope gnome

The Works word processor has an envelope tool that is really designed for doing bulk printing of envelopes. (I like to refer to the envelope tool as the envelope gnome — it works automagically like a wizard, but it's uglier.) If you really want to print a large number of envelopes using a database of addresses, see Appendix A. In this chapter, I'm just going to talk about printing a single, simple envelope. But here's how the gnome is supposed to work:

This tool or gnome lives in the Tools menu; and when you call it into existence, it gives you the dialog box with eight cards on it, as shown in Figure 8-4.

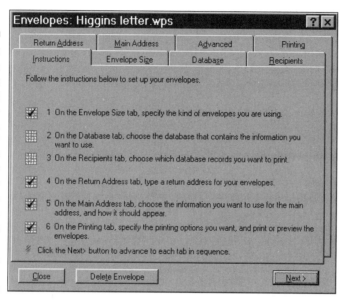

**Figure 8-4:**
The Envelope tool's Instructions card. Only four or fewer steps are really necessary for a single envelope (the ones shown with check marks here).

The top card (the Instructions card) is a checklist of things that have to be set up before Works can print envelopes for you — but some of the check boxes apply only if you are printing a large number of envelopes by using a database.

The Works envelope gnome is designed to take you through each item on this list. To do this, you can click the Next button on the lower right; the gnome moves you to the next item on the checklist, taking you to the next card. (Alternatively, you can click the button next to each step or on the card tabs.) The gnome steps you through the process, always returning to the Instructions card and showing you check marks for the steps that are done now.

When the gnome is done with the checklist, the gnome then creates a new and special page at the start of your document, all properly formatted. When you go to print your document, you can choose to print either the envelope (this special page) or the rest of the document. Works conveniently remembers the return address and fills it in for you automatically whenever you go to print an envelope after that. (You can change the return address if you like.)

# Creating and printing a single envelope

If you want to print only a single envelope, going through all eight cards of the Envelope gnome is confusing, boring, and unnecessary. Here's how to bypass all the unnecessary stuff and print a single envelope.

I'm going to assume that you've written a letter or some other document and that you have that document open in Works. If you're just, say, sending a clipping to a friend but want a nicely printed envelope, then start a new word-processor document.

   1. **Save your document: Press Ctrl+S.**

      If you're working with a letter or other existing document, completing this step is insurance in case you mess up something. (You can just close the messed-up document without saving it and then reopen the original document.)

   2. **If your document is a letter and already has the recipient's name and mailing address in it, select the name and address portion.**

      Otherwise, move on to Step 3.

   3. **Choose Tools⇨Envelopes.**

      If this is the first time that you have printed an envelope since you started Works, you may get one of Works' First-time Help dialog boxes. It offers to help you 1) take a tour of envelopes and labels, 2) create an envelope, or 3) print an envelope. I suggest that you take the tour once, for fun: click the Quick tour of envelopes and labels button and follow directions. When you return to the First-time Help dialog box, click Don't display this message in the future, and First-time Help never bothers you again. Then click the To create envelopes button.

      The envelope gnome pops up the Instructions card of the Envelopes dialog box.

   4. **Click the Envelope Size tab.**

      Choose a size from the list. If your envelope doesn't match any of the ones listed, click the Custom button and enter your envelope's dimensions.

   5. **Click the Main Address tab.**

      If, in Step 1, you initially highlighted the recipient's name and address in your letter, it appears in the Main Address text box when the Main Address card comes up. You can edit the recipient's address now if you like. If you didn't select an address, this text box is blank, and you can fill it in by clicking it and typing. Press the Enter key at the end of each line.

      Ignore all the field choosing and other junk on this card.

6. **Click the** Return Address **card.**

   If you have never printed an envelope before, the Return address text box is empty. Type in your name and address. If you have printed an envelope before, the return address is the same as last time you printed an envelope; edit the return address if you need to.

7. **To preview or print your envelope, click the** Printing **card.**

   Click the Preview button to see your envelope in Print Preview.

   Click the Print button to actually physically commit ink to paper. After a minute or so, your printer is ready to print. Your printer may wait for you to put an envelope in it manually, unless it has a stack of envelopes already in an envelope feed. Every printer handles envelopes differently; insert the blank envelope the way the printer manual tells you. You may also have to press a button to tell the printer that you have inserted an envelope; on most common printers, you won't have to.

8. **Click the** Close **button.**

   Ptooey! The envelope gnome spits out a properly formatted envelope page, leaving it sticking to the top of your document. A special envelope/page break (the dotted line) separates the envelope page from your document. (Thank goodness: gnome spit being what it is.)

The envelope page that you just created is now attached to the document. You can edit the envelope page or format it just like any other page of your document. You can also call on the envelope gnome again to edit the text, if you prefer.

If at any time you decide you won't need the envelope again, you can delete it. Choose Tools⇨Envelopes from the menu bar; then click the Delete envelope button at the bottom of the Envelopes dialog box. Works asks you if deleting the envelope is okay; click the Yes button.

After you have attached an envelope to a document, you have a choice of what to print whenever you print your document: the envelope or the rest of the document. Here's how to print an attached envelope.

1. **Choose File⇨Print (or press Ctrl+P).**

   A Print dialog box scurries out of the woodwork. Make sure that your printer is turned on.

2. **Click** Envelope **in the** What to print **area of the Print dialog box; then click the** OK **button.**

   (As a convenience, if you have been working on the envelope and your insertion point is still on the envelope page, Works has already selected Envelope. If you left your insertion point in the main document, Works has selected Main Document.)

3. **Click the** OK **button of the Print dialog box.**

If all has worked well, you soon have a nicely printed envelope. If not, well, there's always the ball-point pen. Here are a few things that go wrong and information on how to fix 'em:

- ✔ **Nothing appears to happen when you print:** Your printer may be waiting for you to manually feed an envelope into it. If no way is available to manually feed an envelope into it, follow these steps: Click the envelope page. Choose File⇨Page Setup from the menu bar. Click the S̲ource, Size & Orientation card; and (in the Paper dialog box) in the drop-down menu for Sou̲rce, choose Default Tray. Try printing again.

- ✔ **The envelope jams:** After you carefully extract the smushed envelope, try printing again with a new envelope; this time, sharpen the crease of the edges of the envelope by running a hard object across them (or use your thumbnail and middle finger). If this fails, try adjusting the paper thickness control of the printer or using a thinner weight of envelope.

- ✔ **Stuff is printed in *very* wrong places:** In the previous instructions for "Creating and printing a single envelope," Step 4 is to choose the envelope size. Probably the real envelope is not the size you specified. Or you may not be putting your envelopes into the printer properly. Some printers have a special manual-feed guide that you should use. Finally, check to make sure that Windows 95 is set up for exactly the model of printer that you are using (see Chapter 4).

- ✔ **Stuff is printed in *somewhat* wrong places:** See the possible reasons given in the preceding paragraph. Another possible remedy is to click the envelope page; then adjust margins by choosing File⇨Page Setup.

# Part III
## Setting Sail with Spreadsheets

The 5th Wave    By Rich Tennant

I DON'T KNOW - MY SPREADSHEET TELLS ME WE SHOULD BASE OUR OVERHEAD BUDGET ON SALES FIGURES RATHER THAN FIXED, MY PLOT CHART INDICATES WE SHOULD ESCALATE OUR MARKETING THRUST, AND MY PSYCHOANALYSIS PROGRAM TELLS ME I DEPEND TOO MUCH ON OUTSIDE INPUT AND SHOULD TRUST MY INSTINCTS MORE.

## In this part . . .

*E*ver since the invention of the spreadsheet, PC users have been able to circumnavigate the world of calculations with ever-increasing ease. If you've been left standing at the dock, looking wistfully out to sea, Part III is your ticket to adventure on the high seas.

Here are the fundamentals of entering data and doing calculations with Works' spreadsheet tool, with tips for making the job faster and easier. Whether you're planning your finances or just making lists, Works' spreadsheet tool can save you a lot of tedious hours on the calculator.

> "Heigh, my hearts; cheerly, cheerly, my hearts; yare, yare: take in the top-sail; 'Tend to the master's whistle. — Blow till thou burst thy wind, if room enough!"
>
> *The Tempest,* Wm. Shakespeare

# Chapter 9

# Spreading Your First Sheets

. . . . . . . . . . . . . . . . . . . . . . . . . . . . . . . . . . . . . . . . . .

## In This Chapter

▶ Understanding spreadsheets

▶ Using and abusing spreadsheets

▶ Getting under way

▶ Examining the spreadsheet window and toolbar

▶ Using cells and ranges

▶ Typing text

▶ Typing numbers

▶ Changing column widths

▶ Saving your work

. . . . . . . . . . . . . . . . . . . . . . . . . . . . . . . . . . . . . . . . . .

So, you're ready to set sail into the uncharted seas of calculation? Well, batten down the hatches, hoist the anchor, strop the strmf'r'sq's'l, and add a few other such nautical allusions. With the Works spreadsheet hoisted squarely to the wind (hold it open to this page, which is about as windy as they get), you can reach exotic lands where budgets, business plans, alphabetized lists, expense analyses, profit-and-loss statements, surveys, scientific experiments, and sales forecasts live.

Once you get the general idea of spreadsheets, you'll discover all kinds of exciting things to do with them — most of them legal, moral, and non-fattening (but still rather nice). But before you set out on any transatlantic odysseys here, take a look at what's what on the spreadsheet — a little day-cruise, so to speak, staying close to shore. In this chapter, I discuss what to do with a spreadsheet, what's what in the spreadsheet window, how to navigate around in spreadsheets, and how to enter text, numbers, and calculations.

# If You've Never Used a Spreadsheet Before

If you've never used a spreadsheet before, try to think of it as a table of numbers and calculations where all the calculations are done for you, or as a calculator that shows you all the numbers you're adding up or multiplying. Or you may think of it as gnomes sitting on a chess board with calculators, where the pawns are numbers and the rooks add up rows and columns, and the queen is actually a copy machine, and, um, well . . . Hmmm. This isn't helping, is it?

Truth to tell, you can't fully appreciate a spreadsheet until you've used one. It's sort of like an electric toothbrush that way, but even more fun (if that can be imagined). The best idea to start with is to imagine something that automatically adds up rows and columns of numbers in a table.

## So what's the big deal?

The first big deal with spreadsheets is that they make doing most calculations a great deal easier than doing them on a calculator — especially long or complex calculations, such as mortgages, retirement plans, or statistics. One reason why calculations are easier is that, because spreadsheets are tables, you can see and change all the numbers at any time. Few calculators let you see all the numbers you've entered (unless you have a printing or other fancy sort of calculator).

Even fewer calculators let you back up and change a number and then recalculate. This ability to change a number in a spreadsheet, and then immediately see the result, lets you do "what-if" analyses. For example, what if inflation goes to 8 percent; when can I afford to retire? Or, what if I switch to no-tillage corn farming; do the labor savings offset the higher pesticide use? What if I sell this computer? Can I then afford to pay someone else to do all this stuff?

Like calculators, spreadsheets can do all kinds of fancy calculations on the numbers they contain: sums, averages, net present value, sines, cosines — all kinds of stuff. They can even do calculations based on the results of other calculations, or calculations based on time — 30-day running-average annualized yield from an investment, for example.

The second big deal with spreadsheets is that they let you visually organize your data into rows and columns; try to find a calculator that does that. You can even have several different tables of rows and columns. The Works spreadsheet lets you dress up your tables with borders, colors, lines, and text formatting so that you can easily see what's going on.

Because spreadsheets are laid out on a grid, you can use them to create business forms of various kinds. You can even fill in those forms right within Works, do calculations on the data you've filled in, and print out the results.

The third big deal with spreadsheets is that they can be used for simple lists and collections of data — the number of students in your class and their grades, inventories of equipment and their dollar values, and so on. Spreadsheets kind of overlap with databases in this sense, with spreadsheets being used for smaller collections of stuff or for projects involving large amounts of calculation.

The final big deal is that once you have data in a spreadsheet, you can turn that data into a chart in minutes. I look at this in more detail in Chapter 19.

## *What can you do with a spreadsheet?*

People use spreadsheets for all kinds of stuff. Examples include:

- ✔ doing budgets
- ✔ recording and plotting your daily weight and calorie count
- ✔ recording lists of people and how much they owe or have paid
- ✔ creating invoices, bills of sale, and other business forms
- ✔ recording, totaling, and forecasting sales
- ✔ tracking and computing expenses
- ✔ financial planning
- ✔ analyzing statistics
- ✔ recording experiments
- ✔ convincing your spouse that you're working when you're really playing Minesweeper

Nearly anything you can do with a calculator works better on a spreadsheet. Some of the things you can do in a Works spreadsheet are the following:

- ✔ add columns of numbers
- ✔ add rows of numbers
- ✔ compute the average, standard deviation, and other statistics on rows or columns of numbers
- ✔ compute depreciation, net present value, and other financial results
- ✔ find the minimum or maximum value in a set of values
- ✔ compute the number of days between two dates
- ✔ compute the number of dates that you've eaten in two days
- ✔ sort lists alphabetically or numerically
- ✔ find specific items in a list

In general, you should use spreadsheets for anything that involves creating tables, making charts, doing calculations, or keeping short lists of things.

## What shouldn't you do with a spreadsheet?

You should not plot to overthrow the world or cheat on your taxes. It reflects badly on the software industry. (Like you care, right?) But mostly, you should not do anything that can be done better with another Works tool. For example:

- ✔ If you are writing a report that includes spreadsheets, don't write the report using the spreadsheet tool. That's as bad as using the knife blade in your Swiss army knife for a screwdriver. Write the report in the word processor and copy the spreadsheets into the word-processing document.

- ✔ If you're making long lists of things — say, more than a couple hundred items or so — use the database tool of Works.

- ✔ If you're making a list of names and addresses to use for mailings, use the database tool.

## Starting Out

Enough woolgathering. Time to collect our crew, spread our spreadsheets to the wind, and set forth into the Sargasso sea of making calculations.

To review how to start Works and the different ways of starting a spreadsheet document, check out Chapter 1. That's also where you can find stuff about using the mouse, keyboard, commands, menus, and dialog boxes. Refer there whenever you need to. (The book won't tell anybody if you ask a dumb question.)

Otherwise, fire up Works, and you get the Works Task Launcher. (If you've already been using Works and aren't currently looking at that screen, press Alt+F and then N.) Press Alt+T (or click the Works Tools card tab) to bring up the Works Tools card. Then, click the Spreadsheet button.

This starts you on a nice, shiny, untrammeled, new spreadsheet document. You are now gazing at the spreadsheet window and its toolbar and other assorted paraphernalia.

But wait! Maybe you don't want a nice, shiny, untrammeled, new spreadsheet document. Maybe you want a predesigned, pre-trammeled spreadsheet, such as an invoice spreadsheet or a spreadsheet for recording your students' grades. Well, okay. You can get those by starting up with a template. (See Chapter 1 for more on starting with a template.) But until you know a bit more about spreadsheets, you may find these templates a bit tricky to use. The folks who designed them did a lot of fancy formatting, locking certain areas so you don't accidentally change them, and other tricks that I explain later.

## What's what in the spreadsheet window

Figure 9-1 shows you what's what in your spreadsheet window. (Spreadsheet window is my name for how the Microsoft Works window looks when you're using the spreadsheet tool.) Works has given the spreadsheet document shown the forlorn name of `Unsaved Spreadsheet 1`— one of the nerdy sort of startup names Works gives new documents that haven't yet been saved as a file. Near the top of the Works window is the usual Works menu bar with all the commands, and underneath that is the spreadsheet toolbar with all its buttons and icons.

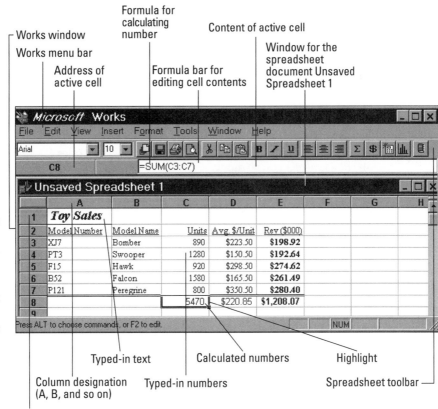

**Figure 9-1:**
Your
window into
the
spreadsheet
world.

Don't try to memorize all this stuff unless it's 3 a.m. and you really, really need to get back to sleep. Stick a pencil or small inanimate object of your choice here and come back whenever you need to refresh your memory.

## *The spreadsheet menu*

As in fine restaurants and programs everywhere, one way you give commands to the Works spreadsheet tool is by using a menu. You click on the item you want.

Using Works, however, is like dining at a franchised fast-food joint: the menu looks pretty much the same for whatever joint — or tool — you're in. So the menu bar (the line with File and all the other command words on it) for the spreadsheet tool looks exactly as it does for the word-processor tool. Of course, there are some interesting differences when you go to use the menu bar. The little menus that drop down when you click on these command words are somewhat different.

Many of the basic commands are the same, however, especially the ones in the menus that drop down when you click on File or Edit. The File and Edit menus include commands for starting a new document, opening an existing document file, closing a document, saving a document to a file, and making basic edits. Even the Find command is practically the same as in the word processor. Most of these commands are discussed in detail in Part I. Basic printing is discussed in Chapter 4 (which is cleverly named "Basic Printing").

I get into the other basic commands — the important ones for spreadsheets — one at a time, as you go along.

## *The spreadsheet toolbar*

The other popular way to give commands to Works (other than traditional shouting methods) is with the toolbar: the thing with all the picture-laden buttons under the menu bar as shown in Figure 9-2. The toolbar is just a faster way than the menu bar to do some of the same things. You click on a button and stuff happens.

That's toolbar, not crowbar. No matter how much you are tempted, do not use a crowbar to give commands to Works.

Most of the spreadsheet toolbar is similar to the toolbar in other Works tools. All buttons but four (the AutoSum, Currency, Easy Calc, and New Chart buttons), for example, are the same as the ones in the word processor. (For more on Works' toolbars, see Chapter 2.)

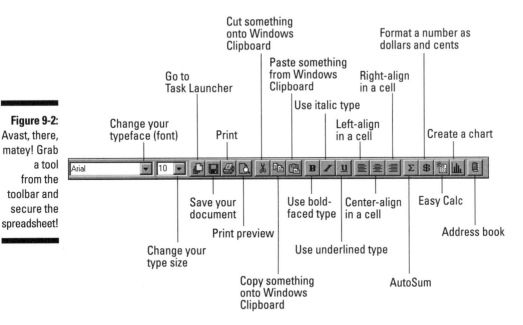

**Figure 9-2:** Avast, there, matey! Grab a tool from the toolbar and secure the spreadsheet!

I don't go into detail about these buttons here, but I bring them up as we go along. Here's where to go to read about the buttons that are particularly interesting for spreadsheets:

- **Left, Center, and Right Align:** See "Changing Alignment in a Cell" in Chapter 11.

- **Format a number as dollars and cents:** See "Formatting numbers" in Chapter 11.

- **AutoSum:** See "Creating Formulas the Point-and-Shoot Way" in Chapter 10.

- **Create a chart:** See Chapter 19.

## The spreadsheet document

The spreadsheet document (the window with the title bar Unsaved Spread-sheet 1 in Figure 9-1) looks like a big table. That's because it is one. Each row in this table has a number, given at the far left, in tasteful battleship gray. Each column has a letter, at the top, also in gray.

You can change the width of a column to accommodate the widest entry in that column. The height of a row changes to accommodate whatever the tallest thing is in that row. If you use large type, the row height increases.

As is often the case with Windows programs, you only look at a small piece of the document at a time. (This is good. Otherwise, how could you read the type in a long document?) To see more, scroll the document up or down, left or right, using the gray scroll bars along the right and bottom sides (see Chapter 1 for information on scrolling).

A spreadsheet has no pages; it's one vast table. The size of your spreadsheet — in theory only — can be more than 16,000 rows by more than 250 columns. In reality, you'll run out of memory long before you can make a spreadsheet that big. So will your PC.

# Working in Cells

No, no, not *those* kinds of cells. A lot of people use spreadsheets in those little office cubicles, which can feel very imprisoning — but that's not what this section is about.

A *cell* is one of those little boxes on the spreadsheet. It's the intersection of a row and a column. Everything you type goes in a cell. Sometimes, if you type text that exceeds the column width, the text will run over into empty neighboring cells. Works tolerates such overcrowding of cells.

Each cell has an address so that you can talk to Works about it in your calculations and other activities. "Hey, Works! Multiply the number at this address by 18," to paraphrase. The address is made up of the column letter and row number, smushed together like this: B12, which would be the cell at column B and row 12.

You don't have to use capitals. Lowercase letters work just fine. (Lowercase numbers would probably work, too, but I haven't seen any lying around.)

## The three kinds of cell-dwellers

There are three kinds of things that live in a cell, and Works treats each of them differently. All three kinds coexist in the example in Figure 9-3 (which is still a few pages away), but they each stay in their own cells and never mix. They are:

- ✔ text (in the figure, the model names are text)
- ✔ a typed-in number (the revenues)
- ✔ a number that results from a calculation (the totals in the last row)

The most frequent and most frustrating spreadsheet mistakes occur when the spreadsheet's creator thinks that a cell contains one kind of object, and Works thinks that it contains another kind of object. When you work with a cell, you always have to keep in mind what kind of cell it is.

## *Moving from cell to cell*

When you've been in your cell too long, it's time to move — to another cell, that is. The easiest way to do that is to move your mouse so that the mouse cursor (a big, fat plus sign: +) hovers over the new cell (where the grass is undoubtedly greener), and then click. The newly clicked-upon cell is then surrounded by a rectangular halo that Microsoft calls the *highlight*. (In computer heaven, the halos are rectangular.) This highlight indicates which cell you're about to type in, edit, or otherwise muck around with. Microsoft calls this the *active cell*. In reality, the active cell just sits there waiting for you to do something to it, which doesn't sound all that active to me. But "passive cell" just doesn't have the same zing, I guess.

Of course, you can't click what you can't see. To cruise around your spreadsheet, use the scroll bars on the right side and bottom of the document window. As you navigate around the spreadsheet with your highlight, notice that the address of the cell you've currently selected appears near the upper-left of the Works window, under the font window of the toolbar.

You can also navigate with (surprise, surprise) the navigation keys on your keyboard. Those are the arrow keys, the PgUp and PgDn keys, and the Home and End keys. And, as a special added bonus in the spreadsheet tool, you can also use the Tab key. These keys move the highlight (and your viewpoint with it) according to the listing in Table 9-1.

| Table 9-1 | Navigating Spreadsheets with Keys |
| --- | --- |
| *Navigation Key* | *Where It Moves the Highlight* |
| Left-arrow/right-arrow | One column's worth left or right |
| Up-arrow/down-arrow | One row's worth up or down |
| Tab | One cell to the right |
| Shift+Tab | One cell to the left |
| PgUp/PgDn | One window's worth up or down |
| Ctrl+PgUp/PgDn | One window's worth left or right, respectively |

*(continued)*

**Table 9-1** *(continued)*

| Navigation Key | Where It Moves the Highlight |
|---|---|
| Home | To column A of the row you're currently in |
| End | To the last column you used, in the row you're currently in |
| Ctrl+Home | To cell A1 |
| Ctrl+End | To the last row and column you used |

If you know the cell address you want to go to and it's nowhere nearby, here's a faster way to get there: press the F5 key. An itsy-bitsy Go To dialog box appears. Type the cell address — **Q200**, for example — and click the OK button.

## *Typing stuff in cells*

How do the cell-dwellers get into their cells? You put them there, of course, either by typing or by copying and pasting. The first cells, naturally, have to get there by typing, because there isn't anything to copy yet. So I'll start there. This chapter explains typing text and numbers into a cell. Chapter 10 will cover calculations.

Typing something into a cell involves the following simple procedure:

1. **Click on a cell.**

   Or move your highlight to it with the arrow or other navigation keys.

2. **Type.**

   Use the Backspace key to delete any mistakes.

3. **Once you have the text, number, or formula the way you want it, press the Enter key or move to another cell with a mouse click or a navigation key.**

If, while typing, you get a change of heart and decide not to type anything at all into the cell, press the Esc key or click on the X that currently appears next to the formula bar.

If your text doesn't fit, or worse, if your number turns into a bunch of ######, your column is too skinny. See "Changing column widths," later in this chapter.

That's it. You don't have to do anything more complex than that. If you want to change what's in a cell, the brute-force-simple way to do it is to just type something new into that cell. To be a little more elegant or to save typing, you can also edit as you type. Read on.

### Typing text

To simply enter some text, such as a column heading or title — something that's not going to be used in a calculation — just click on the cell and type the text. You should be careful of two things:

If you're typing all numerals (a zip code, for example)

— or —

If you're typing something that begins with the symbol =, +, -, or "

Type a quote (") character before you type anything else. This tells Works that it should treat this cell's contents as text, not as numbers or math signs. (Beginning a text cell with a quotation mark never hurts. Works just very quietly says, "Thanks for reminding me that this is text," and doesn't consider the quotation mark to be part of the text.)

After you've typed your text and pressed the Enter key, you may notice that, up in the formula bar, Works sticks a quote character in front of what you typed. The quote mark doesn't appear in the cell, just in the bar. This character is Works' subtle way of saying that it interprets the contents of this cell as text, not as a number or calculation.

There's a little tricky point to remember if you want your text entry to begin with a quotation mark ("). Say, for example, that in Figure 9-3 (a few pages ahead) the company wanted to put the model names in quotes, such as "Bomber" in cell B3. If you just typed in "Bomber," Works would interpret that first quote as its interpret-this-as-text mark, and what would appear in the cell (after you pressed the Enter key) would be Bomber". Strange as it sounds, you need to start with two quotation marks, not one. (Type: **""Bomber".**) This tells Works, "Yes, I really wanted to start this cell with a quotation mark."

### Typing numbers

Entering numbers into a cell is as simple as entering text into a cell. Just click on a cell and type the numbers in. Here are a few options you have for entering numbers.

✔ You can precede a number with a minus sign (-) if it's negative, or you can use a dollar sign ($) if it's money, or — do like I do in my check register — use a (-$) to represent negative money. (Works displays negative dollar amounts in parentheses: negative five dollars is displayed in a cell as ($5). Typing it in that way works, too.) Use as many decimal places as you need, but Works displays the numbers rounded off to two decimal places if you use the dollar sign or parentheses.

✔ You can put commas at the thousands point, but Works throws them out (unless you tell it differently — see Chapter 11).

✔ For percentages, follow the number with %. Remember that 100% is the same as 1.00.

✔ If you're a scientific type, you can use scientific notation: 1,253,000,000 can be typed `1.253e9`, or `1.253E+09`, for example. In fact, if you type in a big number, Works will automatically show it in this format. (You can tell it differently later.)

Don't follow a number with units, as in *36 fathoms.* If you do, Works thinks the entire entry is supposed to be text, not a number, and won't be able to do calculations with it. If you want to use units, you have to type them in as text in another cell. It's best to use the same units throughout your data because Works doesn't even think about units.

When you finish typing the number and press the Enter key (or move the highlight), notice that the number is smushed against the right side of the cell (or right-aligned, in dweeb-speak). If you've previously typed any text, notice that the text is smushed against the left side of the cell. This is how Works aligns numbers and text unless you tell it differently. I'll get into "telling it differently" in "Changing Alignment in a Cell" in Chapter 11.

## *Editing things in cells*

Those of you with good wide-angle vision will have noticed something a bit odd on the horizon as you typed things into cells. Specifically, you will have noticed that you're typing in two places at once: the cell you've selected and the formula bar (under the toolbar of the Works window).

The formula bar shown back in Figure 9-1 is actually more of an editing bar: it's a place where you can easily fool around with what you're typing until you get it right. (They serve cheap red wine and cheese doodles at the editing bar. Editors are a thrifty bunch.)

Here's how to use the formula bar to edit the contents of a cell:

1. **Click the cell.**

   This should give the cell it's little halo and move the contents of the cell up to the formula bar.

2. **Press the F2 key or click in the formula bar.**

   A vertical line — an insertion point like the one in the Works word processor — shows up to help you in your editing task.

3. **Move the insertion point to the place you want to edit.**

   To do this, move your mouse pointer over the formula bar; the mouse pointer changes to an I-beam shape. Position that I-beam where you want to type or delete something, and then click. The insertion point jumps there.

4. **Use the Backspace or Delete keys to get rid of the old stuff you don't want.**

5. **Type in the new stuff you do want.**

If you prefer, you can use the arrow keys instead of the mouse to position the insertion point in the formula bar.

You can also select characters within the formula bar by clicking and dragging the I-beam. If you then type something, those characters will be replaced; if you press the Delete key, they'll be deleted.

Two interesting buttons are located next to the formula bar, one with an X and the other with a check mark. Here's how to use them:

✓ **Click the X to cancel your edit and return the cell to its original condition.**

   This works just like pressing the Esc key.

✓ **Click the check mark to enter the contents of the formula bar into the cell.**

   This works just like pressing the Enter key. If you're entering a formula, Works also checks for errors.

You really can't use very many of the commands in the menu or the buttons on the toolbar while you're using the formula bar. Press Enter or Esc to exit from the formula bar if you need to use the menu or toolbar.

# Working with Lots of Cells

If you always had to work on cells one-by-one, large spreadsheets would never have caught on. One big advantage of spreadsheets over, say, ledgers, is that you can select a bunch of cells and work with them all at once, just as you can do things simultaneously to many paragraphs in the word processor.

## *Feeling at home on the range*

If you're more at home on the lone prairie than on the ocean, you'll be pleased to know that a spreadsheet has plenty of range land. A *range* in spreadsheet terms is any block (rectangular block, that is) of cells. (A cell block, as they say at Sing-Sing.) A range can be two adjacent cells, a column, a row, or even the entire spreadsheet.

Sometimes you need to do a calculation with a range of cells: sum them up, average them, or round them off, to name just a few examples. (Sorry, cowboy, you can't round 'em up!) When you want to refer to a range, you describe it by combining the addresses of the two endpoints, or opposite corners, with a colon (:) in between. It doesn't matter which cell comes first.

Here's how you refer to a few of the ranges in Figure 9-3.

| | |
|---|---|
| All the model names | B3:B7 or B7:B3 |
| Everything concerning the XJ7 | A3:E3 or E3:A3 |
| All the column sums | C8:E8 or E8:C8 |
| All cells representing amounts of money | D3:E8 or E8:D3 |

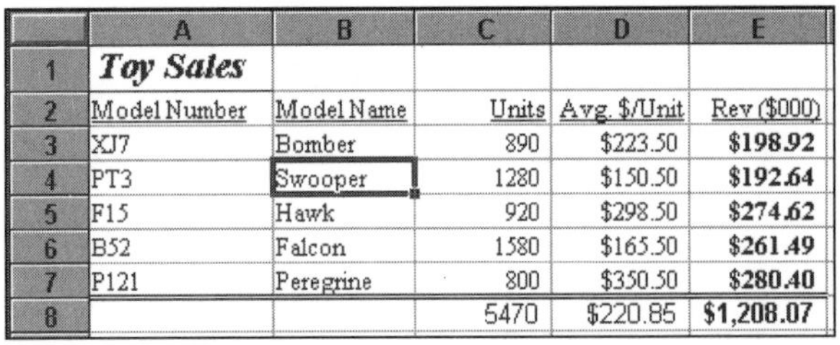

**Figure 9-3:**
Stake out some range land, cowpoke: just use the endpoints or opposite corners to define a range of cells.

| | A | B | C | D | E |
|---|---|---|---|---|---|
| 1 | *Toy Sales* | | | | |
| 2 | Model Number | Model Name | Units | Avg. $/Unit | Rev ($000) |
| 3 | XJ7 | Bomber | 890 | $223.50 | **$198.92** |
| 4 | PT3 | Swooper | 1280 | $150.50 | **$192.64** |
| 5 | F15 | Hawk | 920 | $298.50 | **$274.62** |
| 6 | B52 | Falcon | 1580 | $165.50 | **$261.49** |
| 7 | P121 | Peregrine | 800 | $350.50 | **$280.40** |
| 8 | | | 5470 | $220.85 | **$1,208.07** |

# Selecting your cells

Ask any ex-con: selecting your cells is important. And with spreadsheets, it's key to doing anything useful at all.

In order to do anything to the text, numbers, or formulas (I talk about them in the next chapter) that you enter into the spreadsheet — such as format them, move them, or copy them — you have to tell Works exactly which cells you're talking about. This is called *selecting* or *highlighting*. When you click on a cell, you are selecting that cell, and the cell becomes proud and happy.

Selecting a bunch of cells is pretty much the same as selecting bunches of stuff in all Works' tools, so see Chapter 3 for more details.

For spreadsheets, you have three methods of selecting multiple cells:

- ✔ Click and drag the mouse cursor across the cells you want to select. You can move across or up and down, highlighting any row, column, or rectangular area. Release the mouse button when done.

- ✔ Click, or move your highlight to one end or corner of the range of cells you want to select. Then press the Shift key together with an arrow key or another navigation key to expand the highlight. Release the keys when done.

- ✔ To select an entire row or column, click the column letter or row number (in the gray area of the spreadsheet). To select the entire spreadsheet, click the unmarked button where the row-number and column-letter areas intersect (the upper-left corner).

To select an entire column full of cells, click the top cell and then press Ctrl+Shift+down-arrow. To select an entire row of data, click on the leftmost cell and then press Ctrl+Shift+right-arrow. The selection stops at the first blank cell in the column or row. But if you start with a blank cell, it stops at the first cell with data.

When you select a range of cells, you may wonder why one cell, usually the one in the upper-left corner of the range, is not reversed out. It's not that this cell isn't selected — it is. This distinction tells you that the cell is your current active cell. If you should happen to enter anything in the formula bar while a range is selected (which you normally don't), what you enter goes in this cell.

I actually prefer the second method for spreadsheets because it's an easier way to expand the highlight to include exactly the cells you want. When you press an arrow key, you move precisely one row or column. With the mouse, I tend to slop around too much. Of course, if I were not riding on the Kancamagus Highway with my mouse pad on my knee, I might do better. (Hey, that could be a catchy little tune for the '90s, ". . . for I come from Kancamagus with my mouse pad on my knee. Oh, Susannah! . . .")

## Deleting blocks of cells

Deleting stuff from a block of cells is another of these highly complex tasks requiring years of training. It goes like this:

1. **Select the cell (or cells).**
2. **Press the Delete key.**

## Changing column widths and row heights

One of the big juggling acts with spreadsheets is getting the column widths just right. (While I'm at it, I'll cover row heights, because you adjust them more or less the same way.) There you are, traipsing along, making, say, a list of the students in your class: Smith, Jones, Yu, and then . . . Okiniewskiwitz! If there's nothing in the cell to the right of Ms. Okiniewskiwitz's name, the text just slops over into that cell. If there is something in the cell to the right, Ms. O's name will look like it's been chopped off. (The full name is still there in the cell — Works hasn't forgotten it or anything — it just looks truncated.)

You need a wider column. The simple way to change the width of a column (or the height of a row) is to do the following:

1. **Put your mouse cursor in the gray area that has the column letter (or row number) in it.**
2. **Slowly move the cursor toward the right-hand edge of the column (or the top edge of the row); the cursor changes to a double-headed arrow labeled** Adjust.
3. **Click and drag to the right, and the column gets wider. Drag to the left, and it gets smaller. (For rows, dragging up makes it taller and down, shorter.)**

TIP

---

### $!@($?)&$!!! What's all this ######### ?

If you're typing a number that's too wide for the column, you often get a distressing result. You get a bunch of ###### in the cell, which is a message from Works saying, "I can't print this here; make the column wider, willya?" Sometimes this situation occurs because the cell in question has the wrong number format — some formats are wider than others. If you use Works' default format for numbers, called General format, Works simply switches to nice, compact scientific notation when a number gets too large. You may or may not approve of this switch. For details on number formats, see "Formatting numbers" in Chapter 11.

The very precise way to change the width of a column or the height of a row is with the Format Column Width or Format Row Height dialog boxes:

1. **Click or otherwise highlight the column (or row).**

2. **Click F̲ormat⇨Column W̲idth (or Row H̲eight) in the menu that drops down.**

   The Format Column Width (or Format Row Height) dialog box springs into action.

3. **Type a new width number into the box marked C̲olumn width (or R̲ow height).**

   These numbers may not seem to have a lot of meaning, but the width number is roughly the number of digits that a number in the column can have if you're using 10-point type. The height number is the largest point-size of type that could live in the cell without scraping its head.

4. **Click the OK button.**

   ✔ One of the handiest ways to set column widths or row heights is to let Works automatically choose them based on what is in the cells. Use the dialog box approach just given, and then, in Step 3, click the check box marked B̲est Fit. The column or row is sized to fit the largest entry.

   ✔ To set a group of columns to the same width, click the leftmost column (at any row) and drag to the rightmost. This action selects those columns. Now set the column width using the dialog box approach just given. A similar trick works on rows.

# The Big Picture

Now that you know about cells, what goes in them, and a few tricks you can make them do, it's time to look back at the Big Picture. What the heck are you going to do with all this knowledge, anyway?

## Laying out your spreadsheet

A spreadsheet looks like a table with rows and columns. It usually will have a title in the upper left-hand corner, column headings across the top, row headings down the left side, and numbers and stuff in the middle, just like Figure 9-3 had. Fine. But when you create your own spreadsheet, what are those rows and columns going to represent? In Figure 9-3, the rows correspond to the individual toy models, allowing the company to show how sales vary from model to model and then to sum up to get total sales. The columns correspond to things someone may want to know about those toy models.

But that wasn't the only way that spreadsheet could have been laid out. It could have been arranged the other way, with the models corresponding to columns. (That layout would be a nuisance, though, if the company had 100 different models.). Or the table could have been arranged with the model name first and the number second.

✔ The most important thing is to decide what needs to be in rows and what needs to be in columns, because there isn't any easy way to turn rows into columns or columns into rows.

✔ Don't worry so much about exactly how many rows or columns you may need or what order to put them in. You can add or rearrange rows and columns easily later on.

## *Trying out an example*

Here's an example of what you can do with what I've talked about so far. Figure 9-4 shows the first week of a diet plan for an anonymous, but very earnest, calorie-counting person.

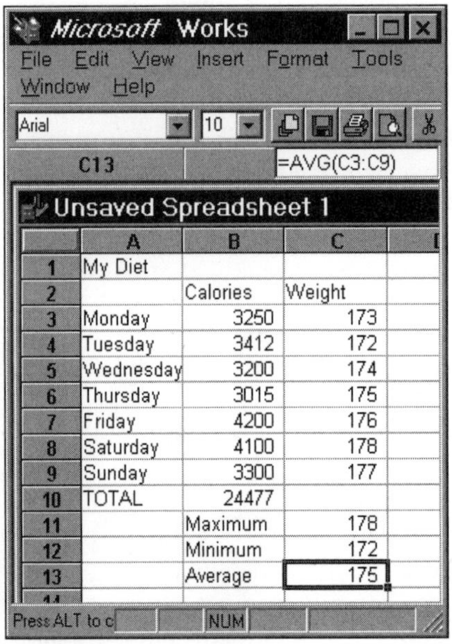

**Figure 9-4:**
A typical first-week diet, with typical first-week results.

| | A | B | C | |
|---|---|---|---|---|
| 1 | My Diet | | | |
| 2 | | Calories | Weight | |
| 3 | Monday | 3250 | 173 | |
| 4 | Tuesday | 3412 | 172 | |
| 5 | Wednesday | 3200 | 174 | |
| 6 | Thursday | 3015 | 175 | |
| 7 | Friday | 4200 | 176 | |
| 8 | Saturday | 4100 | 178 | |
| 9 | Sunday | 3300 | 177 | |
| 10 | TOTAL | 24477 | | |
| 11 | | Maximum | 178 | |
| 12 | | Minimum | 172 | |
| 13 | | Average | 175 | |

*Microsoft Works*

File  Edit  View  Insert  Format  Tools  Window  Help

Arial  10

C13  =AVG(C3:C9)

Unsaved Spreadsheet 1

Press ALT to c    NUM

Here's how to duplicate this spreadsheet (18 quick steps to weight control!):

1. **To get a fresh spreadsheet, press Ctrl+N. When the Task Launcher screen appears, click the** Works Tools **tab and then click the** Spreadsheet **button.**

2. **The current active cell (where the highlight is) is A1. Type** MyDiet **and press the Enter key.**

3. **Click on cell B2 (column B, row 2). Type** Calories **and press the Enter key.**

4. **Press the right-arrow key to highlight cell C2. Type** Weight **and press the Enter key.**

5. **Click on cell A3 and type** Monday.

6. **Press the down-arrow key and type** Tuesday. **Keep pressing the down-arrow key and entering days of the week through** Sunday. **On the seventh day, rest.**

If typing the days of the week seems more disagreeable than learning a new feature, you could try out Autofill here. See the following section, "Automatic Row and Column Heads with Autofill."

7. **Click on cell B3 and type** 3250.

8. **Press the down-arrow and type** 3412. **Refer to Figure 9-4 for the other calories and keep on like this through** Sunday.

9. **Click on cell C3 and type** 173. **Refer to Figure 9-4 for the other weights and keep on like this through** Sunday.

10. **Wake up, it's about to get interesting.**

11. **Click cell A10 and type** TOTAL.

12. **Press the right-arrow key to highlight cell B10 and type** =SUM(B3:B9). **Press the Enter key. Wow! Magic! The total calories for the week.**

13. **Press the down-arrow key to highlight cell B11 and type** Maximum.

14. **Press the down-arrow key to highlight cell B12 and type** Minimum.

15. **Press the down-arrow key to highlight cell B13 and type** Average.

Now we're about to type in some Formulas. Don't worry if you don't understand them right now; just type them in. I explain formulas in Chapter 10.

16. **Click cell C11 and type** =MAX(C3:C9).

17. **Press the down-arrow key to highlight cell C12 and type** =MIN(C3:C9).

18. **Press the down-arrow key to highlight cell C13 and type** =AVG(C3:C9). **Press the Enter key.**

With any luck, you should be looking at an exact duplicate of Figure 9-4. And you did it all yourself.

Notice that you save some effort by not pressing Enter every time you type something (although you may press Enter, if you like). All you need to do is highlight a new cell to enter whatever you've typed in the previous cell.

Try changing some of the calorie or weight values and see what happens to the calculated values at the bottom.

# Automatic Row and Column Heads with Autofill

Good row and column headings usually follow some predictable pattern, such as 1, 2, 3; or January, February, March; or Monday, Tuesday, Wednesday. After all, you don't want the readers of your spreadsheet to have to exercise their imaginations to figure out what your rows or columns have to do with each other. (People who spend their days reading a lot of spreadsheets sometimes don't *have* imaginations. You don't want to strain them.)

Unfortunately, typing in these predictable patterns can be really boring. After a while, you find yourself thinking, "This pattern is so predictable. This thing I'm typing on is a computer. Couldn't it, like, *predict* or something?"

The answer is yes. In general, you only need to type in the first two items from one of these patterns, and Works can take it from there. To try this, follow these instructions:

1. **Type the first two items from the pattern in adjacent cells.**

   In the example in Figure 9-4, for example, you would type **Monday** in A3 and **Tuesday** in A4.

2. **Select the two cells that you just typed in.**

3. **Move your mouse cursor to the lower-right corner of the two-cell block that you just selected, until the word** FILL **appears under your cursor.**

4. **Click and drag over all the cells that you want filled automatically.**

   In the example in Figure 9-4, you would drag until the highlighted area included the two cells that you had typed, plus the next five in the same column.

5. **Release the mouse button.**

Presto! Works extends the pattern to fill the selected cells. Was it worth figuring this out just to avoid typing the names of five days? Maybe, maybe not. But if you ever need to type the days of the *year* into a row or column, you may come to think very fondly of Autofill.

This trick is actually a special use of the Fill Series command in the Edit menu. You can read more about the use of Fill Series in "Fill 'er Up: Filling Cells with Numbers" in Chapter 24.

# Saving Your Work

As the banking industry says, "Save regularly, and watch your interest grow," or some such avuncular aphorism. (Bankers are, or used to be, fond of avuncular aphorisms and kept hothouses full of them at their country estates.) Likewise, you should regularly save your spreadsheet document as a file. It won't make your interest grow — unless the electricity fails, in which case your interest will grow immeasurably.

Saving your spreadsheet document is very much like saving any other Works document. If you need a refresher, see Chapter 2. For basic information on files and disks, see Chapter 1.

The executive summary on saving is as follows:

- Unless you save your document as a file on a disk, the document vaporizes when you stop Works or turn off your PC.

- Save early and often. You never know when the power will fail; if it does, your work may be lost.

- Save your document either by clicking the Save button on the toolbar (the one with the diskette icon) or by pressing Ctrl+S.

- If you're working in some distant corner of the spreadsheet when you save it, you are returned to that distant corner when you reopen the spreadsheet.

# Chapter 10
# Making Calculations

● ● ● ● ● ● ● ● ● ● ● ● ● ● ● ● ● ● ● ● ● ● ● ● ● ● ● ● ● ● ● ● ● ● ● ● ● ● ● ● ● ● ● ● ● ●

### In This Chapter

▶ Using formulas and functions

▶ Understanding operators

▶ Doing calculations

▶ Copying formulas

▶ Creating formulas by pointing and shooting

● ● ● ● ● ● ● ● ● ● ● ● ● ● ● ● ● ● ● ● ● ● ● ● ● ● ● ● ● ● ● ● ● ● ● ● ● ● ● ● ● ● ● ● ● ●

*T*o ensure your chances of success upon the seas of calculations, you need to be able to launch a variety of calculations. Works gives you the means to create darn near any calculation you need. In this chapter, I show you how to create formulas, use Works' built-in "functions," save effort by using a special "point-and-shoot" technique, and save time by copying formulas.

## Using Formulas

The Works spreadsheet tool lets you do a broader variety of calculations than you may ever use in your lifetime. Works calls these calculations *formulas*. To do a calculation, you type a formula into a cell. For example, you may type:

**=(SUM(B1:B8))/(SUM(C9:C17))\*A17-3.7**

or something equally pithy. Believe it or not, this is not a random collection of symbols. It means something, or at least it does to Works.

Works doesn't care whether you write formulas, cell addresses, and ranges in uppercase or lowercase letters. Works may convert some of the lowercase letters to uppercase letters, but that's its business.

## *Entering a formula*

When you type a formula into a cell, the formula appears in both the cell and the formula bar. The formula bar gives you a place where you can easily do all the fooling around that's often required to get a formula just right.

There's a disconcerting result of entering a formula, though:

After you've entered the formula, the formula itself doesn't appear in the cell; the *result* of that formula (the answer) appears there!

You can check out this phenomenon back in Figure 9-4. (You may have noticed it for yourself if you did the example.) The function bar says =AVG(C3:C9), which is what got typed in. But in the active cell (C13, also known as the one with the box around it), you don't see anything remotely like that. You see 175, which is what Works got by carrying out the instruction =AVG(C3:C9). (In other words, Works averaged the cells between C3 and C9 and got 175; then it stuck the answer into C13.)

Disconcerting, perhaps, but very tidy. After all, you're interested in the answer, not the formula. Your calculator shows you only answers, right? A calculator doesn't show which buttons you pushed to get an answer. Neither does Works. So you pick where on your spreadsheet you want the *result* to appear, and that cell is where you type in the *formula*.

To enter a formula into a cell, do this:

1. **Click the cell where you want the formula.**

   Or use the navigation keys to move the highlight to that cell. Use a blank cell; don't try to put the formula in the same cell that holds the numbers that you're using in the calculation. You can use any blank cell; it's okay, for example, to put a formula in cell A56 that uses values in the cells A22 and Q256.

2. **Type an = sign and then a mathematical expression.**

   More about this in a minute. As you type, use the formula bar for easier editing.

3. **Press the Enter key.**

   Or move the highlight (clicking in another cell is one method).

   This enters the formula into the cell and computes the result. *The formula remains in the cell*, but only the result is displayed.

Spreadsheet formulas are mathematical expressions, so you type things like:

**=5.24+3.93**

Starting Works formulas with an = sign is usually necessary so that Works knows that you're doing a calculation and not entering text or a number. Sometimes Works can figure that out for itself, based on what you type, but why trust to luck?

If you are doing a calculation, only enter the right side of the equation, (=**5.24+3.93**, for example). Don't enter the left side. Some folks try to assign the value to a cell by typing **A1=5.24+3.93**, for example. If you type such an equation, however, the equation would end up as text, not a calculation.

I know that some teacher in junior high pounded into you that an equation has to have two sides, but really, just try to accept this fact. Okay, okay, I give in. If you can't accept it, here's what you do: Look at the function bar. See over on the left, where the address of the active cell is? *That's* where the left side of the equation is. So if A1 is the active cell, and if you type =**5.24+3.93**, then the *full* function bar reads **A1=5.24+3.93**. Happy?

Anyway, if you typed =**5.24+3.93** into a cell and pressed the Enter key, the cell would show the answer: 9.17. Isn't that exciting! *This* is why people spend thousands of dollars on computers and software. Well, maybe not; you may have been able to do that more easily on a five-dollar calculator. What you can't do on a five-dollar calculator, though, is type something like:

=**5.24+B1**

Hmmm. Shades of algebra. What this formula really means is, "Show me the sum of 5.24 and whatever is in cell B1." If B1 has the number 3.93 in it, you get 9.17. If B1 has the number 6 in it, you get 11.24. You can keep plugging new numbers into cell B1 and watch the answer change in the cell that has this formula in it.

Okay, this is amusing, but wait! There's more! What if you want a formula to add up a bunch of cells? You can type:

=**B1+B2+B3+B4+B5+B6+B7+B8**

You can see where this may drive you back to your calculator. So to avoid losing your business, the software folks came up with a better idea. Rather than type all these cells and + signs, how about saying to Works, in effect, "Sum up the range B1 through B8"? You say this by entering:

=**SUM(B1:B8)**

Because B1 through B8 are all neighboring cells covering a rectangular area — a column, in fact — they can be expressed as a range. (See "Feeling at home on the range" in Chapter 9 for details on ranges.) If you want to include cells or additional ranges that aren't within that range, you can add them to the formula individually, as shown in the following example:

**=SUM(B1:B8, F15:B52, X15)**

Which means *what*, you may ask. Well (aside from being a way to string together the names of a bunch of great airplanes), *B1:B8* is a column; *F15:B52* is a rectangular block of cells; and *X15* is a single cell. If there were numbers in all those cells, this formula would add them up.

SUM and other built-in calculations are called *functions*. And, used correctly, they do — function, that is. Works has a whole passel of other functions for doing all kinds of things. (More about those in the section "You're Invited to a Function," later in this chapter.) You don't even have to remember the functions, as you soon see in "Point-and-shoot for functions," also later in this chapter.

All calculations, no matter how complex, are done this way in the spreadsheet: by mixing numbers, mathematical operations (such as addition and subtraction), and functions all together to make formulas.

## Seeing and editing formulas

The spreadsheet displays only the result of a formula, even though the formula actually remains in the cell. "So," you may well ask, "how can I see my formula?"

You can see an individual formula at any time by clicking its cell (or using the navigation keys to place your highlight on the cell) and looking in the formula bar. Figure 9-4, back in Chapter 9, shows a formula in the formula bar.

You edit a formula the same way that you edit any other contents of a cell: click the cell, click the formula bar, and type. (See "Editing Things in Cells" in Chapter 9.)

To see all the formulas in your spreadsheet, choose View⇨Formulas from the menu bar. This turns on a Formula view that's pretty ugly but does show all your formulas. You can work using this view, if you like. To turn off the Formula view, do the same thing you did to turn it on.

## Hello, Operator?

In a previous section, I employed the + symbol to represent addition in a formula. Table 10-1 shows some of the other common operators (math actions) and other symbols that you can use to create your mathematical formulas. This table also shows the order in which Works does the operation, if two or more operations are in the cell.

| Table 10-1 | **Math Operators** | |
|---|---|---|
| *Symbol* | *Action* | *Order of Evaluation* |
| ^ | raised to the power of | first |
| * | times (multiplied by) | after ^ |
| / | divided by | after ^ |
| - | minus | after ^, *, and / |
| + | plus | after ^, *, and / |

The order in which you use operators in your expressions can be important. Following the basic rules of math, Works (just like calculators) calculates the formula in groups, performing exponential (that's the ^) calculations first and the addition calculations last.

Table 10-2 has some examples of mathematical expressions and what they do. Pretend for the moment that you're typing the function in cell B4.

| Table 10-2 | **How Mathematical Expressions Work** |
|---|---|
| *Function in Cell B4* | *What It Does* |
| =A2+A3 | Adds what's in A2 to what's in A3 and shows the result in B4. |
| =10+A3/D8 | Divides what's in A3 by what's in D8; adds 10 to the first result; and shows the final result in B4. |
| =A2*A3+B12 | Multiplies what's in A2 by what's in A3; adds to that what's in B12; and shows the final result in B4. |
| =A2+A3*3.14+B12^3 | Cubes what's in B12; multiplies what's in A3 by 3.14; adds those two results together with what's in A2; and shows the result of the whole mess in B4. |

By putting an expression in parentheses ( ), you force Works to evaluate that expression first. Works evaluates the expression (2+3)*4 as 5*4, giving 20. Without the parentheses, the expression is 2+3*4. In that case, Works does the multiplication first, creating 2+12; then it does the addition, giving 14. When you use parentheses within parentheses, the expression in the innermost pair is evaluated first. When you use too many parentheses, you may end up being dragged off to be "evaluated" yourself.

# You're Invited to a Function

Works has quite a few of those convenient built-in functions, such as SUM, which are quite inviting. Functions produce some sort of value as a result. Some functions in addition to SUM that people tend use a lot are:

| | |
|---|---|
| AVG(*cells*) | average of the values in the cells |
| MAX(*cells*) | the maximum value among the cells |
| MIN(*cells*) | the minimum value among the cells |
| SQRT(*cell*) | the square root of the value in the cell |
| ROUND(*cell, # of digits*) | the value in the cell rounded off to some number of digits |

The word *cell* here means that you should type in a single cell address, such as **B1**, not the word *cell*. The word *cells* here means that you should type in a range, such as **B1:B8**. For *cells,* you can also type in a bunch of ranges and individual cell addresses, all separated by commas. For example, you can use **=MAX(B1:B8, D5:D13, F256)** to give a result equal to the maximum value among all those cells. (Microsoft uses the term *range reference* instead of *cells*.)

When I say *# of digits*, I mean a number, such as 2 or 3. (Oh, all right. Instead of a number, it may also be a cell that contains the number of digits or another function that produces a number of digits, but that's getting complicated.)

In formulas and resumes, it's against the rules to be your own reference. If one of the cells that a function *refers to* is the cell that it is *in*, you're in trouble. You're also in trouble if the formula in your cell makes reference to another cell, which, in turn makes reference back to it. And so on. In short, if Works needs to know what *is* in C4 in order to calculate what *ought* to be in C4, there's a problem. If you're lucky, Works tells you that you've got a "circular reference" and refuses to go on until you fix the problem. If you're not lucky, Works just merrily calculates something bizarre and does not tell you why.

I could list other functions here, but there are so many of them that doing that would waste a bunch of paper. To be very precise, there is a large gob of functions. These functions are described in two places: in the spreadsheet tool itself and in the Works Help feature. I discuss the spreadsheet tool's listing in "Creating Formulas the Point-and-Shoot Way" later in this chapter.

To read about functions by using the Help feature, do this:

**1. Press F1.**

This step gets you to the Index card of the Help Topics window.

2. **Type the word** functions: **in box number 1.**

   You can see a number of folders having to do with functions. Several of these are the functions arranged by type — date functions, financial functions, mathematical functions, statistical functions, and so forth. If you don't see the folder that you want, scroll down by using the scroll bar on the right side of the window with the folders.

3. **Click the folder covering the type of function that you're looking for.**

   If you want a function that does averages, for example, click the functions:statistical folder. This gets you a list of documents describing all the functions of this type.

4. **Click the document describing any likely-looking function.**

5. **Read the document in the Help window on the right side of the screen.**

   You may need to move the Help Topics window to see the Help document. If the function shown isn't the one that you wanted, click another one in the Help Topics window.

6. **Click the** Close **button in the Help Topics window to return to your document.**

# Creating Formulas the Point-and-Shoot Way

If your fingers are frazzled from typing formulas and your eyes are oscillating from trying to figure out cell addresses, fear not! (Well, fear a little, maybe.) There's this whole other swell method of creating formulas. I call it the "point-and-shoot" approach, and you use it while you are creating formulas in the formula bar.

You can point-and-shoot cell addresses and ranges, and you can point-and-shoot functions. You can do a whole summation just by pointing and shooting. Here's the big picture; details to follow:

**Cell addresses and ranges:** Whenever you need to put a cell address in a formula (such as A1 — you know, the steak sauce) or a range (such as B4:A1, which is what people used B4 steak sauce), you just highlight it while you're typing in the formula. (*It* being the cell or range. Not the sauce.)

**Functions (SUM and so on):** Whenever you're typing in a formula and you need a function, you can insert one by just choosing it from a nice list. Simply click Insert⇨Function in the menu bar to get a dialog box with the nice list in it.

**Autosum:** Whenever you have a column (or row) of numbers that you want to add up, just select the empty cell at the bottom of the column (or the end of the row) and click the Autosum button on the toolbar. The sum then appears in the empty cell.

# Point-and-shoot for cell addresses and ranges

Here's the blow-by-blow for entering cell addresses in a formula that you're creating:

1. **Click a cell and start creating your formula.**

   Type an = sign, for example. Or you can click in the white area of the formula bar and type an equal sign there. Type your formula right up to the point where you need a cell address or range. If you're using the SUM function, for example, type the following (including the left parenthesis):

   **=SUM(**

2. **When your formula needs a cell or range address, select (highlight) whatever cell or range you want to use.**

   Click a cell or drag the mouse pointer to select an area. (Or use the navigation keys.) The cell address or range you select is automatically entered in your formula in the formula bar. How about that?! The address or range is highlighted to show off the fact that you didn't actually type it in but are pointing at it. If you selected the wrong address or range by mistake, just select a different one.

   *Do not* press the Enter key at this point! If you press Enter prematurely, Works thinks that you're done typing the formula.

3. **Complete your formula.**

   Type the closing parenthesis, if it's not already there, or enter whatever the next math symbol is. The next character you type appears right after the cell or range address in the formula. For example, if you started with **=SUM(** and selected the range B5:B15, the formula reads **=SUM(B5:B15**, so type the final parenthesis: **)**.

   If you have additional addresses to enter, do them the same way. To multiply the sum in the example by the contents of cell D5, continue by typing the multiplication symbol * and then pointing to cell D5.

4. **Press Enter when you're done.**

## *Point-and-shoot for functions*

Here are the details on how to pick a function from a list instead of typing it in:

1. **Click a cell and start creating your formula.**

   Type an = sign or click the formula bar. Type your formula right up to the point where you need a function.

2. **Click Insert⇨Function.**

   The Insert Function dialog box swings into action. At this point, the big list box labeled Choose a function shows all the functions that Works offers. Scroll down the list to find the function that you think you want.

3. **If you don't see what you want on the main list, click a category in the** Category **area to reduce the display of functions to a specific type.**

   For example, to see only mathematical and trigonometric functions in the Choose a function box, click Math and Trig. (Oddly, the SUM function is in the Statistical collection.)

4. **Click a function in the** Choose a function **area.**

   You can see a brief description of what the selected function does at the bottom of the Insert Function dialog box.

5. **Click the** Insert **button.**

   The dialog box goes away, leaving you with your chosen function typed into the formula bar. However, Works doesn't know yet what cell or cells you want the function to apply to, so it leaves text as a placeholder in the places where cell addresses go.

6. **Edit the formula to put in cell addresses.**

   You have two ways to go. If you like, you can type in the cell addresses you need and delete any extraneous text. Or you can highlight some of the placeholder text and use the point-and-shoot method described previously to replace it.

7. **Press Enter when you're done.**

## *Point-and-shoot for summing columns or rows*

Thanks to Works' Autosum feature, summing a row or column of numbers is a piece of cake. Here's exactly how to do it.

1. **To sum up a column of numbers, place your highlight on the cell beneath the last number.**

    — or —

    **To sum up a row of numbers, place your highlight on the cell to the right of the last number.**

2. **Click the Autosum button on the toolbar: the button with the Greek letter sigma on it ($\Sigma$).**

3. **Press the Enter key.**

If you use Autosum on a cell that is *both* at the bottom of a column *and* at the end of a row, Autosum sums the column, not the row.

# The Joys and Mysteries of Copying Formulas

Copying is not what most folks think of as an exciting activity, unless they are confused by the sign over their employer's copy department, which often reads "Reproduction." But rest assured that copying can be a far more interesting activity than you suppose when it comes to spreadsheet formulas.

In a spreadsheet, you often have a column or row in which the same formula is used over and over again — when you're summing a set of columns, for example. Rather than retype the same formula over and over with a different range, you can save a great deal of effort by copying the formula. Works automatically takes care of giving the formula the correct range.

Here's how to copy a formula across a row or down a column, but the procedure is really just the same as copying a number or text or anything else:

1. **Enter your formula in an end cell.**

    You typically use the top cell if you're doing a column or the left end if you're doing a row.

2. **With the formula selected, press Ctrl+C or click the Copy button on the toolbar.**

    This copies the formula to the Windows Clipboard.

3. **Select the rest of the row or column.**

    You can include the original formula cell in your selection, if it makes things easier; it doesn't matter. (The pasting happens from the Clipboard, not the original cell, so the pasting isn't a circular reference.)

**4. Press Ctrl+V or the Paste button on the toolbar.**

Bingo, you're done.

The best way to explain what happens when you copy a formula is with an example; Figure 10-1 shows part of a spreadsheet. Three columns of numbers are shown: C, D, and E. The top five numbers in C and E are typed in; the last number in each column is the sum. The D column is calculated from the C and E columns. So the figure contains ten typed-in numbers and eight formulas.

| | A | B | C | D | E |
|---|---|---|---|---|---|
| 1 | *Toy Sales* | | | | |
| 2 | Model Number | Model Name | Units | Avg. $/Unit | Rev ($000) |
| 3 | XJ7 | Bomber | 890 | $223.51 | $198.92 |
| 4 | PT3 | Swooper | 1280 | $150.50 | $192.64 |
| 5 | F15 | Hawk | 920 | $298.50 | $274.62 |
| 6 | B52 | Falcon | 1580 | $165.50 | $261.49 |
| 7 | P121 | Peregrine | 800 | $350.50 | $280.40 |
| 8 | | | 5470 | $220.85 | $1,208.07 |

**Figure 10-1:** Copying formulas can save you a lot of typing time.

Rather than write eight formulas, I had to write only one. Here's how I did all those formulas:

1. **I summed column C by selecting C8 and clicking the Autosum button on the toolbar.**

2. **I summed column E by selecting E8 and clicking the Autosum button on the toolbar.**

3. **I entered the formula =1000\*E8/C8 into cell D8 and pressed Enter.**

   In case you're curious, the 1000 is there because the revenues in column E are expressed in terms of thousands of dollars. Multiplying by 1000 expresses them in terms of dollars.

4. **I clicked the Copy button on the toolbar to copy the formula in D8.**

5. **I selected the range D3:D7.**

6. **I clicked the Paste button on the toolbar to paste in copies of the formula.**

Each copy of the formula uses cells on a different row, which you see in the formula bar when you click those cells. The formula in cell D5, for example, is =1000\*E5/C5; in cell D6, it's =1000\*E6/C6; and so on. Pretty neat, huh?

Here's what happens to cell addresses when you copy formulas:

✔ **When you copy a formula to a new column, the letters change.**

That is, the column portions of any cell addresses in your formula change. They change by exactly the number of columns that you move: if you copy something three columns to the right and you have an address of A1 in your formula, it changes to D1; or Q17 changes to T17.

✔ **When you copy a formula to a new row, the numbers change.**

That is, the row portions of any cell addresses in that formula change. They change by exactly the number of rows that you move: if you copy something three rows down and you have an address of A1 in your formula, A1 changes to A4; Q17 changes to Q20.

If you copy a formula to a new row and column, both the row and column change in any cell addresses in that formula.

When you *move* a formula (by dragging it), or cut and paste the formula, the addresses in the formula do not change. Addresses change only when you *copy* something — either by dragging or by using the Copy and Paste commands (Ctrl+C and Ctrl+V).

## When formulas don't copy right

Sometimes copying doesn't work right. This condition happens when you *don't* want Works to change the address during a copy.

Commonly, this situation occurs when you've got a single value somewhere that you want to use in a row or column of calculations. When you copy a formula to the other rows, the reference to that single cell changes rows and is now wrong. If you copy to the next row down, for example, a reference to A8 would now be A9 — the wrong cell.

To keep a cell reference from changing when you copy, put a dollar sign in front of the column letter and/or row number in the formula. For example, type =F3*$A$8 instead of =F3*A8. When that formula is copied to the next row, the F3 changes to F4, but $A$8 remains the same. This is called *absolute addressing*.

What this all boils down to is: *Put a dollar sign in front of any portion of a cell address that you want to keep from changing when the formula is copied.* For example, a formula using A$8, copied down one row, still reads A$8. If A$8 is copied one column to the right instead, A$8 changes to B$8. The part with the dollar sign does not change; the rest does.

The dollar sign, here, has *absolutely nothing to do with dollars* (U.S. or Canadian) *or currency formatting;* use of the dollar sign is just an ancient convention in spreadsheets, probably started by Dan Bricklin when he did VisiCalc or by one of the other spreadsheet pioneers.

# Recalculating

Works recalculates all its formulas whenever you change any cell's contents. As a result, a really big spreadsheet can slow you down; you have to wait for Works to recalculate every time you enter something.

If your spreadsheet seems to take a long time to recalculate, you can switch to manual calculation, which makes Works put off recalculating formulas until you press the F9 key. To switch from automatic to manual calculation (and vice versa), choose Tools⇨Options from the menu bar. The Options window is a collection of cards, one of which is named Data Entry. Click the tab of that card. Now click the Use manual calculation check box.

# Chapter 11

# Editing and Dressing Up Your Spreadsheets

*I*t's one thing to be able to create a spreadsheet; it's quite another to convince the program to do all the things that you want — jump through computational hoops and whatnot — without your having to make a career of spreadsheeting. In this chapter I go over some timesaving things you can do. I also explore inner space: how to move things around and insert rows and columns into your spreadsheet.

Are your spreadsheets looking kind of clunky, industrial, and bland? I examine how to use AutoFormat and borders to add beauty and grace and how to use alignment and other formatting to add style and deep, philosophical significance. (Didn't know it was that easy, did you?)

Are your dates always late? Or do your dates seems to last forever? This chapter helps by describing how to deal with dates, time, and basic date-and-time arithmetic. (The chapter helps because you can read it while you're waiting for your date to begin or end. Reading this chapter also gives you that air of elevated intellectual capacity that always attends someone seen reading a *...For Dummies* book, thereby impressing the heck out of your date.)

# Copying, Moving, and Deleting

Works provides a variety of features that lets you move chunks of your spreadsheet around, delete them, and copy them. These features work pretty much the same way in every tool in Works. For the general picture, go look at Chapter 5.

Here's how these things work in your spreadsheet. Note that copying and moving are a little different in spreadsheets from how they are in the word processor:

- ✔ To delete a cell or range, select it and then press the Delete or Backspace key.

- ✔ To move a cell or range, select it and then slowly move your mouse cursor across the thickish frame that appears around the selected area until the cursor changes to an arrow labeled drag. At that point, click with the mouse button and drag a copy of the frame that appears to the new location. Release the mouse button, and the cells are moved.

- ✔ To copy, do the same thing as for moving, but hold down the Ctrl key while you drag.

- ✔ Another way to copy is to select the cell or range to be copied and then press Ctrl+C to copy to the Windows Clipboard. Click the cell where you want the copy, and press Ctrl+V to paste. If you're pasting a range of cells, click where you want the upper-left corner to go.

- ✔ To make multiple copies of something, click the cell to copy and press Ctrl+C. Then highlight a range and press Ctrl+V. All the cells in the range will be filled with a copy.

- ✔ To cut something out and paste it elsewhere, select the something to be cut and then press Ctrl+X; then click wherever you want a copy and press Ctrl+V. If you're copying a range, select the range and then just click where you want the upper-left corner to go.

You can use the buttons on the toolbar in place of the key combinations:

Ctrl+C is Copy, the button with two documents overlapping.

Ctrl+V is Paste, the button with the clipboard.

Ctrl+X is Cut, the button with the scissors.

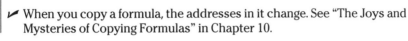

Here are a few things to remember when moving and copying things around:

✔ When you move or copy something to already-occupied cells, the original contents are replaced by what you moved or copied.

✔ When you move a cell (say you're moving what's in A1 to B5) that is used in a formula (say, =A1/3), the formula changes to use the new address (in this example, B5/3).

✔ When you copy a formula, the addresses in it change. See "The Joys and Mysteries of Copying Formulas" in Chapter 10.

# Inserting and Deleting Rows and Columns

There you are, a high-priced lifestyle consultant, typing up your monthly invoice for September. You've got a row for each day that you worked. You've made it to September 30, and suddenly you remember that you taught your client country-and-western line dancing on Saturday the 18th. Swell — what do you do now?

Well, you can select everything after the 18th and move it down a row, but how tedious and pedestrian! No, no, a with-it, '90s kind of person like you should be inserting rows. Or columns — whatever. Here's how:

1. **For a row, click anywhere in the row that your new row will be *above*.**

   For example, to insert a row above row 5 and below row 4, click row 5.

2. **For a column, click anywhere in the column that your new column will be to the *left* of.**

   For example, to insert a column between C and D, click column D.

3. **Click Insert⇨Insert Row *or* Insert Column.**

Deleting a row or column (as opposed to just deleting its contents and leaving the row or column blank) is a similar procedure: Click anywhere in it; choose Insert⇨Delete Row *or* Delete Column. It may seem odd to click Insert in order to delete, but (as Walter Cronkite used to say) that's the way it is.

When you insert a row or a column (say, a new row 5), and one of your formulas includes a range that spans that row or column (say, =SUM(A1:A10)), the new row or column is included in the formula. However, if you insert a new row or column *on the edge* of a range of numbers (say, a new row 1 or a row 11), this method doesn't work. So if you have an alphabetic list and add an Aaron or Zykowski, you may want to check and see that your totals are defined right.

# Formatting in One Swell Foop!

Back when disco ruled and quiche was the trendy food of the day, spreadsheets were dull, boring grids. No more! Today's spreadsheet sports designer colors, shadings, lines, borders, 3-D shading, and fancy fonts in different sizes and styles.

Works is no slouch when it comes to formatting; you can apply all of these fancy formats as you like, where you like. But Works has also combined a bunch of formatting into various stylish ensembles, which it refers to as *automatic formatting*. Automatic formatting (*autoformatting*) is truly a great idea.

## Autoformatting your entire spreadsheet

Figure 11-1 shows what happens to the toy sales spreadsheet when it's decked out in an automatic format called 3-D Effects 2. All kinds of stuff have changed here, even the formats of some of the numbers. Zowie! All these changes resulted from a few mouse clicks!

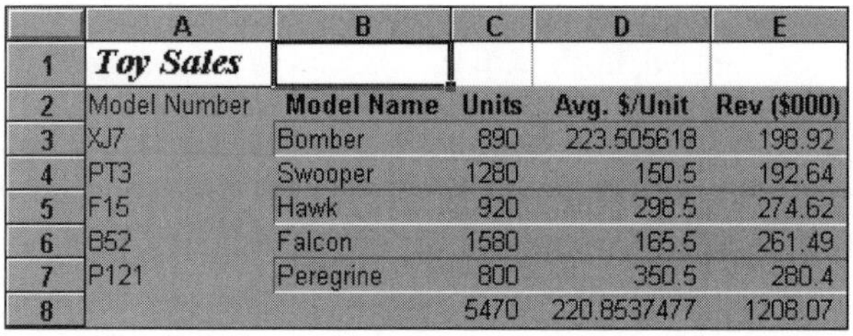

**Figure 11-1:** Autoformatting: Just a few clicks can get you a whole new look.

| | A | B | C | D | E |
|---|---|---|---|---|---|
| 1 | *Toy Sales* | | | | |
| 2 | Model Number | Model Name | Units | Avg. $/Unit | Rev ($000) |
| 3 | XJ7 | Bomber | 890 | 223.505618 | 198.92 |
| 4 | PT3 | Swooper | 1280 | 150.5 | 192.64 |
| 5 | F15 | Hawk | 920 | 298.5 | 274.62 |
| 6 | B52 | Falcon | 1580 | 165.5 | 261.49 |
| 7 | P121 | Peregrine | 800 | 350.5 | 280.4 |
| 8 | | | 5470 | 220.8537477 | 1208.07 |

The AutoFormat feature presumes that you have a fairly classic table structure: rows, columns, and maybe (though not necessarily) totals. If you meet these standards, AutoFormat away:

1. **Make sure that you have column and row headings.**

   Or, if you don't have 'em, at least have a blank row above and a blank column to the left of your table. Use these rows for your title row and column in Step 2.

2. **Select all the rows and columns, including title row and column and total row and/or column.**

   If you have a title for the whole spreadsheet, you can include or exclude it, as you like. I excluded the "Toy Sales" line in Figure 11-1.

**3. Click Format⇨AutoFormat.**

The AutoFormat dialog box of Figure 11-2 leaps into action.

Click a format here.

What the selected format looks like.

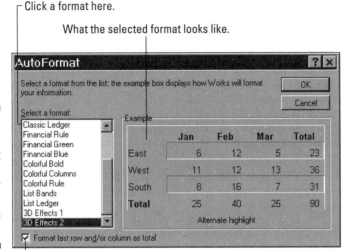

**Figure 11-2:**
The
AutoFormat
dialog box.
If only
reformatting
my car was
this easy.

Click here to turn on/off the special formatting on the last row and column.

**4. Click any interesting-sounding format in the** `Select a format` **list box.**

The Sample area shows you what the format looks like. If you don't like this format, click another format. If you don't like any of 'em, press the Esc key.

**5. Look at the** `Format last row and/or column as total` **check box.**

If you haven't used a total row or column, or if you have your total somewhere other than at the end of the range, make sure that this box is blank. If you do have a total row or column, check the box, but look at the example to see whether this particular format puts the total in the same place you did.

In the toy sales example, I chose to leave the box blank because cell D8 is an average, not a total.

**6. Click the** `OK` **button.**

Foop! There's a brief flurry of activity, and suddenly your spreadsheet looks like the inside pages of a quarterly report. If you don't like the results, press Ctrl+Z immediately to undo the formatting — before you make any other changes to the spreadsheet — and try again.

**7. Throw in some finishing touches if you want.**

In Figure 11-1, I would probably do something to get rid of the long decimal expansions in D3 and D8, either by using the ROUND function (see "Point-and-shoot for functions" in Chapter 10) or by selecting column D and changing to currency format. (See "Formatting numbers" later in this chapter.)

## Formatting the appearance of characters

One of the ways that you can fool with the appearance of the text, numbers, and formulas in your spreadsheet is to change the font, size, style, or color. Appearance formatting is one of those things that works the same way for all the tools of Works.

For the full details, refer to Chapter 3. The executive summary goes like this:

You have three ways to change how your type looks as you enter it:

**Alternative 1.** Choose the font, size, and style from the toolbar.

**Alternative 2.** Choose font, size, style, or color from the Font card of the Format Cells dialog box. To get this dialog box, click Format⇨Font and Style.

**Alternative 3.** (To change style only) Press Ctrl+B for bold, Ctrl+I for italic, and Ctrl+U for underline.

To change the appearance of characters that are already typed, just select them first and then use one of these three alternatives.

## Formatting numbers

Numbers? You want numbers? Works has got your number. In fact, you've probably never realized how many ways there are to write numbers.

Formatting numbers is not quite like formatting text. After all, when you change the formatting of text, the characters themselves don't change; just their font and style change. But when you format numbers, the actual characters and punctuation change to different characters and punctuation, adding dollar signs or parentheses, for example. The number itself doesn't change, but it puts on a radically different face. Sometimes it doesn't even look like a number any more.

For example, if you put the number 3284.2515 in a cell and use your formatting options, you can make that number look like any of the stuff in the How It Looks column of Table 11-1.

**Table 11-1    Different Formatting for the Number 3284.2515**

| *How It Looks* | *Format Name* | *About That Format & Options You Can Specify* |
|---|---|---|
| 3284.25 | General | As precise as possible for the column width; this is how Works formats numbers unless you tell it otherwise. |
| 3284.251 | Fixed | Specifies decimal places (in this example, *three*). |
| $3,284.25 | Currency | Dollar sign, comma, specifies decimal places; negative numbers appear in parentheses. Optional: negative numbers also in red. |
| 3,284.25 | Comma | Like Currency, but no dollar sign. |
| 328425.15 percent | Percent | Displays number multiplied by 100, adds percent symbol; specify your decimal places. |
| 3.28 E+03 | Exponential | Single digit number with power of ten; specify your decimal places (here, *two*). |
| 03284 | Leading Zeros | No fraction, displays as many digits as you specify (here, *five*); adds zeros or trims leading digits to do so. Good for zip (postal) codes. |
| 3248 3/10 | Fraction | Expresses fractional part as fraction: Choose halves, thirds, quarters, eighths, tenths, and so on (here, *tenths*). |
| TRUE | True/False | If zero, displays FALSE; if not zero, TRUE. |
| November 21, 1908 | Date | Interprets number as number of days since 12/31/1899; Works uses this format when you enter a date. |
| 6:02 AM | Time | Interprets fractional part of number (only) as fraction of one day, displays it as that hour; Works uses this format when you enter a time. |
| 3284.2515 | Text | If format applied *before* number is entered, turns number into text. Useful for serial numbers or other numeric codes. |

Date and time formats are among the weirder ones in this list because they make numbers look like text. For more on using them, see "Formatting dates and times," later in this chapter.

Currency format is the easiest to apply: just select the cell or cells to format and click the button with the $ icon on it, on the toolbar.

You don't actually format numbers in the spreadsheet tool; you format *cells*. The cell can be empty when you format it; and when you type a number in that cell, it takes on that format. If you type text in that cell, the text is not affected. If you delete an entry from a cell, the number format remains.

Works starts with every cell having the General format. The way to change specific cells is as follows:

1. **Select a cell or bunch of cells.**

   Click it or highlight them.

2. **Choose Format⇨Number.**

   The Number card of the Format Cells dialog box presents itself for duty.

3. **Click any format in the Format area of the dialog box.**

A sample appears in the Sample area near the bottom of the dialog box. If a number is already in the cell, that number is used in the sample. If you don't like what you see, click another format. See Table 11-1 for notes about these formats.

Some formats allow you to specify how many digits are to the right (or left, in the case of Leading Zeros format) of the decimal point. Normally, Works uses two digits here. To change this situation, just type a number to go into the Decimal places box.

The Currency and Comma formats let you optionally put negative numbers in red; just click the check box marked Negative numbers in red.

The Fractions format will normally reduce fractions: if you choose $^1/_{32}$, and your number ends in .125, it will show $^1/_8$. If you really want $^1/_{32}$ or whatever fraction you've chosen, click the check box marked Do not reduce.

4. **Click the OK button.**

# *Changing Alignment in a Cell*

Another way to change the appearance of something in a cell is to change its alignment: smushed left, smushed right, or smack dab in the center of a cell are the basic choices. Normally, Works aligns text to the left and numbers to the right, but you don't have to live with that.

Alignment is another one of those things that works pretty much the same (at least for the basics) in all the Works tools:

✔ Select a cell or cells and then click the Left, Center, or Right Align buttons in the toolbar. (These buttons are the ones with the lines on them.)

When you specify an alignment, the alignment sticks to the *cell*, not what's in the cell. If you specify alignment for a blank cell, whatever you type later gets aligned accordingly. If you delete what's in a cell, the alignment remains in the cell.

✔ You can tell how any cell is aligned by clicking it and observing the alignment buttons on the toolbar. If one of them is depressed, then the cell is aligned in that way.

✔ To remove an alignment, click the alignment button that is depressed.

These basic alignments, plus some other fancier alignments, can also be found on the Alignment card of the Format Cells dialog box. I don't get into those things here, but if you want to experiment with that box, click Format⇨Alignment.

# *Making Dates*

You've probably made your share of bad dates; now try good dates. Works provides date arithmetic, formatting, and functions so that you can calculate things based on time without having to recite to yourself, "Thirty days hath September, April, June, and December . . . or was it November?"

## The clockwork behind dates and times

Here's what's behind the scenes: Works computes dates by giving every day a number; Works starts the sequence at January 1, 1900, which it represents as 1. Days are whole numbers. Hours and minutes in that day are represented by a fractional portion. So the number that represents 8:00 AM on January 1, 1900 is 1.333333333. Works runs out of dates on June 3, 2079, so don't make any hundred-year plans.

If you type in a date or a time, Works shows it to you as a date or a time, which is nice. But Works secretly changes the entry to a number. If you type 8 AM, for example, Works enters 0.333333333 and chooses a *time format* for the number. If you type in a date, Works enters the number for that date and applies a *date format* that resembles the one that you typed the number in.

## Entering dates

If you're North American, you can enter a date into a cell in most of the normal ways. If you're European, you have to use the weird, backward American way. Table 11-2 shows good and bad ways to enter the date of August 28, 1945:

| Table 11-2 | Good and Bad Dates |
|---|---|
| *Good* | *Bad* |
| August 28, 1945 | August 28 1945 |
| 8/28/45 | 28/8/45 |
| 8/28/1945 | Aug. 28,1945 |
| 8 / 28 / 1945 | 8-28-1945 |

The bad aren't really bad; Works just takes them as text, so you won't be able to do any calculations with them. If you want them simply for labels, though, feel free to type them the "bad" way.

To enter a date in the current year, just enter the day and month part (8/28, for example).

To enter today's date, press Ctrl+; (that's Ctrl and the semicolon key). Amazing!

To enter a date that's current all the time, like on a day/date watch, type in the formula =**NOW( )** and format the cell with a *date format* (see "Formatting dates and times" later in this chapter). The date gets updated every time that you change a cell or press the F9 (recalculate) key. (If you're using *manual* recalculation rather than the normal *automatic* recalculation, you have to press the F9 key. See "Recalculating" in Chapter 10.) The NOW function is one of the standard Works time functions; so if you forget how the NOW function works, you can pull it off of the list in the Insert Function dialog box. (See "Point-and-shoot for functions" in Chapter 10.)

## Entering times

As with entering dates, there are "good" ways to enter times that Works understands as time; any other ("bad") way causes Works to interpret the entry as text. But, as they say, you gotta (everyone together now . . . ) "take the good times with the bad." Sorry. Had to do that. See Table 11-3 for good and bad ways to enter times.

| Table 11-3 | Good and Bad Times |
| --- | --- |
| *Good* | *Bad* |
| 2:30PM | 230PM |
| 14:30 | 1430 |
| 8:00 | 0800 |
| 8 AM | 8 AM EST |
| 8am | |

To enter the current time, press Ctrl+Shift+; (that's Ctrl+Shift+semicolon).

To enter a time that's always current, like the time on a clock, type in the formula **=NOW()** and format the cell with a *time format* (see "Formatting dates and times," later in this chapter). The time gets updated every time that you change a cell or press the F9 (recalculate) key. (Again, if you're using *manual* recalculation rather than the normal *automatic* recalculation, you have to press the F9 key.)

## Doing basic date and time arithmetic

Works' spreadsheet tool lets you do calculations based on time, but you have to be a little careful. Works secretly uses numbers to represent dates and makes them look date-ish by using a *date format*. If you do calculations, the results may come out as funny numbers instead of the date, number of days, or number of hours that you were hoping for. The following instructions can generally keep things working well.

### Subtracting dates; adding days to dates

If you have two dates, you can easily calculate by subtracting exactly how much time elapses between them.

Calculating intervals between dates can be depressing if you're single and your social life is less than satisfactory.

You subtract dates just as you would subtract regular numbers, except that each date either has to be in its own cell or, if you're using the dates in a formula, in single quote marks (apostrophes) and in the slash-date format, as in **9/15/94**.

✔ To use dates in a formula, write the dates in single quote marks and in the slash format: =**'9/15/95' – '4/14/95'**.

✔ To write a formula using dates that are in separate cells, write something like =**B4-B8**, where cell B4 has one date and B8 has the other. Dates can be entered in cells B4 and B8 in any acceptable format.

✔ The first date in a subtraction should be the later of the two if you want a positive number.

✔ The result that you get is the number of days between the dates.

After you've read "Formatting dates and times," later in this chapter, you may be tempted to format the result of date subtraction with a date format, just on general principles. Do *not* do it! Such an action has confusing results. For example, the answer to '9/15/95' – '4/14/95' is 154 days. If you now put that into date format, Works gives you June 2, 1900 — day 154 for Works. (See the sidebar "The clockwork behind dates and times" earlier in this chapter.) Unless the space-time continuum is more complicated than we think, this information is useless. Leave the result as a number of days, with a regular old number format.

Adding dates sounds like the logical complement to subtracting them but, in fact, is complete nonsense. (Christmas plus the Fourth of July equals . . . what?) You can, however, add *days* to dates by using a formula. Just as in subtraction, to put the date right into the formula, use single quotes around the date and use the date-slash format. For example, =**'9/15/94' + 35** adds 35 days to September 15.

If you're adding days to a date to compute another date, such as adding 35 days to September 15, 1994, *do* use a date format; otherwise, you just see a weird number. See "Formatting dates and times," later in this chapter.

### Subtracting and adding times

You subtract time much as you subtract dates. You can use times either in cells by themselves or as parts of a formula:

✔ If you're going to enter a time directly in a formula, put single quotes around it (**'10:00 PM'** or **'22:00'**, for example). For minutes, the hour should be zero, as in **'0:30'** for thirty minutes.

✔ If the times are in cells of their own, you can omit the single quotes.

The only trouble with subtracting times is that the result may need a little fixing up because Works uses units of days for time, not hours or minutes. Here's a quick example.

If you're a hotshot lawyer making, oh, $450 an hour, you of course want to bill your clients precisely for your time. So perhaps you keep three columns for each client: one (say, column B) for starting time, another (column C) for ending time, and the third (column D) for the difference between the two.

In row 3, you can make the following entries:

| Column B | Column C | Column D |
|----------|----------|----------|
| 10 AM | 10:15 AM | =C3-B3 |

The only problem is that the result in column D will probably look like 0.010416667! That number is equal to the fraction that 15 minutes is of a day. There are two problems with this:

- It doesn't look like minutes or hours.

  To fix this situation, use a time format (see "Formatting dates and times" and "Formatting numbers," elsewhere in this chapter); the best time format to use is one of the 24-hour formats — the ones without AM or PM after them.

- If you use it to calculate your fee, you'll go broke!

If you multiply that result by $450, you will only earn $4.65 — a pittance to a high-priced person such as yourself. You spend more than that for a cup of cappuccino in the lobby coffee shop.

Your problem is that Works keeps track of hours as fractions of a day. One hour is $1/24$ of a day. So to fix the problem in this example, you would multiply by 24. The "fix" rules go like this:

- To convert the result of time subtraction to hours, multiply by 24. The formula in column D of the example would be (C3-B3)*24.

- To convert the result of time subtraction to minutes, multiply by 24*60. The formula in column D of the example would be (C3-B3) *24*60.

Now for time addition. Adding *hours of the day* together is just as nonsensical as adding dates together. (What is noon plus midnight?) But you can certainly add *times* together or sum up a bunch of times. (Two hours plus three hours is five hours. No problem.) If you bill by the hour, this type of calculation is a nice thing to be able to do. It allows you to eat, for one thing, which is always useful.

To add or sum times, entering your times by using time format as you type (for example, **1:36** for one hour and 36 minutes) is easier on your brain. Also, format the formula cell that sums them up with a 24-hour time format (without the AM or PM). If you're going to enter the times right into the formula, make sure that you put the times in single quotes: **'1:36'**.

## *Formatting dates and times*

Every now and then, while you're doing some date arithmetic, instead of seeing a nice, date-looking result, you get a weird number, such as 16679. No problem. What you've got there is the date serial number that Works actually uses when it handles dates. (Quick, how many puns can you make out of "date serial"?) Most of the time, Works manages to hide from you how it really handles dates. When Works fails, you need to format the number as a date. (Unless, of course, you don't care what the date looks like.)

Also every once in a while, you may want dates formatted a little differently than Works normally does them. Instead of August 28, 1945, you may want 8/28/45, or maybe even 8/45, ignoring the day; heck, you may just want the month: August. No problem again. Works can do all of these tasks.

When you enter a date or time in a format that Works recognizes, Works actually stores a secret serial number and then formats the cell with a date or time format pretty close to the one you typed.

Here's how to format numbers as dates (or reformat dates):

1. **Select the cell or cells to format.**

2. **Click Format⇨Number.**

   The Number card of the Format Cells dialog box appears on the screen.

3. **Click Date in the Format area of the dialog box.**

   Date will already be selected if the cell is currently date-formatted; if this is the case, you can skip this step.

4. **Click one of the date formats in the Date area of the dialog box.**

5. **Click the OK button.**

You can also change formatting for time. If you don't like 2:30 PM and prefer 24-hour time, you can change the time to read 14:30. Use the same step-by-step procedure as for dates, except make these changes: in Step 3, click Time in the Format area of the dialog box, and in Step 4, choose a time format in the Time area of the dialog box. Among the formats are also choices for displaying seconds, as in 9:56:48 PM, if seconds are important to you.

Changing formatting does not change what's really in the cell — just its appearance. If you reformat August 28, 1945, to appear on-screen as just August, the number in the cell remains 16677. If you aren't convinced, press Alt+V and then F to turn on the Formula view. The Formula view shows the true contents of every cell. Press Alt+V and then F again to go back to the Regular view.

# Adding Borders and Gridlines

There's no excuse for ugly spreadsheets anymore. Pity. Now folks have to spend a lot of time duding up stuff in order for it to be appreciated by anyone else. Fortunately, Works takes much of the pain and strain out of prettying up spreadsheets with its AutoFormat feature (see "Formatting in One Swell Foop!" earlier in this chapter).

Alas, sometimes you still need a few lines to dress things up further. A line along a column, or across a row, or outlining a table. For this effect you need borders.

*Borders* are lines along the top, bottom, or sides of a cell. Combined properly, these lines can create the appearance of a border on or around a single cell, a range, or any given area of your spreadsheet. Used individually, borders are useful for such things as the summation line at the bottom of a column.

If you use borders, notice that some of them are so thin that they're masked by the gridlines that normally cover a spreadsheet. To turn off the gridlines, click View⇨Gridlines. (Or press Alt+V and then G.) The same action turns them back on.

Here's the step-by-step procedure for putting a border on cells:

1. **Select (highlight) the cell or cells that you want to apply a border to.**

   You can apply a border to either a single cell or a range of cells at one time.

2. **Click Format⇨Border.**

   The Border card of the Format Cells dialog box materializes.

3. **Choose what line style you want for your border(s).**

   Click any of the Line style examples shown in the dialog box. The top style signifies no line at all; choose it for turning off borders.

4. **Choose what type of border or borders you want in that line style.**

   Click one or more of the boxes in the Border area of the dialog box.

   Outline applies your chosen line style to all sides of the cell. If you've highlighted a range, you get a border around that range.

   Top, Bottom, Left, or Right can apply your chosen line style to that side. If you've highlighted a range, the border is applied to every individual cell in that range, *not to the range itself.*

   To select a border and turn it on, click its box. The chosen box gets outlined, and your chosen line style appears there. To turn off the border, click its box again once or twice until no line remains in the box. (If the box becomes shaded, that signifies to Works that it should neither add nor remove that border.)

   To choose a color for whatever border is currently outlined, click the down-arrow button to the right of the box marked Color and choose a color from the list that drops down.

5. **If you want different line styles on other borders, repeat Steps 3 and 4.**

**6. Click the** OK **button.**

A typical thing to do with borders is to put a line over a row of column sums. To do that task, highlight the row of sums and apply a Top border to the range.

# Doing Lists

One of the things that you can do with a spreadsheet — that you can also do with a database — is keep a list. Now, keeping a list may not seem particularly exciting; and if you were just "keeping" a list, you'd be silly to lay out the bucks for a spreadsheet program to do it with.

But given a sufficiently long list, you may have several things you want to do with it: sort it alphabetically or numerically, find particular entries in that list, or do calculations based on things in that list. Works' spreadsheet tool can help you do these things. If your list is going to be more than a couple of hundred entries long, you may want to consider using the database tool instead.

The nice thing about using spreadsheets for doing lists is that they have lots of rows — one row for each item on your list. You can treat these rows the way that you would treat file cards, by using one row per "card" and putting the different things that you would put on a file card in different columns. In geek-speak (computer gibberish), each row is a *record*, and each column is a *field*.

Figure 11-3 shows a simple list that you can keep in spreadsheet form: a list of pledges and a note of whether they've been paid.

Here are some tricks that you can use to create this list. One of the basic tricks is *preformatting* entire columns, which means applying a number format before any data is entered. (Or "data *are* entered," if you're an unreconstructed classicist.)

**Figure 11-3:** Keeping a list of donors in a spreadsheet.

| | A | B | C | D | E | F | G |
|---|---|---|---|---|---|---|---|
| **1** | **Pledge List** | | | | | | |
| 2 | Pledge # | Last Name | First Name | Phone | Pledge Date | Amount | Paid? |
| 3 | 1 | Snodgrass | Mortimer | 555-8750 | September 15 | 50 | TRUE |
| 4 | 2 | Horstwhipple | Gertrude | 555-9165 | September 15 | 40 | TRUE |
| 5 | 3 | Meulhueser-Eck | Henrietta | 555-1826 | September 15 | 50 | TRUE |
| 6 | 4 | Cheeseworthy | Stilton | 555-9190 | September 16 | 20 | TRUE |
| 7 | 5 | Phoghorne | Legolas | 555-1725 | September 16 | 15 | TRUE |
| 8 | 6 | Towcester | Bill | 555-2462 | September 16 | 80 | |
| 9 | 7 | Eelgrass | Steve | 555-9152 | September 16 | 50 | |
| 10 | 8 | Dibblesby | Horst | 555-6152 | September 19 | 40 | |
| 11 | 9 | Wikketton | Florence | 555-4625 | September 19 | 35 | |
| 12 | 10 | Smith | Alan | 555-4628 | September 19 | 45 | |
| 13 | 11 | Smith | Alan, Jr. | 555-2451 | September 19 | 25 | |
| 14 | | | | | | | |

✔ Give each pledge (row) a number so that if you later rearrange the rows, you can get them back in the original order. This setup also helps keep the Alan Smiths separate, giving you a unique tracking number for the pledge so that you can, say, put the right person's name on dunning letters and not harass the wrong guy. (Now if you can just tell their checks apart.)

✔ As each pledge is contacted by phone, the date of the call and the amount pledged are entered. The easy way to enter today's date is to press Ctrl+; in the date column. To preformat the entire column with the kind of date format you want, select the whole column by clicking the column letter (E, in this example) and then applying date formatting.

✔ I chose not to format the Amount column because what else would it be but currency? I don't accept barter pledges in chickens or corn. If you do want to preformat the column in currency, preformat it by clicking the column letter (F, in this example) and then clicking the $ button in the toolbar.

✔ When the pledge is received, you can just make any sort of mark in the Paid? column. I chose to get fancy, preformatting the column with the True/False number format. Typing **1** into that column when someone pays results in a TRUE appearing there.

## *Sorting lists*

One of the nice things that Works can do for you is sort lists. (I'm still working on getting it to sort laundry; I'm starting with laundry lists.) You may, in the example in Figure 11-3, want to alphabetize the list by last name so that you can more easily compare it to, say, a purchased list of prospects. (You don't want to call someone twice.) Or you may want to order the list by amount pledged so that you can single the generous out for special attention next year.

Works can sort your list in alphabetical or numerical order. Before you go running off to sort your list, however, decide on the following sorting options:

✔ Which column to sort by primarily (for example, last name).

✔ Which column to sort by secondarily, for those instances when the primary column has duplicates (for example, first name).

✔ Which column to sort by if duplicates exist in the secondary column (if you care about sorting those duplicates).

✔ What order you want the list in: A — Z and 1, 2, 3, . . . (ascending) or Z — A and . . . 3, 2, 1 (descending).

(The order can be different for the primary and secondary sorts, such as having last names in ascending order and dollar amounts pledged in descending order.)

In the pledge example, where you want to compare the list to an alphabetical list of prospects, you probably want to sort on column B (last name) primarily, and in ascending order. In case of redundant last names, use column C (first name) as the secondary sort column, also in ascending order. You probably don't care about any tertiary sort.

If you have any calculations or spreadsheet work of any kind (other lists, other tables) off to one side of your list (in the rows you are going to sort), highlight the area you want to sort before using the Tools⇨Sort command. Then choose Tools⇨Sort, and in the Sort query box that appears, choose Sort only the highlighted information. Otherwise, when you sort the rows of your list, the entire width of each row is reshuffled (all columns), which mangles anything typed off to one side.

The procedure for sorting goes like this:

1. **Save your spreadsheet as a file, in case anything goes wrong.**

   If anything does go terribly wrong and Ctrl+Z doesn't undo it, close the messed-up spreadsheet without saving it and then reopen the original file.

2. **Select (highlight) all the rows in the list.**

   You can use any column or columns in this selection; your choice doesn't matter. Make sure that you don't include any column sum row, or that row is sorted along with your records. You may include the header row or not, as you like. I deal with header rows later.

3. **Click Tools⇨Sort.**

   The Sort dialog box appears with its first question: Do you want to sort only the columns you selected, or all columns? (It asks this question even if you have selected all the columns already.)

4. **Click OK.**

   This action produces the second Sort dialog box, displayed in Figure 11-4, which asks which column to sort on and whether to sort in ascending or descending order. It also asks whether one of the rows you've selected is the header row, so it will know to leave it alone.

**Figure 11-4:**
Sorting on one column. Clicking Advanced will get you a triple-decker version.

5. **If you want to sort only on one column, choose that column from the** Sort By **list box and go to Step 6. If you want to sort on a second or third column when duplicate entries are in the chosen column, click the** Advanced **button and skip to Step 7.**

6. **Click either the** Ascending **or** Descending **check box and go to Step 10.**

   If you chose Advanced back in Step 5, you should be looking at a triple-decker version of the previous Sort box.

7. **Select a column in the** Sort By **window and click either the** Ascending **or** Descending **check box.**

8. **Select a column in the** Then by **window and click either the** Ascending **or** Descending **check box.**

9. **If you're concerned about sorting when the 2nd column has duplicates, select a column in the** Then by **window and click either the** Ascending **or** Descending **check box.**

10. **Click either the** Header row **or** No header **row check box.**

11. **Click the** Sort **button.**

Works sorts your list (that is, your rows are shuffled around in the order that you specified). To return to the original order, you can press Ctrl+Z as long as you haven't made any other changes. If you're clever and give each record a unique number, you can always sort by using that column for Sort By and restore the original order.

You can dress up your list with the AutoFormat feature, just as you can with any other spreadsheet. A couple of formats are even made especially for lists: List Bands and List Ledger. See "Autoformatting your entire spreadsheet" earlier in this chapter.

## Calculating in lists

Putting your formulas in the right place is important. If you're going to do a calculation based exclusively on data in a single row, put the formula in that row. If you're going to do calculations on multiple rows in a list, doing them in the area above the list is best. If you put them at the bottom, you're going to have to continually insert new rows for data as the list expands. If you put them off to the side, they are likely to be mangled by the sorting process.

In general, don't write formulas that refer to specific cell addresses within your list because, when you sort the rows, those cell addresses will have new data. Unless you're very clever and that's what you had in mind, the result will be nonsense.

Also be very careful about using formulas with ranges that include a group of rows, such as =SUM(F3:F13). If you sort the rows, the range in the formula remains unchanged (F3:F13), but it refers to different data. Any formula including a group or rows generally applies only to one particular order of data.

It *is* safe to write a formula that refers to all the rows: for example, one that sums up the Amount column. But you must be careful to make sure that the range in the SUM formula expands to include new rows that you add. The easiest way to do this task is to put a dummy row at the bottom of the list (maybe with a border on it so you can see it). Put your SUM formula above your list or below the dummy row. When you write the SUM formula, start the summing range with the column headings row and end it with the dummy row at the bottom. (Make sure that the cell in the heading row doesn't contain a number, or that number will be added to the sum; text is okay.) When you add new rows, do it by inserting a row (Alt+I and then R) above the dummy bottom row. The range in the summing formula will expand to include the new row.

# Dealing with Printing Peculiarities

Printing spreadsheets is pretty much like printing anything else in Works, so for the general, gory details, see Chapter 6. There are a few peculiarities about printing spreadsheets, however.

✔ To print only a range of the spreadsheet, not the entire spreadsheet, select a range and use the Set Print Area command: click Format⇨Set Print Area. To go back to printing the entire spreadsheet, select the entire spreadsheet (Ctrl+A) and repeat the Set Print Area command.

✔ Works splits up your spreadsheet to get it to fit on a printed page. If the spreadsheet is bigger than the page, you literally have to cut and paste pages together to re-create the original layout. Use the Print Preview feature to see how your spreadsheet is going to print.

✔ To control page breaks yourself, you can cut up the document horizontally and vertically and create page-sized pieces.

✔ To split the document along a vertical line, begin by selecting a column. Click the column letter (in gray at the top of the spreadsheet) to the *right* of where you want the break. Now click Insert⇨Page Break. A dashed line appears along the left edge of the selected column, indicating the break. The break runs the entire length of the spreadsheet, although it may not show up where you have fancy formatting.

✔ To split the document along a horizontal line, select the row *below* where you want the page break and do the same command as for a vertical line. (To select a row, click the row number in gray along the left of the spreadsheet.) The break runs the entire width of the spreadsheet.

✔ If you forget to select a row or column first, a tiny Insert Page Break dialog box appears. In this dialog box, click <u>C</u>olumn for a vertical break or <u>R</u>ow for a horizontal one and then click the OK button.

✔ If you go to insert a page break and the cell currently highlighted is adjacent to, say, an existing vertical page break, Works assumes that you want a horizontal one now and gives you the horizontal page break you want with no preamble or discussion! Conversely, if a horizontal break is above the cell you highlight, Works assumes that you want a vertical page break.

✔ To get rid of a page break, put your cursor to the right of it (for vertical), or under it (for horizontal); click <u>I</u>nsert⊅Delet<u>e</u> Page Break.

# Part IV
## Doing Active Duty at the Database

# In this part . . .

*W*hen you need to get your data to follow orders, march in neat rows and columns, or report on developments in the field, you need a database. When you have large squadrons of names, numbers, or other data, the Works database can help you marshall your facts into usable form.

The database tool helps you sort, list, find, and report on anything from membership lists to inventories. In this part, you'll discover how to create a database, interrogate it, and make reports based on the data contained within.

> "Therefore my lords, omit no happy hour; that we may give furtherance to our expedition."

*King Henry V*, Wm. Shakespeare

# Chapter 12

# Reporting for Duty at the Database

- - - - - - - - - - - - - - - - - - - - - - - - - - - - - - - - - - - - - -

### In This Chapter

▶ Understanding databases

▶ Getting started with databases

▶ Designing your database

▶ Understanding views

▶ Entering fields and data

▶ Navigating your views

▶ Creating an example database

▶ Editing formulas

▶ Adding and removing fields

▶ Using printing options

▶ Saving your work

- - - - - - - - - - - - - - - - - - - - - - - - - - - - - - - - - - - - - -

*1*t's time to give your data a little discipline. Have your scraggly collections of names and addresses, inventory lists, and what-have-you report for duty at the database and give them the Works. Here's where your data learns to get organized, march in rows and columns, and respond promptly to your orders and questions.

## Using a Database

If you've never used a database before . . . well, actually, you probably have used a database before. It's just that it was on paper, a more sensible (able to be sensed) medium than a computer. If you've ever used a library card index, a Rolodex, a dictionary, or a phone book, you've used a database. A *database* is just a collection of information that has some organization to it. (For example, every card in a Rolodex has the same structure: a line for a name, usually last name first; a couple of lines for an address; a line for the phone number; and so on.)

The thing that you may never have used before is a database manager or (as in Works) a database tool. When you put a database on a computer, a *database manager* or *tool* is the thing that you use to read the database and to put information into the database. Because databases are always accompanied by database tools, people get lazy and lump the terms together, calling the whole ball of wax a database.

## What's the big deal?

The big deal with computer databases and database tools is that not only does the tool let you read the database, it helps you find things quickly. (Not your car keys. Sorry.) Making a list of everyone in your Rolodex who has the same zip code (postal code) will take you a while. But use a computer database, and the whole task will take hardly any time at all. (Of course, you've got to learn how to use the database in less than six months in order to make it worthwhile. That's where this book comes in.) Looking for something (or things) in a database is called *querying*.

A database helps you do other things that would be a pain in the wrist to do by hand. To organize a meeting of people who live in the same general area, you may want to find everyone in your Rolodex who works for the Acme Corporation and whose zip code is one of, say, three possible codes. Or you may want to sort things. You may want to sort your organization's membership list by street so that you can organize neighborhood meetings.

Computer databases are great for storing numerical information because the database tool lets you make statistical reports. If you store your business inventory in a computer database with each item's value and department recorded there, you can find out the total inventory value for each department. If you record the item number and salesperson for every sale, you can quickly figure out sales commissions and the remaining inventory levels. Analyses such as these are generally called *reports,* and Works has a special ReportCreator tool in the Tools menu to help you get them just right.

## Fields and records: how information is stored

The Rolodex metaphor is great for understanding the basic parts of a database. Each card on your Rolodex has the same blank areas to fill out: Name, Telephone Number, and Address, at the very least. These blank areas are called *fields* in computer databases. Each field has a name, as in *Address* field.

Each card in your Rolodex has the same set of fields, but the actual content of those fields differs from card to card. In a computer database, the card is called a record. A *record* consists of a set of related information and may correspond to a person (as in the Rolodex), a transaction (such as a sale or a phone call), an object, or a location.

## *Sorting, filtering, and reporting: finding only the information you want*

Although it's very nice to have a lot of information well organized into fields and records, that benefit alone wouldn't convince *me* to use a database instead of a Rolodex or card file. No, what sells me on databases is that they can help you find the information you want. If a database is very small, of course, you can just rummage through it. But the reason that you have a database is because you have a lot of data, and rummaging through it to find the information is just not practical. Three ways in which the Works database helps you find and display data are:

✔ **Sorting** — which lets you organize records alphabetically (by last name, for example) or numerically. Sorting your database records also groups similar records together. For example, when you sort based on zip code, all the records sharing a common zip code will be grouped together.

For the full scoop on sorting see Chapter 15.

✔ **Filtering** — which shows you only certain records in your database. For example, to find all 12-year-olds in your school database, you can create a filter that, using the "Age" field of your database, screens out every child but the ones you want. You can also filter based on multiple fields. If you want all the 12-year-olds who are, say, not in your charming town of Mudville, that can be accommodated, too.

For information on filtering see Chapter 14.

✔ **Reporting** — which filters, sorts, and organizes records into a report or summary form for printing. For example, you can create a report of your customers in the state of California, grouped by zip code, with subtotals of, say, sales for each group for the month of December.

To learn how to create reports, see Chapter 15.

# *Doing Database Duty*

To review the method for starting Works and the various ways of starting a database document, check out Chapter 1. If you're a little vague on using commands, menus, and dialog boxes, stick a bookmark, a small inanimate object, or a slow-moving hard-shelled insect in Chapter 2 and refer back there, too, when you need to.

Otherwise, launch Works, and you get the Task Launcher. (If you've already been using Works and aren't currently looking at the Task Launcher, choose File⇨New or press Ctrl+N.) Choose the Works Tools card, and click the Database button there.

## The spreadsheet connection

Works' database tool and its spreadsheet tool have a great deal in common. The List view of a Works database looks very much like a spreadsheet. Row, column, and cell selection; editing; formatting; data types; borders; gridlines; inserting and deleting rows and columns; and more are very similar. In fact, you can easily cut and paste between the List view of a database and a spreadsheet without too much confusion. You may want to learn about spreadsheets at some point in order to pick up some tricks for working with databases in the List view.

This action starts you on a nice, shiny, untrammeled new database document. Of course, you don't have to start with a nice, shiny, untrammeled new database document. Works has many predesigned, pretrammeled databases for such things as an address list and a membership list for your soccer team. You can get a predesigned database by starting with a TaskWizard, and then choosing it off the TaskWizard card in the Task Launcher. For more on using specific TaskWizards and dealing with some of the fancy tricks that TaskWizards do, see Appendix A. But a TaskWizard just creates the structure for your database. Until you know a bit more about databases, you may find that the databases created in this way are a bit tricky to actually use. You still have to know how to work with fields, enter the data, make queries, change views, and do reports — and that's why you have this book!

## *The database window*

Figure 12-1 shows you what's what in your database window. (*Database window* is my name for how the Microsoft Works window looks when you're using the database tool.) Your window will look like this once you have created or opened a database.

A slightly modified version of the usual Works menu bar appears near the top of the Works window, and the database toolbar is underneath the menu bar.

Don't try to memorize all the stuff in these figures. Stick a pencil here or an unused stick of gum or turn back the corner of the page and come back whenever you need to refresh your memory.

Make a mental note that Figure 12-1 is showing you one of two main *views* of a database. The view shown here is called *Form* view, and the other, *List* view. (A third view, *Form Design* view, looks like Form view, but is designed as an editing feature to let you change how Form view looks.)

To first record    Database toolbar

Menu bar

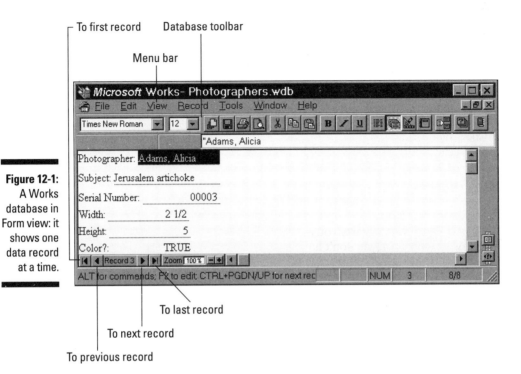

**Figure 12-1:**
A Works
database in
Form view: it
shows one
data record
at a time.

To last record

To next record

To previous record

# *The database menu*

As in fine chili stands and programs everywhere, one way to give a command is
by using a menu. You point and grunt (or in Works, click) at the item you want.

Using Works, however, is more like dining at a fast-food franchise: the menu
looks pretty much the same everywhere. In the database tool, the menu bar
(the line with File and all the other command words on it) looks almost exactly
as it does for the word-processor and spreadsheet tools. The menus display
some differences when you go to use them, and they differ slightly between the
three views: Form view, List view, and Form Design view.

Many of the basic commands are the same, however, especially the ones in the
menus that drop down when you click File or Edit. The File and Edit menus
include commands for starting a new document, opening an existing document
file, closing a document, saving a document to a file, and making basic edits.
Even the Find command is practically the same as in the word processor or
spreadsheet. Most of these commands are discussed in detail in Part I, the basic
skills chapters.

The other commands — the commands that are specific to databases — I get
into one at a time, as I go along.

## *The database toolbar*

The other popular way to give commands to Works (other than the traditional scrawling of curses on the screen) is with the toolbar: the thing with all the decorative buttons under the menu bar. The toolbar is just a faster way than the menu bar to do some of the same things. You click on a button and stuff happens.

Many of the buttons on the database toolbar are similar to those in other Works toolbars (see Figure 12-2). For more on Works' toolbars, see Chapter 2.

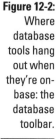

**Figure 12-2:** Where database tools hang out when they're on-base: the database toolbar.

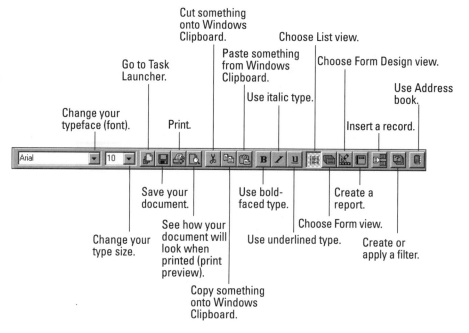

Most of the buttons on the toolbar are the usual suspects mentioned in Part I for starting, saving, printing, doing basic cut-and-paste edits, changing fonts, and getting help. The remainder are specific to databases. Here's where to go for a discussion of what each of these buttons refers to:

- ✔ **List, Form, and Form Design view:** See "Selecting a view" in this chapter.

- ✔ **Insert a record:** See Chapter 13.

- ✔ **Create a report:** See Chapter 15.

- ✔ **Insert a field:** See Chapter 13.

- ✔ **Create or apply a filter:** See Chapter 15.

- ✔ **Use the Address book:** See Appendix A.

To quickly see what a button on the toolbar does, place your mouse cursor over the button (don't click) and wait half a second. A tiny yellow sign appears and gives you a tiny description.

# Designing Your Database

Unless you're using a TaskWizard, you do have to design your own database. Well, no, that's not quite right; you can slap it together in a devil-may-care fashion, but you will pay a price later as you add or rearrange things and must reenter data. Your first step in designing a database is to determine both the fields and the rules for entering information.

*Fields* are the categories common to your records. Name, Address, and Phone Number are the equivalents of fields on your Rolodex cards. (*Records* are like the individual cards in your Rolodex.)

Take a piece of paper (remember paper?) and a pencil (digital printing instrument) and write down a list of field names and standards for entering information. (Or, if you're pretty good with the Works' word processor, use that.) Here are some guidelines for choosing your fields:

- Provide a field for anything that you may want to search for or report on: date, manufacturer, color, price, vendor, nickname, neck size, and so on.

- Use a separate field for things that may not exist in every record. For example, will you always enter the area code for phone numbers, or will you leave it off for local numbers? If you may occasionally leave it off, it's a good idea to create a separate field for the area code.

- Use a separate field for things that are separable. For example, the names of many people in your database may begin with Mr., Ms., or Mrs.; when you use your database, it makes life easier if this type of title is in a separate field.

- Provide a serial number field if you want. This is a good idea so that each record has something unique to identify it with and so that you can reconstruct the original order.

- Decide on standards for data that may accidentally vary. Arbitrarily decide, for example, to always call copy paper *copy paper,* not *copier paper.* Or standardize on *purple,* shunning *violet.* If you refer to the same thing by two different names, you have to work twice as hard to find all the data again.

The next step is actually to create your database document. Read on.

# Creating Your Database

Works bends over backward to help you create your database. First of all, there are a variety of TaskWizards for such functions as address books, inventories, personnel files, and the like. (There is even a "start from scratch" TaskWizard, although, frankly, I think you can do as well or better without it.) Second, even when you start without benefit of a TaskWizard, Works guides you step by step through the initial tasks.

For more on starting a database with some of the more popular TaskWizards, see Appendix A. In this chapter, I'll take you through the more flexible process of creating a database yourself. To start a fresh, untrammeled database document, do the following:

1. **If the Task Launcher is not on your screen, choose File⇨New from the menu bar or press Ctrl+N.**

2. **From the Task Launcher, choose the Works Tools card and then click on the Database button.**

The first time that you start a new database document after starting Works, Works guides you through the creation of fields by popping up the First-time Help dialog box, shown in Figure 12-3.

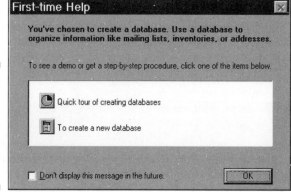

**Figure 12-3:**
Ever-helpful, Works lets you either take a tour or get down to business.

3. **Take the tour once, just for fun.**

Works will return to the First-time Help dialog box when you're done. Click the box labeled Don't display this message in the future, and Works won't bother you with this dialog box again but will go straight to the Create Database dialog box of Figure 12-4.

**4. Click on the button marked** `To create a new database` **in the First-time Help dialog box.**

The Create Database dialog box of Figure 12-4 leaps into view. (So does the Help panel, most likely. You don't need it, so minimize it by clicking the `Shrink help` button on that panel.)

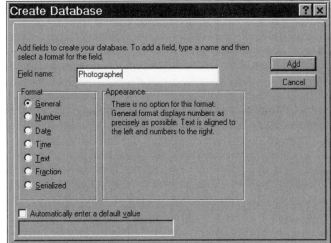

**Figure 12-4:**
Enter fields
one a time
with the
Create
Database
dialog box.

Works is now ready for you to begin creating your database fields. Read on!

## New fields of endeavor

When you create a new database (without using a TaskWizard), your principal job is entering fields. Here in New England, we wear our rubber boots and watch where we step when we enter fields. No such precautions are necessary for your database.

Here's the procedure for creating new fields by using the Create Database dialog box of Figure 12-4. Repeat this procedure for each field that you think that you need. If you discover that you need to change an earlier field, it's easier to wait until you have all the fields done and then go back and make changes.

**1. Enter a name for a field in the** `Field name` **box, less than 15 characters long.**

For example, in Figure 12-4, I'm starting to create a database of photographs that I use in my business. The first field I want is one for the photographer's name. (Don't bother to dress up your field name by adding a colon at the end of the name; Works will add one for you in Form view.)

**2. Choose a format for the field (in the** `Format` **area of the dialog box).**

These formats are very much like the number formats for spreadsheets. Refer to the section on formatting numbers in Chapter 11 of this book.

**General:** You can use the General format for most fields, but there are a few special circumstances where you might want to choose something other than General. Formats can also be changed later, after you have the database built. You can change the format even after data has been entered, but it's best to decide on the format before you enter your data.

**Number:** Use this if you want dollar signs, commas, percentages, or scientific notation to appear without having to type them in. A list of examples appears; choose a format from the list. Number format also includes TRUE/FALSE for fields like the Color? field in Figures 12-1, 12-5, and 12-6, where you can enter a 1 for TRUE or a 0 for FALSE.

**Date or Time:** Use these if you want the flexibility to be able to change the way dates or times appear in your database. Use this, too, if you will need to take advantage of Works' capability to subtract dates, such as calculating elapsed time.

**Text:** Use this if you will be entering data with a mix of letters, numbers and symbols, or codes (like some zip codes) that begin with zero. Otherwise, the zip code 01776 will turn into 1776.

**Fraction:** Use this, and Works automatically rounds off data entered in decimal form, like 2.125, into mixed-number fractional form, like 2 $1/8$. Choose what fraction you want the number rounded off to in the list that appears. This is useful for listing things in nonmetric dimensions, such as inches. Works will "reduce" a fraction like $4/8$ to $1/2$ unless you click on the check box marked Do not reduce.

**Serialized:** This is a very useful format when you want to create a serial number field (and most databases do need some unique number for each record, which a serial number provides). Choose this, and you won't even have to enter a number in this field; Works will do it for you automatically, each time that you enter a new record. In the Next value box, enter the number that you want the next record to start with. If you want the number to increment by something other than 1, enter that increment in the Increment box.

At the bottom of the Create Database dialog box, you can optionally specify a "default value" by clicking in the check box and typing the value in the box at the very bottom. A *default value* is data that appears automatically whenever you create a new record, and it saves you time. For example, if most of the photographs in my photography database are done by the same person, say Johnson, I could make Johnson my default value. Then whenever I record a new photograph in my database, Johnson would automatically be typed in. (I could replace it with another name if the

the photographer were not Johnson.) Fields that use default values behave oddly, however, when you go to enter data into a record: *the default value will not appear until you enter data in at least one other field.*

**3. Choose the A\underline{d}d button (in the Create Database dialog box).**

This action adds the field you just specified to the database, and it lets you move on to the next field. If you are done creating fields, choose the D\underline{o}ne button.

When you're done, your database is ready for you to add some data. But wait! How come it looks like a spreadsheet? Shouldn't it look more, um, database-y? Well, the odd thing about databases is that they can look like darned near anything. Read the following section for the details on viewing your database.

## *Selecting a view*

One reason why people sometimes get a bit confused when using a database tool is that the tool can show you data in different ways, called *views*. Unlike your Rolodex, which has real pages that you can touch, feel, and scribble notes on, computer databases are pretty ethereal. The computer can display the data in various ways, depending on what you tell it to do.

Works has a total of four views. Two of those are views you will use most often for casually browsing through your records: the *Form view* and the *List view.* These are illustrated by Figures 12-5 and 12-6. Works also has a special *Form Design view,* which lets you design the page you see in Form view, specifying where each field appears. The fourth view is the *Report view,* which sounds useful, but is a bit too weird for most people to use easily. See Chapter 15 for a cursory discussion of using that view. Some tasks can be done only in one view or another. For example, you can add fields only while in List view or Form Design view.

**Figure 12-5:**
My database for cataloging photographs in Form view, showing record 6.

**Figure 12-6:**
Same
database as
Figure 12-5,
in List view,
showing
records 1-6.

| ☑ | | Serial | Subject | Photographer | Color? | Width | Height | |
|---|---|--------|---------|--------------|--------|-------|--------|---|
| ☒ | 1 | 00001 | Golden eagle | Johnson, George | TRUE | 5 1/2 | 3 1/4 | |
| ☒ | 2 | 00002 | Black bear cub | Ferguson, Al | TRUE | 2 1/4 | 2 1/4 | |
| ☒ | 3 | 00003 | Jerusalem artichoke | Adams, Alicia | TRUE | 2 1/2 | 5 | |
| ☒ | 4 | 00004 | Curly dock leaves | Adams, Alicia | TRUE | 5 | 7 | |
| ☒ | 5 | 00005 | Laser light, abstract | Hogg, Charley | TRUE | 10 | 8 | |
| ☒ | 6 | 00006 | Wachusett sunset | Hogg, Charley | TRUE | 10 | 8 | |

Zoom 100% — + ◄

Press ALT to choose commands, or F2 to edit. | NUM | 6 | 6/6

If you have just finished creating a new database, you are looking at it in the List view.

✔ *Form view* lets you look at data the way you do on your Rolodex: one record at a time. Figure 12-5 shows a database in Form view.

✔ *List view* looks like a pad of lined paper on which you copied all the information from your Rolodex, using columns for the fields of, say, Name, Address, and Phone Number. You can see several records at once. Figure 12-6 shows the same database as Figure 12-5, but in List view. In this view, your database is a big spreadsheet-like table with rows and columns. The rows, which are numbered along the left side, are individual records. (Blank rows are records in which you haven't entered data yet.) The columns are your fields.

List view looks and works a lot like a spreadsheet! Many of the methods and commands that work in spreadsheets — such as selecting, formatting, copying, pasting, and dragging — also work in the List view of a database document.

✔ *Form Design view* lets you edit the Form view. It provides features that let you move, resize, reformat, or otherwise change how the fields will look in Form view. You can also add text, such as headings or explanations, or even add illustrations to your forms by using Form view.

To switch between views, you can do any of the following:

✔ Click the List view, Form view, or Form Design button on the toolbar. (They are the buttons just right of the **B/U** (Bold/Underline) buttons. If you don't know which is which, pause your mouse cursor over one and read the tiny yellow tag that appears.)

✔ Press the F9 key to go to Form view.

✔ Press Shift+F9 to go to List view.

✔ Press Ctrl+F9 to go to Form Design view.

✔ Choose View⇨List, Form (or Form Design) from the menu bar.

## *Moving and resizing fields*

If you don't like the position or size of your fields in either Form view or List view, changes are a simple matter. Just remember the following:

- When changing how things look in Form view, you must use Form Design view.
- When changing how things look in List view, you can make changes in List view.

### *Moving where fields appear in Form view*

To move the position of a field as it appears in Form view, do the following:

1. **Switch to Form Design view. (Click the Form Design button on the toolbar or Choose View⇨Form Design from the menu bar or press Ctrl+F9.)**

2. **Click and drag the field where you want it.**

   To move a bunch of fields at once, select them first. One easy way is to hold down the Ctrl button and click each field that you want to move. Then click and drag the whole lot of them.

### *Moving where fields appear in List view*

To move a field (column) in List view, do this:

1. **Click the top cell of the column — the one with the field name in it. This action selects the field/column.**

2. **Click on that top cell and drag the column to the left or the right. A dark vertical line that appears between columns indicates where the column will be placed when you release the mouse button.**

### *Resizing fields as displayed in Form view*

If a field is too small to display your data in Form view, you can resize the field. You may have to move adjoining fields to allow for the change in size.

1. **Switch to Form Design view. (Click the Form Design button on the toolbar or Choose View⇨Form Design from the menu bar or press Ctrl+F9.)**

2. **Click the underlined area to the right of the field name. The field is highlighted, and three tiny gray squares, called *handles*, appear in the highlight. Figure 12-7 shows a blown-up view of the highlighted area.**

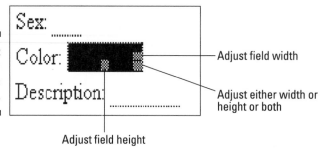

**Figure 12-7:**
Getting a
handle on
field size.

Adjust field width

Adjust either width or
height or both

Adjust field height

✔ To make a field wider, drag the handle at the center of the right edge to the right. To make the field higher (to add lines), drag the handle at the center of the bottom edge down. The handle at the corner lets you drag both width and height at the same time.

✔ To adjust field size more precisely in Form view, click the underlined area next to the field name; then choose Format➪Field Size to get the Field Size dialog box. Enter a width (how many characters) and a height (how many rows) for the data entry.

### Resizing fields in List view

To resize a field (change column width) in List view, you can either drag a column edge or use the Field Width dialog box:

✔ To change the width of the column by dragging, move your cursor to the gray row at the top of the columns, where the field names are. In this row, slowly move your mouse pointer across the right-hand edge of the column that you want to change. When the pointer changes to a double-headed-arrow-sort-of-deal with the word Adjust attached, click and drag the column edge left or right.

✔ To set the width of a column more precisely, use the Field Width dialog box. First click any cell of that column to select it. Then choose Format ➪Field Width from the menu bar. When the Field Width dialog box appears, type a number slightly larger than the maximum number of characters you expect for data in this field and press the Enter key.

To make your field size just large enough to hold the longest entry in your database, double-click on the field name (in the top cell of the column).

# Navigating in Different Views

An important part of your basic training at the database is navigation. We don't want our metaphoric half-tracks wandering all over our metaphoric field. Here's how to get around with minimal casualties and good gas mileage.

If you've applied a filter, some records will be hidden as you navigate your database. To see them all, choose Record⇨Show>>All Records from the menu bar. See Chapter 14 for more information on using filters.

## *Navigating in Form view or Form Design view*

In Form or Form Design view, you're looking at a representation of a page that is 8 ¹/₂ x 11 inches unless you've fooled with the Page Setup commands. You can look at any part of the page or type anywhere on the page.

To scroll around vertically or horizontally, use the scroll bars on the right side and bottom of the document window (see Chapter 2 if you don't recall how to use scroll bars).

To move around vertically on the page, you can also use the navigation keys (arrows, Home, End, PgUp, and Pg Dn).

The dashed lines indicate page boundaries, so you need to keep your fields above and to the left of them.

To advance from one field to the next, press the Tab key. Press Shift+Tab to move in the opposite direction.

To move between records:

- ✔ To advance to the next record, press the Tab key after the last entry on the page (record).

- ✔ Another way to advance one record is to press Ctrl+PgDn. To go backward, press Ctrl+PgUp.

- ✔ Yet another way to advance or go back one record is to click the inner left- or right-arrow in this gadget in the bottom-left border of your document window:

- ✔ To go to the first or last record in your database, click the outer left- or right-arrow in that gadget.

- ✔ Or, to go to the first record, press Ctrl+Home; to go to the last record, press Ctrl+End.

## *Navigating in List view*

Navigating a database in List view is almost exactly like navigating a spreadsheet, so if you know how to do that, you're in fat city. If not, here's the scoop.

To look around your database in List view, use the scroll bars on the right side and bottom of the document window (see Chapter 2 if you don't recall how to use scroll bars). To see more fields, use the horizontal scroll bar; to see more records, use the vertical scroll bar.

To change a cell (the intersection of a row and column), simply click that cell. (Notice that your mouse cursor is a big, fat plus sign in the database tool, as it is in the spreadsheet tool.) Around the cell appears a rectangle that Microsoft calls the *highlight*. This highlight indicates which cell you're about to type in, edit, format, or otherwise muck around with.

Table 12-1 describes how to move the highlight by using keys on the keyboard.

| Table 12-1 | Navigating the List View with Keys |
|---|---|
| *Navigation Key* | *Where It Moves the Highlight* |
| Left-arrow/right-arrow | One column's worth left or right |
| Up-arrow/down-arrow | One row's worth up or down |
| Tab | Go to the next field |
| Shift+Tab | Move backward to the preceding field |
| PgUp/PgDn | One window's worth up or down |
| Ctrl+PgUp/PgDn | One window's worth left or right, respectively |
| Home | To the first column of the row you're currently in |
| End | To the last column in the row you're currently in |
| Ctrl+Home | To the first row, first column |
| Ctrl+End | To the last row and column in the database |
| Ctrl+down-arrow | To the last row in the database |
| Ctrl+up-arrow | To the first row in the database |

# Entering Data

To enter data into your database, you generally fill out one record at a time, starting with the first record. In a nutshell, the procedure is just to click on a cell (List view) or in a field (Form view) and type!

Use any of the techniques mentioned in the preceding section to move from one field or record to the next. A popular method is to use the Tab key to advance from one field to the next (Shift+Tab to go backward). If you press Tab at the end of one record, you'll automatically move to the first field of the next record.

- ✔ To put a new record into your database, just add it at the end: press Ctrl+End in Form view; press Ctrl+End and then pressTab in List view.

- ✔ When you use other-than-General formatting for a field, the appearance of the data you enter may change after you enter it. This procedure can be a convenience for data entry. For example, if you choose a Date format of the form, "January 5, 1996," you can enter the date as 1/5/96, but Works will display it as January 5, 1996.

- ✔ For fields formatted as TRUE/FALSE fields, you can enter the number 1 for True, or 0 for False; or you can type the words TRUE or FALSE.

- ✔ If the symbol ####### appears after you have entered some data, the field is not wide enough to display the data. Make it wider! (A quick fix is to double-click the field name in the top cell of the column, if you're in List view.)

# Creating an Example Database

It's show time! Here's an example of how to create a database. The example is a very simple, five-field database for cataloging photographs.

The Rule of This Design as dictated by its omnipotent creator (me) is that there shall be five fields: Photographer, Subject, Width, Height, and Color?.

The standards for the data are as follows: the Photographer field contains the last name first, a comma, and then the first name; the Subject field contains some short description of what's in the photo; the Width and Height fields give the dimension in inches and $1/8$ fractions of an inch; and the Color? field is a TRUE/FALSE field indicating whether the photo is in color (TRUE) or black and white (FALSE).

1. **To start a new database document, press Alt+F and then N. When the Task Launcher appears, choose the** Works Tools **card and then the** Database **button.**

2. **A First-time Help dialog box may appear. If it does, click the button marked** To create a new database.

3. **The Create Database dialog box arises. Type** Photographer **into the** Field name **box and click the** Add **button. (Do not press the Enter key.) We'll use the General format, so there's no need to change the format. A new, blank field form appears in the Create Database dialog box.**

4. **Type** Subject **into the** Field name **box and click the** Add **button.**

5. **Type** Serial **into the** Field name **box. In the** Format **area, choose** Serialized. **Click the** Add **button.**

6. **Type** Width **into the** Field name **box. In the** Format **area, choose** Fraction. **In the** Appearance **box, choose** 1/8. **Click the** Add **button.**

7. **Type** Height **into the** Field name **box. In the** Format **area, choose** Fraction. **In the** Appearance **box, choose** 1/8. **Click the** Add **button.**

8. **Type** Color? **into the** Field name **box. In the** Format **area, choose** Fraction. **In the** Appearance **box, scroll to the bottom and choose** True/False. **Click the** Add **button and then the** Done **button.**

Your database is created! Well, the structure of it, at least. It's still empty of data.

Now start entering data. You can do this in either List view (which is what you are looking at) or Form view. Simply click a cell (in List view) or a field (in Form view) and type. Or you can use the Tab key to advance to the next field.

## Printing Your Database

Printing databases is pretty much like printing anything else in Works, so for the general details, see Chapter 4. There are a couple of peculiarities about printing databases, however.

✔ When you print in Form view, you normally print one record on a page. If your records are small, you may prefer to combine them on a page. To do so, choose File⇨Page Setup to get a Page Setup dialog box. Click the Other Options card in this box, and then click the check box marked Page breaks between records to clear the check mark from it. Adjust the spacing between records by clicking the up-/down-arrows in the Space between records box.

✔ When you print in List view, you normally see just data, no headings. You can have the field and record headings print out if you choose. You can also have gridlines printed. Choose File➪Page Setup to get a Page Setup dialog box. Click the Other Options card in this box. Click the appropriate check box: the one marked `Print gridlines` and/or the one marked `Print record and field labels`.

✔ To force a page break at a particular point in a List view of records, first select the row you want at the top of the next page. (Click the numbered gray button at the leftmost end of that row). Then choose Format➪Insert Page Break.

✔ To force a page break between columns in a List view, first select the column you want on the next page. (Click the gray button with the field name at the top of the column.) Then choose Format➪Insert Page Break.

✔ To print only certain records, first mark them: switch to List view and click the check box in the leftmost column of each row that you want to print. Choose Record➪Show➪2 Marked Records from the menu bar and then print. See "Using Selected Records: Marking and Hiding" in Chapter 14.

# Saving Your Work

Databases are in dire need of salvation — yours is no exception. I urge you to save your work promptly because I don't want to be accused of making a "salvator" dally. What I mean to say (having perhaps exercised a little too much artistic license) is that you should save your database document as a file, regularly, so that you don't lose data.

Saving your database document is very much like saving any other Works document, so see Chapter 2 if you need more information. For basic information on files and disks, see Chapter 1. For more on Salvador Dali, see your local library.

The executive summary on saving is as follows:

✔ Unless you save your document as a file on a disk, the document vaporizes when you stop Works or turn off your PC.

✔ Save early and often. You never know when the power will fail; if that happens, your work may be lost.

✔ Save your document either by clicking the Save button in the toolbar (the one with the diskette icon) or by choosing File➪Save.

✔ If you're working on a particular record in the database when you save it, you will be returned to that record when you reopen it.

# Chapter 13

# Making Changes in Your Database

**In This Chapter**

▶ Editing in the formula bar

▶ Inserting and removing fields

▶ Formatting fields

▶ Adding, inserting, and deleting records

▶ Copying and moving data

*A*ll is flux, and before you can say *tempus fugit*, you may need to make some changes to your database. Your friends move, so you have to change your address database; your customers grow successful (thanks to you) and sprout new divisions, so you have to create a Division field in your customer database; or maybe you just decide to make your database a bit more readable. Here's how to keep your database up to date and looking snazzy!

## Editing Data and Field Names with the Formula Bar

The story of *Why Editing Is Done with a Formula Bar:* Editors traditionally do some of their best work in bars. Some have done so since infancy, when they worked in crayon, sitting at bars where they were able to get a nice, warm mug of baby formula. Today, in commemoration of that tradition, you, too, can work within a formula bar to edit data in your database.

(Brief pause for groans. Thank you.)

Seriously, folks — when you need to change some data or a field name in your database, the tool you use is called the formula bar.

To find the formula bar as shown in Figure 13-1, look just under the toolbar. The formula bar's purpose is to make editing a little easier. It works just the same as the formula bar in the Works spreadsheet, if you're familiar with that.

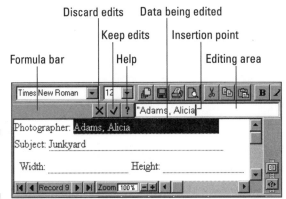

**Figure 13-1:**
Using the
formula bar.

The formula bar works the same in List view and Form view, allowing you to edit data values (someone's last name, for example, in an address database). In Form Design view, you can also use the formula bar to edit field names.

✔ To edit data, click the data; then either press the F2 key or click the formula bar.

✔ To edit a field name, first switch to Form Design view; click the field name; then either press F2 or click the formula bar.

In addition to editing data, you can also edit a field name in List view: Click anywhere in the column; then choose Format➪Field from the menu bar. Edit the field name in the Format dialog box that appears and click the OK button.

The formula bar works like this:

1. **Works copies the data value or field name into the white text box of the formula bar.**

2. **You edit the data value or field name in that text box.**

3. **When you're done, you either click the check mark button on the formula bar or just press the Enter key.**

   The new, edited stuff replaces the old stuff in the database.

In the formula bar, you use the *insertion point* — the vertical line that you also see in the Works word processor — to edit text and data. The insertion point is where characters appear when you type and where they vanish when you backspace or delete.

To move the insertion point, move your mouse pointer over the formula bar, which causes the pointer to change to an I-beam shape. Position that I-beam where you want to type or delete something and then click. The insertion point jumps there. When you type, the characters are inserted at the insertion point. When you press the Backspace key, the character *before* the insertion point gets deleted. Press the Delete key, and the character *after* the insertion point gets vaporized.

If the data you're editing is very long, you may not be able to click near the end. In that case, click where you can and use the navigation keys to move the insertion point.

The *X* next to the formula is the "whoops" button. Clicking this *X* has the same result as pressing the Esc key. Either one abandons your edits and leaves whatever you were editing in its original state.

Clicking the check mark has the same result as pressing the Enter key. Either one enters the contents of the formula bar into the cell.

You can also edit data right in its cell in List view: Just double-click the cell, and the insertion point you need for editing appears in the cell.

# *The Protection Racket*

If you find that Works complains when you try to edit data, the complaint probably arises because the field that you're working in is *protected* against data changes. This situation happens when you use certain TaskWizards. Here's what to do to defeat this protection scheme:

1. **Switch to either List view or Form Design view.**

2. **Click the protected field.**

3. **Choose Format➪Protection from the menu bar to get a Format Protection dialog box.**

4. **If you find a check mark in the** Protect field **check box, click that check mark to clear it. Then click the** OK **button in that dialog box.**

On the other hand, you may want to use this protection racket yourself. By protecting a field, you can help avoid accidental changes to important data. This protection is especially valuable if you are working with another person who may not realize how important some data value is. To protect a field, you follow the same four steps just listed, only you turn the check mark *on* in Step 4 by clicking the P̲rotect field check box.

# Conducting Field Exercises

Strategically speaking, there is a time to advance upon a field and a time to retreat from a field. This stratagem is general knowledge (known by generals). Likewise, in database work, there's a time to add fields and a time to remove them. Well, no problem (as certain teenagers and hotel personnel are tiresomely fond of saying instead of "You're welcome"). Here's how to add or remove a field.

## Adding new fields

You can add new fields in either the List view or the Form Design view. The advantage of using List view is that the process is very simple. The advantage of using Form Design view is that, after you add a field, you are then conveniently in the right view for positioning or sizing the field. You decide!

### Adding new fields in List view

In List view, the fields are columns. Here's how to create new fields in that view:

1. **New fields are columns that go to the right or left of existing columns. Click in the column *next to which* you want to add a new column.**

2. **Choose R̲ecord⇨I̲nsert Field from the menu bar; then choose 1̲ Before (to put a new field to the *left* of your chosen column) or choose 2̲ After (to put a new field to the *right* of your chosen column).**

   An Insert Field dialog box graces your screen, bearing a familiar face: It looks and works just like the Create Database dialog box you used in the beginning. See the section of Chapter 12, "New fields of endeavor," if you need instructions.

3. **Type in a name for the field (and a special format if you need it) and choose the A̲dd button.**

4. **For additional fields, repeat Step 3.**

5. **When you're done adding fields, click the D̲one button in the Insert Field dialog box.**

### Adding new fields in Form Design view

Here's how to add fields in Form Design view:

1. **Click where you want the field to appear. Don't click to the right or below any dashed line you see at edges of the window: That's the page margin area, which is visible when your Works window is sufficiently large.**

   A set of coordinates tells you where you are on the page, if you care. Look in the upper-left corner of the Works window, just under the font box in the text bar. The number after X gives the horizontal position from the left edge of the page; the number after Y gives the vertical position from the bottom edge.

2. **Type a field name of fewer than 15 characters, followed by a colon (:) — as in** Last Name: **— and press Enter.**

   A dialog box appears, asking for a field name and format, just as the dialog box appeared when you first created your database. Click the OK button when you're done.

When you enter a field name in Form Design view, don't forget to end the field name with a colon. If you don't, Works assumes that you are just putting an annotation on the form, not adding a new field.

## Removing fields

Removing a field is so easy as to be a little scary. Removing a field is scary because when you remove a field, you also remove all the data that is in it — data that represents a lot of work on somebody's part. But if removing a field along with all the data that is in it is what you really intend to do, go for it.

Removing a field in List view is a little safer than removing a field in Form Design view because you can "undo" the deletion if you accidentally delete the wrong field. For no particularly good reason that I can think of, Works allows you to undo (with Ctrl+Z) in List view, but not in Form Design view.

- ✔ **Form Design view:** Just click the field name and press the Delete key. A warning box appears on the scene and asks, Delete this field and all of its contents? and warns that you won't be able to undo this delete. If you really do want to delete the field, click the OK button.

- ✔ **List view:** First, click anywhere in that field's column; then click Record⇨Delete Field in the menu bar. A warning box appears, asking whether you in fact want to Permanently delete this information?. If you really do want to delete the field, click the OK button.

Zap! It's dead, Jim.

---

### Laying waste to a field

Invading armies used to sow salt in their enemies' fields. This trick turns out to be a bad idea if you want to use that field later. Don't do the modern equivalent when you eliminate fields in your database, unless you're sure that you won't want that data ever again.

Removing a field is pretty simple, but saving your database just before doing so is a good idea, in case you mess up. To save your database in its current state, press Ctrl+S or click the Save button in the toolbar.

If you think that you may want to access the field and its data again sometime, do this: Before you delete the field, save your unmodified database with a new name, using the File⇨Save As command. A good way to rename the field is by appending a number to the filename. For example, if the name was Hummels (full name, Hummels.wdb), use Hummels 01 (full name, Hummels 01.wdb). Because both old and new files begin the same way, they can stay together in the alphabetized file listings on your PC and be easier to find. After you have done this step, delete your field and do another File⇨Save As command using the original name (Hummels) again.

---

# Adding, Inserting, and Deleting Records

Many unprincipled people have wished, over the years, that they had the ability to add or delete certain records in their files. If only they knew how easy adding or deleting records is to do when you've got a Works database.

## Adding a record

When you want to add another record to your database, the easiest way to add one is to add it to the end of your database:

- ✔ In Form view, press Ctrl+End.
- ✔ In List view, press Ctrl+down arrow and then press down arrow again.

A *record* is an entire page or row of related data, not just one piece of data. (If you are of the pre-compact disc, or *vinyl*, generation, think of these records as albums, not singles.)

## *Inserting or deleting a record*

To add a record at a particular point in your database, you *insert* it. First, indicate to Works where you want to insert the new record. In Form view, just move to that record. In List view, click that row. Then do the following:

- ✔ **To insert a record:** Choose Record⇨Insert Record from the menu bar. Or click the Insert Record button. If you're uncertain which button that is, slowly move your mouse pointer across the buttons and read the labels that pop up. A blank record appears for you to fill in.

- ✔ **To delete a record:** Choose Record⇨Delete Record from the menu bar. That record is then deleted and you are left gazing upon the next higher record in the database.

All the records following the one you inserted or deleted are renumbered.

You can alternatively delete just the *contents* of a record rather than the record itself. This trick is useful if you are replacing an item listed in your database (say, a deceased computer in your inventory). In List view, click the row number (in the gray area on the left) to highlight the entire row — or highlight just as much as you want to delete — and then press the Delete key. The record is now blank (except for serialized fields), and you can enter new data into it.

# *Copying and Moving Data*

Years ago, in school examinations, the consequences of copying data were severe. That's too bad, because today copying is an essential skill for entering data into databases. (So *there*, Mr. Schweinkopf!) Copying is a great time-saver and helps enforce your rules for consistent data, such as using *copy paper* and not *copier paper.*

In any database, many records may have exactly the same data. In a pediatrician's medical database, the term *otitis media* (middle ear infection) would sum up the better part of a week's work. Kids get ear infections like lawns get dandelions. It's surprising that there aren't fast food-style drive-through kids' ear exam and dispensary outlets. ("Stick your head in the clown's mouth, Junior; we'll get a toy at the window with our antibiotics.")

Anyway, what a boon to the bored pediatrician-in-a-box to be able to just copy the Diagnosis field data from one encounter record to another, rather than retype it. Copying prevents typos, too. Nine out of ten doctors recommend copying.

# Copying with the Clipboard

Newly minted military officers sometimes have an unfortunate tendency to strut around with clipboards as if the clipboard somehow enhanced their, um, likelihood of reproductive success. Well, it turns out that they were right. The Windows *Clipboard,* an invisible holding area that you can copy things onto and then paste from, can enhance your success in reproducing (copying) data.

To copy data from one record to another, I suggest that you switch to List view — working in List view is just easier. (Press Shift+F9 to switch.) To copy a single piece of data, do this:

1. **Click the cell that you want to copy and press Ctrl+C to put a copy on the invisible Windows Clipboard.**

   (Or instead of pressing Ctrl+C, click the Copy button, the one to the right of the button with the scissors icon in the toolbar.)

2. **Click the cell where you want a copy and press Ctrl+V to paste from the (still invisible) Windows Clipboard.**

   (Or instead of pressing Ctrl+V, use the Paste button, the one with the clipboard icon in the toolbar.)

You can also make a bunch of copies of that single cell (such as you may need if you get a busload of kids at your Doc-in-the-Box, all with *otitis media*). Copy as in Step 1. When you go to paste, click and drag in that same column across several rows; this action highlights a bunch of cells. Then press Ctrl+V. Each cell gets a copy of the original cell.

You can also copy multiple fields (such as multiple fields to duplicate the date and the diagnosis) at once, as long as the two fields are in adjoining columns. Highlight any group of cells in the row that you want to copy and press Ctrl+C. Then click the leftmost cell where you want to paste a copy and press Ctrl+V. To paste copies in multiple rows, highlight the leftmost cells in several rows before pressing Ctrl+V.

# Copying and moving by dragging

Another way to move or copy data is by dragging (in either List view or Form view). To copy data by dragging it, hold down the Ctrl key; then click and drag a copy of that data to any other field. To move data, simply click it and drag it to the new field.

# *Applying and Changing Formats*

Just like your mother said, appearances are important. You can do a number of things to change the way your fields and data appear in a Works database. You choose a *Field* format for your fields when you first create your database (see Chapter 12) or add a new field. You can use other formats, however, including

- **Alignment:** Whether data is left or right justified or centered, for example.
- **Font:** What typeface and style the data appears in.
- **Border:** For borders around data in selected fields.
- **Shading:** To apply a background color or shade to data.

To change any of these formats, do the following:

1. **Choose either List view or Form Design view.**
2. **Click the field to select it (or select several fields by highlighting them).**
3. **Choose Format from the menu bar; then choose either Field, Alignment, Font, Border, or Shading.**

The Format dialog box of Figure 13-2 appears, displaying the card that matches your choice in Step 3 in the preceding numbered list of steps.

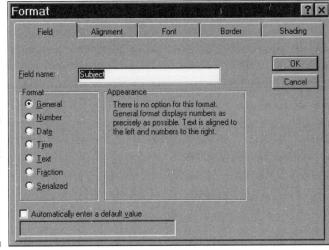

**Figure 13-2:**
The Format
dialog box,
where
appear-
ance is
everything.

✔ In the Field card, you can specify the same sort formatting that you specified when you first created the field, telling Works to display the value as a date, a fraction, or a dollar amount, for example.

If you change a field from General or Text to a Date or Time format, you may have to reenter the data in that field.

✔ In the Alignment card, you can left- or right-justify or center text in its field area (or in its cell, in List view). In List view, you can choose to make text wrap around within a cell; if your rows are higher than a single character height, you can also align text vertically. In Form Design view, you can choose to remove extra spaces between fields on the same line by clicking the Slide to left check box.

✔ The Font card works just as it does elsewhere in Works. See Chapter 2 for more information.

✔ The Border card lets you put an outline around a field, for emphasis, if you like. Click a line style from the list presented. Click the top line-style box (with no line in it) to turn off a border.

✔ The Shading card lets you apply a background color or pattern to the field. Choose a pattern from the Pattern box; patterns are made up of two colors, given by your selection of foreground and background colors. Unless you have a color printer or don't intend to print at all, sticking to Auto for both colors is best.

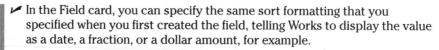

"I JUST BOUGHT THIS NEW COMPUTER THAT COMES WITH ADDITIONAL MEMORY, AND FOR AN EXTRA $100 DOLLARS, IT'LL CARRY A GRUDGE. BUT SERIOUSLY FOLKS,..."

# Chapter 14

# Finding and Filtering in Your Database

*W*hen interrogating an enemy prisoner, a certain reluctance to impart information is to be expected. When interrogating a database, you have the opposite problem: The database offers too much information — volunteering, as it were, name, rank, serial number, birth date, sock size, and mother's middle name, a thousand times over. Finding out just one piece of data becomes tremendously difficult.

You have three ways to solve this problem and find the data that you're looking for with Works' database tool:

✔ **Find:** The simplest solution, if you're looking for those records that contain one particular piece of data (such as the word *tubular*), is to have the database tool *find* records containing that specific word, number, or phrase.

✔ **Filter:** If you're looking for the records that contain some combination of information in specific fields (such as *tubular* in the Description field and the number 90210 in the zip code field), you apply a *filter*.

✔ **Sort:** If you just need an ordered list — ordered alphabetically or numerically by the contents of a particular field — you perform a *sort*.

If you apply a filter or a find, Works shows you the records that you requested and *hides* the rest. To see all the records again, click View⇨Show⇨All Records.

# Finding Specific Data

To locate records that contain a specific word, phrase, or number, the simplest thing you can do is to perform a find. (The Find command is very much like the Find commands in the word processor or spreadsheet, if you're familiar with those.)

You can tell Works to find either the *first* instance of that word, phrase, or number, or to show you *all* instances. Here's how to do it:

1. **Press Ctrl+Home so that Works begins its search with the first record of the database.**

2. **Choose Edit⇨Find from the menu bar.**

   A small but helpful Find dialog box appears.

3. **Type the word, number, or phrase you're searching for in the box marked** Find what.

   You must specify lowercase or uppercase. Searching for *Copy Paper* won't find records containing *copy paper*.

   Type only as much as you remember or need. To find copy paper, printer paper, or any kind of paper, type **paper**. (On the other hand, don't type too little: *pa* will also find padding and packing material if those words are lying about in your database.)

   The symbol ? can substitute for a single character and help you find a broad range of records. When searching for zip codes, for example, the number 0792? will find all the zip codes beginning with 0792.

   The symbol * can substitute for one or more characters as long as the * is preceded by at least one other character. For example, M*. can find Mr., Mrs., and Ms. (but not Miss — because this particular search specifies that a period must come at the end).

4. **To find all records that contain your word, phrase, or number, click** All records **in the** Match **area of the Find dialog box. To find just the next record, click** Next record.

5. **Click the** OK **button.**

If you choose to find All records in Step 4, Works shows you only those records that meet your search text criterion. It hides the others! When you're done reviewing or printing the result of your Find, choose Record⇨Show>>1 All Records to reveal all the records in your database again.

# Using Selected Records: Marking and Hiding

Do you have certain records that you just don't want to appear on your printout, on your screen, or in your database report? Well, do as millions do when the auditor comes to call: hide those records! (Not that I recommend hiding those particular records; auditors know about databases, too!). Works uses three concepts to help you hide or display only the records that you want:

- ✔ **Hiding** is a way to make records invisible in List or Form view, in printouts, or in reports.

- ✔ **Showing** is the opposite of hiding.

- ✔ **Marking** is a convenient way to identify a group of records for hiding or showing.

To hide an individual record, first either click it in List view or move to it in Form view; then choose Record⇨Hide Record from the menu bar. To show hidden records, choose Record⇨Show>>4 Hidden Records.

To hide several records, mark them first: In List view, click the check box in the leftmost column (*marking column*) of each row that you want to hide. (To mark a group that's all together, click the top record's check box; then drag down the marking column.) In Form view, choose Record⇨Mark Record for each record. Then choose Record⇨Show>>3 Unmarked Records from the menu bar.

To hide most of the records and only show a few, mark the records that you want to *show,* by using the method the preceding paragraph describes. Then choose Record⇨Show>>2 Marked Records from the menu bar.

To show all records, hidden, marked, or otherwise, choose Record⇨Show>>1 All Records from the menu bar.

To clear all marks, go to List view and click the check mark at the very top of the marking column.

# Filtering Your Data

Doing the Find command is nice and simple, but it can be done equally well in the spreadsheet tool or even the word processor. The database tool earns its keep when you need to find records with certain combinations of data in various fields, such as all the members of your organization who have more than two kids and who live out of town. Or maybe you want to find members who have contributed $100 or more, in the hope of pressing them for another contribution.

To find these big givers, you would need to filter your data — strain out all the poor of purse or soul. When Works filters your data, it goes through your database, record by record, comparing what's in those records to certain criteria that you've given it and hiding from view those records that don't meet the criteria. Did Widow Jones give only $50 from her pension? If you are filtering for an amount of $100 or more in your Contributions field, Works hides Mrs. Jones' proud record. (Sorry, there is no filtering for moral character.)

The gadget that you use for applying a filter is the Filter dialog box, shown in Figure 14-1. To get one of these little gems:

✔ Choose Tools⇨Filters from the menu bar, or

✔ Click the Filters button on the toolbar.

You can have many criteria at once.

Filters are stored by name.    Each criterion has three parts.

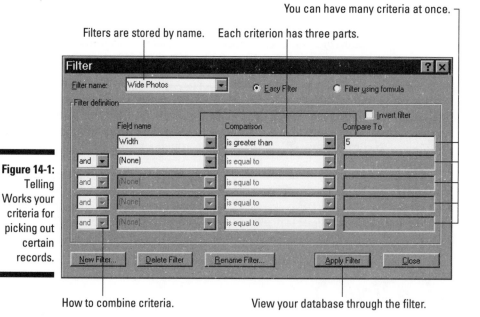

**Figure 14-1:**
Telling
Works your
criteria for
picking out
certain
records.

How to combine criteria.          View your database through the filter.

The first time that you create a filter, Works displays a First-time Help dialog box and lets you choose to either take a tour of filtering or get down to work. Take the tour once (click the `Quick tour of filters` button); then, when you are returned to the dialog box, click the `Don't display this message in the future` check box if you want to keep this dialog box from showing up again. Finally, click the `To create and apply a new filter` button.

If you have not previously created any filters for your database, a Filter Name dialog box springs up; enter a descriptive name that's no more than 15 characters long for your filter. For example, if you are filtering to display big contributors and hide the rest of the data, you can type **Big Contributor**.

The trick to applying a filter is figuring out how to describe the data that you're looking for. Having the capability to write regular sentences, such as "Show me all the records for families with more than two kids and who live out of town" would be nice. It would be nice if we could all go to Barbados for the winter, too, but that's not going to happen any time soon, either. Filters in Works are a little bit like sentences, but not like sentences that your sixth-grade English teacher would approve of.

To construct the description of what records you want, you need three pieces of information:

- **The field name:** This is where you want Works to look — for example, the No. of Children field if you had such a field and wanted to find families based on the number of children they have.

- **The "comparison":** The way to test the data in the field — for example, to test that the data in the No. of Children field is greater than some value.

- **The "compare to" value:** What you want Works to compare the data to — such as *2* for two kids.

For a single criterion, you enter these three pieces of information in the top, three-part line of the Filter dialog box. The `Field name` and `Comparison` boxes allow you to choose from drop-down lists that are available when you click the down arrow adjoining those text boxes.

Some other examples of single-criterion filters are:

- The entry in a No. of Children field *is equal to* 2.

- The entry in a Description field *contains the word* Mikado.

- The entry in a Town field *is not* Mudville.

- The entry in an Age field *is greater than or equal to* 21.

Here's how to perform a single-criterion filter, step by step. Performing a single-criterion filter is like building a sentence out of three parts; when you're all done, you can read the three parts in sequence, and the parts read like a sentence.

1. **Choose Tools⇨Filters from the menu bar.**

   If you have not previously created any filters for this database, the tiny New Filter dialog box pops up and asks you to enter a name for your new filter. Do so.

   The Filter dialog box now takes up residence on your screen.

   If you have previously created filters, the name of your most recent creation appears in the Filter name box, and the filter criteria are displayed. You can click the down arrow adjoining the filter name to choose from previous filters. To create a new filter, click the New Filter button in the dialog box and enter a filter name in the New Filter dialog box that pops up.

2. **Choose a field: Click the down-arrow button next to the box marked** Field name**; then click any field name in the list that drops down.**

   Works has tentatively chosen the first field name in your database, and that field name is initially displayed here. Pick whatever field you need Works to search through.

3. **Choose how to compare: Click the down-arrow button next to the box marked** Comparison**; then click any comparison in the list that drops down.**

   Works has tentatively chosen *equal to* only because equal to is the first comparison in the list. Choose any comparison that you like.

   For purposes of comparison:

   > Later dates are greater than earlier dates.

   > Later times are greater than earlier times.

   > Letters that fall later in the alphabet are greater than earlier ones.

4. **Choose a value for the comparison: Click the box marked** Compare To **and type in a word, phrase, or number.**

   In filters (unlike in finds), Works doesn't take note of capitalization. The words *Potato* and *potato* are identical as far as Works is concerned.

   You can use the ? and * characters just as you do in a Find command, if you like. See "Finding Specific Data," earlier in this chapter.

When you're done, read across the line that you just entered in the Filter dialog box and combine the three parts of the criterion into a crude sentence, such as "Width . . . is greater than . . . 5." This is your criterion; Works can then find those records in which the Width field contains a number greater than 5.

5. **Press the Enter key or click the** `Apply Filter` **button to execute the filtering.**

If you're not in List view at this point, switch to it (press Shift+F9 if you're in Form view). Seeing what's going on is just easier if you're in List view.

You're done! In List view, you see only those records that meet your criterion. The other records are hidden to get them out of your way. When you're done looking over your success, choose Record⇨Sh̲o̲w̲>>1̲ All Records to make the other records reappear.

# Managing Filters

It takes a bit of work to create a filter; so, for your future convenience, Works saves your filters, storing all that criterion stuff you did in the Filter dialog box. Works saves each filter under the name that you gave it.

The reason that Works saves filters is (A) so that you can fool around with them until they're correct and (B) so that you can easily switch from one to the other, applying them to your database when you need them (see "Applying filters," coming up). The idea is that you're likely to want to have a few standard filters that you make on your database regularly.

One quirk is that you can't have more than eight saved filters — any more than eight, and you have to delete one in order to create a new one.

## Editing filters

One nice change between Works 3 and Works for Windows 95 is that you can edit your filters in Works for Windows 95. Simply return to the Filter dialog box, call up a filter by name, and adjust the criteria. Here's the blow-by-blow description:

1. **Click To̲ols⇨F̲ilters in the menu bar (or click the Filters button on the toolbar).**

The Filter dialog box springs into life.

2. **Click the down arrow adjoining the** Filter name **box and choose the filter that you want to edit from the list.**

3. **Change stuff.**

4. **Click the** Apply Filter **button to see how the filter works.**

To change the name of a filter, click the Rename Filter button. Enter a new name in the Filter Name dialog box that appears.

## Applying filters

To apply the filter that you've used most recently, just press F3.

To apply any other filter to your database:

1. **Choose** Record⇨Apply Filter.

2. **Choose any filter in the Filter list that drops down.**

Zap. You're looking at all the records that match your filter criteria. To restore all the hidden records, choose Record⇨Show>>1 All Records.

## Deleting filters

If a filter isn't quite right or you don't need it anymore, deleting the filter is easy:

1. **Click** Tools⇨Filters **(or click the Filters button on the toolbar).**

   The Filter dialog box forces its attentions upon you.

2. **Click the down-arrow adjoining the** Filter name **box and choose the filter that you want to delete from the list.**

3. **Click the** Delete Filter **button.**

   Works puts up a warning box to make sure that you want to do this. Choose the Yes button.

4. **Click the** Close **button of the Filter dialog box when you're done deleting.**

# Using More Than One Criterion

You can have Works use up to five criteria at one time in a filter, which is why the Filter dialog box has five rows. This feature lets you narrow down or expand your search.

For example, if you want only the families in your database that have more than two kids and also live out of town, you create a second row for the Town field, specifying that the town selected should not equal your town of Mudville. Figure 14-2 shows such a two-part filter.

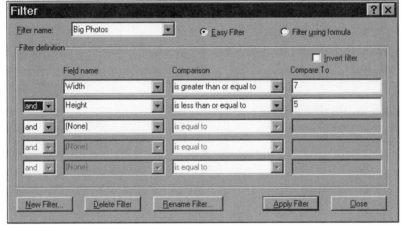

**Figure 14-2:**
Using two
criteria for
a query.

To do more than one criterion, just fill out the first one as usual. Choose either and or or in the box that begins the next line; then fill out the second criterion in a similar fashion. Do the same for any other criteria that you need.

For the example in Figure 14-2, you need to tell Works that both criteria must be met on each record that it finds:

> The photograph width is greater than or equal to 7 inches.
>
> AND
>
> The photograph height is less than or equal to 5 inches.

So you click the and selection.

You use the or selection to specify that a record can meet either criterion. If and is changed to or in Figure 14-2, the search results in photographs that are less than or equal to 5 inches high (but can be any width) as well as photographs that are at least 7 inches wide (but can be any height).

You can also have multiple criteria lines using the same field, one on each line: for example, width is greater than or equal to 7 on the first line *and* width is less than or equal to 14 on the second line. This search would find all photos with a width between 7 and 14 inches.

If you set your logic up incorrectly and end up filtering *out* things that you wanted to filter *in,* click the Invert filter check box in the Filter dialog box. This method is also a good way to look at the filtered-out crowd and make sure that the filter is working correctly.

# Trickier Filtering Using Formulas

Sometimes you need to filter on something that just isn't in your database. For example, in my Photographs database, there's a *width* and a *height*, and I can create a filter for a certain range of those dimensions. But if I wanted a photograph that fits a certain ratio of height to width, I couldn't make a filter using straightforward criteria. No field for *ratio* is available.

One solution to this sort of problem is to use formulas, using field names, mathematical expressions, and Works functions to describe the filter that you want. For example, if I wanted to filter for all photographs where the height was 80 percent or less of the width, I would enter the criterion you see in Figure 14-3.

**Figure 14-3:**
By using a field name and some math, I can filter for height-to-width ratio.

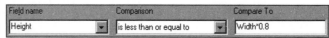

| Field name | Comparison | Compare To |
| --- | --- | --- |
| Height | is less than or equal to | Width*0.8 |

These *functions* I refer to are the same as for the spreadsheet. For a complete listing of functions by type, choose Help⇨Index from the menu bar, and type **functions:** (note the colon). Click any folder that begins with Functions:.

You can use formulas in the Compare To box, for example. In Figure 14-3, I am comparing the value in the Height field to 80 percent of the value in the Width field. The formula in the Compare To box, Width*0.8, does the trick.

Formulas and functions can get pretty powerful and complex. For this sort of work, if you are familiar with computer programming or complex logical and mathematical expressions, you can switch to a Formula view of your filter. In the Filter dialog box, click the Filter using formula option.

This stuff is not for the faint of heart or mathematically challenged!

To get the idea of how this view works, click Easy Filter and set up a few criteria. Then switch to Filter using formula. You can see how field names and operators combine to create a logical expression that evaluates as *true* when the right criterion is met. Some of the operators you can use besides > are =, <, #NOT#, #AND#, #OR#, and the ever-popular <>, which means not equal. If how to use these operators is not obvious to you, then don't use them.

# Chapter 15
# Sorting and Reporting

## In This Chapter

▶ Sorting

▶ Creating standard reports

▶ Viewing your report

▶ Improving the appearance of reports

▶ Reporting on fewer records

▶ Creating sorted reports with subtotals

*N*othing like a few *sorties* on the fields of your database to keep the troops well organized. In the Works database tool, you can sort on any field; in fact, you can sort on several fields at once. You can sort on all sorts of things (sort of). You'll never be "out of sorts" with Works. ... (*Whack! Ouch! Okay, okay, I'll stop with the sordid puns. For now.*)

Sorting not only lets you see records in a convenient order, but it naturally groups things together, such as all the members of your softball league who have similar batting averages. Reports are also an important feature of any database tool. Reports let you list records, summarize data, and organize this information in a nice, readable form to give to other people. Sorts and reports can be also combined with filters so that you can focus on a subset of your database and not have to peruse the whole thing at once.

## Sorting

Give your data its marching orders. Tell the data what order to march in: alphabetical or numerical. Do you want your inventory sorted alphabetically by location or numerically by value? No problem; it's your choice. Do you want your mailing list sorted numerically by zip code and then alphabetically by street name within each zip code? Works does it all.

As it turns out, the spreadsheet tool sorts almost as well as the database tool does. A couple of things make sorting a little easier in the database; but if you already know how to sort in the spreadsheet, the database sorting process may seem very, very familiar to you.

Before you go running off to sort your database, decide how you want it sorted. Works lets you sort by up to three fields. This, in turn, lets you have a list in which your records are sorted by:

Categories (say, by zip code),

Subcategories (by street name within each zip), and

Sub-subcategories (last names on the street)

You can also choose what order you want the various groups in: A–Z and 1, 2, 3 . . . (ascending) or Z–A and . . . 3, 2, 1 (descending).

Here's how to sort. Seeing the results of sorting in List view is generally easier, so if you're currently in Form view, I suggest that you switch to List view (press Shift+F9).

### 1. Choose Record⇨Sort Records from the menu bar.

The first time that you sort, Works displays a First-time Help dialog box and lets you choose to either take a tour of sorting or get down to work. Take the tour once (click the Quick tour of sorting button); then, when you are returned to the dialog box, click the Don't display this message in the future check box if you want to keep this dialog box from showing up again. Finally, click the To sort a database in alphabetic or numeric order button.

The Sort Records dialog box of Figure 15-1 jumps gaily into your lap (so to speak). In Figure 15-1, you can see how Works makes selecting a field for sorting easy by providing a drop-down list of all your field names.

**Figure 15-1:**
Choosing
what fields
to sort on in
the Sort
Records
dialog box.

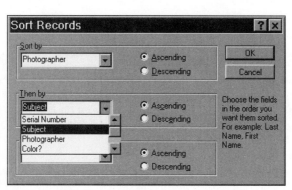

**2. Choose the principal field to sort on.**

Click the down-arrow button next to the box labeled <u>S</u>ort by and then click a field in that list. In a mailing list database, you may choose zip code for this field. In Figure 15-1, I chose the Photographer field in my catalog of photographs.

**3. Choose a sorting direction for that field.**

Click <u>A</u>scending to go from A–Z or in the order 1, 2, 3. . . .

Click <u>D</u>escending to go from Z–A or in the order. . .3, 2, 1.

**4. Optionally, do the same for second field and third field.**

If you fill out the <u>T</u>hen by information (for example, choosing the Street Name field in a mailing list), Works sorts based on that field when two or more records have identical data in the first, or primary, field. (Plenty of folks have the same zip code, for example. The <u>T</u>hen by field lets you sort the records by, say, street name within the zip code.) If you don't fill out this information, the records won't be in any particular order within each zip code. (The final <u>T</u>hen by field does the same thing for duplicate entries in the second field.)

**5. Click the OK button.**

If you're in List view, you see your database with its records shuffled around in the order you specified. Figure 15-2 shows the result of sorting a database by photographer's name and then subject.

**Figure 15-2:**
**Sorting**
**groups of**
**records with**
**identical**
**data**
**together.**

| ☑ | | Serial | Subject | Photographer | Color? | Width | Height |
|---|---|--------|---------|--------------|--------|-------|--------|
| ☒ | 1 | 00004 | Curly dock leaves | Adams, Alicia | TRUE | 5 | 7 |
| ☒ | 2 | 00003 | Jerusalem artichoke | Adams, Alicia | TRUE | 2 1/2 | 5 |
| ☒ | 3 | 00007 | Red sails in the sunset | Adams, Alicia | TRUE | 10 | 8 |
| ☒ | 4 | 00008 | Earthworms | Allworthy, Fred | FALSE | 7 | 5 |
| ☒ | 5 | 00002 | Black bear cub | Ferguson, Al | TRUE | 2 1/4 | 2 1/4 |
| ☒ | 6 | 00005 | Laser light, abstract | Hogg, Charley | TRUE | 10 | 8 |
| ☒ | 7 | 00006 | Wachusett sunset | Hogg, Charley | TRUE | 10 | 8 |
| ☒ | 8 | 00001 | Golden eagle | Johnson, George | TRUE | 5 1/2 | 3 1/4 |

Works sorted on this field . . .

. . . then on this field

✔ Note that records don't keep their original record numbers (the number at the far left of each row in List view) when they're sorted. This is one reason why having a serial number field is important: The serial number field lets you reconstruct the original order by sorting on that field.

✔ You can combine a sort with a filter if you just want to sort a portion of your database. Do the filtering first, which hides all records you don't want. (See "Filtering Your Data" in Chapter 14.) Then sort on the remaining records. When you're done, you can bring all the records back into view by choosing <u>R</u>ecord⇨Sh<u>o</u>w>><u>1</u> All Records.

# Reporting

Reports seem to be what make the world go 'round in some organizations. If that's true for you, Works is ready to help you make a report "heard 'round the world." But first, let me make sure that you know what I'm talking about when I say *report*.

A Works report is intended to be printed, not viewed on your PC screen.

A Works report is made up of two kinds of information:

- ✔ A list of records very much like the List view
- ✔ A summary based on your records

For example, a mail room may have a database consisting of the packages that have shipped, the date of shipping, their destination zip codes, their weights, the shipper, and the cost of shipping. (The mail room may also have a database with the football pool bets; but if the employees are smart, they won't keep their football pool database on the hard disk where the boss can see it.)

From the shipping database, management may want reports on how cost-effective various shippers are; how much product is being shipped by weight every month; how much is shipped to each zip code; the average weight shipped; and other typical nosy management requests. All these reports require either a summary of some sort or a list or both.

## What's a standard report?

To make it easier for you to create a report, Microsoft took some of the basics of report creating and made dialog boxes that help step you through the process of using them. The result of using these dialog boxes is a what I call a *standard report*. You can then make a more elaborate report by modifying this standard report.

A standard report from the shipping department's database may show all the packages sent, together with a summary of total weight and total cost of all the records. Such a standard report would look something like the one shown in Figure 15-3.

The report in Figure 15-3 contains lists of shipments grouped by shipper, with total weight and average weight shipped for each group, and total and average weight at the bottom. Not bad for a little database program!

```
                                          shipping.wdb - Wt. by Shipper

        Shipper    Weight


        CityZIP       0.73
        CityZIP       0.94
        CityZIP       0.21
        CityZIP       0.67
        CityZIP       0.75
        CityZIP       0.95
        CityZIP       0.18
        CityZIP       0.82
        GROUP TOTAL Weight:          5.26
        AVERAGE Weight:              0.66


        DinEx         0.80
        DinEx         0.44
        DinEx         0.63
        GROUP TOTAL Weight:          1.86
        AVERAGE Weight:              0.62


        Hercules      0.05
        Hercules      0.03
        Hercules      0.37

        ---- ( I cut out some stuff here )----


        PSU           0.04
        PSU           0.76
        PSU           0.60
        GROUP TOTAL Weight:          1.40
        AVERAGE Weight:              0.47


        Rural Xpres   0.87
        Rural Xpres   0.58
        Rural Xpres   0.08
        GROUP TOTAL Weight:          1.53
        AVERAGE Weight:              0.51


        Zowiefast     0.98
        Zowiefast     0.80
        Zowiefast     0.96
        Zowiefast     0.76
        Zowiefast     0.86
        GROUP TOTAL Weight:          4.36
        AVERAGE Weight:              0.87


        TOTAL Weight:        14.98
        AVERAGE Weight:       0.58
```

**Figure 15-3:** One of the standard reports Works can make (I chopped out the middle so it would fit on this page).

# What a standard report doesn't give you

A standard report doesn't give you a couple of things that you may want:

✔ First, a standard report doesn't give you a report that gives answers calculated from two or more fields. For example, a report can compute average shipping cost per package by summing all the costs, counting all the records, and dividing the total cost by the total number of packages. Again, you can do this task in Works by modifying a standard report.

✔ Second, it doesn't give you labels and special report formatting to make the report easier to read. Works' database tool has a lot of the same formatting features that the spreadsheet and word-processor tools have, such as different fonts and styles, alignments, and borders.

In this chapter, I look at how to create a standard report and then show you how to do these few useful modifications.

## Creating a standard report

Works makes it fairly simple to create a standard report, but you have to play your cards right! Six different "cards" that you have to fill out are dealt to you by the ReportCreator dialog box.

To begin your quest for a standard report, execute the following mystical command:

**Choose Tools ⇨ ReportCreator from the menu bar.**

A tiny Report Name dialog box requests that you name your report. Use 15 characters or fewer. This name doesn't appear on your report; it just identifies your report so that you can use it again.

Then the ReportCreator dialog box of Figure 15-4 swings into action.

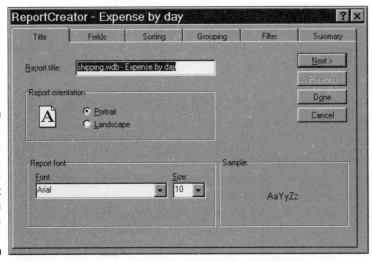

**Figure 15-4:** The ReportCreator's Title card. Fill out all six cards and you win a report!

You don't have to take the six cards in strict left-to-right order, but Works presents them to you in that order when you use the Next button on the ReportCreator dialog box. To work on a different card at any time, just click its tab.

### First card: title, orientation, and font

The top card of the hand that the ReportCreator deals you is the Title card. The *title* is what appears on the top of your report. Works suggests a title for you, made up of the database filename and the name that you gave the report, but you can come up with a better one. Works also suggests that the report be created in the portrait orientation (taller than wide) and the 10-point Arial font, but Works also allows you to change these selections.

1. **Click the** `Report title` **text box and enter a title if you don't like Works' suggestion.**

   How about a title like *Commander of North American Operations.* No, just kidding, type in something boring and industrial, such as **Shipping Costs.**

2. **Choose** `Landscape` **orientation, if you are making a w – i – d – e report (a report with a lot of fields on it — how many? — it depends on how wide your fields are).**

3. **Choose a font and size in the** `Report font` **area.**

When you're done, click the <u>N</u>ext button or the tab for the Fields card.

### Second card: choose your fields

The second card the ReportCreator deals you is the Fields card, shown in Figure 15-5. Here, you choose which of the fields in your database that you want to appear in your report and in what order. (Fields appear in columns, in left-to-right order.) Also, you can specify whether you want field names heading those field columns.

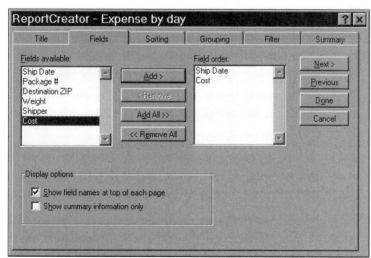

**Figure 15-5:**
Copy field
names from
the left box
to the
right box.

1. **Click a field name in the left-hand box** (`Fields available`).

   This list is a list of the fields you have in your database. The basic procedure in this dialog box is to copy field names from the left box to the right box.

   Click a field that you want to appear in your report.

2. **Click** Add **to copy that field to the right-hand box** (`Field order`).

   The right-hand box is where you accumulate a list of the fields that are to appear in the report.

   (Every time you add a field, the highlight in the left-hand box moves down, for your pleasure and convenience. So to copy a series of field names, you can just keep clicking the Add button.)

3. **Repeat Steps 1 and 2 for each field that you want in the report.**

   If you want them all, click the Add All button.

   If you change your mind about a field, click that field in the *right-hand* box and then click the Remove button. To remove all the fields from the right-hand box and start again, click the Remove All button.

4. **If you don't want the field names at the top of your page, click the** Show `summary information only` **check box.**

   Normally, you want them. Figure 15-3 has 'em.

5. **After you have copied to the right-hand box all the fields that you want in your report, click the** Next **button.**

Works moves you on to the Sorting card.

## Third card: all sorts of stuff!

This card may look familiar to you if you have already done sorting in the Works database tool. Sorting is the ordering of records alphabetically, numerically, or by date or time. (In Figure 15-3, for example, I sorted by the Shipper field. That is a text field, so Works sorted it alphabetically: The report starts with CityZIP and ends with Zowiefast.) In Figure 15-6, I've decided to sort by date.

Here's the procedure — bear in mind that you don't have to sort at all. Your report can just display stuff in the order in which it was entered (or previously sorted). You do have to specify sorting if you want groups in your report (see the Grouping card). But if you're feeling "out of sorts," just click the Next button.

1. **Choose the principal field to sort on.**

   Click the down-arrow button next to the box labeled Sort by and then click a field in that list. In Figure 15-6, I want to see things in order of shipment date; I don't care about ordering shipments within a date, so I don't sort on any other field.

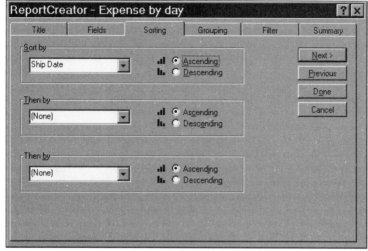

**Figure 15-6:**
What order
do you want
your data
listed in?

2. **Choose a sorting direction for that field.**

   Click Ascending to go from A–Z or in the order 1, 2, 3. . . .

   Click Descending to go from Z–A or in the order . . . 3, 2, 1.

3. **Optionally, do the same for a second and third field.**

   If you want additional sorting, use these fields. (For example, if for each date I wanted shipments listed in order of increasing cost, I would choose Cost as my second field.)

When you're done, click the Next button or the tab for the Grouping card.

### Fourth card: groupings

Works can group records together that have identical values in some field. For example, if I have a bunch of shipments all on the same date, Works can group those together. Not only that, but (as you can see in the last card) Works can, at the end of each group, display a calculation based on that group, such as a sum of the Cost or Weight field. For example, in my shipping database I can group by Ship Date (as you see in Figure 15-7). When I get to the Summary card, I can choose to total the cost of all the packages shipped on that day.

Here's the scoop on grouping:

  ✔ You don't have to group at all. Not feeling groupish? Just click the Next button.

  ✔ To create a group, click the When contents change check box. The other check boxes then come alive because they all control things that you can do to a group. The When contents change check box is so called because Works puts a space between groups when the contents of the specified field change. (For example, when the date changes in the Ship Date field.)

✔ You can group only on fields that you have selected to appear on this report (on the Fields card) and have chosen for sorting (on the Sorting card). If I wanted to group on, say, the Cost field, I would have to go back to the Sorting card and add that field. Each field you have selected for sorting appears on the Grouping card.

✔ You can have groups, subgroups, and sub-subgroups — that's why three identical areas are on this card. For example, I can group shipments by date, "then by" shipper, "then by" zip code. The order in which you chose your fields on the Grouping card determines the order in which your fields appear on this card; and that order, in turn, determines whether you can use a field as a group (top area), subgroup (middle area), or sub-subgroup (bottom area).

✔ You can create groupings based strictly on the first character of a data entry. For example, if you had a list of last names, you probably wouldn't want to group by each name (many groups would be only one name long), but by initial letter: all the As together, the Bs together, and so on. To do this type of grouping, click the Use first letter only check box.

✔ You can put a heading to identify each group. For example, if you were grouping by zip code, you can head each group with its zip. Heading each group with its zip code is somewhat redundant, however, because the zip code appears in every line of that group anyway, making it rather obvious what group it is. Nonetheless, if you like this sort of thing, click the Show group heading check box.

In the initial release of Works for Windows 95, the ReportCreator didn't do a good job of handling dates as group headings; the ReportCreator didn't format them correctly, so that dates appeared as numbers (the number of days since January 1, 1900)!

✔ For some reports, you may want to print each group on a separate page. For example, in a national sales database, you may need to send a separate page to each region's sales office. To do this task, click the Start each group on a new page check box.

When you're done, click the Next button or the tab for the Filter card.

### Fifth card: filters

Filters let you separate the sheep from the goats, so to speak (or the wheat from the chaff, if you are a vegetarian). Filters are a bit lengthy to discuss, and this book has already discussed them back in Chapter 14 (see "Filtering Your Data" in that chapter). The filters that you can use here are exactly the same as the ones discussed in Chapter 14. In fact, if you created any of those filters, they appear in the Select a filter box here.

The executive summary on filters is that filters allow you to selectively *hide* certain records from your report: For example, packages shipped by the regular postal service may not belong in this report, so you would create a filter that says (in filter-ese) *Shipper . . . is not equal to . . . U.S. Postal Service.*

To create a filter, click the Create New Filter button and see Chapter 14. After you have created a filter, it appears in the Select a filter text box. You can modify that filter with the Modify Filter button, if you need to.

If you have not created any filters, the ReportCreator gives you two options anyway, in the Select a filter text box. Choose one:

✔ (**Current Records**) means display any records that are not *hidden* in your database. If you apply a filter, certain records are hidden and do not appear in the report.

✔ (**All Records**) means just that: display all the records in the database.

Be brave; you are almost done. Click the Next button, or click the Summary tab of the ReportCreator, to wrap up your report with a few summaries.

### Sixth card: statistical summaries

At this point, you are gazing (glassy-eyed) at the Summary dialog box of Figure 15-8.

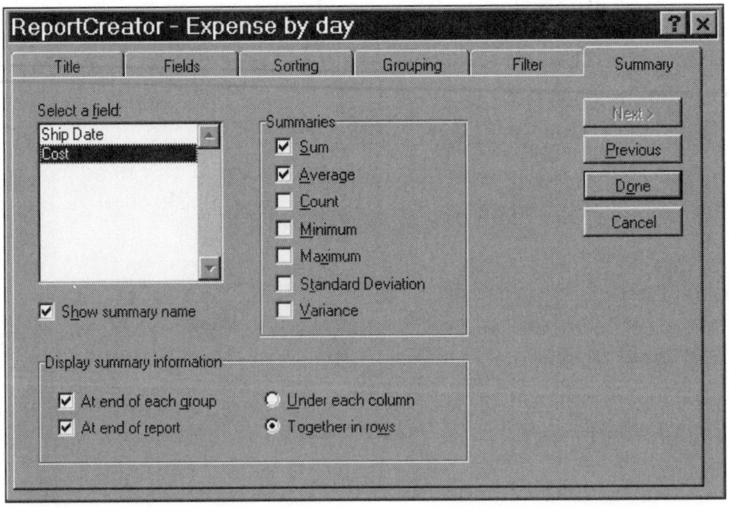

**Figure 15-8:**
Time to
sum up,
counselor!

Statistical summaries are useful things. Statistical summaries are how you get the answers to such questions as, "What are the total sales for January in the Eastern region?" or "What is the batting average for each team?" or "Why are my eyes glazing over?" (Just kidding about the last one. The answer is, your eyes are going buggy from staring at your computer screen or reading this book too long.)

Summaries are optional. If you don't specify any summaries, and you just click the D̲one button in the ReportCreator, you get a report that simply lists all the records in your database, displaying the fields that you chose on the Fields card — sorted and grouped, if you chose those features.

If you want statistics (including sums) on a certain field or fields, here's what to do.

1. **Click the field in the** `Select a f̲ield` **box.**

2. **Choose the kind of statistical summary (or summaries) that you want for that field.**

   Click a check box in the `Summaries` area to select a particular kind of summary. Heck, click a batch of 'em if you want several different kinds of summaries.

   A̲verage computes the average of all the numbers in the field, M̲inimum shows you the smallest (or most negative) value, and so on.

3. **Repeat Steps 1 and 2 for each field that you want summarized.**

   Each field can have its own set of summaries.

   It's important to do this card carefully because summaries can't easily be changed after you've clicked the D_one button. Be careful that you don't sum when you want to count. S_um adds up the numerical value of all the records in the selected field. C_ount just counts the records in a field. Also, don't accidentally sum up the wrong field (such as the date field)!

4. **Click** S_how summary name. **This option makes Works label the summary as a sum, or an average, or whatever you choose.**

5. **If you created groups on the Grouping card, you can have a summary appear under each group by clicking** At end of each group.

6. **Choose where you want your summaries to appear in the report.**

   Click U_nder each column to put your field summaries at the bottom of their respective columns.

   Click Together in ro_ws to put each of your field summaries in a separate row at the bottom of the report (or at the bottom of each group, if you chose that option).

7. **Click the** D_one **button.**

   Things whiz around on your screen, ultimately delivering . . .

   . . . a big, confusing mess, and then one of those little boxes with the exclamation point in it! What the heck?!? This isn't what you had in mind! Where's that nice report??

Hang in there. Read the little dialog box, which is assuring you that The report definition has been created and asking whether you wish to preview it or modify it. I suggest that you choose P_review. Choosing M_odify doesn't gain you much — it just leaves you gazing at the big confusing mess (called the *Report view*).

Click the P_review button, and Works shows you your report in Print Preview mode. Remember, the main purpose of a report is to make a nice report to print out — not to view on your screen. Read on to figure out exactly what's going on here.

### Laying your cards on the table: viewing your report

If you've been following along, you are now viewing your report in Print Preview. Here's a quick summary of how to use Print Preview:

1. **Click anywhere on the image with your mouse cursor (now a magnifying glass) and the image gets larger.**

   You can do this trick twice more before the image gets small again. Scroll around to see a whole page.

2. **Click the** Next **or** Previous **buttons to see other pages.**

3. **If you want to print out your report, click the** Print **button.**

4. **When you're done viewing the report, click** Cancel **or press the Esc key to make the Print Preview window go away.**

After you exit Print Preview mode, what's on your screen at this point is not your actual report. Instead, what is on your screen is the *Report view* — a view most people don't find very comprehensible, and a view that's not necessary for most work. This view displays the rather intimidating *report definition* that tells Works how to construct your report. Don't be too upset — if it weren't for that nice ReportCreator dialog box, you would have had to enter all that intimidating stuff by hand.

You probably want to get out of the Report view and go back to a List or Form view. To go back, just click View and then click either List or Form in the menu that drops down.

Now that you're done defining a report, your named report exists as part of your Works database document. As with filters, you can call up this report at any time, and the report takes into account any new or changed data in your database. Also, as with filters, you can have only eight reports; any more, and you have to delete one: Choose Tools⇨Delete Report and double-click the report name in the dialog box that appears.

You can reuse this report over and over as you add data. Just click View ⇨ Report. Double-click the report name in the dialog box that appears.

## *Modifying your report — the easy way*

Works makes it easy to modify your report — within limits. You can easily modify the sorting, grouping, and filtering. You can't as easily change fields or summaries. Here's the scoop on how to modify report settings:

✔ **Sorting:** Choose Tools⇨Report Sorting.

✔ **Grouping:** Choose Tools⇨Report Grouping.

✔ **Filtering:** Choose Tools⇨Report Filtering.

All of these steps take you to a Report Settings dialog box, where the cards look exactly like the cards in the ReportCreator, except only these three functions (instead of six) are available. Refer back to the preceding discussions of sorting, grouping, and filtering for instructions.

## Modifying and enhancing your report — the hard way

If you can't make the changes that you want from the Report Settings dialog box (the easy way), or if you want to get a better-looking report than the standard one, you need to use the hard way: by using the Report view.

Using Report view is not for the easily confused! Explaining how to use the Report view in detail would take too long in this book, so I only give you the executive summary and a few instructions on how to change things. Fortunately, you may rarely need to resort to editing this report definition to create the reports you need.

You can use Report view to create the report you need by using one of two ways:

- ✔ Create a report from scratch by writing one of those scary-looking *report definitions* you see in the so-called Report view
- ✔ Modify the standard report definition

My money's on the second option.

To modify an existing report definition, switch to the Report view: choose View➪Report, click the report name in the View Report dialog box that appears, and then choose the Modify button. You are confronted with a strange-looking spreadsheet-kind-of-thing.

Each row in the Report view has a special function. Down the leftmost side are special labels that identify what part of the report is being controlled by that row. For example, report titles are entered in a row labeled *Title;* blank rows of any type just provide extra space.

The vertical position of the row corresponds to the position of that row in the final report. Title rows, for example, are at the top; summary rows are at the bottom.

You can add these sorts of special rows if you think that you understand their functions. I tell you about a few of their functions in the upcoming sections. Click the row above which you want to add a row and then choose Insert➪Insert Row from the menu bar. Choose a row type from the list in the Insert Row dialog box that appears and click the Insert button.

### Adding or deleting fields

To add a new field to your report in Report view (which is the only view in which you can do this task), see Figure 15-9 for an example, and do the following:

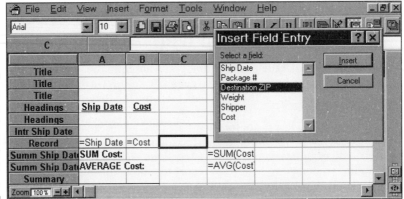

**Figure 15-9:**
Adding a
field to your
report using
the yucky
but essential
Report view.

1. **Locate the row labeled** Record **in the leftmost column.**

2. **Find the first blank cell available in that row and click it.**

   A black border appears around that cell as shown in Figure 15-9.

3. **Choose** Insert⇨ Field Entry **from the menu bar, and the Insert Field Entry dialog box shown in Figure 15-9 appears.**

4. **Choose the field that you want to add to your report from the list in the Insert Field Entry dialog box.**

   In Figure 15-9, I'm adding the Destination ZIP field.

5. **Click the** Insert **button.**

6. **Add a heading, if you wish.**

   Find a row above the current cell labeled Headings (which probably has other headings in it), and simply type in a heading. (If no row is labeled Headings, choose Insert⇨Insert Row from the menu bar and choose Headings from the Insert Row dialog box that appears.) Format the text that you type with bold, underline, or any other font, style, or alignment formatting that you like. If a Summ something-or-other field appears under the cell that you have just typed, you want an underline. (See "Adding or deleting summaries" later in this chapter for more information about adding summaries.)

7. **Add an underline by choosing** Format⇨Border, **choosing** Bottom **in the Format dialog box, and then clicking** OK.

To delete a field from the report, look in the row labeled Record for a cell containing an equal sign (=) followed by the field name. Click that cell and then press the Del key.

To see if these mysterious actions really gave you what you wanted, go to Print Preview. (Click the document-with-a-monocle icon button or choose File⇨Print Preview.)

### Adding or deleting summaries

A report may have two kinds of summaries: group summaries and overall summaries. In Report view, group summaries are controlled by rows labeled Summ (and then the field name). Overall summaries are controlled by rows labeled Summary.

You can create a new row for your new summary, or you can add a summary to an existing summary row.

To add a new row with a new summary:

1. **Click any row above which you want to add a summary.**

   A good choice is the row below an existing Summ or Summary row.

2. **Choose Insert⇨Insert Row from the menu bar.**

3. **Select Summary or Summ [some field name] from the list of row types in the Insert Row dialog box and click the Insert button.**

   For example, if you are adding a new summary to a group grouped by zip code, you can choose Summ zip code.

4. **In the *A* column of your new row, type a label for this summary, such as** TOTAL: Weight.

5. **Click in the column where you want the summary to appear in this row.**

   You can choose any column of this row (column D, for example) that is not overlapped by the label that you typed.

6. **Choose Insert⇨Field Summary from the menu bar.**

   The Field Insert dialog box appears.

7. **Choose a field from the list and click the kind of summary you want in the** Statistic **area of the dialog box; click the Insert button when you're done.**

To see if you really created the summary you wanted, go to Print Preview. (Click the document-with-a-monocle icon button or choose File⇨Print Preview.)

To add a summary to an existing Summary row, start with Step 5 in the preceding list, in which you select an unused cell in that row. That cell is where your new summary appears.

### *Fixing up appearances*

When they first appear, most reports don't look any better than I do when I first appear in the morning. Here are a few things you can do in Report view to improve your report's appearance.

To switch to Report view, choose <u>V</u>iew⇨<u>R</u>eport, click the report name in the View Report dialog box that appears, and then choose the <u>M</u>odify button.

Much of the report's appearance can be set the same way that spreadsheet appearances are set. The commands and procedures are similar, if not identical. If you're familiar with Works' spreadsheets already, you probably know how to do many of the formatting tasks in the following list:

- ✔ **Adjust report column widths:** Click and drag the crack between the column letters (the gray cells with the letters A, B, C, and so forth, across the top of the columns).

- ✔ **Align data within the report columns:** Click the column's letter to select the column. (Click and drag to choose multiple columns.) Either choose one of the alignment buttons on the button bar, or choose F<u>o</u>rmat⇨<u>A</u>lignment to get to the alignment page of the Format dialog box. Double-click the Alignment you need. (Typically, <u>L</u>eft, <u>R</u>ight, <u>C</u>enter, or Center <u>a</u>cross selection does the job.)

- ✔ **Edit the column headings:** Click a report heading (in a row labeled Headings) and make edits to the heading text by using the formula bar.

- ✔ **Change font, font size, or style:** Select either a report heading (click it in a row labeled Headings), an entire column (click its column letter), or the entire report (press Ctrl+A). Then choose a new font, type size, or style (bold, italic, or underlined) by using either the toolbar or the F<u>o</u>rmat⇨<u>F</u>ont and Style command.

- ✔ **Change number formats:** To make your numbers look right — with dollar signs preceding monetary figures and zeros leading zip codes — you need a *number format*. Select the column that needs fixing (click its column letter) and choose F<u>o</u>rmat⇨<u>N</u>umber from the menu bar. The Number card of the Format dialog box appears. Click a Format, choose any Options, and then click OK. See "New fields of endeavor" in Chapter 12 for more information on number formats.

- ✔ **Borders:** To put lines and borders around rows and columns, first select the row (click its label, such as Headings, in the gray column at the left of the row) or column (click its column letter) and choose F<u>o</u>rmat⇨<u>B</u>order. Click a Line Style, then click a Border, and then click the OK button. See "Applying and Changing Formats" in Chapter 13 for more information.

# Part V

# Exploring the Communications Wilderness

After spending hours trying to get the system up and running, Carl discovers that everything had been plugged into a "Clapper" light socket when he tries to kill a mosquito.

# In this part . . .

The information highway is yours for the riding with Works' communications tool. But the highway can be a bumpy road through a vast communications wilderness. This part gives you skills for surviving in the vast uncharted regions of computer communications. Here's how to catch the bus for the information highway, what to do if the bus breaks down, and how to make yourself at home in the wilderness. From Works' Easy Connect feature, to communications procedures, setups, and protocols, Part V teaches you the tools you need for survival.

"I pr'ythee, let me bring thee where crabs grow;
And I with my long nails will dig thee pig-nuts; Show thee a jay's nest, and instruct thee how to snare the nimble marmozet; I'll bring thee to clust'ring filberts, and sometimes I'll get thee young sea-mells from the rock: Wilt thou go with me?"

*The Tempest,* Wm. Shakespeare

# Chapter 16

# Preparing for the Communications Wilderness

........................................................

## In This Chapter

▶ If you've never communicated by computer before

▶ What the big deal is

▶ Modems and communications ports

▶ A few notes about the Internet

▶ Online services

........................................................

*J*ust this side of the information superhighway is a mess of communications quagmires, modem morasses, and sudden data drop-offs — in short, a wilderness. And whenever you're about to enter a wilderness, it pays to look around and take your bearings before you embark on a wilder ride than you're ready for.

This chapter provides a scenic overlook before you plunge into the wild and woolly world of computer communications. You can view the basics of Works' communications tool: what you need to have and to know to connect with just about anybody in the far-flung corners of computerdom.

## If You've Never Communicated Before

If you've never communicated by computer before, here's a quick overview of what you need, with whom you can communicate, and why you may want to communicate in the first place.

✔ First, you need a device called a *modem*. The modem can be either inside your computer (internal) or outside (external) but connected to it. The modem plugs into the phone line. (This assumes that you need to communicate with a computer that's located in another building. If you're communicating within the same building, you don't need a modem, just a special cable.)

✔ Second, you need some communications software that can run the modem — this is where Works comes in. (You still need the software, even if you don't use a modem.)

✔ Third, you need somebody else (another person and/or computer) with a similar setup to communicate with.

## *With whom can you communicate?*

Quite often, that somebody else that you communicate with is a computer communications service, also called an *online service,* such as CompuServe or America Online (AOL) to name just two. Such services have lots of information stored on their computers that you can use, and because lots of other people use these services too, you can exchange messages with these folks. These services have computers all over the world, linked to each other by special connections that can handle messages very quickly. So with some services, you can actually "chat" with other users who are sitting at their PCs. These services, of course, charge you for the time you spend and the things you do.

That other user can be a person who has a PC, or it can be one of your employer's computers. The other user can also be a smaller version of the commercial online services — a *bulletin board service (BBS)*. Usually bulletin boards serve a local area, although they may be able to forward messages to

---

## When you may not want to use Works' communications tool

Online services and other vendors often offer special software that makes connecting to those services a lot easier. Some services even require you to use their software. CompuServe, for example, is truly ugly and confusing without a special program to help you use it. CompuServe offers the Windows CompuServe Information Manager, WinCIM, which is a heck of a lot easier to use; but CompuServe charges about $25 for this software. (If you have problems with CompuServe, though, it has been known to send WinCIM free.) Another vendor, Ashmount Research, offers WigWam for CIS, a different program that can be used for CompuServe. If you're using a service that offers graphical software, you may be a lot happier using WinCIM or WigWam for CIS rather than using Works.

and from other computers around the world. Sometimes BBSs are run by volunteers and are free (except for what your telephone company charges you for making the call).

Some of these somebody-elses may also simply serve as connection points. Many individuals, companies, universities, and online services are part of what is called the *Internet:* a vast web of interconnected computers.

## What's the big deal?

The big-deal payoff for learning to connect your computer to other computers takes various forms:

- ✔ **Education:** A vast amount of up-to-date information is available.

- ✔ **Fun:** Game programs, forums about your hobbies or special interests, and "chat" features let you converse with people around the world and even shop for stuff.

- ✔ **Staying in touch:** Electronic mail — *e-mail* — is faster and easier to use than postal mail (although often more expensive) and cheaper than telephoning.

- ✔ **Working at home or on the road:** You can exchange electronic messages with your colleagues, getting or sending the latest information. You can also obtain important information from your company's computers, such as the latest sales presentations, product literature, or prices.

- ✔ **Making your business more efficient or creating new business opportunities:** You can get detailed information on sales or inventory every day from other offices. You can also use e-mail to stay in contact with your customers.

## What do you need?

To explore the communications wilderness, you need to take along a few survival tools, such as a modem and a phone line. If your PC is already wired up with a modem and if that modem is connected to the phone line, you're all set. Skip ahead to the section "What do you need to know to communicate?"

If your PC is not wired up, remember that to communicate over telephone lines, you need a modem and a phone cable. If that modem is not built into your PC, you also need a couple of cables and a communications *port connector* on your PC.

## Communicating on the Internet

You need to know lots of technical and non-technical things if you are going to explore the ultimate computer wilderness — the Internet. At the very least, you want to know about the "manners" of the Internet, as well as the who, what, where, when, and how of getting around. For more information on the Internet, pick up a copy of *The Internet For Dummies* (IDG Books Worldwide, Inc.) by John Levine and Carol Baroudi.

Communicating on the Internet using Works is possible, although you won't be able to do many of the fancy graphical things you may have heard

about, such as using the World Wide Web. To use Works on the Internet, you must find a *service provider* that offers a *shell account*, which you can access by using Works and your PC as a *terminal*. Many colleges and businesses offer Internet access. To do the fancier tricks on the Internet, you need software other than Works. *The Internet Starter Kit For Windows For Dummies* (also from IDG Books Worldwide Inc.) by John Levine and Margaret Levine Young, includes a diskette of software, instructions, and an introduction to the Internet.

### The modem

Modems come in two varieties: internal and external. Internal modems save space on your desktop, don't require a communications port connector, and cost less, but internal modems are harder to turn on or off if they don't behave properly. External modems can be switched off in an emergency and sometimes have pretty lights to watch, but they need a communications port connector to hook up to, and they have a separate power cord that has to plug in somewhere.

To install an internal modem (which comes in the form of a plastic board covered with lots of electronic stuff), you have to unplug your PC, take its case off, and insert the board. Follow the installation instructions that come with the computer and internal modem. The connectors for the phone (standard phone jacks) then appear on the back panel of your PC (which is one way to tell whether your PC already has an internal modem).

The external modem connects to a communications port on your PC with a cable. (See "The communications port," next.) Plug the cable into the PC and into the modem (this cable can go only one way); then plug the modem's power cable into the modem and into a power outlet. A phone cord connects the modem to the wall jack.

Modems vary in the maximum speed at which they can transmit data. Typically, the more expensive the modem, the higher its top speed. Speed is measured in *baud* or *bits per second (bps),* and goes up to about 28000 bps. A fast modem saves you time (and may save you money) if you are going to send or receive a lot of files or very large files, such as graphics images. If you are just going to send electronic mail and read text on other computers, high speed is not very important. If a fast modem encounters a slow one, the two of them generally manage to get together on a slow speed.

### The communications port

If your computer doesn't have a built-in modem, you may need to identify special connectors on your PC that belong to communications ports. (These ports are not the same as printer or parallel ports.) Check your PC manual or look on the back of your computer where the various connectors are located to see if any the ports are marked as communications ports. These ports are also referred to as *serial* ports, *RS-232* (or *RS-232C*) ports, or *COM* ports.

If you have only one port connector, your mouse may already be using it. Some mice use the communications port; others have special mouse connections. If your only communications port is already being used for your mouse, you have a bit of a problem. Here are some solutions: Buy a new *board* to install in your PC that adds a communications port; buy a new mouse and install a special board in your PC for the new mouse to connect to; buy an *internal* modem, which is a modem on a board that installs in your PC and therefore needs no separate communications port. If you have a laptop computer, you can also buy a PCMCIA or other type of modem card that plugs into your PC and therefore needs no communications port.

If you have more than one port, figuring out what the *port number* is for the one you intend to use is helpful (although not essential). Communications ports are numbered COM1, COM2, COM3, COM4, and usually stop there. Again, check your PC's manual or the back panel of your computer.

# What do you need to know to communicate?

Ask any explorer: If you're going to explore foreign lands, you need to find out about the native customs and language. So if you're going to explore someone else's computer, you need to know a few things about how it behaves, how it expects you to behave, and the *language* it speaks. For this tour, taking the Easy Connect bus, you probably need only the absolute essentials. But I include some important but nonessential things as well.

### Things you absolutely need to know

The absolutely essential things that you need to find out from the person or service you're going to communicate with are the following:

✔ **The phone number:** The first thing you need to know to communicate with another computer is the phone number to call! Online services often have phone lines all over the place, so get the number closest to your location.

✔ **Details of logging on:** If the other computer is an online service, a business computer, or otherwise is not being controlled directly by another person sitting at the keyboard, you also need to know the *logon procedure:* what words or phrases the other computer is going transmit to you and what responses you have to give back. If you do not correctly log on to the other computer, it won't accept you as a user. The logon procedure usually involves, at the very least, your typing in a personal identification name or number (a *login*) and a password. You may also need to type some other key phrases.

✔ **How to use the other computer:** If a computer with no human operator is going to be at the other end, you need to give certain commands to that computer. You have to know what that computer expects of you and how that computer may respond. You especially should find out how it wants you to disconnect, or *log off.*

This may be enough information to do the job. Works has an Easy Connect feature that can, if you like, take a shot at connecting to this other computer. In order to do so, though, the Easy Connect feature makes a few guesses about the correct settings that this other computer requires. If those guesses don't work, you may need the "Things you may well need to know," described next.

Hey, what the heck — give the Easy Connect feature a try. See Chapter 17. If you have problems, you may need to come back here to check out the "Things you may well need to know" or turn to Chapter 18.

### Things you may well need to know

If Works' Easy Connect feature doesn't work out, you need to find out how the other computer communicates. Computers have a lot of different standards that they can use to communicate with each other, but when one calls the other, both computers have to use the same standards, usually called *communications parameters*, *protocols*, or *settings*. So before you can communicate with another computer (or an online service), you may have to either ask about, read about, or guess what communications parameters the other computer expects you to use. You set these parameters by using the Settings menu on the menu bar, and they are saved with your Works *communications document.*

The most important parameters to ask about are the following:

✔ **Speed (baud rate):** Commonly 2400; 9600; or 14400 bits per second or bps; newer modems reach 28000 bps. Works uses the fastest rate your modem can handle, unless you tell it otherwise.

✔ **Number of data bits:** 7 or 8. Works uses 8, normally. Eight data bits are necessary for transmitting anything but plain typewriter text, such as graphics or special typing characters.

✔ **Parity:** Odd, Even, or None (also called *O, E,* or *N*). Works uses None, unless you tell it otherwise.

✔ **Number of stop bits:** 0 or 1. Works uses 1, normally.

Sometimes these parameters are written all lumped together, like *1200 8 N 1.* Two common combinations for the last three settings in this list are 8*N1* and 7*E1,* so Works provides two buttons on the toolbar for these combinations.

### *Occasionally important things to know*

You may eventually need to ask the person with whom you are communicating about the following parameters, although you can usually ignore these particular parameters. (Many computers today can figure out what your computer is using for many of these parameters and follow suit.)

✔ **Full- or half-duplex:** Most computers use full-duplex today. Half-duplex is also called *local echo.*

✔ **Line endings:** This parameter normally takes the form CR/LF (carriage return/line feed). Computers that talk mostly to Macintosh computers sometimes take the CR form, in which case you need to add an LF.

✔ **Data flow control (or *handshake*):** This parameter is almost always Xon/Xoff if you're using a modem.

✔ **ISO translation:** If you are using a foreign language to communicate with people, you may need to specify the language, or your computer may improperly translate certain text characters.

✔ **Terminal emulation:** The other computer may expect your PC to *emulate* (respond as if it were) a particular make or model of computer terminal, in which case, you need to tell Works to play that role. Usually, other computers assume that you are a TTY-type (Teletype) terminal, which is just fine because Works pretends that your terminal is a TTY-type terminal unless you tell it otherwise.

# *Looking Around the Communications Window*

One thing about the wilderness is that there's a lot to see and do that you may never need to experience. Likewise, you may never need most of the things in the communications window, either. Depending on whom you are connecting to and what you want to do, you may simply be able to fire up the communications tool, enter a phone number in the Easy Connect dialog box, and communicate away.

On the other hand, if you wander just a tiny bit off the trodden path or are just a tiny bit unlucky, you may need to turn to a few tricks and tools. In fact, you may discover that these tricks and tools make the whole experience a lot more fun and effective.

Don't spend a lot of time here, memorizing all this stuff. Stick a bookmark or a coffee stirrer here and come back whenever you need to refresh your memory.

"The communications window" is my term for how Works looks and runs when you use the communications tool. The communications window looks like Figure 16-1.

Communications
document window title bar.

Communications menu bar.

Communications toolbar.

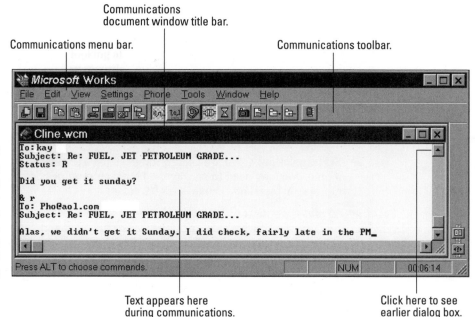

**Figure 16-1:**
Works
communica-
tions tool in
action. (Me,
answering
some mail.)

Text appears here
during communications.

Click here to see
earlier dialog box.

## *The communications document*

Ah, yes. The so-called communications "document." I'm not sure that Microsoft did you a favor by calling it a document. The communications *document* is a collection of all the settings that you need in order to call a particular computer. After you've set up Works to deal properly with a certain computer, you save that setup as a communications document file. When you later open that document and tell Works to call the other computer, everything is set up properly.

Even though text appears in the window when you are communicating, as Figure 16-1 shows, that text does not become part of the communications "document"! The text in the communications window can, however, be saved as a separate text file.

The communications document, like all Works documents, is shown in a window within Works. Like other Works documents, you give the communications document a name when you save the document as a file. Because each phone number that you call gets its own document, you generally name the document after the person, company, or online service that the phone number belongs to. You can leave the document window open (whether or not you're in communication with someone) and switch to other Works documents at any time, just by clicking on their title bars.

You create, name, save, close, and reopen the communications document just like every other Works document, by using commands in the File menu on the menu bar. Communications documents are saved with extensions of .WCM appended to the names that you give to them.

## *The communications menu*

As in Chinese-American restaurants and sushi stands everywhere, one way to give a command is by using a menu. You point at the item you want and smile. In Works, you point and click at words on the menu bar. Additional menus then drop down from those words, and you click selections in them; Works waiters scurry around to do your bidding.

- ✔ The File and Edit selections on the menu bar are very much the same everywhere in Works. They let you open and save files, create new ones, print, and cut and paste stuff from one tool to another. For more on these tasty menu selections, see Part I.

- ✔ The View selection on the menu bar just lets you remove or restore the toolbar. No excitement there.

✔ Clicking <u>S</u>ettings gets you various categories of things that you may need in order to adjust the way Works and your modem communicates with a particular computer.

✔ Clicking <u>P</u>hone gives you commands that let you dial, hang up on, or interrupt another computer. The last five parties you dialed are also shown here in case you want them again.

✔ Clicking T<u>o</u>ols gives you a mishmash of stuff, including commands to send or receive things and commands that let you automate all the tedious steps you often have to do when communicating with another computer.

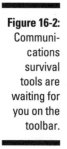

✔ <u>W</u>indow and <u>H</u>elp are selections that work the same everywhere. See Chapter 2 for more information on windows and Help.

I get into more details on some of these commands, one at a time, as I go along.

## The communications toolbar

Besides using the menu bar, the other popular way to give commands to Works (apart from the traditional hollering into the disk drive slot) is with the toolbar: the thing with all the decorative buttons under the menu bar (see Figure 16-2). The toolbar is just a faster way than the menu bar to do some of the same things. You click a button and stuff happens.

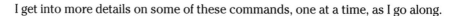

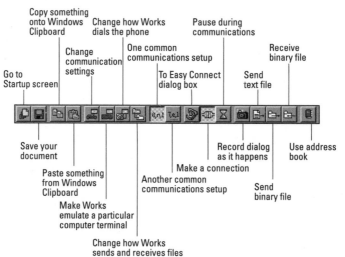

**Figure 16-2:**
Communi-
cations
survival
tools are
waiting for
you on the
toolbar.

Copy something
onto Windows
Clipboard

Change how Works
dials the phone

Pause during
communications

Change
communication
settings

One common
communications setup

Receive
binary file

Go to
Startup screen

To Easy Connect
dialog box

Send
text file

Save your
document

Record dialog
as it happens

Use address
book

Paste something
from Windows
Clipboard

Make a connection

Another common
communications setup

Send
binary file

Make Works
emulate a particular
computer terminal

Change how Works
sends and receives files

The leftmost four buttons of the communications toolbar are similar to buttons in other Works toolbars. For more on Works' toolbars, see Chapter 3.

# If You Have Communicated Before

If you have communicated before, are pretty comfortable with Works in general, and would just like to get down to it, here's an executive summary. For the details of setting up the communications parameters, see Chapter 18.

- ✔ To create a communications document, just fill out the Easy Connect dialog box when it appears.

- ✔ Change communications settings (modem, terminal, and others) by using the Settings menu on the menu bar; change connection parameters by choosing Settings➪Communication and then clicking the Properties button. Default parameters are no parity, 8 bits, 1 stop bit, and maximum modem speed (set by using high serial port speed).

- ✔ Works keeps each dial-up line's phone number and communications parameters as a communications document.

- ✔ To call someone for whom you have created a communications document, open that communications document or start a new document and select that person by name from the Easy Connect dialog box.

- ✔ To disconnect from (or reconnect to) the line, click the two-connector icon in the toolbar or use commands in the Phone menu.

- ✔ To send or receive files, use the Capture Text, Send Text, Send Binary File, and Receive Binary File buttons near the right end of the toolbar. Protocols for binary files are set with the Transfer command in the Settings menu. The default is Kermit.

- ✔ To record a script for dialing up and logging in to a service, or for any automated activity, see the script commands in the Tools menu.

# Chapter 17

# Entering the Communications Wilderness

*W*elcome to the vast, exciting wilderness of computer communications! Oh, you thought that this was an information highway? Well, it *is* crossed by a few stretches of well-paved electronic autobahn; but just a few bits off the side of the road, you find communications quagmires, modem morasses, and sudden data drop-offs — in short, a wilderness. Fortunately, Works has a nice, air-conditioned tour bus called *Easy Connect;* so if you're lucky, you can get where you're going without encountering any nasty communications critters or without even knowing how to drive.

Unfortunately, on about half the roads you may ask this bus to travel, the bus will break down, leaving you to get it started again on your own. If that happens, move on to Chapter 18.

This chapter is the tour guide for the Easy Connect excursion and also gives a brief view of life without Easy Connect. Like any tour guide, this chapter is full of fun and useful facts, aimed mostly at folks who haven't seen the communications countryside before. It includes the basics of starting communications: how you can call and converse with some other computer by using Works. For more about this sort of introductory communications stuff plus advanced communications tricks and tips, read *Modems For Dummies* (IDG Books Worldwide, Inc.) by Tina Rathbone.

If you're already familiar with communications and "don't need no stinking tour bus," come along anyway for the ride; you may find a new route or two. For tips on dealing with the ruts in the road, move on to the next chapter.

# Starting the Communications Tool

If you haven't started Works before, check out Part I. If you're a little vague on using the mouse, the keyboard, commands, menus, and dialog boxes, stick a bookmark, toothpick, or stray diskette in Part I and refer back there when you need to.

## Starting with Easy Connect

Works' Easy Connect dialog box pops up whenever you open a new communications document. The Easy Connect dialog box, shown in Figure 17-1, is a shortcut sort of feature. I think that Microsoft created the communications tool and then said, "Hey, you know, half the time they don't need to fool with all this technical stuff. Why don't we give them something that they barely have to think about?"

So that's Easy Connect; it works best if you don't think about it. Among other things, Easy Connect lets you try to create a communications document by entering only two pieces of information:

- ✔ A name
- ✔ A phone number for the other computer

Works tries to make a lucky guess on all the other stuff by using its default settings. These default settings work about half the time. Works saves the name and phone number you give it for future use.

If you have to change a few settings in order to make things work, well that's okay, too. Easy Connect stores everything about a particular service in the current communications document. Save that document as a file; when you later reopen that document file, Works sets up everything properly.

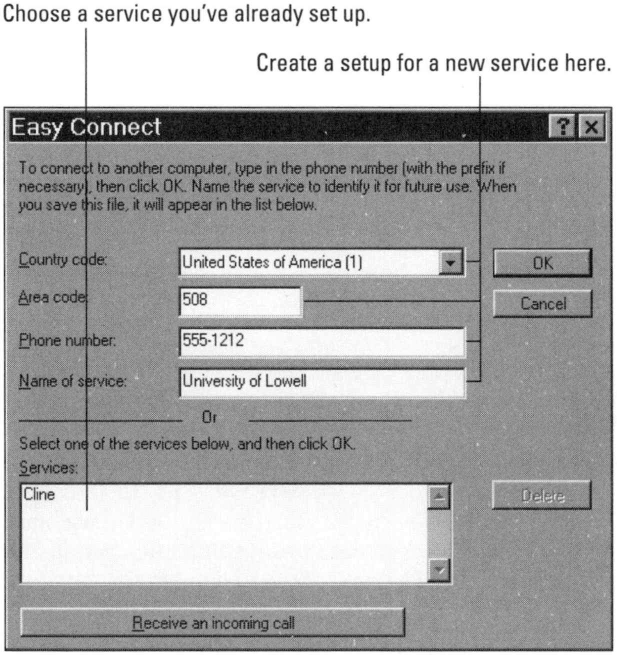

Choose a service you've already set up.

Create a setup for a new service here.

**Figure 17-1:**
The Easy
Connect
tour bus
awaits you.

When you're ready, launch Works and get the Task Launcher. (If you aren't currently looking at that screen, press Ctrl+N or choose File⇨New from the menu bar.) Then:

1. **Turn on your modem if it's an external modem.**

   If your modem is an internal modem, it's already on.

2. **Choose the Works Tools card on the Task Launcher. Click the Communications button there.**

   This step should launch you directly into Easy Connect and start a new communications document — if, when you (or the dealer) installed Windows 95, you set Windows 95 up to know about your modem. If Windows 95 doesn't know about your modem, Works pops up a dialog box saying that There are no valid telephony devices available and asking you, Do you want to run the modem setup Wizard? Click the Yes button, and the aforementioned Wizard can help you fix this problem.

3. **If you have previously set up Works for the person or service you want to call, choose the name you want from the list (the Services text box) in the Easy Connect dialog box.**

   **otherwise**

### 3. Enter information on the person or service you want to call.

Choose the country that you wish to call in the $\underline{C}$ountry code box; then enter the area code and phone number you want to call. Don't enter the long-distance prefix code (the $\underline{C}$ountry code box does that for you), but do enter the area code if you need one. You can use dashes or spaces, if you like, for readability. Works ignores them.

If you are calling from a location where you need to dial a credit card number or an outside-number access code (such as 9) — such as a hotel or an office with a switchboard — you may need to change a few settings. See "If You Need Special Dialing: Modem Settings," in Chapter 18.

Enter a name in the $\underline{N}$ame of service text box. This name identifies the person or service.

Finally, click the OK button.

Now, Easy Connect is about to begin dialing the number and pops up its Dial dialog box of Figure 17-2. (If you're not ready to actually make the call at this point, press the Esc key. If you have entered new communications information in Step 3 press Ctrl+S to save that information as a communications document. The filename of the document will be the same as the name you entered in Step 3.)

### 4. Check the number that you're about to call and modify it, if necessary.

Works is about to dial the number you see in the Dial dialog box. If you see that the number is missing necessary long-distance or other prefix codes (such as the number "1"), try clicking the Dial $\underline{a}$s long distance check box. (If you are using a laptop PC from a remote location, and you have set up Windows 95's Control Panel to handle that location, choose the proper location by clicking the $\underline{L}$ocation box.)

**Figure 17-2:**
The Dial
dialog box
tells you that
Works is
ready to dial
your
number.

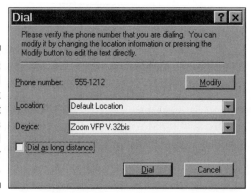

To modify the number temporarily, click the Modify button and edit the number in the Phone number text box. The change won't be saved with your communications document, however.

5. **Click the Dial button.**

This starts the call. You can hear the dial tone and the modem dialing out (assuming that your modem has a speaker; most do). A Dial Status dialog box appears, displaying the name of the party that you're calling and the number that the modem is dialing. The Dial Status dialog box also shows the seconds that remain in a 60-second countdown period, after which Works gives up and cancels the call.

## Reconnecting

To reconnect with a service after hanging up — or if the first attempt to connect failed

✔ **Choose Phone⇨Dial Again from the menu bar, or**

✔ **Click the Dial/Hangup button in the toolbar.**

This Dial/Hangup button is supposed to look like two connectors joining. I think that it looks like two snakes facing each other, one with teeth. To make sure that you're on the right button, position your mouse cursor over the button without clicking, and a yellow tag gives the button's name.

# Establishing a Connection

Now that the modem has started to dial and a call is in progress, Works displays the Dial Status dialog box. This dialog box remains visible until the two modems have *connected* — that is, successfully turned the phone line into a computer data line. The process goes like this:

1. **The Dial Status dialog box is on the screen; check the number that Works is calling.**

If the number is wrong, click the Cancel button in that dialog box to cancel the call. If you don't hear any dial tone, see "Problems Getting Connected" in Chapter 18.

2. **The phone rings at the other computer until the other computer answers or until Works gives up.**

Works gives up (*times out*) after 60 seconds, and the Dial Status dialog box disappears. If you think that 60 seconds doesn't give the other computer enough time to answer the phone (most computers answer within a few rings), you can add some time and try again. See "Hold the Phone — Phone Settings" in Chapter 18.

If the line is busy or for some reason doesn't ring, Works gives up after a few seconds. You may see the word Busy on your screen. See "Disconnecting" page 288 later in this chapter. If the line is busy a lot, see "Hold the Phone — Phone Settings" in Chapter 18.

**3. The other computer answers.**

Some horrendous noises ensue, distressing dogs and arousing infants. If you're lucky, they soon stop (the modem noises, anyway), and the Dial Status dialog box disappears. Most likely, the word Connect will appear on your screen, followed by some number, such as 2400 or 14400. This message actually comes from your modem and means that the two modems have successfully negotiated the terms under which they are going to communicate. The number that appears on your screen is the speed (*bits per second* or *bps*) at which the two have decided to communicate. (Nearly all, but not quite all, modems transmit the Connect message; some may have the message turned off, but connect anyway.)

If you're not so lucky, the word Connect does not appear on your screen, and you get three lemons in a row. No, just kidding about the lemons; you probably get some other gibberish on your screen. This gibberish means that the two modems can't understand each other.

After your computer's modem and the other computer's modem have connected and the Dial Status dialog box has disappeared, the time for the computers to see if they can speak the same language has come. If the computers can communicate properly, some text appears on your screen, and you are expected to type something in return. If the computers can't communicate properly, see the next chapter.

# Conversing with the Other Computer

If the computers do communicate properly, you're ready to have a conversation with the other computer. What happens next depends entirely on what the other computer has been programmed to do. At this point, you need to refer to the instructions you received from the other computer's owner or operator.

Your document window acts like paper in a typewriter on which the two communicating parties take turns typing. As you each type and press the Enter key, the screen fills up, and after the screen is full, it begins to scroll. If you need to see something that was typed earlier, click the arrow at the top of the scroll bar (at the right of the document window) to scroll back. If you can't see the scroll bar, choose <u>W</u>indow⇨<u>T</u>ile to fit that window (and all open documents) into your Works screen.

Here are a few tips:

- ✔ Generally, after you have typed something to the other computer, it waits for you to press the Enter key. This way, you can press the Backspace key to correct any errors in your typing before you press the Enter key.

- ✔ If you forget to press the Enter key or otherwise do nothing (as far as the other computer is concerned), the other computer will probably disconnect from you after a few minutes.

- ✔ If you type a password at some point, it probably won't appear on your screen, or it may appear as a string of dots or asterisks. This is in case you have spies looking over your shoulder, reading your password.

- ✔ If nothing appears on your screen (except the `Connect` message), press the Enter key once or twice.

- ✔ If pressing the Enter key doesn't work, try pressing Ctrl+Q, an ancient and mystical command meaning, "Hey! If somebody told you to wait, it's time to start talking again."

- ✔ If nothing appears on your screen when you type, choose <u>S</u>ettings⇨<u>T</u>erminal from the menu bar and click `Local echo`.

- ✔ If the other computer prints a short line of text on your screen, the other computer is probably requesting some information. Such requests are called *prompts* from the other computer. At this point, you have to rely on the login procedure and other directions that you have obtained from the other computer's owner to know what to type in response. You may have to supply certain code words or numbers.

- ✔ You can have Works automatically perform the login procedure, if you like. See "Automate Sign-On" in Chapter 24.

- ✔ The other computer may give you a welcome message, instructions, a list of commands that you can type, or a numbered list of menu selections, followed by a prompt. Type something from the list or menu.

- ✔ If the other computer transmits a lengthy message that is going by too fast to read, click the hourglass icon (Pause) on the toolbar. Click it again to restart the transmission.

Besides conversing and reading, you may also want to send or receive files or save some of the text that is appearing on your screen. For more on this topic, see Chapter 19.

## Disconnecting

In our society, one generally does not just hang up on the other person at the end of a phone call. A certain amount of preamble and love and kisses always takes place. You can just hang up, but the other party may be (at the very least) confused by your action.

With computers, the situation is often the same. The proper way to disconnect from another computer depends on that computer. Obtain instructions from the computer's owner on how to disconnect. Usually you need to give a command such as *exit*, *quit*, or *logout* before you hang up; in fact, you may have to exit or quit from several different programs before disconnecting. Some computers, however, don't mind too much if you just hang up on them.

To physically disconnect from (hang up on) the other computer, you have several alternatives:

- ✔ Click Phone⇨Hang Up.
- ✔ Click the Dial/Hangup button on the button bar. (The Dial/Hangup button looks like two connectors being joined together and is usually found right next to the button with the phone icon.)
- ✔ Close the communications document.
- ✔ Exit Works.

Any of these options causes Works to display a query box asking whether it's OK to disconnect. Click the OK button in that box.

Actually, if you have an external modem, you have a final option: Switch off the modem. Works may be a little confused afterward, however, and still think that you're connected. Check the Dial/Hang Up button on the toolbar; if the connectors are connected, click the button.

Do not disconnect by just turning off your computer. Besides the fact that turning off your computer without exiting Works and Windows will leave your computer in a confused state, your modem may remain connected for quite a while, running up your phone bill!

## Saving Your Settings in a Document

If you plan to call this same computer again later, save the phone number and any other settings that you have made as a document file. Saving a communications document works the same as saving any other Works document. See Chapter 4 for full details.

A reasonable person may assume that because Microsoft refers to this communications thing as a *document,* saving the document would save all the text displayed on your screen — text that resulted from your communications session. After all, that text is in the document window. A reasonable person would be wrong.

Here's a refresher course on how to save your communications document: Press Ctrl+S. The Save As dialog box appears. Type a filename and press the Enter key. When you next see the file, the filename will have an extension of .WCM appended to it.

To use this saved file again later, follow these steps: From the Works Startup screen, either click Open an Existing Document and open the file as you do other Works documents, or click Communications (as if you were going to create a new communications document), and then click the computer's name in the Easy Connect dialog box that appears.

# Leaving the Communications Tool

When you're done communicating, you can close the communications tool (close the document) or leave it running and just switch to another tool. If you close the tool, Works insists on hanging up on any communication currently in progress.

To close the communications tool:

1. **Click File⇨Close.**

2. **If you are still connected to the other computer, Works puts up a query box asking whether it should disconnect; click the** OK **button in this box.**

If you're in the middle of a communications session and suddenly realize that you need to do something with another document (copy some text from a word-processor document, for example), you don't need to hang up or close the communications document. Just open or switch to that other document. When you're done, switch back. (Switch back by clicking the communications document window or by choosing Window on the menu bar; then click whatever ends in .WCM (your communications document) in the list that drops down.

## *Reconnecting at a Later Time*

After you have set up a communications document, you can always dial that person or service again by just opening that document. (For example, press Ctrl+N and choose the document from the Existing Documents card of the Task Launcher.) If you follow that sequence, you can skip the Easy Connect dialog box and just go right to the Dial dialog box.

# The 5th Wave

## By Rich Tennant

"WE OFFER A CREATIVE MIS ENVIRONMENT WORKING WITH STATE-OF-THE-ART PROCESSING AND COMMUNICATIONS EQUIPMENT; A COMPREHENSIVE BENEFITS PACKAGE, GENEROUS PROFIT SHARING, STOCK OPTIONS, AND, IF YOU'RE FEELING FUNKY AND NEED TO CHILL OUT AND RAP, WE CAN DO THAT TOO."

# Chapter 18

# Surviving in the Communications Wilderness

• • • • • • • • • • • • • • • • • • • • • • • • • • • • • • • • • • • • • • • • • • • • • •

*In This Chapter*

▶ Fixing dialing and connection problems

▶ Fixing other communications problems

▶ Making your own communications settings

▶ Making text look right on your screen

• • • • • • • • • • • • • • • • • • • • • • • • • • • • • • • • • • • • • • • • • • • • • •

*1* f the tour bus has broken down, leaving you stranded at the side of the information highway, the time has come to buckle down and pick up a few survival tricks. In the last chapter, you gambled on using Works' out-of-the-box communications settings. Here you get into the nitty-gritty of making your own communications settings. You also see how to fix specific things that may be going wrong.

## Problems Getting Connected

One type of problem that arises is just never getting connected (or not staying connected). Following are some typical connection problems and causes and where to turn to find a solution.

> ✔ **You don't hear any dial tone, dialing tones, or other noises when the Dialing Status dialog box appears.**
>
> Your modem may not be properly connected to the phone line. Check to see if the wire from the phone line is plugged into the correct (wall) jack on the modem.

Your modem may be dialing just fine, but it may not make any sounds because it doesn't have a speaker (unlikely, but possible) or its speaker is turned off (also unlikely). Check the modem's manual.

✔ **Works doesn't dial the phone number correctly.**

This situation is probably due to settings in Easy Connect that specify what country you are calling or whether you are dialing locally. See "When Easy Connect Doesn't Connect," later in this chapter.

You may need special dialing if you need a long-distance access code other than *1,* if you're calling from within an office or hotel with a switchboard, or if you are traveling with a portable PC. See " If You Need Special Dialing: Modem Settings," later in this chapter.

✔ **You hear the modem dialing, but the dial tone never goes away.**

You have a telephone line that works only with rotary dial telephones. You need to change the phone settings of Works. See "If You Need Special Dialing: Modem Settings," later in this chapter.

✔ **Nothing appears on your screen after the Dialing Status dialog box disappears. (Normally, the word** Connect **appears on your screen.) Or the other computer seems to pick up the phone but then hangs up.**

One or both of the modems can't negotiate a common speed. You need to find out what speed the other modem is set to and change your own communications settings. See "Cryptic Technobabble — Communications Settings," later in this chapter.

✔ **The other line is always busy. (You should hear a busy signal, if this is the case.)**

If the other line is often busy, you can have Works automatically redial. See "Hold the Phone — Phone Settings," later in this chapter.

✔ **It took more than 60 seconds to complete the connection, and Works timed out (gave up).**

You can extend the time. See "Cryptic Technobabble — Communications Settings," later in this chapter.

✔ **The noise of the modem is waking the kids.**

See "Cryptic Technobabble — Communications Settings," later in this chapter.

✔ **Your modem doesn't answer when someone else's computer calls you.**

See "Hold the Phone — Phone Settings," later in this chapter.

# Problems That Occur after You Connect

If you manage to get connected to the other computer, things can still go wrong. Some typical problems are:

- **The other computer doesn't respond at all after the initial** `Connect` **message, or hangs up.**

  This problem probably means that you need to change communications settings, such as parity, number of stop bits, or speed. If you have call waiting, you may need to disable it (see "If You Need Special Dialing: Modem Settings," later in this chapter).

- **The other computer transmits strange characters.**

  This problem also probably involves communications settings.

- **The other computer transmits huge quantities of gibberish, or it disconnects and the words** `No Carrier` **appear on your screen.**

  This circumstance sometimes indicates that a problem with the quality of the phone line exists and can often be fixed by using a lower speed. Communications settings are the answer.

- **Everything the other computer transmits is more or less readable, but it overtypes itself, runs off your screen, or has wide line spacing.**

  This difficulty is most likely a problem with your terminal settings, in particular the End of Lines setting. See " Making Text More Readable — Terminal Settings," at the end of this chapter.

- **You can't see what you are typing.**

  Another terminal settings problem — check the `Local echo` setting.

- **Lines wrap strangely; lines alternate between short and long.**

  Yet another terminal settings problem — take a look at the `Wrap around` setting.

# When Easy Connect Doesn't Connect

Easy Connect can get confused and add or leave off important digits if you don't enter the right types of data in the right fields. If you notice that the number Works dials doesn't match the number that you thought you had entered, use the following check list to scrutinize the Easy Connect box. (To edit the Easy Connect box, choose Phone⇨Easy Connect from the menu bar or click the button with the telephone icon on the toolbar.)

✔ Make sure that you don't have any extraneous digits in front of the phone number in the Phone number box — no area code, no *1-800*, no *9* to dial out. Just the three-digit exchange (in the U.S.) and the four-digit number.

✔ Make sure that you put an area code in the Area code box — even if the number you're dialing is local. If your call is a toll-free call, the area code is 800.

✔ If the area code that you are dialing is the same as your own, but your call is long distance, you may still need Works to dial a *1* or other long-distance access code. Don't put that code in the Easy Connect box, though. Wait until the Dial box appears and click the Dial as long distance check box. See "If You Need Special Dialing: Modem Settings" coming up next.

✔ If Works is dialing the wrong long-distance access code, it's not Easy Connect's fault. See the next section of this chapter, "If You Need Special Dialing: Modem Settings."

# *If You Need Special Dialing: Modem Settings*

Life is complicated these days, even when you need to dial a regular voice phone call. Pity your poor dialing software. You have outside-line access codes, codes for long-distance providers, and credit card calls. To make matters worse, you may drag your laptop PC from point to point to point (to the point where it doesn't know where the heck it is dialing from). If any of these descriptions fit you, you may want to automate this special dialing box by using the Modem settings of your software.

If you don't mind entering codes yourself, you can always use just a regular telephone to do so, and let Works dial the rest of the numbers. (By regular telephone, I mean that thing with the buttons on it on your desk that you often talk into!) For an access code, for example, just pick up the phone and dial the code (don't hang up yet); use Phone⊅Easy Connect to have Works dial the rest of the number; then hang up the phone. For a calling card call, just pick up the phone after Works dials the number, enter the calling card number, and hang up the phone.

The following steps bring the Dialing Properties dialog box to the screen so that you can automate the special dialing you need:

1. **Choose Settings⊅Modem from the menu bar.**

   The ugly-sounding Modems Properties dialog box pops up. (Actually, this dialog box is a Windows 95 Control Panel dialog box called in as a consultant by Works, but who cares?)

**2. Click the** Dialing Properties **button.**

The rather attractive Dialing Properties dialog box of Figure 18-1 appears. All the Modem settings I am going to talk about are centered on this dialog box.

For long-distance access or calling cards.

Other "locations" can be set up differently.

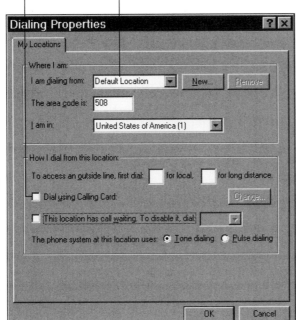

**Figure 18-1:**
Dialing
Properties
helps you
handle
today's
phone
system.

Here's how to handle those special dialing needs.

## Using calling cards and special access codes for long distance

You specify either of these choices in the same place:

**1. Click the** Dial using Calling Card **check box (as shown in Figure 18-1).**

The Change Calling Card box of Figure 18-2 appears.

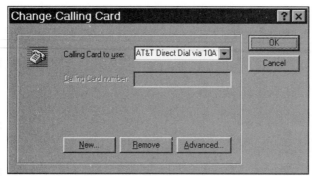

**Figure 18-2:**
Amazing!
Works
knows about
calling
cards!

2. **Click the** `Calling Card to use` **box and choose a calling card.**

3. **If you need to use just an access code (not a calling card), here's the trick: Choose from the calling cards in the list that specify "Direct Dial," such as AT&T Direct Dial. This type of selection makes Works precede your call with the access code for that company — but not try to put a credit card number in, too.**

4. **If you need to use a calling card, choose one of the non-Direct Dial selections and enter your calling card number in the space provided.**

5. **If your calling card is not on the list, click the** New **button. Enter the calling card's name; then click** OK. **Click the** Advanced **button to get to the Dialing Rules dialog box; in the Dialing Rules dialog box, put a G in the top box, your access code (if any) followed by FG$TH in the middle box, and your international access code followed by EFG$TH in the bottom box. (Use *$* if your service provides a *bong* signal before accepting the calling card number; otherwise, leave *$* out, and Works uses an eight-second delay.) Click** Close **when you're done. Enter your calling card number as in Step 4.**

## *Getting an outside line*

If you need to dial *9* or some other code to get an outside line, or (as in some hotels) a different code to get a long-distance outside line, here's where to set those codes in the Dialing Properties dialog box of Figure 18-1. Find the line:

```
To access an outside line, first dial: ____ for local, ____ for
long distance.
```

Enter the *9* (or other code for a local outside line) in the first blank area. If you use the same code for a long-distance outside line, enter that code in the second blank area, too. If the code is different for long distance, say *8*, put an *8* in the second blank area.

A delay may occur between the time that you dial *9* (or whatever) and the time that the outside dial tone appears. If so, follow each number with a comma for a two-second delay.

## Calling from various locations

If you're one of these folks who spend half their time in remote offices, and you bring a portable PC with you, you need a slightly different setup for each location. For this trick, click the New button in the Dialing Properties dialog box. This lets you construct a new My Locations card similar to the one shown in Figure 18-1.

When you are in a given location, proceed normally to make your call; but when the Dial dialog box pops up, choose your new location from the Location box.

## Disabling call waiting

If you have call waiting, incoming calls can interrupt your data transmission and cause you to lose the connection. Most call-waiting systems now allow you to temporarily disable the feature on outgoing calls by entering a special code.

If you want Works to dial the special code before making your call, find the line in the Dialing Properties dialog box (see Figure 18-1) that reads:

```
__This location has call waiting. To disable it, dial:___
```

Check the check box and enter the disabling code in the blank area provided.

## Dialing without tones

Some countries, towns, and other locations (such as rented vacation homes) don't provide tone dialing. In that circumstance, find the line in the Dialing Properties dialog box (see Figure 18-1) that reads:

```
The phone system at this location uses: __ Tone dialing __
Pulse dialing
```

Click the proper setting for the phone system at the location from which you want to call.

Just because the telephone at your location has a rotary dial doesn't mean that the line won't support tone dialing! Try using tones first.

# Hold the Phone — Phone Settings

If you have trouble getting the other computer to pick up the phone, the first place to turn is Phone Settings:

- **Choose Settings⇨Phone from the menu bar:** The Phone card of the Settings dialog box appears.

- **To have Works redial the phone when it encounters a busy line:** Click `Redial`. Works makes as many attempts as it says in the `Redial attempts` box. Between attempts, Works waits the number of seconds shown in the `Redial delay` box. To change the number of seconds in either of these boxes, double-click the box and type in a new number.

- **If you are trying to receive a call from another computer:** Click `Auto answer`. The modem picks up after one ring. Alternatively, choose Phone⇨Easy Connect>>Receive an incoming call.

- **Click the `OK` button when you're done.**

# Cryptic Technobabble — Communications Settings

The communications wilderness has lots of biodiversity. Each different computer that you connect to has its own preferred communications settings or parameters. Sometimes, the other computer adjusts to your settings. Usually, though, *you* have to adjust to *its* settings. Works stores your communications settings as part of the communications document, along with the phone number and name of the other computer.

A lot of computers use two popular settings. You can switch between these settings at any time without using the Settings dialog box. Just click the toolbar button marked 8,n,1 or 7,e,1. The three terms in these labels refer to the Data bits, Parity, and Stop bits settings, respectively: *8* means 8 data bits, *e* means even parity, and *1* means one stop bit. Using these buttons affects only these particular settings.

If you discover that the computer you want to call uses other settings, here's how to adjust them:

1. **Choose Settings⇨Communication.**

   This action puts you on the Communication page of the Settings dialog box.

2. **Click the Properties button.**

   This step puts you in a Properties dialog box for your modem, as shown in Figure 18-3.

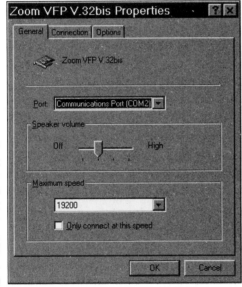

**Figure 18-3:**
The
Properties
dialog box
for your
modem,
General
stuff.

Here's how to modify the individual communications settings. Click the OK button in the Properties dialog box when you're done:

✔ **Changing the speed:** Click the General tab. You may want to lower the speed if you have trouble staying connected to the other computer. The speed is generally set by Works to a number that is higher than or equal to the maximum speed that your modem can deliver. Many of the other computers you call adjust their speed to match yours, but not all of them do that. Find out what maximum speed the other computer can accept. Then, to set your speed to match, click the Maximum speed box and choose the correct number in the list that drops down.

Some online services charge you more per hour if you use higher speeds. If you don't send or receive large files, such as graphics images, programs, or big documents, it may pay you to switch to a lower speed.

✔ **Changing data bits:** Click the Connection tab of the Properties dialog box. Different computers use either 7 or 8 data bits. Click the Data bits text box and choose a number to match the other computer's setting.

For *text communication* (typing and being typed back at) and transmission of text files (also called *ASCII files*), 7 data bits is usually fine. For computers that you want to use to transmit or receive binary files, you may have to change this setting to 8 bits.

✔ **Changing Parity:** Click the Connection tab of the Properties dialog box. Click the Parity text box and choose a parity. The parity you use doesn't make a whole lot of difference, as long as you and the other computer match.

✔ **Changing Stop bits:** Click the Stop bits text box and choose a number to match the other computer's number.

Here are a couple of other valuable settings tucked away with the modem Properties dialog box:

✔ **If your modem gives up too soon when making a call:** Click the Connection tab and change the value in the line that reads Cancel the call if not connected within __ seconds.

✔ **If you tend to forget that you are connected, running up phone bills:** Click the Connection tab. On the Connection card, click the check box marked, Disconnect a call if idle more than __ minutes; then set the idle time to a convenient value.

✔ **If you find the modem noise objectionable:** Click the General tab and drag the Speaker volume pointer to the left.

# Making Text More Readable — Terminal Settings

If the text that the other computer sends you is more or less readable but doesn't seem to be printing properly on your screen or has a small quantity of gibberish in it, you need to fool with the terminal settings.

## PCs in disguise — terminal emulation

When your PC is connected to another computer, your PC is not really acting much like a computer. It's acting like a typewriter or teletype: You type stuff, and stuff appears on the screen. In geek-speak, your computer is *acting like a terminal.* Before PCs existed, large, hulking computers lurked in a back room somewhere; these huge computers had wires running off to *terminals* (keyboards with screens) in peoples' offices. Under Works, your PC can pretend to be (*emulate*) certain terminals. If you emulate the wrong terminal, you see gibberish called *escape sequences* every so often on your screen. To make them go away, you must emulate the correct terminal.

To change the terminal settings: Click S̲ettings⇨T̲erminal. This action puts you on the Terminal page of the Settings dialog box.

Here's how to change the individual settings on the Terminal page. Click the OK button when you're done:

- ✔ **To change terminal emulation:** Find out from the person operating the other computer what terminal you are supposed to be emulating and click that terminal's name in the list box marked T̲erminal.

- ✔ **If lines don't wrap properly:** Choose a new selection in the End of Lines area. Click either A̲dd CR or Add L̲F and see how things work out. Use Add CR if lines appear in a staircase pattern. Use Add L̲F if lines overwrite each other. Changing the End of Line setting is sometimes necessary when communicating with Macintosh computers or online services that expect you to be using a Macintosh.

- ✔ **If lines are too long:** Some computers use a very wide screen and type too many characters to appear on your screen in a single line. To make these lines wrap at the end of the screen, click W̲rap around.

- ✔ **If you're communicating with a foreign country:** Special symbols of that country's language may not come out right. Click the country name in the list marked I̲SO Translation.

- ✔ **If you can't see what you're typing:** Click Local echo.

The general idea behind the terminal settings is that the other computer is sending special characters called escape sequences that are supposed to control how the text appears on your screen. If your terminal settings don't match those of the other computer, these special characters are not interpreted properly, and text appears weird.

# Chapter 19

# Homesteading in the Communications Wilderness

In This Chapter

▶ Saving text to a file

▶ Capturing text to a file

▶ Sending and receiving files

▶ Copying text with the Clipboard

*A*fter you've been tramping around in the communications wilderness, you may want to settle down and start making things a little more homelike. You can settle down by the data stream; capture a nice, fresh bit of text now and then; and maybe cook it up as a word-processor document. Or maybe do a little file-trading with the neighbors. And please do something about this tedious logging business! Maybe you can automate your logging-in. Build yourself a nice login cabin to live in.

## *Preserving and Capturing Screen Text*

Hungry for a little more substance than the fleeting messages drifting across your screen? Set your snare and capture or preserve some wild text. Reading things on your screen is great, but sometimes keeping it in a file is nice, too. If you're getting e-mail, for example, you can keep your correspondence in files. Or, if you're getting stock market reports, you may want to analyze the data at a later time.

## Preserving what's in your document window

The simplest way to save text as a file is to save whatever has so far appeared in your communications window. To do this task at any time:

1. **Choose File⇨Save As from the menu bar.**

2. **Click the** Save as type **list box and choose** Session Data.

3. **Give the file a name and specify a directory as you usually would in Save As; then click the Save button.**

This action saves everything that passed by on your screen during your communications session as a text file.

## Capturing text

If you would rather save just a portion of what is being transmitted to you, you can capture the text. *Capturing* is like turning on a tape recorder for a while; so you must turn on the capture feature *just before* the text you want to save is transmitted. Here's how capturing text goes:

1. **Click the Capture Text button on the toolbar (the camera icon).**

   Or you can click Tools⇨Capture Text in the menu bar. Same thing.

2. **Give the capture file a name and folder.**

   The Capture Text dialog box arrives on the scene, looking for all the world like the familiar, old Save As dialog box. The Capture Text dialog box works the same way as the Save As dialog box does.

3. **Roll 'em.**

   Do whatever you need to do to have text transmitted to you (perhaps give a command to the remote computer).

4. **Click the Capture Text button again.**

   (Or click Tools⇨End Capture Text in the menu bar.)

That's it. You've captured the elusive communications transmission as a text file! Now you can open that file and read it, edit it, or dress it up.

## Cooking with captured files

You've captured some text, so what are you going to do with it? To open the file, choose File⇨Open from the menu bar. In the Open dialog box that appears, specify that text file: select its directory in the Look in list box and then type its file name (with the .TXT extension) in the File name box. If you can't remember its name, type **\*.TXT** instead, press Enter, and double-click the name when it appears in the File name list box.

The Open File As dialog box appears on the scene and wants to know what kind of document it should make from this text file: word processor, spreadsheet, or database. The choice is yours; but unless the text is in table form, I suggest that you click Word Processor. Phwzap! In a few seconds, you've got your file in the word processor.

# Sending and Receiving Files

A little trading is always good for the communications homesteader. Send a file, get a file, and pretty soon all us homesteaders are fat and happy, information-wise. But sending and receiving things on the frontier requires a little more care than just calling United Parcel Service.

First, decide whether you truly want to send a file or just send the contents of a file. "Huh?" you say (and not without reason).

> ✔ **If you want the recipient to actually end up with a file:** Use the Send Binary File command (or button).

> ✔ **If you want to send text from a file as if you were typing it:** You can send the *contents* of a file. You can use two different ways to do this task: copying and pasting or using the Send Text command (or button). Copying and pasting works with a variety of other Works documents. Send Text works only with files of the *text* type (files with an extension of .TXT on their filenames, typically).

## Send a file: the Send Binary File command or button

To send or receive a file, do this:

1. **Find out what file transmission protocol the other computer uses.**

   Don't panic. A *file transmission protocol* is just a name describing how a file is sent; you don't have to understand the protocol, just find out its name. The other computer may have several file transmission protocols available to use. The protocol you choose must be a protocol that Works can use, too. Zmodem is usually the best protocol to use with Works; if Zmodem is not available, try Ymodem, Xmodem/CRC, and Kermit in order of preference.

**2. Choose Settings⇨Transfer on the menu bar.**

The Settings dialog box appears, displaying the Transfer card as shown in Figure 19-1. Click the chosen protocol in the list box marked Transfer protocol.

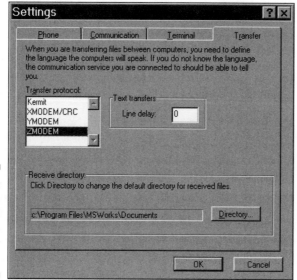

**Figure 19-1:** Observing protocol with the Transfer settings.

If you are going to be receiving files, you need to tell Works where to put them. Click the Directory button in the lower-right corner. Choose a directory in the aptly named Choose A Directory dialog box that appears. The Choose A Directory dialog box works like a simple version of the Save dialog box. Click the OK button when done.

**3. Click the OK button in the Settings dialog box.**

**4. Command the other computer to send you a file or prepare to receive a file yourself.**

How you command the other computer depends on the other computer. You may have to type several commands, one of which involves telling the other computer what protocol to use. (Sometimes a computer mentions being able to send or receive only binary files. Don't worry. If you have a text file, send it along in the same way as I describe here.)

If you are directly connected to a user such as yourself, sitting at a PC screen, that person must give the command for his or her own computer to send or receive a file, using the same protocol that you are using.

5. **To send, click the Send Binary File button in the toolbar (a file folder with an arrow pointing out of it). To receive, click the Receive Binary File button (same thing, but the arrow points in).**

   A Send File or Receive File dialog box appears, describing your progress in terms of, among other things, *percent complete*. After that reaches 100 percent, you're done, and the dialog box goes away. If the transmission process appears to get stuck for a long time (like minutes) at some percentage, click Cancel.

Sometimes Works decides to send a Pause signal to the other computer when it finishes transmitting. If everything appears to come to a halt during or immediately after a transmission, see if the hourglass-icon button on the toolbar is depressed. If it is, take it out to lunch, give it a good sing to cheer it up, then click it.

## Send content: the Send Text command or button

Works' Send Text command (or toolbar button) is good for sending text that you would otherwise type on the screen, but the text just happens to be in a file. The Send Text command sends the *contents* of a text file without sending the file itself. (The other computer just figures that you're a speedy typist; it has no idea that you're sending contents from a file.)

For example, if you use an electronic mail program that runs on a remote computer, you can compose a text file first on your PC. Then you can connect to the other computer, tell it that you are about to type text for a message, and send the contents of your text file instead of typing.

Sending content works only with *text* files — files that typically have an extension of .TXT on their filename — not Works' word-processor, spreadsheet, or database files.

1. **Connect to the other computer.**

2. **Give that computer whatever command it may need to prepare to receive text.**

   For example, the command may be to start creating the body of an electronic mail message. Whatever you transmit afterward would then be the message text.

3. **Click the Send Text button in the toolbar (to the right of the camera icon in the normal toolbar setup) or choose Tools⇔Send Text.**

4. **Carry on as if you had just typed a bunch of text to the other computer. (Tell the other computer to send the e-mail, or whatever, and log off.)**

It's possible that the other computer may think that you are *too* speedy a typist and get confused. If this situation happens, choose Settings⇨Transfer, find the box marked Line delay, and enter the number 1 into that box. If things still don't work, increase this number until things do work.

# Sending and Receiving Text by Copying and Pasting

Windows provides a nice facility for copying things from one program to another. This facility is called the Windows Clipboard, and you can read more about using it in Chapter 3. The Windows Clipboard works for communications, too. In a nutshell, to use the Clipboard to send something by copying and pasting, you do this:

1. **Select something in any document window.**

2. **Copy it onto the Clipboard with Edit⇨Copy.**

3. **Paste it into the communications document while you are communicating, using Edit⇨Paste.**

You can send text as long as you are connected to another computer when you go to paste the text. (You can't press Ctrl+V to paste in the communications tool; choose Edit⇨Paste instead.) The text is transmitted as if you had typed it.

The Clipboard works the other way, too (for copying text between the communications tool and other Works tools). You can copy text from your communications window to the word processor, for example.

When you send or receive text in this way, much of the formatting can be lost or even jumbled. The recipient of pasted text must redo some of the formatting to get your text to look as it did originally.

# Part VI
# Creating Great Works of Art: Graphics

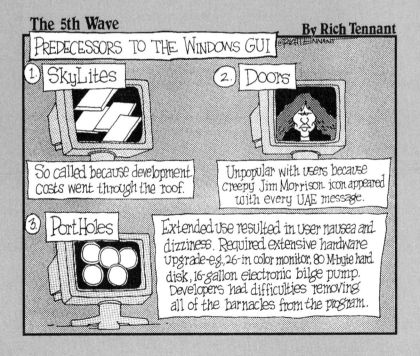

PREDECESSORS TO THE WINDOWS GUI

① SkyLites

So called because development costs went through the roof.

② Doors

Unpopular with users because creepy Jim Morrison icon appeared with every UAE message.

③ PortHoles

Extended use resulted in user nausea and dizziness. Required extensive hardware upgrade-e.g., 26-in color monitor, 80 M-byte hard disk, 16-gallon electronic bilge pump. Developers had difficulties removing all of the barnacles from the program.

# In this part . . .

1 f you can't even draw a straight line, you've come to the right place. Works is good at drawing straight lines; curved lines, too. In fact, Works can give you great works of art — or great works of "chart" — with little more than a few sweeps of your mouse.

In this part, you'll learn how Works can turn your spreadsheet into a bar chart, pie chart, or even a "radar" chart, with only a few hints from you about how you want the chart to look. Need some basic diagrams? Works includes Microsoft Draw where you can sketch nice, clean rectangles, circles, and other "blobs" without ever the need for an eraser. Works even provides a gallery of clip art to liven up your documents, and a fun WordArt tool to give you some eye-catching headlines.

"Art for art's sake."

Anonymous

# Chapter 20

# Creating a Work of Chart

- - - - - - - - - - - - - - - - - - - - - - - - - - - - - - - - - - - - - - - - - -

## In This Chapter

▶ Strolling the gallery of charts

▶ Getting from spreadsheet to chart

▶ Laying out your spreadsheet for charting

▶ Understanding series and categories

▶ Creating any chart

▶ Using the chart window, menu, and toolbar

▶ Changing chart types and variations

▶ Saving your work of chart

▶ Printing a chart

▶ Using charts in documents

▶ Leaving the chart window

- - - - - - - - - - - - - - - - - - - - - - - - - - - - - - - - - - - - - - - - - -

*B*e done with the tyranny of words and numbers. Stroll Works' gallery of charts and find one that expresses the pent-up yearnings of your soul. (Assuming a soul with comparatively modest yearnings, of course. 3-D area charts always do the job for me.)

For a multitool package with plenty of other things on its mind, Works offers a rather nice selection of chart types and variations and makes the job of charting a breeze. Or is it a snap? Whatever. A snapping breeze, perhaps. Very easy, in any event. In this chapter, explore the mysterious link between spreadsheets and charts, learn how to exploit this connection to your advantage, and turn mere rows and columns into graphical eye candy to delight the soul and satisfy the intellect.

# A Gallery of Chart Types and Variations

Works offers a veritable optical smorgasbord of charts. Here's a representative listing of types:

- ✔ **Bar:** For multiple categories, bars are differently colored and can be side by side or stacked to show the sum.

- ✔ **Line:** Creates lines, lines with dots (data points), dots alone, or high/low/close (for stock values).

- ✔ **Stacked Line:** For multiple lines: Each line adds to the preceding line (that is, it stacks).

- ✔ **Area:** Looks like Stacked Line, but shaded underneath the line.

- ✔ **Pie:** Shows values in a single row or column as pieces of a pie: together, with one piece removed (common in our house), or exploded (must have microwaved it).

- ✔ **Scatter:** Lotsa dots. Used for showing correlation between two types of measured phenomena, like degree of baldness and IQ in men (strongly correlated; the dots cluster into a nice, straight line).

- ✔ **Radar:** Shows data in a connect-the-dots picture of Radar O'Reilly from the TV series *M*A*S*H*. No, just kidding (but it's not a bad idea, is it?). Shows variations in cyclical events — for example, popularity over several months of different flavors of ice cream by phase of the moon. Which, come to think of it, does resemble . . .

- ✔ **Combination:** Lets you mix lines and bars in a single chart.

I'm not going to get into all of these chart types here. After you learn the basics, you can pick up the others pretty easily.

You can get these basic types of charts in several variations:

- ✔ **Bar, line, and pie charts in 3-D:** No, you don't have to wear special glasses. Works doesn't really mean 3-D; the chart appears to have thickness and shading so that it looks as if it's made of chunks of plastic. Very trendy.

- ✔ **Titles:** You can have two lines in the title.

- ✔ **Labels:** You can put numbers on the data points (data labels) along bars or lines, or put in text identifying bars or lines. You can label categories, as with the stuff along the horizontal axis in a bar chart.

- ✔ **Legends:** Identify lines or bars by color or shading.

✔ **Axes:** You can have two Y axes if you plot two different kinds of data. Plus you can have logarithmic scales for things that increase rapidly, such as national debt over time.

You can also size the charts to any size you need; put a border around them; change the fonts, the colors, the shading, the gridlines, and even the shapes of the data points. There. Is that enough? I don't discuss all of these variations here, but you should be aware of what's possible.

Don't worry that everything on-screen is shown in color. If you have a black-and-white printer, the chart comes out with shading to substitute for the various colors. To see how things will look on your printer, use the command View⇨Display as Printed in the menu bar.

# *From Spreadsheet to Chart: The General Procedure*

Charts and spreadsheets go together like itch and scratch (or Ben and Jerry, or Pinky and The Brain, or whatever your favorite combination is). In fact, the only way you can chart something in Works is by first creating a spreadsheet.

Here's the general procedure for making a chart:

1. **Make a spreadsheet, planning and laying it out carefully for the best charting results.**

2. **Select (highlight) a portion of that spreadsheet, making sure to include row and column headings.**

3. **Choose Tools⇨Create New Chart from the menu bar.**

4. **A New Chart dialog box lets you select a bar, line, pie, or other type of chart based on the data and headings in your spreadsheet. It even shows you a sample to help you choose.**

5. **A chart window opens up, displaying your basic chart in color.**

   You are now in the Works charting tool. The menu bar and toolbar now contain charting commands, not spreadsheet commands.

6. **Embellish the chart with titles, labels, and other chartish features.**

7. **Print the chart or put it into another document by copying and pasting it.**

   (You could also *link* it, although I don't recommend this for beginners — see "Using Charts in Documents" later in this chapter.)

# Laying Out Your Spreadsheet for Charting

Like an artist preparing a canvas, you should lay out your spreadsheet to simplify your chartwork. Works is pretty good at dealing with various kinds of spreadsheet layouts, but a little care can make your life easier and give you better results.

Here is a checklist for preparing your spreadsheet:

✔ Keep together numbers that you want to chart together. If practical, keep them grouped in the upper-left corner of the spreadsheet so that they are adjacent to the row and column headings.

✔ Put headings on rows and columns.

✔ Don't use blank rows or columns.

✔ If you're going to use data labels (numbers printed on the chart), format your data the way you want it to appear on the chart. For currency, for example, use currency formatting.

# What the Heck Are Series and Categories?

It sounds like a TV quiz show: As you work with charts, Works keeps yammering about series and categories. (As in, "I'll take the charting category for 10 points, Pat!") What the heck are these, anyway?

A *series* is a set of numbers in a single row or column. In a line chart, a series would be shown as a single line of a given color. A chart can have several series; each series with its own color.

A *category* is a name for each number in the series (January, February, and March could each be a category). If the series is contained in a row, these categories are the column headings. You can make these categories automatically appear along the X axis by including the column headings in your initial selection of cells.

A series label is a description of what the numbers represent, such as Sales or Rainfall. If a series is contained in a row, you can put a series label in the first cell of each row (the first column). If you include that column in your initial selection of cells, the labels appear automatically in the legend.

# How to Create Any Chart

To create a new chart, start with a spreadsheet — preferably one laid out with row and column headings, but any spreadsheet can be charted.

1. **Select a range with the data you want to chart.**

   If you can select a range of cells that includes both row and column headings, so much the better. See Figure 20-1.

   For a pie chart, select just the one column (or row) containing the numbers to be charted. If you can, include the adjoining column to the left or the row above that has the headings. If you can't, don't worry.

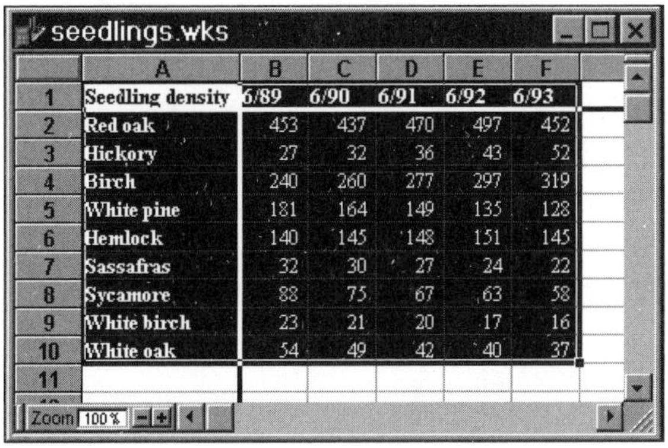

| | A | B | C | D | E | F |
|---|---|---|---|---|---|---|
| 1 | Seedling density | 6/89 | 6/90 | 6/91 | 6/92 | 6/93 |
| 2 | Red oak | 453 | 437 | 470 | 497 | 452 |
| 3 | Hickory | 27 | 32 | 36 | 43 | 52 |
| 4 | Birch | 240 | 260 | 277 | 297 | 319 |
| 5 | White pine | 181 | 164 | 149 | 135 | 128 |
| 6 | Hemlock | 140 | 145 | 148 | 151 | 145 |
| 7 | Sassafras | 32 | 30 | 27 | 24 | 22 |
| 8 | Sycamore | 88 | 75 | 67 | 63 | 58 |
| 9 | White birch | 23 | 21 | 20 | 17 | 16 |
| 10 | White oak | 54 | 49 | 42 | 40 | 37 |
| 11 | | | | | | |

**Figure 20-1:** Highlight headings and data if there are no blank rows or columns separating the two.

2. **Click Tools in the menu bar and then click Create New Chart in the menu that drops down. Or click the New Chart button on the toolbar (it looks like a tiny bar chart).**

   The Create New Chart dialog box of Figure 20-2 swings into action. It shows you a sample of a bar chart based on the data you selected. It also tries to figure out if you have included line and column headings; if so, it uses them as labels in the chart.

3. **Choose a chart type from the graphical picture gallery.**

   The sample area on the right shows you what your chart will look like. Works always starts out by showing you a bar chart. If you're not quite sure what type of chart is being depicted, read the text description that appears in the `Chart type` line, atop the gallery.

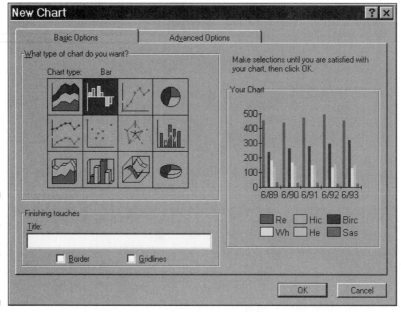

**Figure 20-2:**
The New Chart dialog box initially suggests a bar chart.

**4. If the chart looks like the wrong things are being plotted, use** Advanced Options.

It's possible that Works has misinterpreted your spreadsheet data and is reading your data series across instead of down, or vice versa. If your chart is displaying the wrong data along the X axis, click the Advanced Options tab on the New Chart dialog box.

**a. If necessary, change item 1, Which way do your series go?**

Frankly, I find thinking about this too confusing. If the chart looks wrong, I just choose the alternative: either Across or Down. If you want to think about it, though, see the sidebar "How does Works decide what to do?"

**b. If necessary, change the settings for First column contains and First row contains.**

If you have numbers in the first row or column and you actually intend them to be labels for your data, not the data to be charted, click Legend text.

If you have dates or times in the first row or column and you actually intend them to be data and not labels, click A value (Y) series.

All better now? Click the Basic Options tab.

**5. Enter a title for the chart.**

Click the text box marked Title and type in something descriptive, like *Sales by Quarter*. The sample chart in the dialog box reflects your choice.

6. **If you want a border around the whole chart, click** Border**; if you want gridlines, click on** Gridlines.

The sample chart shows you what you'll get. You can improve on these features later, too (more gridlines, for example).

7. **Click the** OK **button.**

A chart window appears with your lovely work of numeric art in spunky primary colors. To see how it will really look on your (probably black-and-white) printer, click View⇨Display as Printed in the menu bar. (Repeat to go back to color viewing.) Then run out and buy a color printer!

# The Chart Window, Menu, and Toolbar

When you finish creating a new chart, things look a bit like Figure 20-3. (The chart window usually covers up the spreadsheet window a bit more than Figure 20-3 shows.) The chart window has the same name as the spreadsheet, but with Chart 1 appended.

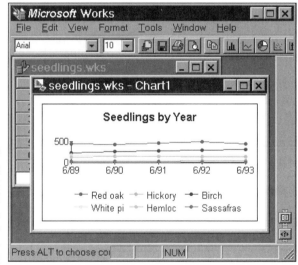

**Figure 20-3:**
The chart window and its brother, the spreadsheet.

Notice that the menu bar has changed a little, and the toolbar has changed a lot. That's because as long as the chart window is active, you're in the chart tool. If you switch to the spreadsheet (by, say, clicking its title bar), you're in the spreadsheet tool. And if you click your heels together three times, you're in Kansas, where the bars don't have menus and you leave your tools in the truck.

## How does Works decide what to do?

Works guesses how you want your data organized by looking at the rows and columns in the area you selected in the spreadsheet. If you have more rows than columns selected, the rows become the *categories* (individual lines or bars) of the chart, and Works picks Across (across a row) for the direction of the data series. If your data series actually run the other way, click Down.

Works also tries to figure out whether or not you have included labels. Works looks at both the first row and the first column that you selected. If they contain numbers, Works charts them. If they contain text (or dates or time), Works uses the text for the legend.

You can always switch between windows by clicking Window in the menu bar and then clicking the window of your choice in the list that drops down. With charts and spreadsheets, you can also switch from one to the other by pressing F3. You can choose from several charts, so a dialog box comes forth with the list of charts available. Double-click the one you want.

If the chart looks rather squished and crowded and the words are chopped off, don't panic. It's just how Works deals with a too-small chart window. Click and drag a side or corner of the chart window to make it bigger.

## *The chart menu*

The chart menu looks and works like menus everywhere but is actually pretty different:

 ✔ The File selection on the menu bar is very much the same everywhere in Works. See Chapter 2. When you save from the chart menu, you save the whole spreadsheet file because charts are part of their associated spreadsheet.

 ✔ The Edit selection gives you not only the usual cut-and-paste stuff described in Chapter 3, but also everything you need for changing what range in the spreadsheet is being charted, or editing the text in the chart.

 ✔ The View command lets you switch between the spreadsheet and any of the charts that are attached to it. (Yes, you can have several different charts attached to a spreadsheet.) The chart windows don't have to be open; this command opens them.

✔ Clicking on Format⇨Chart Type lets you change the type and variation of the chart. See "Changing Chart Types and Variations," coming up soon. The toolbar buttons are another place to do the same thing.

✔ The Format menu also gives you commands that control appearances: fonts, patterns, colors, axes, borders, legends, and 3-D-osity. (Try formatting your text in Wingdings font for that trendy, Museum-of-Fine-Arts Egyptian hieroglyphic look!)

✔ Clicking Tools gives you commands to create, name, and delete charts attached to the spreadsheet.

✔ Window and Help are selections that work the same everywhere. See Chapter 2 for more information on windows and help.

I get into more details on some of these, one at a time, as I go along.

## *The chart toolbar*

The toolbar, as always, is just another way to give commands to Works (instead of the traditional semaphore flags). About half the buttons (the ones on the left side) are identical to the buttons on the spreadsheet toolbar, covering options such as font, size, saving, printing, and copying.

You can always find out what a button is for by placing your mouse cursor over it (don't click). A tiny tag appears with actual English words on it.

The buttons on the right half of the toolbar are, for the most part, WYSIWYG (What You See Is What You Get). That is, they have pictures of charts on 'em. (Really! Just get out your magnifying glass.) Click 'em, and your chart can look something like the icon, only bigger and prettier. See "Changing Chart Types and Variations," next.

The second-to-last button (with the white arrow and the number 1) is a secret passage to the spreadsheet — specifically, to the first data series in the spreadsheet. If you have a big spreadsheet and are charting just a portion of it, this is a quick way to get to the right place.

# *Changing Chart Types and Variations*

You can change the chart's *type* or *variation* on that type either by clicking Format⇨Chart Type or by clicking a toolbar button. Either way, you get a lovely graphical display of various ways to display your data. For example, if you click the button that looks like downtown Chicago (the 3-D Bar Chart button), you get the dialog box shown in Figure 20-4.

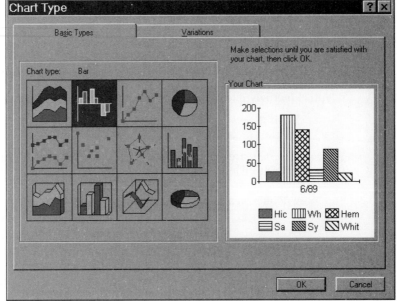

**Figure 20-4:**
A graphical
selection of
*basic* chart
types; for
*variations*
on that type,
click the
Variations
tab.

The top card in the Chart Type dialog box shows you the basic types of chart available, such as bar, line, or 3-D bar. (If you clicked a toolbar button to get here, your chosen type is already selected.) Choose a different type by clicking one of the pictures.

Click the Variations tab, the second card in this dialog box, for different versions of the basic type. Click the chart variation of your choice in this dialog box and then click OK. Some look a lot alike; to see the differences, watch the example chart closely as you switch between the variations.

If you change your chart type or variation, do so before you apply finishing touches, such as data labels (discussed in the next chapter). Changing the chart type or variation may remove these niceties if they aren't used in the new type of chart. If you change back to the old type, they will be gone.

# Saving (or Not Saving) Your Work of Chart

Lest your work of chart suffer the depredations of time and crumble, like the fabled facades of Venice, into the sea, you should take pains to preserve it. In other words, save that sucker.

To save your chart, you save the entire spreadsheet. Do this in the ordinary way: choose File⇨Save. If the spreadsheet is a new document, the Save As dialog box appears, and you give the file a name and a directory to live in.

If your chart is utterly wrong and you don't want to bother trying to rehabilitate it (see instructions in Chapter 21), just get rid of it. If you don't, it hangs around in your spreadsheet file, always getting underfoot when you try to use other charts.

To delete a chart, choose Tools⇨Delete Chart in the menu bar. A modest Delete Chart dialog box comes forth. Click the chart's name (if the chart's window is still on-screen, you can compare the name in the dialog box against the title bar in the chart's window to ensure that you pick the right one) and click the Delete button.

You must click the OK button in the Delete Chart dialog box for the deletion to take effect. Even though the name disappears when you click the Delete key, it's not gone until you click OK.

# Printing a Chart

A great piece of industrial art like your chart deserves to be proudly displayed on canvas. Because your printer probably doesn't do canvas very well, you'll have to settle for printing your chart on paper (and proudly displaying it on the refrigerator door, perhaps).

If your chart is going to become part of a document, you'll print that document. See "Using Charts in Documents," the following section.

If your chart, like the cheese in the nursery rhyme, is to stand alone, use the same printing commands that you use in any other tool: the Page Setup and Print commands in the File menu.

Here are a few tips for printing charts, mostly having to do with the Page Setup dialog box:

✔ Preview the printout (choose File⇨Print Preview). You may be a bit surprised at what your chart is going to look like. It will probably be taller than you had in mind and will have patterns instead of colors if you have a black-and-white printer. Click the image in Print Preview to enlarge your preview on your screen.

✔ Many, if not most, charts will fit better if printed sideways *(landscape* mode). Call up the Page Setup dialog box (File⇨Page Setup); click the Source, Size and Orientation tab; and choose Landscape to change to sideways printing. Click the OK button.

- ✔ To proportion the chart just as it is in the chart window, call up the Page Setup dialog box (File⇨Page Setup), click the Other Options tab, and choose Screen size. Click the OK button. The graphics keep the same proportion; the text is whatever point size you have selected.

- ✔ Other options are (not surprisingly) also on the Other Options page of the Page Setup dialog box. The Full page, keep proportions option keeps the same proportions as the chart window but fills the page to either the side margins or the top and bottom margins. Full page expands height and width to the margins and doesn't worry about proportions.

- ✔ To set the dimensions more precisely by using the Page Setup dialog box, choose either of the two Full page options on the Other Options page and then set the page margins on the Margins tab.

## Using Charts in Documents

No doubt about it: Charts liven up a document. But putting charts in a document can be a little mysterious at times. You have two basic ways to put a chart in a document:

- ✔ Paste a copy.
- ✔ Insert it (link it).

The pasting method is straightforward and can be easily done in either a word-processor document or a database document. You just paste a copy of the chart — a snapshot of the chart at the time you copied it. If the data changes, the chart is not updated by Works; you have to paste a new copy. The process, in a nutshell, is to press Ctrl+C while in the chart window and then switch to another document window and press Ctrl+V. To resize the chart, drag the handles around the image.

For more detailed instructions on how to copy and paste a chart into a word-processor document, see Chapter 8. To copy and paste a chart in a database document, use the same instructions. Copying and pasting a chart won't work in a communications document or another spreadsheet, although it will often work in programs outside Works.

The inserting (or linking) method is nice, but a bit fragile and tricky, and in Works this method is limited to word-processor documents. Its advantage is that if the data in the spreadsheet changes, the chart in the word-processor document changes. Its main disadvantage is that if you move or rename the spreadsheet document, or rename the chart, the link between the two documents can be broken. Also, controlling the size of the chart in the final document can sometimes be a frustrating experience.

If you decide it's worth the trouble, the inserting procedure goes like this:

1. **Both documents (the spreadsheet with the chart and the word-processor document) must be open. Set up the chart window so that it looks exactly how you want it to appear. Save your spreadsheet (press Ctrl+S).**

2. **Switch to the word-processor document window and choose Insert⇨Chart.**

3. **In the Insert Chart dialog box that appears, your spreadsheet will be listed in the** Select a spreadsheet **box. Click it, and then click the name of your chart (for example, Chart1) in the** Select a chart **box. Click the** OK **button.**

# Leaving the Chart Window

To leave the chart window, simply close the window: Double-click the X symbol at the right end of the chart window's title bar (not the worksheet title bar or the Works title bar). This action puts you back in the spreadsheet window. Your chart remains part of the spreadsheet. To return to the chart window from the spreadsheet, choose View⇨Chart; then double-click the chart's name in the dialog box that appears.

If you close by using the Close command in the File menu, you will close the entire spreadsheet. If you exit by using the Exit command in the File menu, you are actually shutting down Works. With either of these actions, Works may ask whether you want to save changes to your spreadsheet — probably a reference to the charts you just added. If you click No, those charts will be lost.

# Chapter 21
# Polishing Your Work of Chart

· · · · · · · · · · · · · · · · · · · · · · · · · · · · · · · · · · · · · · · ·

## In This Chapter

▶ Adding horizontal and vertical lines

▶ Formatting X and Y axes

▶ Using fonts and style

▶ Formatting numbers

▶ Making chart and axis titles

▶ Changing the legend text

▶ Changing X- and Y-axis labels

▶ Adding data labels

▶ Pasting labels and data

▶ Using multiple charts

· · · · · · · · · · · · · · · · · · · · · · · · · · · · · · · · · · · · · · · ·

*W*hen Leonardo da Vinci painted *The Last Supper,* did he finish one apostle and move on to the next? Or did he go back, add a little wrinkle here, a little twinkle in the eye there, fixing and refining and polishing until the apostles' mothers themselves would not have recognized their kids? Well, we'll never know, and neither will the apostles' mothers, but I thought I should ask. Not out of idle curiosity, either, but to illustrate the point that, like da Vinci, you will want to fool around with your charts until their own mothers wouldn't recognize them, if they had mothers.

So, "Leonardo," here are your tools. In this chapter are most of the things you are likely to want to fool around with in a chart. Go forth and finish your masterpiece.

# Horizontal and Vertical Lines and Axis Stuff

All these spiffy types and styles of charts, like 3-D area charts, are artistic as all heck but may occasionally leave your viewers wondering exactly what values they're looking at. If you're an economist or corporate PR honcho, you may value this vagueness — no, no, I mean *moderation of precision* — in your presentation. Folks with jobs requiring somewhat more precision will probably want gridlines, more precision on the intervals along the axes, and other axis-related refinements.

The absolutely simplest way to get horizontal or vertical lines is to choose a style that gives them to you. That is, when you choose a chart type by choosing Format⇨Chart Type in the menu bar (or by using the buttons on the toolbar), among the several styles that are presented to you are a couple with vertical and/or horizontal lines. Click one of these. You may have to reenter data labels or other fine points of your chart, however. Choosing a style is best done before getting fancy with labels and lines.

Otherwise, you can get lines and other axis options by formatting the axes. Figure 21-1 shows some options for a 3-D bar chart. Lines that run horizontally from the vertical Y axis are perhaps most in demand. To get these, see "Formatting the Y axis," next. For lines that run vertically from the X axis, see "Formatting the X axis" later in this chapter.

**Figure 21-1:** Horizontal lines at intervals of 25 along the Y axis improve this chart.

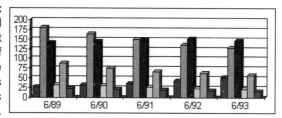

## Formatting the Y axis

To extend horizontal lines out from the Y axis, or otherwise fool around with the Y axis, click Format⇨Vertical (Y) Axis in the menu that drops down. The Format Vertical Axis dialog box descends from the ether, looking a bit like Figure 21-2.

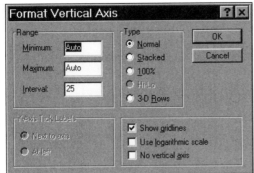

**Figure 21-2:**
The place
to go for
a more
refined axis.

✔ For gridlines at each interval along the axis, click Show gridlines to put an X in that check box.

✔ For more or fewer intervals along the axis, click Interval and type a new value. For example, for a numbered tick-mark along the axis every $50 (or 50 ducks or 50 inches of rain, whatever), enter 50.

✔ To start or end the axis at a different value, edit the values in the Minimum or Maximum text boxes, respectively. This is good when you have a couple of extreme values you're embarrassed about and don't care to present.

✔ If you have values over a very wide range (like over several powers of 10; say, from 1 to 1,000), click Use logarithmic scale (not available in all chart types).

✔ To eliminate the vertical axis altogether (economists and PR folks, take note), click No vertical axis. Hey, if you let folks see actual numbers, you'll just get a lot of picky debate.

✔ You can fool around with what I call the chart's variation, by clicking one of the (non-grayed out) entries in the Type area. Sometimes you'll find variations here that aren't available when you use the Format⇨Chart Type command or the toolbar buttons (such as line charts expressed as percent fractions). Certain variations are not available for certain chart types.

## Formatting the X axis

To extend vertical lines up from the X axis, or otherwise fool around with the X axis, choose Format⇨Horizontal (X) Axis in the menu bar. The Horizontal Axis dialog box does a jolly buck-and-wing onto your screen. (No, just kidding about the dance part, but it would be fun if it did.)

In X-Y *(scatter)* charts, the X axis works very much as the Y axis does, so the Horizontal Axis dialog box doesn't work as described here. It works more like the Vertical Axis dialog box. See "Formatting the Y axis," earlier in this chapter.

✔ Click `Show gridlines` to, well, show gridlines — the vertical line thingies at every interval.

✔ In an area-type chart, where gridlines disappear behind the curve, you can also click `Show droplines`: These lines are superimposed on the area curve.

✔ To eliminate the horizontal axis altogether, click `No horizontal axis`.

✔ To trim out some of the category labels along a crowded X axis, type a larger value in the text box marked `Label frequency`. A **3,** for example, shows every third label.

# Changing Chart Text and Numbers

It's enough to give a sensitive artist fits. We go to all the trouble of making pictures of data, and then we have to put text and numbers all over it to make any sense out of it! Works lets you put text — including titles, series labels, and data labels — in several places in your chart.

## Fonts and style

As far as fonts go, one size fits all. In fact, one font and one font style fits all in a Works chart. Everything is in exactly the same type (Arial 10-point bold, for example). You can change fonts in the charting tool just as you do in any other tool:

✔ Click the down-arrow button next to the font or size box in the toolbar and then click a new selection in the menu that drops down.

✔ Press Ctrl+B for bold, Ctrl+I for italic, or Ctrl+* for underline.

✔ Click Format⇨Font and Style in the menu that drops down. Select font, size, and style in the Font dialog box.

If your problem is that the text doesn't seem to fit, it's probably because you're looking at the chart in a rather small window. Works compresses the graphics to fit the window but leaves the type whatever size you make it. Check your chart with Print Preview before you assume that the type is too large.

## Number formats

If your numbers need dollar signs, a different number of decimal places, or any of the other formatting that you're familiar with from spreadsheets — it's not your chart's problem! No, it's your spreadsheet's problem.

Return to your spreadsheet window and change the number formatting of your data. See Chapter 11 for more on this.

## Chart and axis titles

Titles are important. I once had a cartooning teacher who said that if you can't draw a rabbit, make sure the title says *rabbit* somewhere.

> ✔ Chart titles are the one or two lines at the top of the chart.

> ✔ An axis title goes along an axis and tells you what it represents: months, furlongs, doughnuts, and so on.

To create chart or axis titles, choose Edit⇨Titles. The Titles dialog box moves regally into view. Just click the appropriate text box and type.

> ✔ You can enter two lines of title for the chart: `Chart title` and `Subtitle`.

> ✔ To type an identifier to be printed alongside the X or Y axis, click `Horizontal (X) Axis` or `Vertical (Y) Axis`.

> ✔ Right Vertical Axis is for a second Y axis if you have one.

Click the `OK` button when you're done.

If these titles don't look very good in the chart window, don't forget: They probably won't really look like that when they are printed. To see how the chart "really" looks, use Print Preview.

## Series labels in the legend

Series labels are the text that appears in the legend. They identify the contents of a graph by color or pattern.

> ✔ If you include row and column headings when you select the cells for your chart, the series labels are taken automatically from those headings.

> ✔ If you don't include the headings (or cannot because of the spreadsheet layout), you get boring automatic labels, such as Series 1.

To change the series labels, use the Edit⇨Legend/Series dialog box, shown in Figure 21-3.

To change the labels, you can do one of two things in the Edit Legend/Series Labels dialog box, as shown in Figure 21-3:

- ✔ **Thing 1:** Type in the text you want for the series. (Direct, simple, and to the point.) In Figure 21-3, I'm typing in **Spruce** for the first data series.

- ✔ **Thing 2:** Type in the cells where the labels are in your spreadsheet. (Indirect, perhaps, but may save retyping.) In Figure 21-3, all but the first data series (which I'm editing) refer to the cell where the label is.

  For reference, you may want to arrange your windows so that you can see both the chart and the place in the spreadsheet where the labels are. (Choose Window⇨Tile to see all your current windows at once, for example.) Or else just make a note of the cell addresses.

Either way, you start out the same: Choose Edit⇨Legend/Series Labels in the menu bar. In the Legend/Series Labels dialog box that appears, do the following:

- ✔ If you have boring labels of the "Series 1, 2, 3 ..." variety, click the check box marked `Auto series labels` to clear the check mark.

- ✔ To type in the labels, just click the appropriate box and type, as I do with the label "Spruce" in Figure 21-3. There's one text box for each series (each color or pattern).

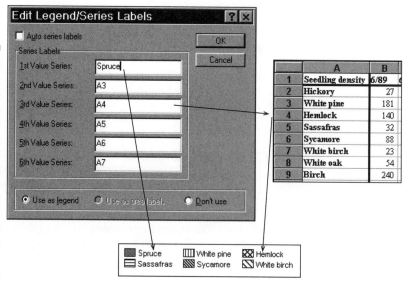

**Figure 21-3:** Labels in your legend can come either from the spreadsheet or from text you enter in the Edit Legend/Series Labels dialog box.

> ✔ To use a cell in the spreadsheet that contains a label, just click the appropriate text box and type the label's cell address.

Click the OK button in the dialog box when you're done.

## Data labels

Data labels are nice when the actual values along the line are particularly important. (Or atop the bars, or alongside the pie slices — whatever.) Just to be clear what I'm talking about, see Figure 21-4, which has data labels in it.

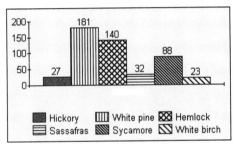

**Figure 21-4:** Data labels leave no doubt about what the numbers are.

To simply print the numbers corresponding to all the points on the chart, do this:

1. **Choose Edit⇨Data Labels in the menu bar.**

   The Data Labels dialog box puts in an appearance.

2. **Click the Use series data check box to put a check mark there.**

3. **Click the OK button.**

Data labels are great but can be confusing if you have several data series on the chart at once. In Figure 21-4, there's only one data series, so it's pretty easy to read. The trouble with the procedure I just gave you is that it puts numbers everywhere.

In order to enter data labels for each data series individually, no check mark should be in the Use series data check box. If a check mark is there, click on the check box to turn it off. Here are a few (more than 2) alternatives:

✔ If you want numbers on your chart, but not for every series, you can enter a range for each series individually. Choose Window➪Tile so that you can see both spreadsheet and chart, choose Edit➪Data Labels to get the Data Labels dialog box, and type the ranges into the series boxes.

✔ Here's a faster way to do the same thing: In the spreadsheet window, highlight the range of numbers to be used as data labels; press Ctrl+C to copy it. Switch to the chart window, choose Edit➪Data Labels, click the box for the data series you want to label, and click the Paste button.

✔ If you want a series marked with something other than the actual data values on your chart — text, perhaps — first, create a column of those labels in an out-of-the-way portion of your spreadsheet, say H1:H10. Then in the Data Labels dialog box, set the range for that series to H1:H10. You can use the paste technique above for this, too.

## Pasting New Data and Labels

If you miss using scissors and paste to create charts, Works has a treat for you. (No, you can't eat the paste.) You can paste new data series, data labels, or category labels from any range in your spreadsheet into your chart. This lets you easily add another series of data, add data from some remote part of your spreadsheet, or specify a new range for a new set of labels.

Category labels are those labels that appear at intervals along the X axis of your chart. Data labels are labels that appear on top of each point in your chart.

1. **In your spreadsheet, highlight a range of cells — data, labels, whatever, in a row or column — and press Ctrl+C (the more-or-less universal Copy command).**

2. **Switch to the chart window and press Ctrl+V.**

   (You can also choose Edit➪Paste Series from the menu bar, but Ctrl+V is the conventional Paste command, so I prefer it. Fewer things to remember.)

3. **In the Paste Series dialog box that appears, click the series that you want to paste data or labels for.**

   If you are pasting new category labels, click Category.

4. **Specify data or labels.**

   If you are pasting data for a series, click Data. (Use this for category labels, too, oddly enough.)

   If you are pasting data labels for a series, click Labels.

5. **Click OK.**

# Using Multiple Charts

Creative artist that you are, you are probably not going to be content with a single chart of your spreadsheet. No, you'll want two charts, maybe a line chart to compare annual sales by region and then a bar chart to show total sales by product.

Works lets you create many new charts and keeps them as part of the spreadsheet file. Your good buddies for handling multiple charts are the Tools and the View menus. Click Tools and then click one of the following selections in the menu that drops down:

**Create New Chart:** This does the customary routine with the New Chart dialog box, described in Chapter 20.

**Rename Chart:** To keep them all straight and to buttress their self-esteem, give your charts names. Choosing this command invokes the Rename Chart dialog box. Click the chart you want to rename in the Select a chart list. Click the Type a name below text box at the bottom of the dialog box and type a name for the current chart. Click the Rename button. The chart name now appears in the chart title bar. Click the OK button.

**Delete Chart:** This command gives you the Delete Chart dialog box (surprise). Click the chart you want to delete in the list of charts and then the Delete button. Click the OK button.

**Duplicate Chart:** This is handy to create a slightly different version of an existing chart. In the Duplicate Chart dialog box that appears, click the chart to duplicate and then click the Name text box. Type a new name, click the Rename button, and then click OK.

To switch between charts, just choose View⇨Chart from the menu bar. A humble View Chart dialog box appears, displaying a list of charts by name. Double-click a name to open that chart window.

# Chapter 22
# Producing Works of Art

· · · · · · · · · · · · · · · · · · · · · · · · · · · · · · · · · · · · · · · · · · ·

## In This Chapter

▶ Starting up Microsoft Draw

▶ Inserting a drawing

▶ Making and modifying shapes and text

▶ Leaving and restarting Draw

▶ Using ClipArt

▶ Using WordArt

· · · · · · · · · · · · · · · · · · · · · · · · · · · · · · · · · · · · · · · · · · ·

As my friend Art says, "Expose yourself to Art." Or, in this case, expose your art to your readers. Scary thought? Don't fret. Works' art tools can help you make quick work of artsy stuff, whether the artwork is functional, decorative, or just to show off.

## Using Draw to Do Basic Blob Art

Few things strike more dread into the heart of the average adult than being asked to draw something. Otherwise brave souls who daily undertake such daunting ventures as business trips, advanced courses in physics, or even (shudder) a field trip with their child's class shiver in their berets at the thought of drawing.

Fortunately, the most artistic endeavor most of us are ever called upon to do is what I call "blob art." This is the art of putting together a bunch of simple shapes with lines and text. Microsoft's Draw tool is great for blob art, which is why Microsoft stuffs various forms of it into various programs that it makes.

# Starting up Draw (inserting a drawing)

The drawing tool is not one of the Big Four tools; it's a sort of helper tool. You can start up Draw only while you're in a word-processor or database document, and the drawing you make can be stored only as part of that document. Works doesn't give you any way to start Draw up by itself or to save drawings as separate files.

It also works only in the word-processor or the database tool. That leaves the spreadsheet tool a bit out in the cold, but I suspect most folks can live with that. (And as far as the communications tool is concerned, drawing while communicating is a swell idea but a little ahead of the technology.)

To start up Draw (that is, to create and insert a drawing into your word-processor or database document), do the following:

1. **Click at the point in the document where you want the drawing.**

   In the database tool, you must be in Form Design view.

2. **Choose Insert➪Drawing from the menu bar.**

The Microsoft Draw tool springs into action. It springs so enthusiastically that, unlike any other tool, it even escapes the boundaries of the regular Works window and has a window of its own. It looks sort of like a bigger version of Figure 22-1, except that it's blank in the middle, where Figure 22-1 has some blob art and says, "This is your canvas area!"

# What's what in the Draw window

**Drawing tools:** Draw gives you a set of drawing tools along the left edge of the window. Except for the top two (the arrow and the magnifying glass), these tools help you create a shape or text.

**Colors:** Along the bottom of the window are two palettes that let you control colors as you draw. The color marked with a check mark is the color Works will use when you next make a shape. The Line palette specifies the color of a line or outline. The Fill palette determines what color fills the shape (if you're using a *filled* or solid shape). Just click a color to use it for the next objects you create.

**Menu bar:** The main job of the Draw menu bar is to let you change or improve the way the tools and palettes work. For example, you may want to use a different line width, change the text font, or get help aligning your shapes. The

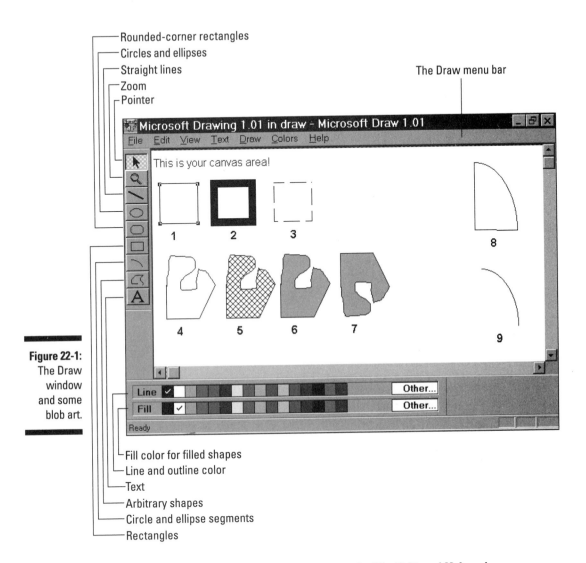

Rounded-corner rectangles
Circles and ellipses
Straight lines
Zoom
Pointer

The Draw menu bar

This is your canvas area!

1   2   3   8

4   5   6   7   9

**Figure 22-1:**
The Draw
window
and some
blob art.

Fill color for filled shapes
Line and outline color
Text
Arbitrary shapes
Circle and ellipse segments
Rectangles

menu also lets you copy and arrange shapes easily. The Edit and Help selections, for the most part, work pretty much as they do in other Works tools. The other menu selections are unique to Draw.

## Making shapes and text

The shapes and text you create in Draw are separate objects, like cutouts lying on a piece of paper. Unless you say otherwise, most of them start out having *fills,* or solid centers. This means that if you draw over an existing object, you cover it up. After you have created objects, you can delete them, copy them, move them to the foreground or background, shift them around, stretch or shrink them, change their color or line style, fill them or not fill them, rotate them, and flip them end-for-end or side-for-side.

To use a tool, click it and then move your mouse cursor into the canvas area. Once you do that, using the tool is generally a matter of clicking at various points in the drawing or clicking and dragging. Pressing the Shift key while you click allows you to get certain "specialized" objects, such as circles and squares, from the more general ellipse and rectangle tools.

✔ **Line:** Click where you want one endpoint and drag to where you want the other endpoint. Shift+click forces a line to be horizontal, vertical, or at a 45-degree angle.

✔ **Ellipse or circle:** Click and then drag in any direction to create an ellipse. Dragging diagonally makes the shape more circular. To *force* it to be a circle, use Shift+click.

✔ **Rectangle or rounded-corner rectangle:** Click where you want one corner and drag to the opposite corner. For a square or rounded-corner square, use Shift+click.

✔ **Ellipse or circle segment:** This tool draws quarter-ellipse segments. (That is, it goes a quarter of the way around an ellipse; see shape 8 in Figure 22-1.) If the Fill is on, then the quarter-ellipse gets connected to its center to make a sort of pie-wedge shape. Click where you want the top or bottom of the curve and drag up or down or to the right or left. Drag in a diagonal direction for a more circular shape, or force a quarter circle by starting with Shift+click. Practice a few times to see what's going on. To make a curved line rather than a pie segment, turn off the fill: press Alt+D and then F. For a different curve or segment shape, see "Modifying objects," later in this chapter.

To draw a curved line between two locations, turn off the fill, click at one location, and drag to the other location (see shape 9 in Figure 22-1). The curve will always bend up if the second endpoint is higher and down if it is lower; so if the curve bends the wrong way, press the Delete key and then try again starting at the other end of the curve.

✔ **Arbitrary shapes:** The arbitrary shape tool combines straight line segments with arbitrary pencil-like drawings. First, click at a starting point. Then, for a straight line segment, click somewhere else; continue clicking around and you'll get a bunch of line segments. To make a segment that's drawn, as with a pencil, just click and drag. To end the line, either click on the original starting point (for a closed shape), or double-click when you make the last point. (See shape number 4 in Figure 22-1.)

✔ **Text:** To specify a font and style to work in throughout the drawing, click Text and then click the commands in the menu that drops down. A check mark indicates the current defaults. To use the text tool, just click anywhere in your drawing and type. Press Enter when you're done.

✔ **Zooming in or out:** Click View in the menu bar and then click any of the percentage selections in the menu that drops down. Smaller percentages make the drawing smaller. You can also use the magnifying glass tool in the toolbar. Click that tool and then click any part of the drawing you want to see close up. Hold down the Shift key while clicking to reverse the action.

## Drawing from the center

All the objects you draw with the Draw tools exist inside imaginary rectangles. One corner of the rectangle is the place you clicked, and the opposite corner is the place you dragged to. The tool fits its particular object (line, ellipse, rounded rectangle, and so on) into that rectangle. This is a fine way to draw rectangles, lines, and stuff like that, but it's an absolutely terrible way to draw circles. You usually don't draw a circle just to have a circle; you usually want to draw a circle *around* something. You want your click to represent the center of the circle, not the corner of some imaginary rectangle containing the circle.

That's what Draw uses the Ctrl key for. In any of the tools, Ctrl+click means that your click is intended to be the center of the object, and as you drag, the object will expand in all directions around that center.

There's a simple way to remember (and keep straight) what the Ctrl and Shift keys do in combination with a click: Remember your *C*s and *S*s. Ctrl means Centered; Shift means Specialized. Or press them both at once to get a centered, specialized object.

This is how Ctrl+click works with all the tools:

✔ **Line:** Ctrl+click where you want the center of the line segment. As you drag, the segment will extend equally in both directions from your original click.

✔ **Ellipse or circle:** Ctrl+click where you want the center to be. As you drag, the ellipse will grow symmetrically. Ctrl+Shift+click where you want the center of a circle to be and then drag to choose its radius.

✔ **Rectangle or rounded-corner rectangle:** Crtl+click where you want the center and drag to where you want a corner. For a square or rounded-corner square, use Ctrl+Shift+click.

✔ **Ellipse or circle segment:** This one gets a bit complicated. Ctrl+click on the midpoint between the two points you want to connect with a curve. Then drag to one of the two points. The curve won't go through the place you clicked at all.

✔ **Arbitrary shapes, Text, Zoom:** The Ctrl key appears to have no effect here.

## Modifying objects

To select an object (shape or text) for modification, click first on the selection tool, which is the arrow at the top of the toolbar. Then click on the object. A frame of four square dots appears around the object to tell you it's selected, as in shape number 1 of Figure 22-1.

To select a whole bunch of objects so that you can modify them all at once, click first on the selection tool (the arrow) and then click and drag diagonally across the shapes to be selected. A dashed rectangle appears (temporarily) as you do so, indicating that whatever objects you've corralled entirely within the rectangle will be selected.

If you want to select a bunch of objects scattered all over the drawing, hold down both Ctrl and Shift, and click on each of them individually.

Here are some things you can do to an object (or bunch of objects) that you have selected. You have to select the object(s) before you can do any of these:

✔ **Move:** Click anywhere within the object and drag. To move straight horizontally or vertically, hold down the Shift key and drag. (Don't forget: you can select a bunch of objects and move them all together.)

✔ **Copy:** Press Ctrl+C and then Ctrl+V. A copy appears somewhere nearby; click and drag it to the place you want it.

✔ **Stretch or shrink:** (For shapes, not text.) Click any of the four squares around the shape and drag. Shift+drag makes the stretch either straight horizontal, vertical, or 45 degrees. To keep the shape, drag at a 45-degree angle while holding down the Shift key.

✔ **Line thickness and style:** Click Draw on the menu bar and then move the mouse cursor down to Line Style in the menu that drops down. A list appears; click any line style, such as dashed; or click any line width (shown in *points* or $1/72$ of an inch). Shape 2 in Figure 22-1 has a thicker line; shape 3 has a dashed line.

✔ **Color:** To change the line or outline color, click a color in the Line palette at the bottom of the window. To change the fill color, use the Fill palette instead. See the shapes numbered 6 and 7 in Figure 22-1, which have a fill color other than white.

- **Text:** To change font, size, style, or alignment, click Text and then click commands in the menu that drops down. The common keyboard short-cuts, such as Ctrl+B for bold, also work for text in Draw.

- **Fill:** To switch between filled and unfilled, click Draw in the menu bar and then click Filled in the menu that drops down. Unfilled shapes are trans-parent, showing objects underneath them. An unfilled circle or ellipse segment turns into an arc, as with shape 9 of Figure 22-1.

- **Fill pattern:** To use a fill pattern instead of or in addition to a color, click Draw in the menu bar and then move the mouse cursor down to Pattern in the menu that drops down. Click a pattern in the box that appears. (The Line and Fill colors must be different for the pattern to show up.) See shape number 5 in Figure 22-1.

- **Outlining:** To remove an outline from a filled shape, click Draw in the menu bar and then click Framed. (To restore the outline, repeat the command.)

- **On-top/underneath:** Objects cover up each other in Draw; to change an object's position in the pile, click Edit in the menu bar and then click either Bring to Front or Send to Back.

- **Rotate or flip:** Click Draw in the menu bar and then click Rotate/Flip in the menu that drops down. Click Rotate Left or Rotate Right to turn the object 90 degrees. Click Flip Horizontal for a mirror image or Flip Vertical for upside down. In Figure 22-1, see shape number 7, which is a copy of number 6 flipped vertically.

If you realize immediately that you've made a mistake (like maybe you moved something that took you a long time to get in exactly the right place), you can undo it. Ctrl+Z works here just like it does everywhere else.

If you get a few objects positioned just perfectly relative to each other, you can freeze them in their relative positions by selecting them all and choosing Draw⇨Group from the drop-down menu. Now Works considers the collection to be one single object, and anything that is done to one is done to all. If you decide later that you want to modify the objects individually, select the grouped object (by clicking any of its pieces) and choose Draw⇨Ungroup.

## Leaving and restarting Draw

When you exit the Draw program, you can either save your work in the docu-ment if the drawing is a keeper or throw away whatever you have done in this drawing session. To exit Draw, click File⇨Exit and Return. A query box appears, asking if Draw should update your document. Click Yes to keep your drawing, or click No to throw away everything you've done since you started Draw.

When you return to your document, the drawing appears in a box with squares around it. To resize the drawing while keeping its proportions, click and drag one of the corner squares. To squish or stretch it, click and drag one of the side squares. To frame it, put it in a paragraph by itself, adjust the left and right paragraph indents to fit it, and apply a border to the paragraph.

You can always do further work on your drawing later. Just double-click the drawing in your word-processor or database document to restart Draw.

# ClipArt

When your document needs a little pizzazz — not functional, industrial art like blob art or charts — use some *clip art.* Clip art is nothing more than a bunch of predrawn illustrations that you can use in your documents. Works comes with a batch; you can buy more by browsing through the pages of computer magazines or sometimes by downloading them from online services or bulletin boards.

Nearly all artwork is licensed for some particular use. Make sure that you have the right to use downloaded or other artwork obtained informally.

Works comes with a clip art feature cleverly called the ClipArt Gallery. The first time you use it, a query box will ask you if you want to install the artwork. Click Yes to respond affirmatively. (It actually doesn't take too long to install, despite an implied warning that it does.)

Here's how to insert a piece of clip art in your word-processor or database document:

1. **Click in your document where you want the art to appear.**

   You must be in Form Design view in a database.

2. **Choose Insert⇨ClipArt from the menu bar.**

   The vast acreage of the ClipArt Gallery appears on your screen. See Figure 22-2.

3. **Click a category in the** Categories **list.**

   The available artwork in that category now hangs in the gallery for your artistic critique and selection.

4. **Click the picture you want from the** Pictures **box.**

   Scroll the gallery to see more, if the gallery appears full. Most categories have pretty sparse galleries, though.

5. **Click the** Insert **button.**

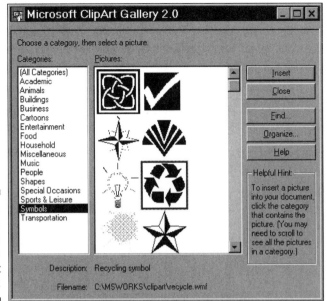

**Figure 22-2:**
Recycle
some
images from
the ClipArt
Gallery.

Once the art is inserted into your document, you can size it the same way you do for your own drawings. See the preceding section, "Leaving and restarting Draw." You can also copy the clip art into Draw for modification: click the art in your document, press Ctrl+X, fire up Draw as described previously, and press Ctrl+V to paste the artwork into Draw.

# *WordArt*

Oh, those madcap Microsoft engineers! First blob art, then clip art, and now word art. What's next, punctuation art? Well, this one is definitely fun, and it's also great for getting someone's attention (see Figure 22-3). The Works WordArt feature lets you create special effects for text, like you see in advertisements and brochures.

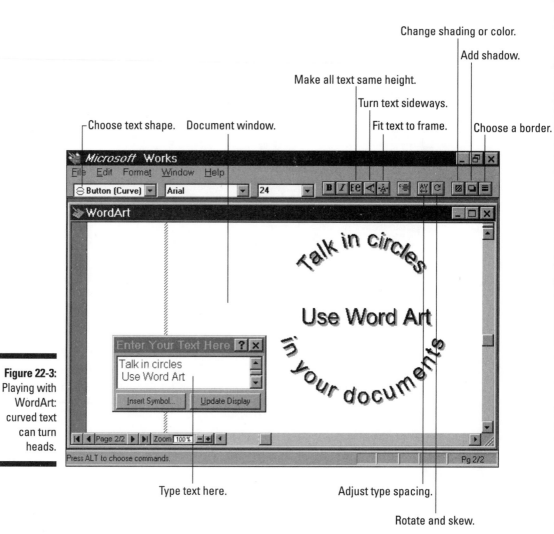

**Figure 22-3:**
Playing with
WordArt:
curved text
can turn
heads.

Here's the basic procedure for getting swoopy, loopy text in your word-processor or database document:

1. **Click at the place you want your text art. (You must be in Form Design view in a database document.)**

2. **Choose Insert⇨WordArt from the menu bar.**

   The menu and toolbar change to WordArt, and an Enter Your Text Here dialog box appears. "Your Text Here" appears there and in your document, where it has a shaded frame around it. The phrase "Your Text Here" probably doesn't quite get your point across, so move on to Step 3.

3. **Type one or more lines of text in the Enter Your Text Here dialog box.**

4. **Click the list box in the toolbar where it currently says** `Plain-Text` **to see a gallery of weird shapes for your text.**

5. **Click any shape in the gallery. (Shapes with multiple lines are intended for multiple lines of text in the Enter Your Text Here dialog box.)**

   When you choose a shape, your text becomes an illegible blur in the document, as Works tries to fit the artwork in a standard-height line. I tell you how to fix that, coming up.

6. **Click the down-arrow button next to where it currently says** `Best Fit` **in the toolbar and click a larger type size in the list that drops down.**

   Works may display a Size Change dialog box babbling about enlarging a frame and asking `Resize WordArt object?` Click `Yes`.

7. **Choose special effects from the toolbar. See Figure 22-3.**

   The special effects are pretty cool, actually. A lot of stuff in Works is fun in a this-beats-working sort of way, but a few of the special effects are fun in a finger-painting, hey-look-at-this sort of way. I'll give a short description of what they do, but you can't really appreciate the fun ones until you've played with them for yourself:

   *The Bold and Italic buttons* are the boring ones — they do the same thing they always do, change your text to bold or italic.

   *The Ee button* makes capital and lower case letters the same height.

   *The sideways-A button* has a confusing label. It doesn't turn your letters sideways, but it does make your text vertical rather than horizontal.

   *The Alignment button* (which has lines on it and a C) gives you a menu with all the usual text alignment choices (centered, left, right, and so on)

   *The AV button* allows you to adjust the amount of space between letters of your text.

   *The Rotate button* (which looks like an arrow going in a circle) allows you to turn your text in any angle. (This button really can turn your letters sideways.)

   *The Shading button* allows you to control what your letters are made of. (This result won't show up very well unless you make really big letters, though.) Want your letters to be made of little silver bricks with blue mortar between them? Why not?

   *The Shadow button* makes your text cast a shadow on the page. You get to choose the direction of the light source, so the shadows can be long, short, forward, backward, and so on.

   *The Border button* lets you put a border around your letters. Of course, unless you've used the Shading button to fill those letters with something other than solid black, you won't see the border.

8. **Click the** Enter Your Text Here **box to edit your text. Click the** Update Display **button to see the results.**

   Works tries to put the box in a convenient place on the screen, but it doesn't always succeed. If the box blocks your text, you can always click its title bar and drag it somewhere else. You can't resize the box, though, so if you have more than two lines of text, you can't see all of the text at once.

   The Insert Symbol button does just what it sounds like: It produces a box full of special symbols, such as accented vowels, copyright marks, and so forth. Click whatever one you'd like to insert into your text.

9. **When you're done, double-click in the document anywhere outside of the gray-shaded frame.**

# Messing Around with Art in the Document

When you return to your document from Draw or WordArt, the drawing appears in some nominal size that Works thought was best, with no frame or text wrapping around it — nothing. What a way to treat a great work of art!

To resize, redimension, move, or make text wrap around the drawing, first click it. The drawing then appears in a box with squares around it.

✔ To resize the figure, click and drag any of the squares.

✔ To modify the figure, double-click it, and you return to the original tool.

✔ To put a frame around your artwork, choose Format⇨Borders and Shading from the menu bar. Click a line width and, if you like, a color.

✔ To change the figure's dimensions, choose Format⇨Picture from the menu bar (or click it with your right mouse button and choose Format⇨Picture from the menu that appears). In the Format Picture dialog box that appears, enter new values for the width and height of the picture.

✔ To make text wrap around the figure in the word-processor tool, choose Format⇨Picture as above, but click the Text Wrap tab, instead. Click the Absolute button.

✔ To position a figure in the database tool, Form Design view, just drag it.

✔ To position a figure in the word-processor tool, Choose Format⇨Picture and then click the Text Wrap tab. Click the Absolute button and then adjust the horizontal, vertical and/or page number settings in the Picture Position area. Click the down-arrows next to those settings to choose standard left/right/center or top/center/bottom positioning. Even easier: once Absolute text wrap has been chosen, click the OK button, and you can just drag the picture anywhere.

# Part VII
## The Part of Tens

The 5th Wave          By Rich Tennant

"It was at this point in time that there appeared to be some sort of mass insanity."

## In this part . . .

As on *Sesame Street*, this part is brought to you by the number 10: ten golden rules, ten nifty tricks, ten things NOT to do, and other digital decalogues. If you didn't find what you wanted in the rest of this book, you might just find it here.

*Tenth Night* — Play by Wm. Shakespeare that never made it to prime time.

# Chapter 23
# Ten Golden Rules

Golden rules? Yechhh. Who wants to hear about rules? Well, as your parents probably told you, you can break the rules, but. . . a little rule-following goes a long way toward being a happy camper in Works.

## Use Works' Formatting

The number one golden rule for Works users is to use Works' formatting. Don't position text by typing spaces and blank lines: Use the alignment and other formatting features. I have had friends with advanced engineering degrees who don't do this and wonder why their software is such a pain to use.

## Save Early and Often

Every so often, press Ctrl+S to save your document as a file. If lightning strikes — well, actually, if lightning strikes, you're out of luck anyway — but someday you will trip over the power cord or something, and your work will be lost. By saving often, you will lose only the last half-hour of work or so, and you will not have to pound your head repeatedly against the wall (the traditional remedy for lost documents).

## Save Before Major Changes

If you are about to do a major change, say, replacing the word *program* with *software* throughout your document, it's best to save your document first. That way, if it turns out that you've made a big boo-boo, you do not have to rend your garment and make other traditional appeasements to the gods of stupidity.

## Back Up Your Files

Every so often, copy your document files from your hard disk to a diskette. Hard disks do not last forever. If you lose your program files, you can always reinstall the software from the original diskettes, but if you lose your document files, they are gone.

In Windows 95, your files aren't really gone, even when you delete them. Double-click on the Recycle Bin icon on your screen, find and click on your file, and choose File⇨Restore from the Recycle Bin menu bar. If, on the other hand, you really want to delete a file forever, click on the file in the Recycle Bin and press the Del (or Delete) key. A tiny dialog box will ask you to confirm the action; click the Yes button.

## Close Your Documents

If you keep opening documents but not closing them, eventually Works is going to get quite slow, and you're going to get quite confused. If you're done with a document, close it (Ctrl+W does the trick).

## Use More Than One Folder

Unless you tell it otherwise, Works stuffs all your files into the same folder. This is like stuffing your invoices, receipts, laundry, and used auto parts into the same cardboard box. See "Saving Files and Creating Folders" in Chapter 2.

# Delete Old Files

Some folks use their hard disk drives like extended-wear diapers, with similar results. Every so often, make it a practice to delete some old files. If you see a file listed in a File Open or File Save As dialog box, or nearly anywhere in Works or Windows 95, you can send it to the Recycle Bin easily: just click it and press the Del (or Delete) key on your keyboard. (How do you know how old it is? Click on the Details button in upper-right corner of the File Open or File Save As dialog box, and then click the word Modified in the column headers that appear to sort by date.)

# Learn Buttons and Other Shortcuts

Works makes it easy to learn the buttons on the toolbar. (It puts up a label when you rest your mouse cursor on a button.) It also tells you the Alt or Ctrl key shortcuts when you choose a command from a menu. You can make Works a heck of a lot more pleasant to use if you just learn the few buttons and other shortcuts for commands you use regularly.

# Look for Similarities

Works was designed so that there are similarities between tools. If something seems like a familiar task, such as aligning text, there's a good chance it works the same way as it did in the last tool you used — or at least in a similar fashion.

# Use Print Preview

Hey, save a tree! And save yourself some money. Use the Print Preview feature to see what your printout will look like before you print it. The command is in the File menu, and there's even a button on the toolbar (the document-with-a-monocle icon).

# Chapter 24
# Ten Nifty Tricks

*R*emember those great ads for magic tricks in the back of comic books? Well, continuing in that tradition, here at the back of this book is a bunch of nifty, nearly magic tricks. You probably won't amaze your friends with these tricks, but you may actually begin to enjoy your PC, which is magic enough.

# Fill 'er Up: Filling Cells with Numbers

For sheer boredom, you just can't beat typing a series of numbers or dates into a spreadsheet or database. So don't do it. First, type a starting number into the top cell of the column you want to fill, or leftmost cell of the row. (Use List view in the database tool.) Then, highlight that cell and the rest of the range to be filled. To fill the range with an increasing or decreasing series, click Edit in the menu bar and then click Fill Series in the menu that drops down. In the Fill Series dialog box that sprouts up, click the kind of units you want (plain numbers or dates). Click the Step by box and type the increment or decrement you want between each cell, like **–1**. Click OK and you're done.

# Automate Sign-On

Logging on or *signing on* to communications services is, let's face it, a bore. In the spirit of pioneering ingenuity, why not automate it? All you have to do in Works is tell it to watch and record what you do while you log on. Later, you can play it back, and Works repeats your every step.

Here's how to record your steps while you sign on to a service. Choose Tools⇨Record Script from the menu bar. When the Record Script dialog box appears, just click the OK button; do *not* type a name for the script.

Connect to the other computer and do all the steps you normally do to sign on. (If you mess up, click Tools⇨Cancel Recording; try again from the start.) When you're done signing on, click Tools⇨End Recording in the menu that drops down.

The script plays automatically the next time you open the same communications document and start your connection.

# Freeze Your Head (ings)

When spreadsheets get larger than one screen's worth, it gets hard to see your column and row headings anymore. So lock them in place, or *freeze* them. Click the cell that's just under your column headings and just to the right of your row headings. Choose Format⇨Freeze Titles from the menu bar. Now you can scroll all over the place and those headings will stay in place. To undo your freeze, repeat the action. To freeze just horizontally, select a row; to freeze just vertically, select a column.

# Freeze-Dry or Customize Your Workspace

If you work on pretty much the same documents all the time, you can tell Works to remember what documents you're using and reopen those document windows automatically when you start the program again. First set up your workspace the way you want it. Then choose Tools⇨Options and click the View tab in the Options dialog box. Click Use saved workspace at startup; then click the Save Workspace button. Next time you start Works, it will reload those documents.

The Options dialog box that you see here holds all kinds of possibilities for customizing Works behavior. One of my favorite changes is getting rid of that Help screen that appears at startup: on the View card, click Show Help at startup to clear the check mark. Another change is to get rid of the jerky word-at-a-time highlighting in the word processor: click the Editing tab and clear the check mark labeled Automatic word selection.

# Import and Export Documents

Works can read files from other programs or create files that other programs can read. When you go to open a file, the Open dialog box offers a Files of type list box. Click that box, and you'll find a whole bunch of programs whose files Works can read. Click one of those programs, and the File name box lists files of that type in the directory you've selected. Choose the file to import, and Works converts it. Exporting a file works similarly: use the Save As command and choose a file type in the Save as type list box.

When you go to save an imported document, use the Save As command and delete the period and three-letter extension in the File name area. Works supplies a proper extension and saves it as a Works file.

# Drag and Drop Documents

This is a trick that nearly every Windows program can do. Have both the Windows 95 File Explorer open (from the Taskbar, choose Start⇨Programs⇨Windows Explorer) and Works open on your screen. When you want to work on a file, just click its icon in the Explorer and drag it over to the Works title bar. Release the mouse button, and Works opens the file. Even if the file is not a Works file, Works will try to import it.

# Wrapping Text in Small Windows

When you're working on a word-processor document in a tiny window, where lines extend beyond the window's edge, it's a pain to have to scroll left and right to be able to read. Instead, choose Tools⇨Options; then choose the Editing tab in the dialog box that appears. Click the check box marked Wrap to window. The document won't appear this way when you print — this just helps you read it.

# Split a Window

To work on two different parts of a document at once, split the window. At the very top of the vertical scroll bar, above the up-pointing arrow, is a microscopic, obscure, shy little rectangle. Click that guy and drag him downward. This action splits the document into two windows that you can scroll independently. It's still only one document, though. To put the split away, drag the horizontal line that separates the two halves back up to the very top of the document window.

# Use Computer Post-It Notes

If you're like me, you live in a small blizzard of those sticky 3M Post-it notes. And now you can even put the computerized equivalent in your word processor or database (Form view) documents. They're great for annotating your text with notes to yourself because they don't print out.

Click where you want one. Click Insert on the menu bar and then click Note-It in the menu that drops down. In the Note-It dialog box that appears, choose one of the adorable symbols in the `Choose a picture` area (scroll to see more). Underneath that, where it says `Type your caption here`, type a few words that will appear with the symbol in your document. To the right, where it suggests that you `Type your note here`, do so.

Click the `OK` button, and you return to the document. Click and drag one of the corners of the frame around your symbol to shrink it to a reasonable size. Now, when you double-click the symbol, your note appears somewhere on your monitor. Click anywhere else to make it go away. To delete the Note-It altogether, click it and press the Delete key.

# The Other Mouse Button

The "other" mouse button (the one on the right side of the mouse, unless you're a lefty and someone has configured your mouse for you) has a surprising amount of stuff behind it. Try highlighting (selecting) something — text or graphics — the usual way and then clicking with the "other" mouse button. You'll find editing commands such as Copy, Cut, and Paste, as well as formatting commands. Use them just as you would commands from the menu bar.

# Chapter 25

# Ten Things NOT to Do

*E*veryone has an idea about how things *ought* to work. Unfortunately, computers don't usually work that way. It's easy to fall into old typewriter habits or form a mistaken impression that Works makes you do something that you don't really have to do. Here's my list of the top ten errors, misconceptions, or just plain boo-boos that you should avoid.

## Do Not Use Extra Spaces, Lines, or Tabs

If you're using multiple, consecutive spaces or tabs in a word-processor document, you're probably making your life difficult. If you're using multiple tabs in every line, it's probably because you haven't set your tab stops or you've forgotten that you can indent a paragraph with a toolbar button. If you are using blank lines to separate paragraphs, try pressing Ctrl+0 (that's a zero, not the letter *O*) to put space above the paragraph instead. See Chapter 6 for additional better ways to do things.

# Do Not Keep Pressing Enter to Begin a New Page

This trick may have worked nicely on your Royal typewriter, but in Works word-processor documents, it creates a royal mess. Press Ctrl+Enter to start a new page.

# Do Not Press Enter at the End of Each Line

I know, I've said this before, but it pains me greatly to see people fighting their word processor. If you press Enter at the end of every line in a word-processor document, Works can't word-wrap for you. As a result, every time you edit a line, you have to manually readjust every line! AAAAAGGGH!! JUST DON'T DO IT, YOU HEAR ME?!!

# Do Not Type Your Own File Extensions

When you save a file, just type the filename, not the .WKS or any other extension. Works automatically puts the proper extension on. If you use your own special extension, it's harder to get Works to display the file in the Open dialog box, and the file is therefore harder to open.

# Do Not Number Your Pages Manually

Works can automagically number your word-processor pages, positioning the numbers where you want them. What more could you want? If you try to number your own pages, you'll be continually adjusting them as you edit the document.

# Do Not Turn Off Your PC before Exiting

Hey! It's time for dinner! But don't just flip the power switch on your PC. Exit Works and exit Windows first. (If you have a computer that can *suspend* the state of all your programs and of Windows, then that's okay. Some laptops do this.) If you don't exit before you turn off your computer, then Windows and Works can become confused the next time you try to do things. At the very least, your hard disk fills up with little Windows temporary files.

# Do Not Use Spaces for Blank Cells

In your spreadsheet documents, when you want to remove an entry, don't type a space: press the Delete key instead. If you put a space in the cell and use a COUNT, AVG, or other statistical function, the cell will be counted.

# Do Not Work in Tiny Windows Unnecessarily

Just because Works starts out with a smallish window, you don't have to stay with it. Click and drag a corner or side of the Works window and enlarge Works. Do the same with your document windows. Better yet, maximize the Works or document window. See Chapter 2 for a refresher on doing this.

# Do Not Stuff All Your Files in the Same Folder

I know, I said this in "Ten Golden Rules," but it bears repeating. See Chapter 2 for ways to make new folders. When you save files, put them in different directories. If you stuff them all in the same directory, you will get very confused.

# Do Not Type in ALL CAPITALS

Particularly when you're using the communications tool to send mail to somebody, don't type in all capital letters. It's considered shouting. In other tools, using all capitals (uppercase letters) makes your documents harder to read.

# Appendix A

# Wisdom and Wizardry
# for Common Tasks

· · · · · · · · · · · · · · · · · · · · · · · · · · · · · · · · · · · · · ·

*In This Appendix*

▶ Creating an address book

▶ Creating your own junk mail

▶ Creating envelopes and labels for mass mailing

▶ Using templates

▶ Working with Wizard-created documents

· · · · · · · · · · · · · · · · · · · · · · · · · · · · · · · · · · · · · ·

*T*hrough the magic of TaskWizards, Works can create some amazing things for you. You would have to study Works for months in order to create some of the delightful documents that TaskWizards do. It can be a little overwhelming dealing with these magical affairs, however, so here are a few instructions and hints to make things come out right.

## Creating an Address Book

It's apparent that Microsoft thinks that it's very important for you to have an address book. After all, it put an address book button on the toolbar. Because none of you wants to disappoint Microsoft, you should probably create an address book. Other good reasons for doing so are:

✔ There are lots of people whom you call often — usually while you are sitting next to your computer.

✔ You have lots of friends and want to keep track of their birthdays and anniversaries.

✔ You are in charge of sending out letters or information to a lot of people on a regular basis.

> ✔ You want to do your own junk mail: "Dear Mr. ___, I know you and others of the ___ family would love to send us your money."
>
> ✔ You are a salesperson and need to keep a record of all your prospects and clients. When Ms. Steinway calls, you want to be able to say, "Oh — hi, Barbara, I was just thinking of you. How are, um, . . . (brief pause while you look up her entry in the address book) George and the kids? Isn't little . . . Sustenuto 12 now?"

Computerized address books make the above tasks easier because you can quickly search for people by name, by birthday, by company, or by other criteria. You can also reorganize your address book easily — for example, grouping together all the people who work for the same company.

You may want several address books — one for friends, another for clients, another for members of the professional organization that you run. You can print out these address books as well as use them on the computer.

Address books are really database documents. Each entry (last name, first name, phone number, and so on) is a *field* in database lingo. For more information on creating, modifying, and using databases, see Part III of this book.

Here's how to create an address book by using one of the cool TaskWizards that Works supplies:

1. **Choose File⇨New and click the TaskWizards tab in the Task Launcher.**

2. **In the Common Tasks category of the TaskWizards list, double-click** Address Book.

3. **If a Works Task Launcher dialog box appears, click the button marked** Yes **to run the TaskWizard.**

   The address book TaskWizard fires up and asks you to choose what type of address book you'd like.

4. **Choose a type of address book that sounds good; if it's not perfect, you can go back and choose another one or modify this one.**

5. **Click the** Next **button to see what sort of information will be in this address book.**

   To go back and try another type of address book, click the <Back button. To add other types of information to this address book, hang on until you get to the next screen.

6. **Click the** Next **button to add fields or specify "reports" (printed versions of your address book).**

For each type of address book, Works has some standard additional fields it thinks you might like, such as extended phone numbers and an area for notes. ("Extended phone numbers" include fax, home/business phone, pager, cellular phone, and electronic mail address.) For these things, choose `Additional Fields`. Click `OK` when you're done.

To add your own fields, such as a Dues Paid field, choose `Your Own Fields`. In the dialog box that appears, you can add up to four fields of your own choosing; click a field check box and enter a name for the field in the adjacent box. Click `OK` when you're done.

To create printed reports, click `Reports`. Works lets you choose between an alphabetized listing of people in your address book or a listing that is broken up into groups based on a "category" field. Click `OK` when you're done.

7. **Click the `Create It!` button to check over your choices before creating the book.**

   To make this address book the one that pops up when you click the Address Book button on your toolbar (or choose <u>T</u>ools⇨<u>A</u>ddress Book), click the option marked `Yes, I want this to be my default address book`.

8. **Click the `Create Document` button. The address book TaskWizard, the world's fastest typist, tosses together a database document: your new address book.**

9. **Save your address book: press Ctrl+S. Give your file a name and folder to live in.**

Of course, now you have to fill out your address book. Ugh. For more details on navigating around your address book database and entering information, see Chapter 12. Here's the executive summary:

- ✔ You are looking at one page, or *record* of your address book.

- ✔ To advance from one field to the next, click it or press the Tab key.

- ✔ Type to enter data, pressing the Enter or Tab key when you're done.

- ✔ To advance or go back one record, press Ctrl+PgDn or Ctrl+PgUp, respectively.

- ✔ If you requested a "category" report in Step 6, decide how you want people grouped (for example, members/nonmembers/prospects), and for each person, enter his or her group in the `Category` field.

- ✔ Edit an entry, click it, press the F2 key, and edit in the formula bar just under the toolbar. Press Enter when you are done.

- ✔ To find someone by name or other information, the easiest way is to choose Edit⇨Find from the menu bar. In the Find dialog box, type the word or phrase you want in the Find what box, choose All records and then click OK. Choosing All records hides records not containing your search word; press Ctrl+PgDn to step through them and then choose Record⇨Show⇨1 All records to make all visible again.

To open your address book

- ✔ If you made this address book your default address book in Step 7, just click the Address Book button (the last one, on the right end).
- ✔ To open an address book other than your default book, open it like any other (database) document with File⇨Open or the Task Launcher.

To change your default address book, choose Tools⇨Options, click the Address Book tab, and double-click an address book in the list shown.

# Creating Your Own Junk Mail

For that personal touch without actually being personal, there's nothing like junk mail. (Miss Manners, please call your office.) Yes, now you, too — <your name here>, of <your address here> — can send junk mail just like the pros!

This popular feature, also known as *mail-merge* or *form letters,* lets you write a single letter in the word processor, leave blanks in the text, and have Works automatically fill in the blanks (*merge*) from a database (such as an address book). Works prints out one letter for each lucky person in your database.

Of course, besides sending falsely personal letters, this feature can be used for more valid personalization, such as:

- ✔ Sending a letter to each member of your organization, telling them how much they have paid, and have left unpaid, of their annual dues or pledge.
- ✔ Welcoming each attendee of some event and telling the attendees what room they will be staying in.

In these examples, some piece of information that your database contains about that person appears in the letter.

Of course, you have to have a database document with this information in it! You can use any database TaskWizard to create one, such as the address book TaskWizard described in the preceding section. In the Task Launcher, look through the various TaskWizard categories (such as Names and Addresses) for wizards with a database icon (a tiny picture of Rolodex-style cards). Or create one from scratch — see Part III of this book.

Once you have a database, you need to create the letter. You have two alternatives:

- ✔ Write the letter from scratch, modifying it for mail-merge.
- ✔ Have Works write the letter with a TaskWizard, although this action typically doesn't do any more than begin the letter with the recipient's name and address.

If you are new to this mail-merge stuff, or if you just need some assistance in writing and properly formatting a letter, I suggest the second option: use a TaskWizard to start the letter and then modify the letter to add any personal information you want in the body of the letter. By seeing how the TaskWizard handles the task, you can learn to create your own form letters. See "Form letters using a letter TaskWizard," coming up.

Otherwise, you can create your own form letters from scratch fairly simply.

## *Form letters from scratch*

There is a tool in Works for creating form letters, but it seems unnecessarily complicated to me for most purposes, requiring you to pop in and out of the tool to write the letter. Here's what I think is the simplest approach: Write your letter by using the word processor. Wherever you need to fill in some personal data for the addressee, do the following steps. This strategy creates a document that prints a letter for every entry in your database. If you want to filter or exclude certain records, see the section "Mailing only to a select few."

1. **Choose Insert⇨Database Field from the menu bar.**

   If a First-time Help dialog box appears, click To write a form letter.

   An Insert Field dialog box appears. Click Use a different database and in the Use Database dialog box that appears, double-click your chosen database.

2. **Click the field that contains the personal data you need, (such as Child name, a field you might have if you were writing an acceptance letter for summer camp using a database of applicants) and then click the Insert button.**

   You can enter several fields from this dialog box.

3. **Click Close when you're done.**

When you've finished composing your letter, you can best see the results of your work by using Print Preview. Choose File⇨Print Preview from the menu bar; click OK in the dialog box that mutters about "all records"; and enjoy the view.

In Print Preview you can see each of the many letters you are going to print! Just click the Next button to see the next one. Continue editing the form letter if necessary and print for real when it's ready. If the data is wrong, you'll need to edit the database. To filter your data, see the section "Mailing only to a select few," later in this chapter.

## Form letters using a letter TaskWizard

There are several TaskWizards to choose from; just about any "letter" TaskWizard will do, but a good, basic one is "Form Letter" in the Correspondence folder:

1. **Choose File⇨New and click the** TaskWizards **tab in the Task Launcher.**

2. **Click** Correspondence **in the TaskWizards list and double-click** Form Letter.

3. **If a Works Task Launcher dialog box appears, click the button marked Yes to run the TaskWizard.**

   The form letter TaskWizard fires up and asks you to choose which layout of a letter you'd like. Choose one that sounds good to you and click the Next button. In the next box, you get to specify the details.

4. **Choose** Letterhead. **Two choices appear. The first takes you to a letterhead specialist; use the second if your letterhead is already preprinted on your paper (or if you don't need a letterhead).**

   If you choose the first, just follow along, substituting your personal or company information in the blanks provided.

5. **Choose** Address. **Choose** I want to use addresses from a Works database **and click the Next button.**

6. **Select the database containing your names and addresses from the next dialog box.**

   If the database you want isn't listed, Works tells you how you can continue to make the form letter and then go back and merge the database later.

7. **Build an address for the addressee area of the letter by using the dialog box shown in Figure A-1:**

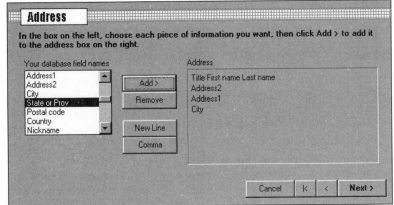

**Figure A-1:**
Select fields
from your
database
for the
Address
area.

The task here is to choose which fields will be printed, in what order, and on which line they will appear. The procedure goes like this:

a) Click a field on the left side and click the Add button to copy it to the right side.

b) If you make a mistake, click the Remove button to remove the last field you added.

c) To begin a new line, click the New Line button.

d) Click the Comma button to type a comma — for example, to separate city from state.

Don't use all the fields! Just the ones you want printed on the top of the letter. When you're done, click the Next button.

8. **Create a greeting or salutation line (Dear ____) in the next dialog box by using the same method you just used for the addressee area in Step 7. Click the Next button.**

For a formal letter, you can do Dear <Title> <Lastname> for Dear Ms. ____ or Dear Mr. ____.

9. **Click OK in the next dialog box and . . . you're not done yet! Back to deciding the other features of your letter.**

10. **Choose Content. Wow! Works provides even prewritten letters! Use one if you like (although many of these are not particularly suited for bulk mailing, such as Acceptance of job offer, unless you live a very interesting life!). I am occupationally predisposed toward writing, so I chose Blank letter. Click OK when you're done.**

11. **All right, you get the idea; finish up by choosing a Text Style and then Extras, if you like.**

12. **Click the** Create It **button! At last!**

Check over the specifications for your form letter in the Checklist dialog box that appears, and if it needs changes, just click Return to Wizard. Otherwise, click the Create Document button.

When all the dust settles, you're left gazing at an ordinary Works word-processor document. Well, not entirely ordinary: as you can see in Figure A-2, there are some odd entries in it.

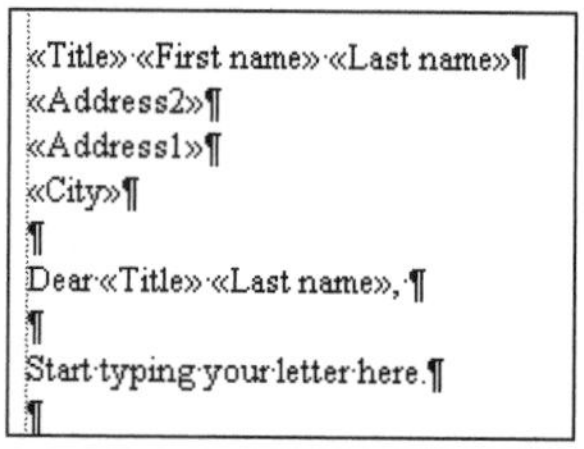

**Figure A-2:**
What you
end up with:
a letter with
odd text in it.

```
«Title» «First name» «Last name»¶
«Address2»¶
«Address1»¶
«City»¶
¶
Dear «Title» «Last name», ¶
¶
Start typing your letter here. ¶
¶
```

The items in << >> symbols are placeholders. Works will replace these with actual data from your database. The thing within the <<>> symbols is the name of the field from which the data will come. (There are also paragraph and space symbols displayed that don't actually print, so don't fret about them.)

Finish your letter. Whenever you come to a place where you need to fill in some personal data for the addressee, do the following:

1. **Choose** Insert⇨Database Field **from the menu bar.**

If a First-time Help dialog box appears, click To write a form letter.

An Insert Field dialog box appears.

2. **Click the field that contains the personal data you need (such as Child name, a field you might have if you were writing an acceptance letter for summer camp using a database of applicants) and then click the** Insert **button.**

You can enter several fields from this dialog box.

3. **Click** Close **when you're done.**

When you've finished composing your letter, you can best see the results of your work by using Print Preview. Choose File⇨Print Preview from the menu bar; click OK in the dialog box that mutters about "all records"; and enjoy the view.

In Print Preview you can see each of the many letters you are going to print! Just click the Next button to see the next one. Continue editing the form letter if necessary, and print for real when it's ready. If the data is wrong, you'll need to edit the database.

## Mailing only to a select few

You may not want to send mail to everyone in your database, so you need to *filter, hide,* or *mark* certain records. To do this, I suggest you use the word-processor's Form Letter tool. This tool is actually designed to step you through the creation of a form letter. You can use it for that, but I think it's a bit confusing, so I suggest that you use it only when you need to filter your records.

For information about what filtering, hiding, and marking are, see Part IV of this book.

With your form letter open in Works, here's how to specify exactly what records you want to use:

1. **Choose Tools⇨Form Letters from the word-processor menu bar.**

   The Form Letter dialog box appears, in all its glory. You have already selected a database, so that task appears checked off on the Instructions card. Now it's time to make some changes in other cards.

2. **Click the Recipients tab in the Form Letters dialog box.**

   This is the control center for what records are used from your database (see Figure A-3).

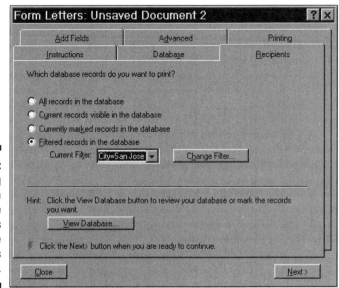

**Figure A-3:** Controlling who gets a letter: the Recipients card of the Form Letters tool.

To use a filter, click `Filtered records in the database` and choose a filter from the drop-down list marked `Current Filter`. To modify the filter, click the `Change Filter` button.

To mark or hide records, you will need to access the database document itself. The way the Form Letter tool manages this is by letting you pop in and out of the database without exiting the tool.

1. **To pop into the database, click the `View Database` button.**

   (If a First-time Help dialog box appears, click `Mark Records`.) Your database document appears, but partly obscured by a small Form Letters dialog box with a `Return` button on it. Drag that out of your way.

2. **Mark the records you want to use, or hide the records you don't want to use (Record⇨Mark Record or Hide Record).**

   Switch views, if you need to.

3. **Find the small Form Letters dialog box with the `Go Back` button on it; click the button.**

   You return to the big Form Letters dialog box.

4. **To use marked records, click `Currently marked records in the database`. Another one of those persistently helpful First-time Help boxes may pop up. Click the `To show or hide marked records` button.**

   To exclude using hidden records, click `Current records visible in the database`.

To see the results of your efforts, click the `Printing` tab of the Form Letters dialog box and choose the `Preview` button. Click `OK` in the dialog box that pops up, and in Print Preview, see if your filtering, marking, or hiding has had the desired effect. Click the `Next` or `Previous` button to move between records.

When you're all done, click the `Close` button in the Form Letters dialog box.

## *Envelopes and labels for mass mailing*

Need to send out your form letter in an envelope, or create mailing labels for your newsletter? Here are the Works tools that do the job for you. They both work very much alike.

Works' envelope tool is specially designed to help you do mass mailings by using addresses from databases. Just choose Tools ⇨Envelopes from the menu bar.

Works' label tool is specifically designed to print on labels made by the Avery company. Choose an Avery label by its model number, and in Works choose

Tools⇨Labels from the menu bar. Works automatically sets up the page size, layout, and printer settings to print precisely on the labels.

Make sure that you use Avery labels that are well suited to your printer. For example, for laser, ink-jet, or bubble-jet printers, use the kind that come on 8 ¹/₂ x 11-inch sheets. For laser printers, make sure that the labels are designed for laser printers, or you may end up with a gummy mess!

Both tools require you to have a database full of names and addresses. As with form letters, Works lets you write a document that is a normal word-processor document in nearly every way except that instead of regular text, it has place-holders for such database fields as Last name, First name, and Address.

Both tools present you with a set of cards. The top card is a checklist of things that have to be set up. These Works tools (I like to call them gnomes) are designed to take you through each item on this list. To do this, you can click the Next button on the lower right; the gnome moves you to the next item on the checklist, taking you to the next card. (Alternatively, you can click the button next to each step or on the card tabs.) The gnome will step you through the process, always returning to the Instructions card and showing you check marks for the steps that are done now.

If you are sending out form letters and want to save some time and effort, use envelopes with windows on them! Just lay out the addressee field so that it shows through the window!

These cards are pretty self-explanatory, except for a few items that I discuss a little later. Here's how to get started:

1. **If your document is a form letter and already has the placeholders for the recipient's name and mailing address in it, select the name and address portion.**

    Otherwise, move on to Step 2.

2. **Choose Tools ⇨Envelopes or Tools⇨Labels from the menu bar.**

    If this is the first time you have printed an envelope since you started Works, you may get one of Works' First-time Help dialog boxes. It offers to help you 1) take a tour of envelopes and labels, 2) create an envelope or label, or 3) print an envelope or label. I suggest that you take the tour once, for fun: click the Quick tour of envelopes and labels button and follow directions. When you return to the First-time Help box, click Don't display this message in the future and First-time Help will never bother you again. Then click the To create envelopes or To create labels button.

The gnome pops up the Instructions card for the dialog box. Click the Next button to move from card to card until you're done. Here are a few tips:

 ✔ **The Main Address or Label Layout card:** This card, shown in Figure A-4, is where the address information goes. If, in Step 1, you initially highlighted the recipient's name and address in your letter, it appears here in a big text box (either `Main address` or `Label layout`). You can edit it now if you like, in that box. If you didn't select an address, this text box will be blank, and you can fill it in as follows:

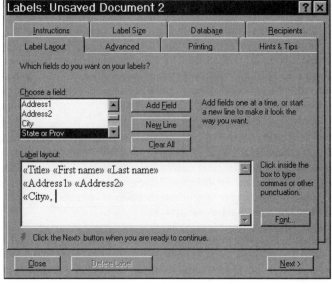

**Figure A-4:**
The Label Layout card in the Label tool is just like the Main Address card in the Envelope tool.

Click on a field in `Choose a field` and click the `Add Field` button to copy it to the address area. For example, to make your first address line, you might add Title, then First name, then Last name from your database.

If you make a mistake or need to add a comma or other fixed text, click in the big text box and edit.

To add a new line, click the `New Line` button or press Enter in the text box.

✔ **The Recipients card:** This card allows you to trim out certain people from your mailing by specifying filters or marking or hiding certain records. If you want to mail to everyone in your database, just click the Next button and continue on. If you do need to select certain people, see the instructions just following Figure A-3, in the section "Mailing only to a select few." Those instructions are for the Recipients card in the Form Letter tool, but this card works exactly the same.

✔ **To preview or print your envelope, click the Printing card.** I strongly suggest you click the `Preview` button to see your envelope or labels in Print Preview. When you think they look correct, click the `Test` button to actually try them out on paper.

✔ **For tips on labels, check out the Hints & Tips card in the labels tool.**

If you created an envelope while you had a form letter open, you end up with a properly formatted envelope page adhering to the top of your form letter. A special envelope/page break (the dotted line) separates it from your document.

# Tempting Templates

Dummies being who we are — intelligent people who would just as soon not do the same thing twice — templates are a fabulous Dummies feature. Templates are the bare bones of a document type that you use over and over again in slightly different form. You can use templates for all the different types of Works documents: word-processor, spreadsheet, or database documents. (Communications templates are possible, but rarely useful, as it turns out.)

For example, if you are a consultant, almost all your invoices look the same, except for the details of date and charges, and who the work is for. To make an invoice template, you create and format an invoice document — but leave the changeable information out — and save it as a template. The next time you need a new invoice, begin with that template, and you need to add only the particulars of this invoice.

## Creating a template

To create a template, begin by creating a document that has all the unchanging text and graphics (such as your address or logo). Format it and set up the page layout. If you want the text that will be added later to have a particular format, put in dummy — or placeholder — text and format that. When you later replace the text, select it, type new text, and the new text will take on the same format.

To save the document as a template:

1. **Choose File⇨Save As from the menu bar.**

2. **Click the** `Template` **button on the lower right of the Save As dialog box. A Save As Template dialog box then requests a name.**

3. **Enter a name for the template.**

   If the only type of word-processor, database, spreadsheet, or communications document you ever do is the one for which you created the template, click the `Use this template for new <whatever> documents` check box. This action turns your template into a *default* template. Now whenever you start a new document of that type — a word-processor document, for instance — your document automatically takes the form of that template. To turn this feature off, open the template with File⇨Open, return to this dialog box by using Steps 1–3, and click the check box again.

Works stores your template in the Template folder, within the MSWorks folder. If you need to modify the template in any way, use File⇨Open and open that folder to find the template.

### *Using a template to start a document*

After you have defined a template, it's easy to use it to start a new document. Using the Task Launcher (choose File⇨New), click the TaskWizards tab. Way down the bottom of the list of TaskWizard categories, you will find User Defined Templates. (That category doesn't appear until you have created one or more templates.) Click User Defined Templates and then double-click the template of your choice.

Your new document is just like any other document, except that it's already partly complete!

## *Tips for Using Wizard-Created Documents*

Works pulls out all the stops when it comes to Wizard-created documents. It uses lots of advanced features in such clever ways that you might not recognize exactly what feature is being used. Here are some tips for working with Wizard-created documents.

### *Working with word-processor documents*

Wizard-created word-processor documents are full of graphical and layout tricks.

✔ In Newsletter Wizard documents, Works shows multiple columns, WordArt, charts, and graphics. The Word NEWSLETTER, for example, is a WordArt box. To change any of these features, double-click it; whatever tool is responsible will appear.

✔ In Letterhead and other Wizard documents, Works uses paragraph formatting and borders extensively. Click some text and use Format⇨Paragraph and Format⇨Borders and Shading to see what's going on.

# *Working with spreadsheet documents*

Wizard-created spreadsheet documents use lots of tricks with borders, column widths, and gridlines.

- ✔ If a spreadsheet appears to have headings with text indented under them, it might be done by using a very narrow column for the heading text and then putting the indented text in the next column over.

- ✔ If you can't edit the text in a spreadsheet, select the area and choose Format⇨Protection. Click the `Protect Data` check box to clear the check mark.

- ✔ If a spreadsheet uses colored text that doesn't work well for you, remember that colors are an option in the Font card of the Format Cells dialog box.

# *Working with database documents*

Wizard-created database documents come equipped with built-in reports and some tricky formulas, as well as fancy formatting.

- ✔ Check out what reports are available by choosing View⇨Report; choose one from the list and then click `Preview` in the dialog box that appears.

- ✔ To pick up some advanced techniques with formulas, check out the built-in reports in Report view.

- ✔ To change the formatting, layout, or content of a database document, Form Design view generally works best.

- ✔ If you need to change a field, but Works won't let you, choose Format⇨Protection and click to remove the `Protect field` check mark.

# Appendix B

# Installing Works

● ● ● ● ● ● ● ● ● ● ● ● ● ● ● ● ● ● ● ● ● ● ● ● ● ● ● ● ● ● ● ● ● ● ● ● ● ● ● ● ●

## In This Chapter

▶ Initial installation

▶ Adding or removing options

● ● ● ● ● ● ● ● ● ● ● ● ● ● ● ● ● ● ● ● ● ● ● ● ● ● ● ● ● ● ● ● ● ● ● ● ● ● ● ● ●

*I*f you're staring balefully at the Works box, dreading the installation process, fear not. Installing software sounds hard and, indeed, used to be hard. But today it's fairly painless, if not quick. It's mainly a matter of inserting disks and pressing a few keys. (If you are installing with a CD-ROM it's even simpler — you just have to insert one disc and press a few keys.) Before you install Works, you need to understand a little about Windows, though; so if you're a little vague on Windows-related things, read Chapter 1 first.

The only time during the installation process that you may need to think much is if you find that your computer doesn't have much room in its memory or hard disk drive. Then you have to decide which features to install and which to leave out. So, chin up! It won't be so bad.

By the way, if you're installing Works on a network, get the network guru to help out. A few additional settings that I don't get into here need to be made for network installation.

## From the Box to Your PC

1. **Turn on your computer and start Windows 95.**

2. **Close any programs you may already be running.**

3. **Open the shrink-wrapped box, open the plastic envelope of disks and find the one labeled "Disk 1 Setup." Or if you have the CD-ROM version, find the only CD in the box.**

4. **Put the disk (or compact disc) in the drive where it fits.**

On most computers, the 3 ¹/₂-inch drive is drive A (occasionally B), and the CD-ROM drive is drive D. Drive C is almost always your hard drive. The 3 ¹/₂-inch disks should go with the metal side in and label up. (That's for horizontal drive slots. If the slot is vertical, you can figure it out for yourself.)

Compact discs always go in drives the same way. Don't turn them over or around. (They have no flip side.)

5. **Use your mouse to click the Start button in the lower-left corner of the screen.**

6. **Click Run in the menu that came up when you clicked Start.**

   This step opens a Run window, which awaits your input.

7. **Type** A:\setup **if you put the disk in drive A, or** B:\setup **if you put it in drive B, or . . . you get the idea.**

   There should be a brief delay while Windows looks at the Setup file on the disk and figures out what to do next. Then a window appears that has your product registration number and a bunch of legalese. Copy down the number. (If you ever need to call Microsoft for help, you need to be able to tell them the number.) Because you are the kind of person who would never do anything that the Microsoft Corporation wouldn't approve of, you don't need to worry about the legalese. (You were probably going to name your first-born after Bill Gates anyway, weren't you?) Click the Continue button.

8. **Type in your name and (optional) the name of your company or organization.**

   Type this information on two separate lines. If you want to put in the name of your company, click that line separately. Don't press Enter until you are done with both lines.

9. **Choose a destination directory.**

   Sounds complicated, but it really isn't. Left to its own devices, Works installs itself in a directory cleverly entitled MSWorks. If you have your own clever way of naming directories, now is your chance to use it. Or just press Enter and leave Works to its own devices.

10. **Choose the options that you want to install.**

   The simplest thing to do is to click Complete Installation. But if you are trying to squeeze Works into that last little sliver of storage space on your hard disk, you can click Custom Installation. That lets you look at a list of features and decide whether or not you can live without them. (You can always install them later if you want to. See "Adding or Removing Options" later in this Appendix.)

   The worst thing about an incomplete installation is that whenever you're having trouble making Works do what you want, you always wonder, "Is this because of some option I didn't install?" Probably it won't be, but you'll wonder.

**11. Decide whether you want a shortcut icon on your desktop.**

I've got one; they're kind of handy, and I recommend them for most Works users. Whenever you want to start Works, you just double-click the icon, rather than winding your way through the Start menu until you find Works. However, if you run a bajillion different programs on your PC, having a shortcut icon for each of them can be a real mess. It's your call.

**12. Insert and remove disks as the Setup program asks for them.**

This is the boring part. If you're installing from a compact disc, go make a sandwich or something. If you're installing from 3 $1/2$-inch disks, every few minutes the Setup program beeps at you and asks for a new disk. There are a whole pile of disks, and they're numbered. If you're doing a complete installation, you use all the disks in order. Otherwise, you may skip some of them. If you insert the wrong disk, Setup just beeps at you again.

A bar that tells you how far along the installation process is and what disk you're currently using appears on the screen while you are installing Works. If you want to stop the whole process and start over some other time, you can click the Cancel button. But usually if you've gotten this far, you may as well finish — unless the power is about to be shut off or something.

**13. Decide whether you want to do Online Registration.**

Registering your copy of Works with Microsoft is a good idea. If you ever need to call them for help, they are nicer to you if you have sent in your registration. The registration also gives Microsoft your address, so they can send you things such as discount coupons for future upgrades.

The old-fashioned way to register is to send in the registration card that is next to the Works manual in the box. The newfangled way is to use your modem (if you have one) to call Microsoft's 800 number and answer the registration questions online.

Smarter people than you and I have debated the merits of online registration. Folks with suspicious minds don't like the idea that Microsoft may be talking directly to their computer (though I've never been able to follow the plot for world domination that this is supposed to be part of). Personally, I take an if-it-ain't-broke-don't-fix-it view. Those old registration cards seem to me to work just fine.

# Adding or Removing Options

If you don't like the choices that you made during the installation, you can change them. Here's how:

1. **Click the Start button.**

2. **Move your cursor up to the Program menu, and then to the Microsoft Works 4.0 folder, and from there to the Microsoft Works 4.0 Setup icon.**

3. **Click the Microsoft Works 4.0 Setup icon.**

4. **Click the** Add/Remove **button.**

    This will open up the Maintenance Installation window, shown in Figure B-1. The options currently installed should have checks in the boxes next to their names.

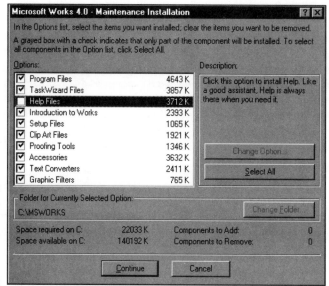

**Figure B-1:**
The
Maintenance
Installation
window.

5. **If you want *to remove* an option that is already installed, click the box next to the option's name to make the box empty.**

6. **If you want *to install* an option that isn't installed now, click the box next to the option's name to put a check in the box.**

    You can add some options and remove others at the same time.

7. **Click the** Continue **button.**

8. **Insert and remove disks as the Setup program asks for them.**

    This part is just like the installation process. Of course, if all you did was remove some options, Setup doesn't need to look at any disks. But if you added some options, Setup has to copy some files off of the installation disks.

9. **After Setup announces that it is finished, click** OK.

# Index

• *C* •

*(continued)*

*(continued)*

*(continued)*

|  |  |  |  |
|---|---|---|---|
| The Internet For Macs® For Dummies® 2nd Edition | by Charles Seiter | ISBN: 1-56884-371-2 | $19.99 USA/$26.99 Canada |
| The Internet For Macs® For Dummies® Starter Kit | by Charles Seiter | ISBN: 1-56884-244-9 | $29.99 USA/$39.99 Canada |
| The Internet For Macs® For Dummies® Starter Kit Bestseller Edition | by Charles Seiter | ISBN: 1-56884-245-7 | $39.99 USA/$54.99 Canada |
| The Internet For Windows® For Dummies® Starter Kit | by John R. Levine & Margaret Levine Young | ISBN: 1-56884-237-6 | $34.99 USA/$44.99 Canada |
| The Internet For Windows® For Dummies® Starter Kit, Bestseller Edition | by John R. Levine & Margaret Levine Young | ISBN: 1-56884-246-5 | $39.99 USA/$54.99 Canada |

## MACINTOSH

|  |  |  |  |
|---|---|---|---|
| Mac® Programming For Dummies® | by Dan Parks Sydow | ISBN: 1-56884-173-6 | $19.95 USA/$26.95 Canada |
| Macintosh® System 7.5 For Dummies® | by Bob LeVitus | ISBN: 1-56884-197-3 | $19.95 USA/$26.95 Canada |
| MORE Macs® For Dummies® | by David Pogue | ISBN: 1-56884-087-X | $19.95 USA/$26.95 Canada |
| PageMaker 5 For Macs® For Dummies® | by Galen Gruman & Deke McClelland | ISBN: 1-56884-178-7 | $19.95 USA/$26.95 Canada |
| QuarkXPress 3.3 For Dummies® | by Galen Gruman & Barbara Assadi | ISBN: 1-56884-217-1 | $19.95 USA/$26.99 Canada |
| Upgrading and Fixing Macs® For Dummies® | by Kearney Rietmann & Frank Higgins | ISBN: 1-56884-189-2 | $19.95 USA/$26.95 Canada |

## MULTIMEDIA

|  |  |  |  |
|---|---|---|---|
| Multimedia & CD-ROMs For Dummies® 2nd Edition | by Andy Rathbone | ISBN: 1-56884-907-9 | $19.99 USA/$26.99 Canada |
| Multimedia & CD-ROMs For Dummies® Interactive Multimedia Value Pack, 2nd Edition | by Andy Rathbone | ISBN: 1-56884-909-5 | $29.99 USA/$39.99 Canada |

## OPERATING SYSTEMS:

### DOS

|  |  |  |  |
|---|---|---|---|
| MORE DOS For Dummies® | by Dan Gookin | ISBN: 1-56884-046-2 | $19.95 USA/$26.95 Canada |
| OS/2® Warp For Dummies® 2nd Edition | by Andy Rathbone | ISBN: 1-56884-205-8 | $19.99 USA/$26.99 Canada |

### UNIX

|  |  |  |  |
|---|---|---|---|
| MORE UNIX® For Dummies® | by John R. Levine & Margaret Levine Young | ISBN: 1-56884-361-5 | $19.99 USA/$26.99 Canada |
| UNIX® For Dummies® | by John R. Levine & Margaret Levine Young | ISBN: 1-878058-58-4 | $19.95 USA/$26.95 Canada |

### WINDOWS

|  |  |  |  |
|---|---|---|---|
| MORE Windows® For Dummies® 2nd Edition | by Andy Rathbone | ISBN: 1-56884-048-9 | $19.95 USA/$26.95 Canada |
| Windows® 95 For Dummies® | by Andy Rathbone | ISBN: 1-56884-240-6 | $19.99 USA/$26.99 Canada |

## PCS/HARDWARE

|  |  |  |  |
|---|---|---|---|
| Illustrated Computer Dictionary For Dummies® 2nd Edition | by Dan Gookin & Wallace Wang | ISBN: 1-56884-218-X | $12.95 USA/$16.95 Canada |
| Upgrading and Fixing PCs For Dummies® 2nd Edition | by Andy Rathbone | ISBN: 1-56884-903-6 | $19.99 USA/$26.99 Canada |

## PRESENTATION/AUTOCAD

|  |  |  |  |
|---|---|---|---|
| AutoCAD For Dummies® | by Bud Smith | ISBN: 1-56884-191-4 | $19.95 USA/$26.95 Canada |
| PowerPoint 4 For Windows® For Dummies® | by Doug Lowe | ISBN: 1-56884-161-2 | $16.99 USA/$22.99 Canada |

## PROGRAMMING

|  |  |  |  |
|---|---|---|---|
| Borland C++ For Dummies® | by Michael Hyman | ISBN: 1-56884-162-0 | $19.95 USA/$26.95 Canada |
| C For Dummies® Volume 1 | by Dan Gookin | ISBN: 1-878058-78-9 | $19.95 USA/$26.95 Canada |
| C++ For Dummies® | by Stephen R. Davis | ISBN: 1-56884-163-9 | $19.95 USA/$26.95 Canada |
| Delphi Programming For Dummies® | by Neil Rubenking | ISBN: 1-56884-200-7 | $19.99 USA/$26.99 Canada |
| Mac® Programming For Dummies® | by Dan Parks Sydow | ISBN: 1-56884-173-6 | $19.95 USA/$26.95 Canada |
| PowerBuilder 4 Programming For Dummies® | by Ted Coombs & Jason Coombs | ISBN: 1-56884-325-9 | $19.99 USA/$26.99 Canada |
| QBasic Programming For Dummies® | by Douglas Hergert | ISBN: 1-56884-093-4 | $19.95 USA/$26.95 Canada |
| Visual Basic 3 For Dummies® | by Wallace Wang | ISBN: 1-56884-076-4 | $19.95 USA/$26.95 Canada |
| Visual Basic "X" For Dummies® | by Wallace Wang | ISBN: 1-56884-230-9 | $19.99 USA/$26.99 Canada |
| Visual C++ 2 For Dummies® | by Michael Hyman & Bob Arnson | ISBN: 1-56884-328-3 | $19.99 USA/$26.99 Canada |
| Windows® 95 Programming For Dummies® | by S. Randy Davis | ISBN: 1-56884-327-5 | $19.99 USA/$26.99 Canada |

## SPREADSHEET

|  |  |  |  |
|---|---|---|---|
| 1-2-3 For Dummies® | by Greg Harvey | ISBN: 1-878058-60-6 | $16.95 USA/$22.95 Canada |
| 1-2-3 For Windows® 5 For Dummies® 2nd Edition | by John Walkenbach | ISBN: 1-56884-216-3 | $16.95 USA/$22.95 Canada |
| Excel 5 For Macs® For Dummies® | by Greg Harvey | ISBN: 1-56884-186-8 | $19.95 USA/$26.95 Canada |
| Excel For Dummies® 2nd Edition | by Greg Harvey | ISBN: 1-56884-050-0 | $16.95 USA/$22.95 Canada |
| MORE 1-2-3 For DOS For Dummies® | by John Weingarten | ISBN: 1-56884-224-4 | $19.99 USA/$26.99 Canada |
| MORE Excel 5 For Windows® For Dummies® | by Greg Harvey | ISBN: 1-56884-207-4 | $19.95 USA/$26.95 Canada |
| Quattro Pro 6 For Windows® For Dummies® | by John Walkenbach | ISBN: 1-56884-174-4 | $19.95 USA/$26.95 Canada |
| Quattro Pro For DOS For Dummies® | by John Walkenbach | ISBN: 1-56884-023-3 | $16.95 USA/$22.95 Canada |

## UTILITIES

|  |  |  |  |
|---|---|---|---|
| Norton Utilities 8 For Dummies® | by Beth Slick | ISBN: 1-56884-166-3 | $19.95 USA/$26.95 Canada |

## VCRS/CAMCORDERS

|  |  |  |  |
|---|---|---|---|
| VCRs & Camcorders For Dummies™ | by Gordon McComb & Andy Rathbone | ISBN: 1-56884-229-5 | $14.99 USA/$20.99 Canada |

## WORD PROCESSING

|  |  |  |  |
|---|---|---|---|
| Ami Pro For Dummies® | by Jim Meade | ISBN: 1-56884-049-7 | $19.95 USA/$26.95 Canada |
| MORE Word For Windows® 6 For Dummies® | by Doug Lowe | ISBN: 1-56884-165-5 | $19.95 USA/$26.95 Canada |
| MORE WordPerfect® 6 For Windows® For Dummies® | by Margaret Levine Young & David C. Kay | ISBN: 1-56884-206-6 | $19.95 USA/$26.95 Canada |
| MORE WordPerfect® 6 For DOS For Dummies® | by Wallace Wang, edited by Dan Gookin | ISBN: 1-56884-047-0 | $19.95 USA/$26.95 Canada |
| Word 6 For Macs® For Dummies® | by Dan Gookin | ISBN: 1-56884-190-6 | $19.95 USA/$26.95 Canada |
| Word For Windows® 6 For Dummies® | by Dan Gookin | ISBN: 1-56884-075-6 | $16.95 USA/$22.95 Canada |
| Word For Windows® For Dummies® | by Dan Gookin & Ray Werner | ISBN: 1-878058-86-X | $16.95 USA/$22.95 Canada |
| WordPerfect® 6 For DOS For Dummies® | by Dan Gookin | ISBN: 1-878058-77-0 | $16.95 USA/$22.95 Canada |
| WordPerfect® 6.1 For Windows® For Dummies® 2nd Edition | by Margaret Levine Young & David Kay | ISBN: 1-56884-243-0 | $16.95 USA/$22.95 Canada |
| WordPerfect® For Dummies® | by Dan Gookin | ISBN: 1-878058-52-5 | $16.95 USA/$22.95 Canada |

*Order Center:* **(800) 762-2974** *(8 a.m.–6 p.m., EST, weekdays)*

| Quantity | ISBN | Title | Price | Total |
|----------|------|-------|-------|-------|
| | | | | |
| | | | | |
| | | | | |
| | | | | |
| | | | | |
| | | | | |
| | | | | |
| | | | | |
| | | | | |
| | | | | |
| | | | | |
| | | | | |
| | | | | |
| | | | | |
| | | | | |
| | | | | |
| | | | | |
| | | | | |
| | | | | |

### Shipping & Handling Charges

| | Description | First book | Each additional book | Total |
|--|-------------|------------|----------------------|-------|
| **Domestic** | Normal | $4.50 | $1.50 | $ |
| | Two Day Air | $8.50 | $2.50 | $ |
| | Overnight | $18.00 | $3.00 | $ |
| **International** | Surface | $8.00 | $8.00 | $ |
| | Airmail | $16.00 | $16.00 | $ |
| | DHL Air | $17.00 | $17.00 | $ |

\*For large quantities call for shipping & handling charges.
\*\*Prices are subject to change without notice.

**Ship to:**

Name _____

Company _____

Address _____

City/State/Zip _____

Daytime Phone _____

**Payment:** ☐ Check to IDG Books Worldwide (US Funds Only)

☐ VISA      ☐ MasterCard      ☐ American Express

Card # _____ Expires _____

Signature _____

**Subtotal** _____

CA residents add
applicable sales tax _____

IN, MA, and MD
residents add
5% sales tax _____

IL residents add
6.25% sales tax _____

RI residents add
7% sales tax _____

TX residents add
8.25% sales tax _____

**Shipping** _____

**Total** _____

*Please send this order form to:*

**IDG Books Worldwide, Inc.**
**7260 Shadeland Station, Suite 100**
**Indianapolis, IN 46256**

*Allow up to 3 weeks for delivery.*
*Thank you!*